ALSO BY STEPHEN KENDRICK AND PAUL KENDRICK

Douglass and Lincoln: How a Revolutionary Black Leader and a Reluctant Liberator Struggled to End Slavery and Save the Union

Sarah's Long Walk: The Free Blacks of Boston and How Their Struggle for Equality Changed America

NINE DAYS

NINE DAYS

The Race to Save Martin Luther King Jr.'s
Life and Win the 1960 Election

STEPHEN KENDRICK and **PAUL KENDRICK**

FARRAR, STRAUS AND GIROUX | NEW YORK

Farrar, Straus and Giroux
120 Broadway, New York 10271

Printed in the United States of America
First edition, 2021

Photograph on page 281: Bettmann / Getty Images

Library of Congress Cataloging-in-Publication Data
Names: Kendrick, Stephen, 1954– author. | Kendrick, Paul, 1983– author.
Title: Nine days : the race to save Martin Luther King Jr.'s life and win the 1960
    election / Stephen Kendrick, and Paul Kendrick.
Other titles: Race to save Martin Luther King Jr.'s life and win the 1960 election
Description: First edition. | New York : Farrar, Straus and Giroux, 2021. | Includes
    bibliographical references and index. | Summary: "A history of the 1960 US
    presidential election with a focus on the role played by the imprisonment of
    Martin Luther King Jr. in the wake of an Atlanta sit-in"— Provided by publisher.
Identifiers: LCCN 2020039720 | ISBN 9781250155702 (hardcover)
Subjects: LCSH: Presidents—United States—Election—1960. | Political
    campaigns—United States—History—20th century. | King, Martin Luther, Jr.,
    1929–1968. | King, Martin Luther, Jr., 1929–1968—Imprisonment. | Kennedy,
    John F. (John Fitzgerald), 1917–1963. | Nixon, Richard M. (Richard Milhous),
    1913–1994. | United States—Politics and government—1953–1961. | Civil
    rights demonstrations—Georgia—Atlanta—History—20th century. | Civil
    rights—United States—History.
Classification: LCC E837.7 .K46 2021 | DDC 323.0973—dc23
LC record available at https://lccn.loc.gov/2020039720

Designed by Gretchen Achilles

Our books may be purchased in bulk for promotional, educational, or business
use. Please contact your local bookseller or the Macmillan Corporate and
Premium Sales Department at 1-800-221-7945, extension 5442, or by email at
MacmillanSpecialMarkets@macmillan.com.

www.fsgbooks.com
www.twitter.com/fsgbooks • www.facebook.com/fsgbooks

10 9 8 7 6 5 4 3 2 1

This book,
with love and appreciation,
is dedicated to our partners in life—
for Liz,
for Kori

Before this thing is over, my son is going to end up bearing the heavy end of this burden.

—MARTIN LUTHER KING SR.

to Rev. Otis Moss Jr. and Atlanta Student Activists

When Judge Mitchell gave Dr. King's sentence, it was like being in a room when someone enters and announces a death. Everyone is shocked, frozen, and emotional.

—REV. OTIS MOSS JR.

Martin told me late one night that when being driven across those rural Georgia roads in the middle of the night, "I knew I'd never see anybody again. That kind of mental anguish is worse than dying, riding mile after mile, hungry and thirsty, bound and helpless, waiting and not knowing what you're waiting for, and all over a traffic violation."

—ANDREW YOUNG

And Dr. King can be heard saying, "We will transform these jails from dungeons of shame to havens of victory." And that is exactly what happened.

—DOROTHY COTTON

CONTENTS

PROLOGUE   3

"IN TROUBLE"   11

"YOU CAN'T LEAD FROM THE BACK"   31

DAY 1: WEDNESDAY, OCTOBER 19   51

DAY 2: THURSDAY, OCTOBER 20   75

DAY 3: FRIDAY, OCTOBER 21   89

DAY 4: SATURDAY, OCTOBER 22   97

DAY 5: SUNDAY, OCTOBER 23   113

DAY 6: MONDAY, OCTOBER 24   121

DAY 7: TUESDAY, OCTOBER 25   131

DAY 8: WEDNESDAY, OCTOBER 26   151

DAY 9: THURSDAY, OCTOBER 27   189

TIME TO DETONATE   209

"IT WAS A SYMPHONY"   229

"THEY JUST ALL TURNED"   237

EPILOGUE: THE DUNGEON SHOOK   255

NOTES   283

SELECTED BIBLIOGRAPHY   323

ACKNOWLEDGMENTS   333

INDEX   339

NINE DAYS

PROLOGUE

Sunday, October 23, 1960

Coretta Scott King eagerly waited to see her husband. The dining room at Atlanta's Paschal's Restaurant was packed on this Sunday night; she was surrounded by the boisterous celebrations of students, friends, families, and professors all greeting one another. After five tense days in jail, the freed student sit-in demonstrators were fast arriving, but Coretta was impatient for Martin to walk through the door.

Martin Luther King Jr. had never spent a night in jail until this week, and Paschal's, where the food had so often sustained his team's impassioned strategy sessions, felt like the right place for a welcome-home party. The word from Mayor William Hartsfield's office was that the last protesters who were still in jail from earlier in the week were now free. This night of their return, there was a sense that last Wednesday's arrests at Rich's department store had successfully seized the attention not only of the city but of the entire nation.

With the presidential election sixteen days away, the students had timed the protest to affect a close national contest between John F. Kennedy and Richard Nixon, both of whom had been mostly silent on issues of race. King had not been the instigator of the massive wave of sit-ins centering on Rich's, one of the largest department stores in the South, and had at first been reluctant to join the students. But, not wanting to let them down, he had followed their lead, backing the Morehouse College activist Lonnie King. Lonnie wasn't related to the King family, though he had once been a youth leader at Ebenezer Baptist Church under the tutelage of Martin Luther King Sr., known as Daddy King.

Martin and Coretta Scott King had endured much in their first seven years of marriage: the bombing of their first home, where their newborn lay sleeping; a knife attack while King was on tour for his first book; harassment by the police and the tax authorities designed to discourage a growing civil rights movement. When King was arrested with more than fifty students, five days earlier, he decided to refuse bail and face an extended stay in jail. If the Atlanta university students were willing to take this risk to desegregate downtown lunch counters, he could not walk away in the face of their resolve.

The businessman and movement supporter Jesse Hill had called Coretta earlier that Sunday evening to invite her to the gathering at Paschal's. Word was spreading through the community that the students had agreed to the mayor's proposal of a monthlong truce and that they would be released. The pause would give Mayor Hartsfield time to negotiate a difficult desegregation agreement with Atlanta's white business elite. As she dressed for the evening, Coretta was delighted at the prospect of welcoming her husband home. Today, Sunday, was the third birthday of their youngest child, Martin III, and perhaps he could even sneak in a kiss for his sleeping son later that night. Despite having to care for their two children (and being five months pregnant with their third), Coretta had managed to visit her husband in the Fulton County Jail nearly every day. She knew her visits were essential to King's ability to endure the despondency of prison life, and they had both been heartened at how, despite King's apprehension, his time in jail had not been as crushing as he had feared. Being surrounded by the students seemed to buoy him up, to steady him. She understood he did not want her to leave the children to be jailed alongside him. Yet when King was behind bars, Coretta once wrote that she felt as though she were imprisoned with him; being on the outside did not help.

Though he was now supposedly a free man, King had yet to appear at Paschal's. The servers were bringing out hot plates of food, manna for those who had suffered nothing but jail fare for days. Students shouted with relief when they saw their liberated friends. Yet there was no sign of King, and Coretta started to feel frightened; she had what she called "a premonition of evil." Finally, a student came over to confirm what was quickly becoming apparent: "They kept Dr. King in jail."

Student leaders ran out of the restaurant, heading back to the Fulton County Jail to figure out what was wrong. All anyone knew was that while the students had been released, King had not.

Unbeknownst to Coretta and everyone else gathered at Paschal's that night, the following days would heighten a crisis that would not only help determine the victor of the 1960 election but transform American politics for decades to come. The Reverend Martin Luther King Jr. would end up spending a total of nine days in three different jails—nine days that changed everything. As Sunday evening gave way to midnight on Monday, those around King experienced the sickening realization that another courthouse was summoning him, that unexpectedly he potentially faced a far more dire predicament than before.

King's family would remember those days in late October 1960 as the time when they most feared for his life.

■   ■   ■

There wasn't much to pack; you traveled light to and from the Fulton County lockup.

Earlier on that Sunday evening, King had sat silently beside his cellmate Lonnie King, who, as the leader of the students, had presided over a heated discussion about Mayor Hartsfield's proposal to get them out of jail. King was content to let the navy veteran and former Morehouse football star lead the way; he trusted Lonnie as a neighbor who shared a newspaper route with his younger brother. The students debated for two hours about whether they should accept Hartsfield's offer: the longtime mayor was, after all, one of the only white politicians in the South who actively courted Black voters. Hartsfield, whose eccentric southern charm masked Machiavellian cunning, was asking for the sit-in leaders' trust, giving white Atlanta business owners time to see the need to desegregate not only lunch counters but also the entire downtown economic core.

But could Hartsfield really pull it off? The sullen, stubborn attitude of the wealthy department store owner Dick Rich showed how difficult this endeavor might be. In the end, the students accepted the proposal, telling the press, "We now await substantial evidence of the good faith."

Guards approached, ordering everyone in Lonnie's cell to come with them. One of them said to King, "You gotta wait, there's people here from DeKalb County." As Dr. King froze, Lonnie saw a look of shock flash across his face.

The very name—DeKalb County—called up a host of terrible associations. DeKalb was Klan country. Unbeknownst to King and the students, DeKalb County had secured a bench warrant to stop King from walking free from neighboring Fulton County's cells. King and his staff, in the midst of their efforts to get the students out of jail, had not discussed the brief newspaper stories indicating that the minister was very much still in the authorities' sights. Even in light of the injustices that Black Georgians had faced for generations, it seemed impossible, even ludicrous, that an old twenty-five-dollar traffic citation, for something as minor as possessing an out-of-state driver's license, could send King to the DeKalb County Jail, and potentially to the notorious Georgia State Prison in Reidsville, where Black people were treated as if they were as worthless as the state's red clay soil.

Just as one jail door was opening, another was quietly inching ajar to receive him.

Everything Lonnie King knew about the authorities in DeKalb County suggested King might never leave their custody alive. King quickly recovered his usual stoic demeanor, telling Lonnie and his stunned fellow students not to worry, to continue walking out. Yet for the first time, the weight of responsibility for King's fate fully hit Lonnie. He was the one who had asked—pressed, even—his childhood friend to put himself in danger alongside them. Now Dr. King would be left behind to confront even more perilous legal troubles, and Lonnie would no longer be there to help him.

King appeared vulnerable to Lonnie with the students leaving the jail. Lonnie realized that Daddy King would never forgive him if anything happened to his son. He was also sure that Coretta believed he was going to get her husband killed.

As King talked with his brother, A.D., who had accompanied their father, he seemed to regain his composure. Despite his own unease, Daddy King reassured the angry students who had not yet left the jail that "M.L. will be all right."

When guards told protesters to start walking out, a student cried, "Why are you releasing us? We are supposed to stay here." The students did not want to leave without King, but he believed they were right to leave jail under the terms of the agreement they had negotiated. He told them to have Coretta call his lawyer. One young woman, Carolyn Long, was in tears, and King went over to let her know it was all right to go. Eventually, the young people staggered through the glass doors of the jail and into the mellow autumn dusk, where some fellow student leaders were waiting for them. King was still in the relative safety of Atlanta's Fulton County Jail, and the movement's attorneys, epitomized by the determined and agile Donald Hollowell, would strive to protect him.

King, however, had left himself dangerously exposed. The Georgia courts were well practiced at finding avenues for retaliation against Black people who dared to raise their heads. At this fateful juncture of King's thirteen-year career, the thirty-one-year-old activist would soon face the possibility of months on a prison work gang. It was difficult to imagine the scholarly King serving such a sentence, but there was potentially even worse in store for him. Whether the result of a guard's outburst of violence or a paid hit job, killings in the Georgia prison system were common and could be covered up with little fuss. While King remained impassive, his father was justifiably fearful; it was impossible to know from what direction his son's enemies might strike.

On the verge of the 1960 election, King was still an emerging leader on the national level, far from the towering figure of the marches on Birmingham, Washington, and Selma he would later become. It was there, incarcerated in Georgia, where King first came to understand and accept the dangers he would face in the course of his fight to change America. Later, when students criticized him for not boarding the bus during the 1961 Freedom Rides, King replied, "I think I should choose the time and place of my own Golgotha." It would be on that week's long night ride to the Georgia State Prison in Reidsville, hundreds of miles from Atlanta, that he discovered the stations of the cross along the way.

The days of heightened peril that followed changed King forever— scarring, fortifying, and galvanizing him. While King's arrest just weeks before Election Day in 1960 has historically been treated as a minor aspect of the presidential race's closing days, the truth of how it actually played out, and its resulting impact on national life, has never been revealed in full. The most well-known narrative centers mostly on John F. Kennedy and his brother Robert's political calculations and the support for King displayed by his staffers Harris Wofford and Sargent Shriver. While the importance of the latter's actions to Black voters may seem obvious, it was a leap into the electoral unknown with regard to white voters. It was not self-evident that the Kennedy campaign's efforts to help King would redound to its benefit.

This intervention would prove to be crucial, but how King emerged from the trials of the dungeon is also the story of King's family and staff, lawyers like Donald Hollowell, Black Atlanta student activists, and a Kennedy campaign aide whom historians have largely ignored: Louis E. Martin, the pioneering Black newspaper editor. These overlooked characters are no less a part of this national drama than the Kennedy campaign itself.

Martin, in particular, played a critical role in helping the Kennedy brothers, Wofford, and Shriver alter the course of the campaign. He quickly perceived the problems with Kennedy's muted support for civil rights and used his experience to move the campaign to action. His verve and immense creativity would help tilt the election. And yet Martin's role has largely been neglected by histories of the Kennedy era. He was the ultimate unseen strategist, making the right things happen, speaking blunt truths without favor to white bosses, and then claiming little of the credit. Martin said, "It wasn't just a job with me. I looked on it as a lever, to move this mountain of racism." Martin's determination would prove pivotal, and he dared his team to act despite orders to desist.

Martin, along with his partner Harris Wofford and their boss, Sargent Shriver, advocated on behalf of King when even the slightest miscalculation might spell disaster as the presidential contest neared its knife-edge conclusion. Despite the relationship Vice President Nixon had built with King before the election, Louis Martin was growing more and more convinced that Kennedy represented greater hope for Black Americans, and he was determined to help Kennedy live up to that potential.

In the last sixty years, America has experienced many "October surprises"—unexpected turns and abrupt shifts in the weeks before a presidential election. Martin Luther King's imprisonment at Reidsville might have been an October surprise neither the Nixon nor the Kennedy campaign wanted, but this trio of Kennedy aides made a daring bet that they could nonetheless turn it to their advantage. Black voters, they thought, were theirs to win, and these same voters would subsequently hold the new president to account on civil rights.

Shriver, Kennedy's brother-in-law (though he was known by the family as the "too-liberal-in-law"), was the head of this groundbreaking effort to reach Black voters, a group seldom accorded much importance before 1960. Shriver proved insightful enough to recognize that as two white men, he and Wofford would fail without Louis Martin's understanding of the Black community. To their credit, they listened, learned, and cleared the way for the editor who would eventually be called, by those who knew his efforts best, "the godfather of Black politics."

The story of Martin, Wofford, and Shriver, and their fight against Georgia's entrenched racial hierarchy, remains an underappreciated example of how the practice of politics—so often perceived as craven when not corrupt—can sometimes make a startling difference. In later years, Shriver told young activists that the "politics of death" is marked by "bureaucracy, routine, rules, status quo." Then he added, "The politics of life is personal initiative, creativity, flair, dash, a little daring." These civil rights iconoclasts all practiced the politics of life during nine fateful days in the fall of 1960.

And though these three Kennedy staffers went rogue to secure King's release, the minister himself was no helpless bystander. The decisions he made over the course of October 1960 proved critical to the unfolding of his career. The agonizing choice to go behind bars and to refuse bail helped determine the future course of the civil rights movement and transformed America.

"IN TROUBLE"

In the spring of 1960, with John F. Kennedy's presidential campaign hurtling toward an undecided Democratic convention in Los Angeles, Bobby Kennedy summoned his brother's new speechwriter, Harris Wofford, into his office. Bobby, who managed Jack's campaign, was famous for his irritability and his slashing ripostes. That day he was his typically blunt self and told Wofford that he would soon have a new role in the campaign: "We're in trouble with Negroes. We really don't know much about this whole thing. We've been dealing outside the field of the main Negro leadership and have to start from scratch."

Secretly delighted by this assignment, Wofford sensed that he was being placed right where he needed to be. He was eager to start working under the successful Chicago businessman Sargent Shriver, a Kennedy brother-in-law whom Wofford had recently befriended. Shriver's chief responsibility was heading up the Civil Rights Section (CRS) of the campaign, an initiative that had yet to produce any meaningful results. Wofford knew that they were starting from behind, working for a candidate with scant knowledge of how to bond with Black voters.

Making matters worse, JFK would be facing a general election opponent with a strong civil rights reputation. This is a Nixon long lost to American memory. Though it is overshadowed by his later actions, this Nixon prided himself on his moderate racial views. Vice President Nixon held an advantage with Black voters over Kennedy, at least when it came to his image. Nixon was seen by many of those voters as a more hopeful and sympathetic figure than the man he served, President Eisenhower. Nonetheless, in his 1956 reelection campaign, Eisenhower had still won nearly 40 percent of the Black vote, the most of any Republican since 1932, before FDR's New Deal. Roosevelt's economic programs won the Democrats a majority of Black votes outside the South, but southern cities (at least those in which Black voters were able to go to the polls) remained a different matter. The Democrats, after all, were the party that violently resisted Reconstruction, leading to the Jim Crow era. Segregationist Democrats were overwhelmingly supported by white voters across the South and reviled by Black voters in equal measure. There was an inevitable spillover effect to other parts of the country, and the CRS was trying to reverse the trend of Black Americans elsewhere once again voting for the party of Lincoln. Their task was made even more difficult by the perception that their candidate was a rich Massachusetts senator who had not been shy about forging connections with southern segregationist colleagues.

Although few Democratic operatives understood the hazards of their campaign's disconnect with Black voters, the Kennedys were finally waking up to a simple truth: all Nixon had to do was improve on Eisenhower's 40 percent, or simply come close to it, and he would be well on his way to winning the White House. Black voters remained the Democrats' to lose outside the South, but it was nonetheless important to make inroads where possible and to stanch the loss of votes in the North and West. In light of Nixon's popularity, it seemed plausible that he might even approach the threshold of 50 percent.

Though Wofford, in the years to come, would be dismissed by politicians as irritatingly idealistic, he was no fool. He knew Bobby's dire assessment was correct. As former counsel to the U.S. Commission on Civil Rights, Wofford had an unusual perspective on where both parties stood on issues of race. Yet as useful as his experience working for the commission had been, it was his role as an adviser on nonviolence to Dr. King that gave Wofford the most insight into the developing civil rights movement.

He knew that Nixon had personally forged a relationship with King, despite the minister's youth, and that King was more and more at the center of a volatile national debate about racial inequality. Wofford sensed that King's stated neutrality concerning the presidential race might not last for long, given the pastor's meetings with, letters from, and seeming goodwill toward Vice President Nixon. Besides, King had been raised in Atlanta's Black community, which for generations had gravitated toward the GOP. It did not help that Kennedy had over the course of his career displayed little interest in the realities of racial discrimination.

Finding himself unexpectedly appointed by Bobby to this new position in the Civil Rights Section of the campaign, Wofford thought it might be the perfect opportunity to help the Massachusetts senator understand the importance of encouraging if not a friendship, then at least an honest and forthright connection with King.

After Kennedy nailed down the nomination, Wofford increasingly stressed King's potential benefit to the campaign, though he sensed he might pay a high price with the Kennedys' inner circle in the future for doing so. Serving as the link between Kennedy and King would never be an easy role, not in this campaign season nor in years to come. Yet even as his efforts were met with resistance, Wofford did not despair; he sensed that King was becoming more responsive to Kennedy's appeals. And King, for one, believed the Democrat surrounded himself with better advisers than Nixon did, and he included Wofford among those he called the "good people, the right people."

King's reservations about Kennedy himself were understandable; Wofford, too, felt some unease about the candidate he now worked for. While the young lawyer admired Kennedy for his wit, his quick intelligence, and his apparent capacity for growth, he had signed on to the campaign in order to move and to motivate Kennedy as much as to elect him. This dynamic was quite different from his devotion to King. Their connection had developed soon after Wofford read about the Alabama minister's use of Gandhian tactics during the Montgomery bus boycott. When he heard how this young pastor was utilizing nonviolent techniques, putting into action ideas the young lawyer Wofford was speaking and publishing about, he resolved they should meet. He began sending King letters with his writings on nonviolence and solidified a working relationship when they met at a conference in 1956. Though never formally a member of King's staff, Wofford offered blunt advice and editorial support for King's 1958 book, *Stride Toward Freedom: The Montgomery Story.*

Wofford was encouraged when the popular singer Harry Belafonte also advised Kennedy to seek out King. The candidate was recruiting Belafonte as a prominent Black supporter, but at their meeting the entertainer bluntly told Kennedy, "You're making a big mistake if you think I can deliver the Negro vote for you. If you want the Negro vote, pay attention to what Martin Luther King is saying and doing. You get him, you don't need me—or Jackie Robinson." He added, "The time you've spent with me would be better spent talking to him, and listening to what he has to say, because he is the future of our people." Suddenly Wofford's advice was starting to look more and more prescient.

Wofford eventually succeeded in arranging two private meetings between King and Kennedy, one before and one after the Democratic National Convention in Los Angeles. King would later say of his first meeting with JFK, which took place in the lavish New York apartment belonging to Kennedy's father, that he could tell the senator was bright but that he sensed little emotional commitment to addressing the depth of the injustices Black Americans faced. King noted that Kennedy "had never really had the personal experience of knowing the deep groans and passionate yearnings of the Negroes for freedom." Kennedy had grown up without knowing many Black people and had not sought out knowing many more since then. Bobby would say later of racial inequality, "I don't think that it was a matter that we were extra-concerned about as we were growing up." But Wofford believed that Kennedy might well possess the capacity, perhaps because of his own family's experience of discrimination toward the Irish, to develop an impulse to take action. King and Kennedy, so different in personality and attitude—one moral and somber, the other coolly ambitious and ironic—were at last beginning to forge some kind of connection, however awkward and halting.

During their second meeting at the senator's Georgetown town house, King told Kennedy, "Something dramatic must be done to convince the Negroes that you are committed on civil rights." Given the candidate's spotty civil rights record and long-standing inclination to accommodate the segregationist sensibilities of southern Democrats, King was only expressing what many Black leaders felt. Kennedy did not disagree, nor did he bristle at King's helpful candor. They agreed they should meet again as soon as the fall campaign began, perhaps in a public forum. Wofford got to work on making that happen.

Little did King know that his earnest admonition to Kennedy— that the candidate would have to do "something dramatic"—would play out with his own life in jeopardy.

Kennedy finally agreed to appear with King in the third week of October, less than three weeks before Election Day. King was not inclined to allow Kennedy to play a double game, talking about civil rights only in northern media markets, so he insisted that the joint appearance take place in the South. Wofford and King first discussed King's home city of Atlanta, but the Democrats running Kennedy's Georgia campaign warned he would lose their state if he appeared there alongside King. Kennedy was not willing to take that risk. So Wofford persuaded a reluctant King to agree to meet in Miami—where Kennedy was scheduled to speak before the American Legion—even if Miami was Deep South more by geography than culture. Wofford hoped this event might be what would allow them to clinch the Black vote.

A bleak, open-plan office in the Investment Building in Washington was home to Shriver's Civil Rights Section. Situated three blocks east of campaign headquarters, the team was grateful to do their work mostly unsupervised by the main campaign staff. Over the summer, the small group started working on a plan that was, by the standards of the time, entirely novel: a substantive, civil-rights-focused program aimed at Black voters that would go far beyond the modest publicity-focused outreach of the past. As summer turned into autumn, however, the CRS learned just how daunting a task this would be. At the July convention, Shriver saw that Kennedy was the least popular of the Democratic presidential candidates with Black delegates, who looked as "cold as fish" toward Kennedy. Making matters worse, the Kennedy brothers belatedly decided that the two Black Washington lawyers they had brought on to head the CRS—Marjorie Lawson and Frank Reeves—lacked the national stature needed to actually rally Black votes. Furthermore, Lawson and Reeves seemed to be intent on spending their time disparaging each other. As a result, Shriver and Wofford found themselves functionally in charge of outreach to the Black community—an untenable situation.

One day in late August, Shriver—a lean, compact man whose blinding smile concealed an obsession with fourteen-hour workdays—wondered out loud if they should bring on someone new, a member of the Black community respected across the country. He had heard good things from organized labor contacts about a Chicago newspaper editor who might be the perfect fit, though the two fellow Chicagoans had never met. The idea sounded good to Wofford, so Shriver started wooing Louis (pronounced "Louie") E. Martin with the aim of persuading him to join their team.

Shriver began by inviting Martin to a Black advisory group that gathered at the start of August at Washington's LaSalle Hotel. As

Martin listened to the morning's presentations, he was dismayed by the lack of practicality. What the journalist heard were banal generalities from people who had never worked in politics. Martin finally spoke up during the afternoon session, saying the Democratic National Committee (DNC) needed to pay its outstanding debts for advertising space it had bought during the previous election in papers like *The Chicago Defender*, the publication he worked for: "These bills had to be paid by the DNC before we could get the full cooperation of the Negro newspapers." Martin added, "We should work for the total involvement of all elements in Black life in this campaign, irrespective of past association, party affiliation." At the end of the day, Shriver and Wofford took Martin aside and asked what the budget for Black outreach should be. Martin answered, "A million dollars." Wofford and Shriver exchanged startled looks; they had expected to be told to spend one or two hundred thousand. Martin scoffed, having spent more than that during his brief adventure doing Black media publicity for FDR's 1944 campaign.

It was then that Shriver asked, because Martin had the experience they needed, would he stay on and serve as their guide?

Martin at first declined, though both Shriver and Wofford had impressed him. Back in Chicago the next day, Shriver telephoned him, insistent that Martin come "get into the act." Martin again demurred, but eventually Shriver got him to agree to work three days a week in D.C. with them. That arrangement lasted all of two weeks; there was no such thing as part-time work, or half-hearted commitments, in the Kennedy world. One meeting would end up leading to eight years of work on behalf of both the Kennedy and the Johnson administrations for Martin.

Still, Martin's first meeting with Robert Kennedy was less than propitious. The first time he walked into Bobby's office, flanked by Wofford and Shriver, he watched as Kennedy tore into his two associates, saying it was "mighty late in the day to find out that the Civil Rights Section had not gotten off the ground." The two silently absorbed the tirade, though they felt they were doing valuable work: Shriver was focusing on civil rights issues instead of merely handing out money (though the campaign would resort to this tactic, too). Nonetheless, Bobby did not think they were securing the connections they would need to turn out the Black vote.

Martin had seen enough and decided to risk his continued involvement in the Kennedy campaign by communicating some salient realities to Bobby. He spoke up: "You don't know anything!" People looked at Martin in shock. "You're talking about what we haven't done. You haven't done what you were supposed to do. You haven't linked up the guys who have been in this party for twenty years. You don't know the officers. You don't know anybody. You're supposed to open these doors, you know."

He added that it was ridiculous that Bobby had not even met with South Side Chicago's representative William Dawson, the honorary chair of the CRS. The traditional, older Dawson had counseled Shriver when they first met, "Don't have any relations with these wild young men like Martin Luther King. That will just get Kennedy into trouble." Dawson even objected to their using "civil rights" in their unit name, because it would "offend our good Southern friends." Still, Martin believed it was scandalous that Bobby had not bothered to sit down with the nation's longest-serving Black congressman. In truth, Shriver and Wofford were just as dismissive as Bobby toward the elderly Dawson. When the congressman was first shown the CRS's open-plan layout, he had demanded a private office for himself, which the team soon referred to as "Uncle Tom's Cabin." Martin, though, had more respect for Dawson. The congressman's views might seem out of touch to the upstart Kennedys, but to fail to respect Dawson was to fail to respect his Chicago voters, and Martin thought that mattered.

Shriver said, "You know, this man is from Chicago," attempting to justify Martin's near insubordination. Martin, for his part, went on laying out exactly what needed to be done in order to win and just how much it would cost. As he walked out of the fractious meeting, Bobby's assistant, the journalist John Seigenthaler, whispered to Martin, "Wait a minute, I wish you'd stay. Bobby wants to talk to you."

Martin prepared himself to be fired.

It turned out that firing Martin was not what Bobby had in mind. Martin's ability to speak Bobby's rough, practical political language had already won him the Kennedy brother's respect.

So Martin posed another tough question to Bobby: Did he really want to win the Black vote? Martin explained, "If you want it, you can get it, but you're going to have to work for it, and you're going to have to fight for it and you're going to have to spend money." The campaign manager's immediate trust in Martin's judgment over that of two well-intentioned white liberals gave him enough confidence in the CRS to allow them to continue their work—at least for now. Martin would walk out of headquarters onto Connecticut Avenue and K Street resolved to give the Kennedy campaign everything he had.

Martin's and Wofford's desks sat side by side in the cavernous CRS office, which was also where other constituency outreach operations were based. The two new colleagues toiled through endless days of calls, meetings, and hundreds of press releases. It would have felt overwhelming, except that they quickly became friends, discovering that they could rely on each other. Many nights, the two of them, along with Shriver, stumbled out late to go to nearby Harvey's Restaurant, where their best ideas emerged over midnight beers and oysters.

Late nights hardly precluded early mornings, because the devout Shriver rarely missed morning Mass. Given the many directions in which the campaign pulled Shriver (who also headed up outreach to the business community and to farmers), Martin—a fellow Roman Catholic owing to his Afro-Cuban father—figured that going to Mass with Shriver followed by breakfast was a good opportunity to take care of CRS business. Though Wofford was not a Catholic, he tagged along, figuring it couldn't hurt.

The thirty-four-year-old Wofford—whose high forehead and arched eyebrows gave him a look of affable curiosity—was a man more comfortable with classical Greek tragedy than raw politics. He admired Martin's ability to maneuver through a world hidden to him and Shriver: the arena of Black newspapers, magazines, and radio stations. Martin had spent the previous year building up independent media in Nigeria, and now he was on the phone each day in D.C., calling as many Black publishers, journalists, and local precinct organizers as he could, opening their minds to Kennedy. When an emissary of Representative Adam Clayton Powell laid out what Powell could do for Kennedy around the country—for a steep price—Martin immediately saw that Powell's proposal was full of big promises he did not have the necessary organization to keep, at least not outside New York. Martin got the congressman on board to do speeches for them at a fifth of the cost. His negotiating skills amazed Shriver and Wofford.

Martin, in turn, respected Wofford's knowledge of young players in the emerging civil rights movement. He relied on Wofford as a walking repository of everything Kennedy had previously said or done regarding civil rights (which, admittedly, was little). The journalist sensed his white partner had more latitude to express his passionate ideals than he did. Though he shared Wofford's vision for equality, Martin figured it was hard political advice for winning this election first that he was here to give.

Martin found Wofford to be someone who listened to him. The only thing that worried him was whether other Black associates of the CRS might see Wofford's self-assurance in discussions as arrogance. On the other hand, Wofford was hardly aloof; for a man operating in the aggressive Kennedy world, he was kind and accessible, and this in spite of a tendency to always be on the go. He was the epitome of a big-city lawyer, constantly hurrying with a bulky briefcase in hand, and yet no matter how busy he was, Wofford was always willing to slow down and tell a funny story about his Tennessee lineage. This ability to make fun of himself saved Wofford from being annoyingly self-righteous. The fact that Wofford had attended law school at Howard University, a historically Black institution (causing his grandmother to literally faint at the news), also fascinated Martin. It showed that his colleague was more than a dreamy idealist; he had spent time learning about realities of Black life before getting a second legal degree at Yale.

Though Martin, like his colleagues, dressed in sharp business suits, his presence was more grounded; his face, at forty-seven, had softened. His steady professional demeanor was conveyed by a staccato voice with Georgia inflections, and he wore thick black glasses and a neat mustache. In addition to appreciating Martin's direct style, Wofford marveled at his partner's sure-footed way of sensing which levers to press, what calls to make. The editor's decades of experience in managing Black newspapers for John Sengstacke's *Defender* empire meant he knew everyone in that world who mattered. Shriver's hunch was clearly paying off.

If Martin seemed confident, he was. He didn't mind the rumors that he was a millionaire; this meant that people would never think he would take a bribe. He had successfully built the *Michigan Chronicle* newspaper for the company that owned the *Chicago Defender*, and his wife Gertrude's father's insurance agency provided financial assurance of a kind few Black families experienced. Today, Martin's daughter Toni says they were hardly rich, but points out that their grandfather achieved setting up a trust fund in the Jim Crow era for all five granddaughters' college educations.

Martin never had a problem being bold. As a young man, he showed up at the University of Michigan without having applied. A shocked admissions officer asked why he had not even brought a transcript, but Martin persuaded the man to allow him to take the entrance exam. He passed, then thrived at school, where he discovered a world of "white classmates, scores of students who were, if anything, dumber than I was. Indeed, a few were so stupid I began to wonder how they would fare in the advanced and highly competitive white society that controlled American life."

Later called a president whisperer, Martin smoothly moved within this rarefied world and built his success while expecting little from white men. He had painful childhood memories from Savannah, Georgia, that left him with a deep-seated skepticism of even those who claimed to have good intentions. Yet since joining the Kennedy campaign, he had judged Shriver and Wofford to be worthy of his trust. They seemed sincere in wanting to take on racism, but did not drone on about how they were going to do it; they just got on with the work at hand, making room for him to operate. Despite what Martin called the "quicksand of racial relations," he thought that Wofford and Shriver asked the right questions, appreciated all they did not know, and didn't take themselves too seriously.

Settling into his new job, Martin scored a major coup by getting John Kennedy and his wife, Jackie—then pregnant—to make an appearance at a forum on human rights at Howard University. Hoping for photographs of Kennedy offering a campaign speech in a place so full of meaning to Black Americans, Martin was pleasantly surprised that the cautious senior staff, known colloquially as the Irish Mafia, approved. This was the first time that Martin sensed that the trademark Kennedy charm, so enchanting to white voters, might possibly resonate with Black voters as well.

Martin felt it was Jackie's appearance at this event that conveyed something especially powerful to the Black community. White politicians, if they appeared at all before Black audiences, rarely brought their wives. If differences in policy and rhetoric between the candidates were marginal—and Black Americans were used to white officeholders delivering little—the aide believed Black voters were looking for clues as to who was even slightly less prejudiced, who could be trusted not to disappoint them more.

After being introduced to an overflowing crowd in Rankin Chapel, Kennedy said, "I regret that the Republican member has not shown up as yet," getting laughter. Kennedy drew blood by making sure the audience knew that Nixon, though he had been invited to the forum, had not bothered to make an appearance. Leaving the campus, they were nearly overwhelmed by excited students. Martin had the photo opportunity he needed to start earning the trust of Black voters.

◼ ◼ ◼

The race was hurtling toward being the closest in generations—tight everywhere, state after state, in all regions of the country. It was excruciating for both campaigns, knowing that the smallest mistake, the tiniest edge surrendered, could cost them the presidency. Both candidates were seen as moderates without strong views—young (perhaps callow) political technocrats eager to please an electorate that was not sure either man was ready to lead. Neither candidate said much during the campaign that was particularly compelling, and the mundane quality of the issues they latched onto, like falling behind the Soviet Union in missile development and China's interest in the obscure islands of Matsu and Quemoy, should have made the election of 1960 uneventful, but that is not how the story unfolded. Voter turnout would be more than 63 percent, the highest in decades. That year's debates, the first in a presidential general election to be televised, drew the intense interest of voters across the country.

Because both men had so much to prove, these four televised debates were crucial, especially for Kennedy. Nixon showed up at the first debate, on September 26, looking haggard, strangely passive, and so pale and five-o'clock shadowed that his mother, watching on television, inquired if her son was sick. Nixon had been up six points in midsummer, but Kennedy found himself up one after the first debate, and up by three after the second. It was at this debate on October 7 in Washington (just hours before Kennedy arrived at Howard University) that the two candidates unintentionally broke their silence on civil rights.

Ten minutes into the debate, Nixon was asked about his accusation that Kennedy avoided speaking about civil rights in the South. Nixon, looking more comfortable and assertive than he had in the first debate, made reference to the sit-in movement, saying, "I have talked to Negro mothers. I have heard them explain, try to explain how they tell their children how they can go into a store and buy a loaf of bread, but then can't go into that store and sit at the counter and get a Coca-Cola. This is wrong and we have to do something about it."

Kennedy replied, invoking stalled progress on equal education and employment: "Those are the questions to which the president must establish a moral tone and moral leadership." But while Kennedy and Nixon could have escalated the battle with a month to go, they retreated to their corners. Neither foresaw that the pastor each of them had cautiously, gingerly, courted would be the one to force open the issue of race in Atlanta.

■ ■ ■

It had taken him years, and much frustration, to get onto the White House grounds, but E. Frederic Morrow was thrilled to leave his job in the Executive Office Building to work on Nixon's presidential campaign. Morrow, the nation's first Black White House staffer, had scheduled two months' leave from the Eisenhower administration to campaign for Vice President Nixon. A former CBS television executive, he had spent the last six years navigating expectations of being "the first," working alongside white colleagues who did not know how to relate to him, much less utilize his executive talents.

He found the experience emotionally draining, and only his deep respect for Eisenhower sustained him. To Morrow, occupying the role of the administrative officer of special projects at the White House meant drafting speeches and occasional memos gently prodding the president out of his passivity regarding race. To the rest of the staff, it meant Black affairs only, whether or not he wanted that. Having given up a groundbreaking position at CBS, Morrow resisted and resented being marginalized. He had once even been asked to arrange White House parking spots.

Morrow's time on the Nixon campaign began auspiciously with the honor of speaking at the Republican convention, where he said, "One

hundred years ago today my grandfather was a slave. Tonight I stand before you a trusted assistant of the President of the United States." However, once he arrived at the national campaign headquarters, he found
himself without money or staff. His excitement was being ground down,
and he was frustrated by the blind assurance of young white staffers who
thought they knew Black voters better than he did. Morrow tried to respond to the cascade of requests directed at him from Black Republicans
around the country, but as he did, he sensed he was being shunted to
the sidelines, without access to his candidate. He was, as he put it, "in
a rear car."

He could not understand why he was being ignored. Morrow believed Nixon needed to hear what he had to say. He sensed the candidate was in a precarious position, paying no heed to all the things
Morrow had learned over his last six years in the White House. They
had a chance to reawaken the party of Lincoln, with all that might
mean to the Black community. The voters in 1956 had clearly responded with increasing support for Eisenhower, despite the sleepiness
and occasional tone deafness displayed by the administration.

In 1958, at a time when Morrow was discouraged by his dealings
with a president he found decent yet oblivious, it was Nixon who went
out of his way to invite Morrow into his office. Vice President Nixon
listened, commiserated, offered career advice. After telling Morrow he
should stick with government work because he was forging a trail for
others, Nixon promised that if he ever achieved a position beyond the
vice presidency—and there was only one—he would use it to open doors
for Black Americans in government. Morrow vowed to stay on, believing
that the president was not racist as much as misguided and that Nixon
was intent on finding a better way forward.

Morrow found Nixon sincere, earnest, and capable of working toward making America more equal. No one else in Washington had
invited Morrow to his home for dinner as he had, or so graciously
greeted his new wife, Catherine. Morrow found Nixon to be a good
listener, a cause for optimism that he would advance civil rights. Morrow was not alone in this view: a 1959 *Jet* survey revealed that Nixon

was the most popular presidential candidate among Black Republicans. Morrow's convention experience affirmed these hopes. When he was invited to participate in Nixon's midnight deliberations regarding his choice of running mate, Morrow advocated for the racial moderate Henry Cabot Lodge, the man Nixon ultimately selected.

Yet Morrow had not been allowed to participate in this level of decision making since the convention, or even to have a direct conversation with his candidate. Morrow was almost at the point of heading back to his post at the Executive Office Building, thinking the frustrations there were no worse than those at the candidate's headquarters. The constant calls and nearly frantic letters from Black leaders all over the country convinced him that the campaign was somehow going wrong.

But finding it hard to blame Nixon, Morrow stayed put, waiting for an opportunity to reassert himself and to help his candidate.

■ ■ ■

Louis Martin looked around the Metropolitan AME Church on M Street in Washington, D.C., a few blocks down Fifteenth Street from his office. He was there, surrounded by Black voters packed into wooden church pews, to observe Jackie Robinson. He would see just how persuasive the legend who broke the color line in baseball could be in his support for Dick Nixon. Now, with the election only a month away, the sight of Robinson tearing into Kennedy in front of an audience of Black voters drove home the problems facing the CRS.

When Kennedy tried to recruit the now-graying Robinson in a July meeting, the senator confessed his shortcomings on racial issues and promised to do better, doing something rare for a Kennedy—asking for another chance. But everything Kennedy said only seemed to make Robinson more suspicious and angry. When Kennedy asked Robinson, now a New York business executive, what he needed in order to view his candidacy more positively, Robinson thought he was being asked what kind of a bribe he might accept. It did not go well.

After leaving his executive position with the coffee company Chock

president's attention. King smiled and explained that he had just been writing to Nixon's office trying to arrange a meeting with the person in Washington he believed was most open to Black concerns. How fortuitous, King added, to meet each other here, so many thousands of miles from home.

Nixon replied, "You're Dr. King. I recognized you from your picture on the cover of *Time*. That was a mighty fine story about you. I'd like to meet with you when you are back in Washington."

They saw each other again at a white-jacket reception that night at the Parliament House, where they were photographed chatting comfortably (though King in fact felt quite ill). At midnight, the Union Jack was lowered forever, and the nation of Ghana was formally declared independent.

Back in Washington, a meeting between Nixon and King was promptly arranged; the vice president was true to his word. That June, a month after King had spoken at the Prayer Pilgrimage for Freedom in Washington on May 17 (a forerunner of 1963's March on Washington), King visited Nixon in his Capitol office. They talked for two hours, Nixon scribbling notes while King explained why Congress should go ahead and pass the 1957 civil rights bill, even though Democrats were busy scaling it back. King pressed for greater presidential leadership on racial equality, and Nixon dutifully offered the administration's perspective, but not defensively. Both were pleased by how well the meeting went and by their easy rapport and seemingly shared purpose.

In a subsequent letter, King thanked Nixon for their "rich fellowship . . . and fruitful discussion." Assessing Nixon's work in helping the first civil rights measure since Reconstruction to be enacted, however limited the bill's impact, King wrote that Nixon had shown "dauntless courage . . . This has impressed people all across the country." Demonstrating King's foresight as a political strategist, he said that Nixon's efforts showed "an expression of your political wisdom. More and more the Negro vote is becoming a decisive factor in national politics. The Negro vote is the balance of power in so many important big states that one almost has to have the Negro vote to win a presidential election." The following year, King sent Nixon a copy of his first book, *Stride Toward Freedom*, with a note that began, "To my friend."

Nixon replied, "My only regret is that I have been unable to do more than I have. Progress is understandably slow in this field, but we at least can be sure that we are moving steadily and surely ahead."

When a mentally ill woman stabbed King at a 1958 book signing in New York and his life hung in jeopardy, Nixon wired support, saying he was "terribly distressed to learn of the attack that was made on you." Though "this incident added to all the unfortunate indignities which have been heaped upon you," Nixon assured King, "the Christian spirit of tolerance which you invariably display in the face of your opponents and detractors will in the end contribute immeasurably in winning the support of the great majority of Americans for the cause of equality and human dignity to which we are dedicated." While corresponding with a biographer of Nixon's that year, King remarked, "It is altogether possible that he has no basic racial prejudice."

Yet King added an interesting paragraph to his letter. Pastors are inclined to think the best of others, but they also see people's shadow selves. King wrote, "Finally, I would say that Nixon has a genius for convincing one that he is sincere. When you are close to Nixon he almost disarms you with his apparent sincerity . . . And so I would conclude by saying that if Richard Nixon is not sincere, he is the most dangerous man in America."

"YOU CAN'T LEAD FROM THE BACK"

Daddy King was a force of nature, with a booming voice and presence that could at times be overwhelming. Martin Luther King Jr.'s father might have lacked his son's diplomatic subtleties, but his elemental strength offered protection. He foresaw such great things for his son that he named him twice: Michael, at birth, and then, after a European trip that elevated his sense of ministerial mission, he changed his own name as well as that of his five-year-old son to Martin Luther. Evoking the radical reformer who transformed Christendom, the change indicated the promise Daddy King saw in his gifted son.

Yet his great shadow was also something the young M. L. King retreated from. The younger King went to Pennsylvania to attend Crozer Theological Seminary, then to Boston University for a PhD, and finally to Montgomery, Alabama, for his first pastorate. As a brand-new twenty-six-year-old minister in Montgomery, King was unexpectedly thrust into the spotlight as one of the foremost leaders of the civil rights movement. Had boycott planning after Rosa Parks's arrest not been held at his own Dexter Avenue Baptist Church, he might have gone home before the meeting ended. Yet when he was asked to speak at the Holt Street Baptist Church mass meeting, a voice flowed out of him that sounded more like that of a prophet than an organizer. His impassioned words helped sustain the Montgomery bus boycott for over a year—longer than many thought possible for a campaign like that.

Near the end of the boycott, King foretold what their mission from that point on would entail: "It might even mean going to jail. If such is the case, we must be willing to fill up the jail houses of the South. It might even mean physical death. But if physical death is the price that some must pay to free their children from a permanent life of psychological death, then nothing could be more honorable."

Yet despite his confident oratorical skills, King had his share of doubts. He confided in Harry Belafonte when they first met, "I need your help . . . I have no idea where this movement is going." King said, "I'm called upon to do things I cannot do, and yet I cannot dismiss the calling. So how do I do this?"

What sustained him then, and would for the rest of his days, was an experience he had one night sitting alone in his kitchen during the most difficult days of the boycott. After receiving a threatening phone call, he suddenly felt the presence of God, promising he would never be left alone, never. But beyond even this experience, he needed something else to justify his hope that he could help America change. He found this additional strength in the organizing tactics of Gandhi. The radical ethos of organized nonviolence, present in both the Sermon on the Mount and the Mahatma's campaign, offered King a path forward, no matter how dangerous it might prove to be.

The Supreme Court intervened to give the bus boycott a surprising victory, but this did little to ease King's worries. He told Coretta, "People will expect me to perform miracles for the rest of my life. I don't want to be the kind of man who hits his peak at twenty-seven, with the rest of his life an anticlimax. Neither do I want to disappoint people by not being able to pull rabbits out of a hat." He wondered if he had reached "the zenith of my career too early . . . I might be on the decline at a fairly early age." Any hopes for a life as a quiet (however proudly intellectual) parish minister were changed forever by fame and the promise others saw in him, and there was no going back. King would later lament in a sermon to his Montgomery congregation, which ended with him in tears, that he was tired of "the general strain of being known." He distrusted this fame that, to his perplexity, kept growing, kept seeking him out as he spoke and organized. The more renowned he became, the more he felt unmoored as he tried to do God's will to the degree he could perceive it.

As King increasingly captured the nation's attention, he felt he was "a pretty unprepared symbol." Yet how could he possibly prepare himself to become a representative of the people? This was something circumstances thrust upon you—no one, from Isaiah on, trained for it; there was only the image of the prophet's lips being singed by hot coals, the admission that "I am undone." Not even being Daddy King's son could prepare you for this. And yet the younger King spoke of the zeitgeist of history plucking him up, his sense that no one else could do what he was seemingly being asked to do.

He would tell Coretta, "I can't afford to make a mistake." Though his hold on being a public figure felt tenuous, he accepted it. Every time he was offered an escape route—and he was offered many, from illustrious pulpits to prestigious professorships—he declined and packed his bag for another road trip, another march. Other Black leaders were often jealous of his gifts, his ability to claim the spotlight, but few understood what came with the weary pursuit. It was a hard road, even harder when he could not see where it was leading.

In late 1959, he acquiesced in Daddy King's plea for him to come home to Atlanta, thinking his father's imposing strength might in some measure protect him from these growing pressures while he contemplated how to lead a national movement as he had led a movement in an Alabama city. There, as head of the Southern Christian Leadership Conference (SCLC), King's headquarters would be just a few doors down the street from Ebenezer Baptist Church. King could now constantly fly in and out of the hub of Atlanta to fulfill dozens of speaking engagements. His scattered life made the prospect of being co-pastor at his childhood church seem like a secure home base, anchored in the supportive locale that had raised him. After all, it was here, in the middle-class, professional surrounds of Atlanta's Sweet Auburn neighborhood, that he had been told he was born to do great things.

Yet five years after the boycott, he was still struggling to figure out—as he put it to increasingly larger audiences—how to save the soul of America, nothing less. There was momentum from what he had begun in Montgomery, but could America be moved, shocked, persuaded to abandon its racial caste system? Just because his twenties were more eventful than the lives of most mortals did not mean King understood where to go in his thirties. In moving his growing family back home to Atlanta in early 1960, King was hoping to avoid being a one-hit wonder, trying to translate his early, signal success into something larger.

As the 1960s loomed on the horizon, however, King was floundering in his efforts to build a mass movement for a civil rights revolution. He had talked of organizing an American version of Gandhi's Salt March, but the conference he planned in Atlanta to bring it to fruition mustered fewer than a hundred sign-ups. He organized voter registration sit-ins around the South, expecting two thousand participants in thirteen locations. There was no response in key cities and a mere handful of protesters in others. *The New York Times* wrote almost mockingly about how small the turnout was. King had championed the Crusade for Citizenship, aiming to double the number of registered voters in the South by the 1960 election, but he was nowhere near this goal. It was unclear to King what his Southern Christian Leadership Conference should even be: a leadership association of ministers, a platform for King, or more of a grassroots organization? Should it focus on the vote or on direct action? How could its impact be more than regional? When describing King in 1960, *The New York Times* still had to remind readers that he was known for an Alabama bus boycott.

Amid these struggles, Daddy King promised city elders and fellow

Black leaders that his son would not make trouble locally, that his reputation as a movement leader would be muted in his hometown. Georgia's governor, Ernest Vandiver, a man King would never meet (but who would end up playing a consequential role in the events of October 1960), immediately denounced King's homecoming, saying that "anyone, including King, who comes across our state lines with the avowed intention of breaking laws will be kept under surveillance at all times." Longtime Atlanta Black leaders, Daddy King's proud Republican allies and friends, were nearly as uneasy with the wunderkind's return, worried that he might disrupt long-standing accommodations forged with local white politicians. Daddy King assured them that America's challenges were vast enough that King did not need to make Atlanta his target, telling friends, "He's not coming to cause trouble."

And he didn't. Trouble claimed him.

After returning home to Daddy King's world, King retained a measure of independence by resisting the old man's partisan loyalties. The self-confident and increasingly economically secure world of King's Sweet Auburn was a strong redoubt of Republicanism. Nationally, surveys at the time showed that Black Americans were split on the question of which party was better for them, narrowly favoring the Republicans. Roosevelt's New Deal had indeed swayed many formerly staunch Black Republicans through job creation, particularly in the North, but Black communities in southern cities like Atlanta remained GOP strongholds. Atlanta's Black Republicanism was more than a residual memory of Lincoln. With a southern Democratic Party that fiercely protected its segregationist power, allegiance to the GOP was a matter of survival for families like the Kings. Yes, FDR had made the party more palatable in many Black communities, but here in the South, men like Daddy King were only being attentive to the reality they saw around them.

In December 1959, King junior told a friend how Nixon was the only candidate who would call him and invite him to his home, which made him inclined to support Nixon, as he thought increasing numbers of Black Americans would. The Reverend Ralph Abernathy, King's close friend, had already made clear that Nixon was his man. King voted Republican in the 1956 presidential election, as did nearly 80 percent of Atlanta's Black voters. In addition to his father, other leaders whom King had respected all of his life such as the real estate broker John Calhoun—head of the Atlanta chapter of the NAACP and a wily Republican wheeler-dealer—held a modicum of political power by way of the organizations they had built with the support of Black Republican voters. But men like Calhoun did not operate in this political world on their own; they needed the power of Black preachers.

While the younger King remained publicly neutral, which both candidates took as an invitation to court him, Daddy King was not at all tempted to back Senator Kennedy. At an event held at Mount Zion Second Baptist Church on October 10, an impressive array of Black Atlanta preachers gathered to champion the Republican ticket. Daddy King was more than ready to support Georgia's GOP. The celebratory event was vintage John Calhoun, deftly rallying Black Atlanta for his party once again. The charismatic, round-faced Calhoun told the sizable crowd that Nixon and Lodge both possessed better records than Lyndon Johnson, a Texan they most certainly did not trust, and that JFK had been vague, at best, in his previous civil rights positions. Daddy King then used this opportunity to offer a full-throated endorsement of Nixon.

Both M.L. and A.D. were spotted at the program, dutiful sons that they were, but neither made an endorsement. Onlookers could only wonder if their father's stance was rubbing off on his uncommitted son. Yet that fall, King continued to refuse to be partisan, labeling both parties "hypocritical" on the subject of equality, saying, "The dearth of positive leadership from Washington is not confined to one political party. Each of them has been willing to follow the long pattern of using the Negro as a political football." Ultimately, King was trying to keep both parties from co-opting him and his movement.

■　■　■

While Louis Martin had persuaded Kennedy to speak at Howard University, Wofford's turn to assert himself came when he led a national, nonpartisan convocation on equal rights in New York City in mid-October, less than a month before the election. The CRS's goal was to burnish Kennedy's lackluster civil rights record, with a conference stuffed with NAACP and National Urban League leaders, academics, community activists, and even a few liberal Republicans. They invited Vice President Nixon to attend, but as they predicted, he declined.

Wofford's and Martin's years of connections gave them the credibility to put the gathering together, and in doing so, Martin felt that the CRS not only surpassed the Nixon campaign but firmly established their candidate as a credible civil rights advocate. When the CRS was later praised for helping turn the election, Martin maintained that helping King had been "the icing on the cake, but the cake was already made." Nonetheless, the event did reveal some deference on the part of the CRS to more conservative elements in the Kennedy campaign. In Wofford's words, some of Kennedy's associates were "tremendously scared of losing white votes." The vice presidential nominee, Lyndon Johnson, recommended that instead of explicitly evoking "civil rights," the convocation should be called the National Conference on Constitutional Rights. If that was what it took to talk about equality, the CRS would happily accept a change of name.

On October 11, a week before the sit-in at Rich's in Atlanta, the National Conference on Constitutional Rights convened at the Park Sheraton, just below Central Park, with its grand awning of golden lights. The chief draw was not Kennedy but Eleanor Roosevelt, given the trust Black leaders had in her. Hence the shock when she proclaimed, in the summer, that "Kennedy can't win the Negro vote." (She famously quipped that JFK needed "a little less profile and more courage.") Now, at last warming to Kennedy, she told the gathering,

"It took courage to call this conference . . . Senator Kennedy will fight to get prompt action on civil rights."

With the conference concluding successfully on the second day, participants boarded buses to head uptown for a Harlem campaign rally. In front of the Hotel Theresa, on a stage erected over the wide sidewalk of Seventh Avenue, Congressman Adam Clayton Powell greeted a crowd of two thousand people. When JFK joined him, Powell proclaimed, "This is the next President!"

Kennedy cried, "Are we going to vote Democratic?" and Harlem roared back. He reminded the crowd how democratic revolutions were once inspired by America: "There are children in Africa called Thomas Jefferson. There are none called Lenin or Trotsky or Stalin in the Congo, or Nixon." After pausing, Kennedy added, "There may be a couple called Adam Powell."

"Careful, Jack!" Powell interjected from behind, and his hometown audience roared with knowing laughter.

Kennedy accused Nixon of concealing his own civil rights record, whereas he was proud of his. He asked the crowd to stand with him in moving the country forward, "until the United States achieves this great goal of practicing what it preaches."

Coincidentally, on the same night and in the same neighborhood, Nixon's vice presidential nominee, Henry Cabot Lodge, wooed Black and Puerto Rican voters at a rally at 116th and Lexington, among searchlights and fireworks. The Republican set off an explosion of his own. Lodge pledged, for the first time in American history, that Nixon would appoint a Black man to the cabinet if he won. Nixon now had to deal with what most white Republicans felt was an unforced error by Lodge.

When Louis Martin heard the news, Lodge's pledge "hit like a bomb." This was a far more specific promise for action than Kennedy's rhetoric on equal opportunity. Should they make a similar commitment? Then it struck him: Nixon would not back up Lodge. Martin and Wofford bet Nixon would not have the courage to support his vice presidential candidate. As they gamed it out, they decided their campaign should not make any panicked promises. It would be better to highlight the substantive policies that had been spotlighted at the New York conference.

They anxiously waited to see how Nixon would react. When the morning papers arrived, their prediction was borne out. While campaigning in his native Southern California, Nixon disowned Lodge's pledge, saying only, "I will attempt to appoint the best man possible without regard to race, creed or color." A Nixon aide told *The New York Times*, lest his statement be less than clear, "Mr. Nixon would not appoint a Negro just because he was a Negro." The Nixon campaign was now in a terrible bind, having offered something, only to yank it away. One Virginia Republican said of Lodge, "Whoever recommended that Harlem speech should have been thrown out of an airplane at 25,000 feet."

In truth, Lodge's promise upset Martin on a deeper level than even Wofford knew. What Lodge proposed, ill-advisedly or not, was exactly what Martin hoped to accomplish. He vowed to ask Kennedy to "move decisively toward the integration of the Supreme Court and the Cabinet." If Martin could bring about these groundbreaking appointments, "there was no job in the federal establishment too big for a black man," or in any part of American life.

The competing Harlem rallies were an unusual interlude in a campaign season largely devoid of talk about civil rights. But there was something else striking about them, too: the conspicuous absence of Martin Luther King.

■ ■ ■

Back in the summer, Lonnie King—the lively, impatient Morehouse student leader—said to King, "Can I get you to go to jail with us? 'Cause if you go to jail with us, because of Montgomery, it will become an international story." The plan, he said, was to stage a sit-in at Rich's.

For generations, Rich's department store had been the place where Atlanta families shopped for fashionable clothes, where kids got to ride the beloved Pink Pig monorail, and where restaurants and bathrooms were humiliatingly segregated by race. Lonnie believed that if the students could force Rich's—the most prominent department store in Georgia, if not the whole South—to desegregate, every downtown business would follow suit.

As a test, Lonnie had visited Rich's lunch counter over the summer with the family of Howard Zinn, a white professor at Spelman College. The staff turned off all the lights, preferring to close the restaurant rather than risk a confrontation. After perturbed white patrons had filed out and Rich's called the police, Lonnie was brought to police headquarters for a warning, by way of a talk in Chief Herbert Jenkins's office. The owner of Rich's, Dick Rich, was also present. To Rich, criticism of his store felt personal, because he thought of himself as a liberal on race. He told the student leader how much he supported the Atlanta University Center and how his store was the first to give Black people charge cards—all true. So he felt justified in asking Lonnie to stop any future student protests at his store.

Lonnie responded that Rich needed to integrate his store fully, even allowing Black shoppers to eat in the elegant Magnolia Room. The meeting fell apart, and Rich's face turned red as he shouted, "If you bring your Black ass in again, I'm telling you, Chief, put his ass under the jail."

Lonnie shot back, "I'm coming back in October, and I'm going to bring thousands of students with me, so Chief Jenkins, get your cells together, 'cause we will be back."

As October approached, Dr. King had encouraged Lonnie's student leadership while keeping his own counsel as to whether he would be participating in the students' direct action. That was fine with Lonnie; King hadn't said no, so Lonnie assumed that meant yes. The pensive King had always been hard to read, but there was no denying his strong support for the exploding sit-in movement across the South. The movement began in February 1960, when four North Carolina A&T students ordered food at a segregated Greensboro lunch counter and refused to leave when asked. Having seen the effects of Rosa Parks's refusal to give up her bus seat five years before, King knew the importance of seizing transformative moments when they unexpectedly presented themselves. Only fifteen days after the Greensboro students first began the sit-in movement, King addressed a group in Durham, North Carolina, praising the bold move. He told his audience, "Remember that both history and destiny are on your side . . . And one day, historians of this era might be able to say, there lived a great people, a black people who injected new meaning into civilization." King spoke words that day that would soon have unforeseen implications for him: "Let us not fear going to jail. If the officials threaten to arrest us for standing up for our rights, we must answer by saying that we are willing and prepared to fill up the jails of the South."

Within weeks, there were dozens, and then hundreds, of similar student sit-ins erupting all across the South. King's success with the Montgomery bus boycott after Rosa Parks's arrest continued to inspire students, showing what could be accomplished by citizens through nonviolent civil disobedience. Now a younger generation was propelling the movement forward, and King could catch up or be left behind. He was quick to support the student sit-ins.

The minister saw in these students a spirit that his own SCLC seemed to lack, and King wondered, as the movement exploded, if he might be able to guide it while also harnessing its power. At Spelman College's Founders Day on April 10, he said, "You're not merely demanding a cup of coffee and a hamburger here and there. You are demanding respect." After watching King put the moral clarity of the sit-ins into words, a student named Marian Wright (later Marian Wright Edelman) wrote in her diary, "There's something almost holy about him."

In the months before the election, the energy was exhilarating. In February, Lonnie King had read in the Black-owned, Republican *Atlanta Daily World* about the North Carolina lunch counter sit-in, and everything about the students' actions resonated with him. Quickly, he organized a team from the adjacent campuses of Morehouse, Spelman, Morris Brown, Interdenominational Theological Center, Clark College, and Atlanta University to follow their example. In preparing students for sit-ins, he taught them that their method of resistance must be nonviolent, but warned them that the other side might not be. In mid-May, Lonnie led nearly three thousand students in a march up the hill to Georgia's capitol on the sixth anniversary of the still unenforced *Brown v. Board of Education* decision. The students had invited Dr. King to walk with them, and as they set out that morning, they wondered if he would make an appearance.

Governor Vandiver, however, had the protesters met with armed troops and fire hoses. As the marchers approached the gold-domed statehouse, Lonnie elected to detour to avoid the capitol and the danger it posed. He would not risk lives being lost—not this time. When the students finally arrived at Wheat Street Baptist Church, King was waiting for them on the church steps, greeting them with pride and relief.

When students returned for the fall semester, planning for the big push against Rich's segregationist policies began. The students had skirted a confrontation with the authorities in their spring march, but there was no guarantee they would be so lucky again. Lonnie understood the fears expressed by Daddy King's generation of leaders: "They were concerned we were going to overshoot the runway; a lot of us were going to get killed—that's understandable."

Lonnie watched the presidential campaign with mounting anger, however. He thought both candidates seemed to talk about every problem in the world except their own country's problem with racism. He reflected, "If you had been from Mars, you wouldn't have known any Black folks were in this country . . . and thousands of young Black kids, and some white kids too, were raising heck all over the South." The students decided the most opportune time to act would be after the third presidential debate, to put "this issue of civil and human rights on the burner and make the Kennedy Nixon people discuss it."

With the planned sit-in at Rich's less than a week away, emotions were running high. Student activists from around the country, including the formidable Nashville crew of John Lewis, Diane Nash, Marion Barry, and James Bevel, descended on Atlanta for a Student Nonviolent

Coordinating Committee (SNCC) conference over the weekend. A message arrived from the Kennedy campaign reading, "The human rights for which you strive are the definite goal of all America." A student leader announced a message from Nixon would be coming as well, but none arrived.

King spoke at the SNCC gathering and praised the students' efforts, but he was upstaged by the Reverend James Lawson of Nashville, who told the students that the next time they went to jail, they all needed to refuse bail. Soon a rhythmic chant of "jail/no bail" filled the conference hall. King had been saying for years that there was "great suffering" soon to come, but many students—some starting to judge the thirty-one-year-old minister as more oratorically gifted than daring—wondered who, precisely, would bear the brunt of this suffering. John Lewis saw the Atlanta students repeatedly pulling King aside, prodding him to make a decision.

King understood how upset the students were about the prospect of his not participating in their planned act of civil disobedience. But an arrest in Montgomery years earlier, when he came close to spending a night in jail, had left him shaken, and he was personally hesitant about the movement's radical tactic of going to jail. John Lewis believed King nonetheless recognized SNCC's increasing influence on the civil rights movement and saw the need to act. "If he stayed on the sidelines much longer," Lewis wrote, "he and the SCLC risked losing us. Basically he knew it was time for him to stick his neck out, as so many of us had been doing for months."

Six students followed King to the airport later that weekend as he was leaving to deliver a series of speeches up and down the East Coast, and they walked with him through the terminal, continuing to pressure him. An onlooker thought King seemed to be on the verge of tears.

Once King was back in Atlanta, a group of students found him eating at his parents' house and invited themselves inside. Feeling trapped, King was forced to listen as they implored him to get arrested alongside them at the upcoming sit-in. When Daddy King walked in, he said angrily, "M.L., you don't need to go! This is the students, not you." Then he kicked the students out of his house.

■ ■ ■

Harris Wofford heard with dismay King's soft Georgia murmur offering conditions that he was certain the Kennedys were not going to like. The minister was laying out his reasons for why their hopes for a joint appearance with John F. Kennedy—not an endorsement, but something close to it—were misplaced. King told Wofford, "I've learned that Nixon is going to be at the veterans' convention, and I have a rule to be bipartisan, and not one or another, so I have to offer that I would meet with him too."

"Do you really feel you have to?"

"Yes," said King, knowing he was thwarting Wofford's efforts. King told him Nixon might not show, but that he needed to invite him and make it a joint appearance. Wofford said he understood and would plead with the Kennedys to not let Nixon's presence in Miami force them to abandon the whole idea. But he knew his perfect event was slipping away.

Putting down the phone, a disappointed Wofford began strategizing with Louis Martin because it was clear that a daunting task lay ahead of them. Shriver was back in Illinois, preparing for the final push in that state. They would have to persuade Bobby, on their own, to accept the conditions offered by a controversial activist with whom the Kennedys were not completely comfortable—a task made even more difficult by the fact that Kennedy was increasingly allergic to getting anywhere near Nixon if he could avoid it.

Wofford got a chance to convince the candidate himself as well, but JFK exploded: "To hell with that, Nixon doesn't have much to lose in this whole situation . . . I lose Southern votes." Kennedy had the white South to hold on to; Nixon had it to gain.

Kennedy seldom lost his temper, usually opting for deft, deflective humor. But months of campaigning had worn down any hope of his showing much sympathy for Nixon—Nixon, whose Senate office was across from his and whose political career had, from the moment they both entered Congress as newly elected navy veterans from the Pacific theater, so closely tracked his own. While they were once friendly, if distant, Kennedy now routinely attacked Nixon with expletives.

Bobby, too, was curt when Wofford floated King's proposal: "No. You can't possibly do that." Wofford argued the Miami event could still be worth it, given that he and Martin were virtually certain that Nixon would decline, just as he had declined invitations to Howard and the New York City conference.

Bobby dismissed this idea; there was no way they were going to risk offering Nixon a large stage to do whatever he wanted. If this young preacher wanted to make demands, then "take it off the agenda, we're not meeting him. That's not going to do us any good."

Wofford's relationship with Bobby had been fraught since the day they had met on the Hill three years earlier. Kennedy was then chief counsel to the U.S. Senate Select Committee on Improper Activities in Labor and Management, and a mutual friend thought that they should know each other. As Wofford looked on, Bobby calmly ate the lunch that a Black attendant set out for him, until at last he picked up Wofford's résumé and perused it. He said, before sending Wofford away, "One thing I just can't understand is, why did you go to Howard Law School? I could understand going and teaching there, but how in the world did you go there to be a student?"

Now, three years later, Bobby dismissed the idealistic Wofford once again. It was Wofford's turn to give King some bad news. When Wofford called King to tell him the Miami event was off, he sensed unexpected disquiet in King's response. To Wofford's surprise, the minister sounded even more distressed than he himself felt.

While refusing to compromise the obligation he felt toward non-partisanship, King confided in his old friend why he really wished for the Miami event to take place: "I'm in a real jam 'cause they're going ahead despite my urging them not to do a sit-in before the election; they're going to go ahead and do it for Rich's department store. I'm under great pressure to go there. I don't really want to, I don't think it's the best thing, but they're doing it and I probably am going to have to go with them."

King had wanted a good excuse to avoid the Rich's protest, which being in Miami would have provided, and now it had been yanked away. He felt boxed in by students whose idealism matched their determination. Without an important event to attend, King conceded, "I have to participate now."

Wofford's disappointment was insignificant compared with what King felt as he canceled his plans to go to Florida. There would be no packing of suitcases for Miami, only a paper bag of toiletries for a booking cell. He had endured much since Montgomery, but this was different.

■ ■ ■

The day before the sit-in, Lonnie King was at the Spelman library trying to inspire more students to join them. He asked his new co-chair Herschelle Sullivan to "call M.L. and just remind him to meet me at ten o'clock on the bridge tomorrow." From his conversations with King dating back to August, Lonnie believed King would join the sit-in. Sullivan didn't know Dr. King, but Lonnie said, "Just tell him that I asked you to call him and he'll talk to you." Though Lonnie did not doubt King's commitment to the cause, he preferred to leave nothing to chance. He knew King was hesitant to take part, which he believed came not from King's own fears but from his father's. Sullivan later wondered if Lonnie chose her to make the call to King because, if the pastor was considering backing out, he might be less likely to do so speaking to a woman.

Sullivan had been studying in Europe in the spring but dove into the student movement upon her return to Atlanta. Her strengths complemented Lonnie's, and she made a solid partner as the crucial day neared, but her call to the King residence was met with a disappointing reply. Sullivan walked back to Lonnie with a distressed look. "Lonnie, he said he can't go."

"Can't go?"

A shocked Lonnie soon had King on the phone, along with Daddy King and the SCLC administrative head, Wyatt Tee Walker. A furious Daddy King replied with what Lonnie thought was a bombastic no, but Lonnie held his ground: they needed King there.

Lonnie said, "M.L., let me say something to you: you are the moral leadership of this movement, whether you like it or not, and you promised me you were going to go."

The younger King stayed silent. Daddy King replied that it made no sense for his son to subject himself to further legal peril, especially because he was supposed to be preparing for a trip to Nigeria. King's return to Atlanta earlier that year had nearly been thwarted when Alabama indicted him for submitting fraudulent tax returns. Though the charges were baseless, they threw King into a depression. He feared all he had worked for could be stripped from him. It took the effort of family and friends to get him back on his speaking schedule to face audiences still eager to hear him. King's response was hardly surprising, though, given that a white Alabama jury would almost certainly find him guilty. Jail time looked like a very real possibility.

At around the same time, he faced another legal entanglement, though it seemed like a minor nuisance compared with the tax indictment. On May 4, 1960, King volunteered to drive the novelist Lillian Smith, a white ally of the movement, to her breast cancer treatment. DeKalb police spotted this Black man and white woman in a 1957 Ford near Emory University's campus on Clifton Road and pulled King over. As he sat in the driver's seat, the police told King his car tags were out of date, though Smith knew that her presence was the real reason why her friend had been pulled over. King explained that the car did not belong to him. The officer ticketed him for this and then, fatefully, also wrote him a ticket for not carrying a Georgia driver's license, though he still carried a valid Alabama one. King took a day off to appear before Judge Oscar Mitchell in nearby Decatur, and in a quick and seemingly uneventful trial he was ordered to pay a twenty-five-dollar fine, which he paid.

To King's amazement, on May 28, 1960, he was declared innocent of all tax charges by an all-white Alabama jury. Suddenly the whole wretched specter of jail evaporated. The fine for an out-of-state driver's license seemed of no importance. Still, King's legal travails left him skittish; he had been in enough courtrooms that May to last a lifetime.

On the phone, Lonnie reiterated the plan: "You and I are going down to Rich's. There's going to be hundreds of us all over downtown." Lonnie interpreted King's silence as a sign that he was torn between an old friend and his father. Lonnie said, "This is your hometown, and I think you need to go with us. If you get arrested with us, it'll be in the national news, and I think that's what the movement needs." King understood Lonnie's sense of urgency; he knew the indignity of not being able to get a hamburger and a coffee at a lunch counter, and would speak later of seeing tears in his daughter's eyes when he had to tell her they were not allowed to go to the Funtown amusement park.

As the call dragged on, Daddy King's resistance aggravated Lonnie. He decided to play a card only someone who'd been attending Ebenezer Baptist Church since 1945 could possibly hold. Every year, without fail, Daddy King preached a sermon about how you must be ready to engage and sacrifice for your cause. So Lonnie quoted the sermon's title by saying, "M.L., you can't lead from the back. You gotta lead from the front."

Daddy King could say nothing to that.

His son slowly replied, "L.C., what time do you want me to meet you?"

"Ten o'clock on the bridge." This was the sky bridge over Forsyth Street that led into Rich's. They all knew it well.

"Okay," King said. "I'll be there."

■ ■ ■

That same day, on the other side of town, the Atlanta Baptist Ministers Union was staging another public endorsement of Nixon. This would be one of two big stories readers of the *Atlanta Daily World* would confront the next morning, October 19. The Republican endorsement appeared on the front page, along with a news item stating that hundreds of students would be heading downtown sometime that day to protest Rich's segregationist policies. There was no mention of the fact that Daddy King's son would be joining them.

The Nixon and Kennedy campaigns were unaware of events in Atlanta. Unusually, both men were appearing in Florida on the same day. October 19 was slated to be another long slog, with a stop for Nixon in Wilmington, Delaware, and speeches for Kennedy in New York City, culminating in their joint evening appearance at the ritual Al Smith Dinner at the Waldorf Astoria hotel.

If all went as planned the next day, Lonnie's friend Otis Moss Jr. would be ready to telegram both Kennedy and Nixon that the Reverend Martin Luther King Jr. had gone to jail in support of desegregation. Lonnie predicted to friends that Nixon was the presidential candidate who would respond.

DAY 1: WEDNESDAY, OCTOBER 19

"Chain Gang" by Sam Cooke and "Georgia on My Mind" by Ray Charles were on the radio. Movie theaters showed *Inherit the Wind* and *Ben-Hur*. Charges against three white men planning to dynamite the historically Black Philander Smith College in Little Rock were dropped. New Yorkers sought tickets for the new musical *Camelot*, opening in a few weeks. Nina Simone wrapped up a two-night appearance in Atlanta's Vine City, King's neighborhood, and University of Georgia fans around the state wondered what the star quarterback Fran Tarkenton had in store for Saturday. Gallup's most recent poll had Kennedy taking the lead at 49–46 percent, with 5 percent undecided. In Atlanta, the fall morning was clear and cool.

The students chose Trevor Arnett Library as their meeting point, well situated between all the campuses of the Atlanta University Center, the consortium of historically Black colleges in the city. From the rounded portico of the ivy-covered brick building, Lonnie King surveyed an empty lawn stretching from Clark all the way to Morehouse. After working a night shift at his post office job, followed by a nap of only a few hours, Lonnie was impatient and on edge, eager for the sit-in to begin. The city was tense, too. Promises had been made, threats ignored, months spent on planning, and now the day had arrived. This was the students' first large demonstration since the spring. How many people would actually show? The few who had already arrived milled about, looking nervous.

Then, as happened during their first sit-in that spring, a trickle turned to a steady stream of students arriving from different campuses. In a few minutes, the quiet collegiate quadrangle was filled with a crowd of nearly two hundred. Lonnie gathered the students and told them that this day would be "the most rewarding experience of their lives." Because all wondered if they would be ending the day in jail, many had textbooks tucked under their arms and toothbrushes in their pockets. After the best speech he could summon, Lonnie instructed them to break into the eleven groups to which they had been assigned. Just before 10:00 a.m., these groups walked to waiting cars to head downtown. Drivers had been given maps, and group leaders made sure their watches were coordinated. Lonnie led them in a final prayer to steady them, but as they walked to their cars, someone broke the silence by calling out, "We're not going to a funeral." The students laughed, and someone started singing "We Shall Overcome" until all the voices around them lifted up the song.

Martin Luther King was right where he said he would be. He waited on the Rich's sky bridge, dressed in his usual dark suit and tie, a Bible under his arm. Lonnie met him there; with his massive chest and athletic physique, he loomed over King. They looked impressive side by side, with Lonnie attired in a gleaming gray suit.

The Crystal Bridge had been built so that shoppers could flow seamlessly between floors two through five of Rich's flagship department store and the newer Rich's furniture emporium across the street. Every Atlantan could picture these gleaming elevated walkways as the Christmas season began on Thanksgiving night. Thousands assembled in the street below to see the great Christmas tree lit on top of the bridge, with choirs singing carols on each level, while the iconic department store clock presided over the intersection of Broad and Alabama Streets.

The students and the two Kings, united on the sky bridge, began, at eleven sharp, "a sit-in exercise as coordinated as a military maneuver on a drill field," according to *The Atlanta Journal*. In the second-floor snack bar, about a dozen students took seats at the lunch counter and stood in the cafe's line to request service. Lonnie instructed the group to ask to be "served or be arrested."

Picking up a ham and cheese sandwich on whole wheat from the silver counter, King stepped forward to purchase it, to no avail. A Rich's staffer immediately sized up the scope of the demonstration and tried to hurriedly close the luncheon space. As he started shutting down the lunch counter, he hurriedly explained, "We don't serve colored."

"We aren't here to buy colored, we are here to have lunch," Lonnie replied.

The student leadership team had called *The Atlanta Constitution* the day before to tell them something big would be happening downtown, so reporters roved through the store hoping to capture any disputes, cameras at the ready. This suited the students, for without coverage the sit-ins would be, as Herschelle Sullivan put it, "a tree falling in the forest." A reporter asked King why he was here today, and he replied, "Because the students asked me to come, and I felt a moral responsibility to join them in this worthwhile movement." He then added, "I am not the leader. It was student planned and student originated and student sustained." Still, it was hard for King not to be seen as the center of the action unfolding all over the city. Another reporter asked how long he would be joining the students in the sit-in, and King identified the Clark College student Carolyn Long as the group's spokesperson: "The decision as to when we leave is up to her."

She took the cue and repeated the day's mantra: "Until we get arrested or served." Long's father was an Atlanta school principal whose job had been threatened because of her protest activities, yet her father still supported his two daughters' involvement in the civil rights movement. Like the other women present, she stood in the cafeteria dressed in high heels and a pressed dress.

As everything shut down around them, the sit-in group started to feel anxious. The problem was not that they weren't being served but that they were not being arrested. In momentary limbo, some of them sat down at the tables and benches around the snack bar. Cars flowed past below on Forsyth Street.

They needed a better leverage point, and high above them, on the sixth floor, the crown jewel of Dick Rich's empire beckoned.

Across the city, student teams hit other sites. Four national chain stores, Woolworth's, Grant's, Kress, and McCrory and McLellan dime stores, had announced that they were integrating lunch counters in more than a hundred cities, but Atlanta had not been on their list. Demonstrators found "Closed" signs posted up and down Broad Street. A middle-aged man kicked a female student in the shins near Kress, but she relied on her training and did not respond. As the women working the lunch counters left, the students filled the emptying restaurants and waited for the police to arrive.

When eighteen students arrived at the seventy-five-yard-long counter of Woolworth's on Broad Street, the manager muttered, "The fountain is closed," and proceeded to rope it off. The Morris Brown College student Bernard Lee, later to become King's body man, announced, "We're going to sit here until they serve us." The students' lawyer, Donald Hollowell, walked through Woolworth's to observe how the students were doing before moving on to the other stores. Earlier in the year, the NAACP chose Hollowell to represent all of those involved in civil rights protests in his state, so he seemed to be everywhere that long day, his military demeanor reassuring and steadying.

At site after site, once a student observer saw that a group had been refused service, he or she sent word back to headquarters by way of a shortwave radio operation set up in the nursery of the Rush Church. Dozens of cars filled with student picketers waited to be sent out. Soon, there were many more sign-carrying picketers outside the lunch counters than sit-in participants inside. At one restaurant, white counterprotesters gathered around the marching students, loudly playing a recording of a recent Stone Mountain Ku Klux Klan rally. One white person yelled that the morning's action was "a beautiful black mess" and proceeded to spin a student so hard that he was thrown off his stool. Another white man waved his KKK card at them, and a white woman knocked down a student by the Rich's subbasement Barbeque Grill. *The Atlanta Journal* described the faces of white witnesses around downtown as displaying "astonishment, uneasiness, or dislike."

Yet a few white people also called out encouragement; students heard, "More power to you," and, "Stick with it, we're behind you." Despite isolated attacks and insults, widespread violence had not yet broken out. How long the peace would last was an open question; tensions rose throughout downtown. Someone called state troopers to the capitol after spotting a long line of Black women, but it turned out they had arrived to take a nurse's exam.

Back at Rich's, Benjamin Brown, president of the student body at Clark College, and his student group waited at the entrance to the Magnolia Room, along with white-gloved ladies lined up for its 11:30 a.m. opening. The first time Lonnie had observed the Magnolia Room, he was appalled at the antebellum-style uniforms Rich's insisted Black waiters wear. The sixth-floor Magnolia Room, the plushest gathering spot in Atlanta, conjured up the old South, so for the student leaders it felt right that this place of elegant insult would be the site of the final, climactic confrontation. The glow of the crackling fireplace; gold-framed oil paintings depicting colonial tableaux; formal soft yellow tablecloths and green walls—all this luxury cosseted diners enjoying chicken salad amandine, the "Plantation Salad," and, as a final indulgence, Rich's famous coconut cake. From the standpoint of the movement, no place could have been more evocative.

The chairman of Rich's board, Frank Neely, arrived with security to confront Ben Brown, waving a paper listing twelve "Atlanta Mixing Organizations," asking, "Which of these organizations do you belong to?"

A student responded, "We don't belong to any organization."

Neely said it would help him better understand exactly what they wanted. The students repeated that they represented themselves. After a few minutes, Captain R. E. Little from the city police arrived and asked the anxious manager, "Have you asked these people to leave?"

Neely replied they would not admit to belonging to one of the "mixing" groups. Captain Little asked if he wanted them to leave, and Neely said of course. Little turned to the students, "An official of this store has asked you to leave the premises, which is his right. Do you refuse to leave?"

They nodded. A curious crowd gathered. Captain Little informed the students he was taking them to the station. As he led them out, they saw a growing crowd of picketers gathering around Rich's. Protesters, most of them women, held light-blue cardboard signs: "1–2–3–4 don't shop at this store" and "Don't spend cash where you can't drink coffee." The arrested students, the first of many that day, were taken to a waiting red arrest wagon, and then the officers reentered the store to see where else sit-ins were happening. The tearoom momentarily returned to business as usual.

A young local minister, the Reverend Otis Blackshear, and Bobby Schley of Morris Brown College went to the Cockerel Grill. A waiter told them there was a restaurant for Black people elsewhere, and if they persisted, they would be arrested. Captain Little arrived, quieting white onlookers, saying, "Now I'm handling this." He placed the two under arrest. Officers took them out to join those arrested from the Magnolia Room.

This first wave of arrested students was taken to the Atlanta Police Station before noon, to wait on benches in the station captain's office for fingerprinting and booking. Donald Hollowell observed everything, preparing to take charge of the legal battle to come.

Growing restless, Lonnie decided he should escort King straight to the Magnolia Room. Looking over his team, he chose two Spelman students, Agnes "Blondean" Orbert and Marilyn Pryce, to go up with them. He thought the two elegant roommates embodied exactly what a lady entering the Magnolia Room should look like. It should be absurd to deny them service.

The night before, Orbert and Pryce had attended a meeting at Spelman's Giles Hall, where a sit-in instructor announced, "If you're going to participate, go right. And if you want to be part of the movement, but you don't think you can go to jail, go to the left." They went to the right. One of their other roommates went left, explaining, "My mother has a weak heart; I can't go." They joked with her that she might be talking about herself. For Pryce, the decision to challenge Rich's was easy: "It was time for Jim Crow to go." For years, Pryce's family had taken a 4:00 a.m. train from their home in Tuskegee, Alabama, to shop at the glamorous Rich's, though it meant eating in the basement, where they would "sit at a little old nasty counter right near the toilet." She would return to change that. Orbert, a North Carolina native, had a Rich's card for college friends' Saturday visits to the store.

Lonnie, along with Orbert, Pryce, and King himself, walked up to the great white columns framing the front of the restaurant. Pryce could observe ladies being served on fine china plates. Seeing Martin Luther King approach, a staff member raced to find Mr. Rich in his office, informing the owner that King was not only now on the premises but literally at the gates of the citadel. When informed that King was there for today's sit-in, Rich started to cry. He wanted to work with the older Black leaders, but now he felt trapped, squeezed between a white customer base demanding segregation and the students, who he believed were out-of-town agitators. Rich foresaw disaster now that Martin Luther King was involved.

Rich's general superintendent, Bennett Tuck, emerged from the restaurant and stepped forward to block the group from going any farther. He said, "We are sorry, we cannot serve you here. We have facilities for you in the basement."

Lonnie said, "Why can't you serve us here?"

"We have facilities for you in the basement."

The minister stared at Tuck, his expression passive and patient.

"Well, we would like to eat here." More pressingly, he then asked, "Why can't you serve us here?"

"We are very sorry we cannot serve you here, and we ask you to leave the store. You know that one group has already been up here and made their point." Tuck added, "You realize it is unlawful not to leave a store when asked to do so?"

"Yes," answered King, "but I would like to point out to you that I have spent, in the last year, over two thousand dollars in your store. I feel it is my moral right to stay here."

Unsure how to respond, Tuck walked away. The students and King stood for about fifteen minutes near the restaurant entrance and the elevator lobby. Never did they actually sit in. Cecil Semple, Rich's vice president of operations, informed the police that they needed their services again up on the sixth floor. Soon Captain Little returned with two other Atlanta police officers. He asked who spoke for the group, and Lonnie jumped in to say he did. Captain Little looked to King to confirm this was true, and the minister slowly nodded yes.

More of Rich's staff had now gathered to block the entrance to the center aisle of the tearoom. Semple spoke up, telling the police that they had asked the group "to leave the store, and they have refused to do so." The police officer informed Lonnie that he was now breaking the law. They had no choice but to arrest him and the other sit-in participants. One last time, Captain Little asked them to exit, because if they did not, he said, "I would have to take them away from the premises."

Lonnie said, "I came here to eat, and prefer to be arrested than not be served." With that, Captain Little declared all four now under arrest.

As Little led them out without handcuffs, Lonnie's friend Constance "Connie" Curry, one of the few white participants in the sit-in movement, had a moment of panic. Standing in the lobby in front of the sixth-floor elevators, she had volunteered to serve as an official observer. As a white woman, she would not be suspected of taking part in the sit-in and could tell Donald Hollowell and sympathetic reporters what she had observed. A graduate of Agnes Scott College in Decatur, she had been part of SNCC's inaugural meeting. Inspired by her beloved mentor Ella Baker, she was elected an adviser of SNCC, though, like King, she was a few years older than the students. She tried to get more white students from local universities involved but got little response.

Suddenly, in terror, she noticed the head of the local Ku Klux Klan chapter, Calvin Craig, just across from her as Lonnie and Dr. King were being escorted out. Seconds before they passed, she feared Lonnie and King would instinctively greet her, thus marking her to the Klan as a white collaborator. She said a silent prayer: "Dear God, please don't let any of the students look at me, speak, or show recognition, because this man will surely do me harm."

Remarkably, Lonnie and King, despite all that was going on around them, kept their wits. Lonnie recognized Craig in an instant, realizing the KKK leader "could have done her in." Passing Curry, they looked past her as if she were just another bystander, to her profound relief.

Once downstairs with the officers, the three students and King emerged through Rich's glass doors and onto the crowded sidewalk and were escorted past student picketers presently enduring a barrage of racial slurs from enraged bystanders. The police cleared the way through a thicket of the students' signs, which displayed messages like "We want to sit down like everyone else" and "A house divided cannot stand."

Police treated Dr. King, Lonnie King, Marilyn Pryce, and Blondean Orbert differently than the other protesters that day. Captain Little placed the four in his personal patrol car. Lonnie felt that Little could barely contain his hostility, but he assumed the officer spared them handcuffs on the orders of Mayor Hartsfield. These images would be in the next day's newspapers, and the always alert mayor wanted to avoid bad publicity. Before the car pulled away, photographers swiftly surrounded them with bursting flashbulbs, capturing King seated next to Pryce in the back seat. There would be no arrest wagon for Dr. King that day.

As Little drove them away, a photographer caught King looking out the window with a troubled expression on his face.

Other sit-in groups, locked out or ignored by other lunch counters and department stores, reassembled at Rich's. When word got out that only at that department store were students actually being arrested, wave after wave of students hit it throughout the afternoon, most heading up to the Magnolia Room. Once arrested, groups of students enthusiastically sang together as they were packed into department store elevators by the police; one officer groused that they were nearly bursting his eardrums. Unlike King's group, later groups were ushered out by way of back exits; the police wanted to avoid being photographed as they lined them up against the walls of back alleys and took down their names.

As arrest wagons headed to the police station, students held impromptu prayer services, singing "We Shall Overcome." A student remembered, "The tin body of the wagon acted as a sounding box for our deeply felt singing." As the vehicle turned right on Forsyth and Alabama, the picketing students heard the muffled singing, and the music spread among them.

En route, one student made his group crack up as he objected, "I can't go to jail, I have exams coming up." They projected bravery and bravado, but they knew this was no game. What was coming would be nothing like the brief jail stays they had experienced in the spring, when they were all released quickly back to their comfortable dorms. Arriving at the courthouse to wait for their appearance before the presiding judge, James Webb, the men were put into one large holding cell, and women in another. Students were thankful the leadership team had anticipated that they would each need to have a person on the outside, one friend who would be responsible for bringing them updates from their classes along with books and other materials. It was dawning on many that they could be incarcerated for weeks, not days. So they sang.

Judge James Webb was not in good spirits, faced with the increasing volume of students suddenly filling his courtroom that day. Luckily for Martin Luther King and this cascade of student protesters, their lawyer was scared of no one and quite used to facing down irritable white court officials. Over the decades, frightened Black clients wondered where their advocate got his nerve. The answer was simple: Donald Hollowell had been a buffalo soldier.

He was one of the last to serve in the legendary Black cavalry unit. During the Depression, Hollowell's family badly needed help, and so he left school to support them, enlisting in the historic Tenth Cavalry at Fort Leavenworth, Kansas. Despite the reputation buffalo soldiers had as formidable fighters from their history on the western plains, when World War II came, Hollowell faced what all Black soldiers did. In his interactions with the larger army, he said, "I was treated with less dignity, less acceptance, and less common courtesy than even prisoners."

After the war, he put himself through law school by working as a freight laborer and trucking clerk. He arrived in Atlanta only eight years before the sit-ins and, because he was determined to protect his vulnerable clients, found himself driving dangerous backwoods roads to defend those who desperately needed representation. He endured judges who turned their backs to him, prosecutors who insulted him with racial epithets in open court, and in at least one instance a bailiff who forced him to argue his case from the courtroom balcony to preserve the separation of the races. Hollowell became a local legend for getting a Black man, Willie Nash, acquitted for the rape of a white woman and the murder of a white man. Facing an all-white Georgia jury, he first got a mistrial (after the prosecutor used a racial slur) and then convinced a second jury that Nash's confession was coerced by police intimidation. The evidence against Nash was weak, but Hollowell knew that wasn't enough; he identified a suspicious lover of the woman and showed the court how flawed the evidence that the rape had even occurred was. Hollowell saved Nash's life in a place and time in which facts rarely prevented a Black man from being executed.

The forty-two-year-old lawyer, still muscular from his quarterbacking days at Lane College, occupied an unusual position in the movement, revered by the old guard and young activists alike. His growing fame as Georgia's foremost civil rights lawyer meant that on October 19, 1960, he was perfectly placed to represent King and the students. He earned this respect working sixteen-hour days, juggling multiple federal cases designed to force Georgia's public education system to desegregate at all levels, and yet he still managed to make time to represent the students. They would say, "King is our leader; Hollowell is our lawyer; and we shall not be moved."

To keep track of the influx of new cases, he made a chart on yellow notepad paper with each student's name, which group they were part of, where they had been arrested. He worried about young people placing themselves in harm's way and told them so. A later jail call from Lonnie would be greeted by Hollowell with "What kind of trouble are you in now?" He was steadfast but not coddling. After the student leader Julian Bond was arrested at a sit-in in the spring, a judge asked him how he pleaded; the student organizer paused and then stammered, not knowing how to answer. Hollowell said to the young man in a stage whisper, "'Not guilty,' you damn fool."

The students declared themselves willing to spend months behind bars, but Hollowell saw his job as getting them out of jail as quickly as possible. He knew that every minute spent in jail was a risk, and despite his heavy caseload the students became his priority the moment they were arrested. Hollowell was used to working through the courts to effect change, following the moderate NAACP playbook, but he also possessed imagination enough to see how the students' actions could be a turning point for civil rights.

Hollowell needed assistance, however, and so he hired a couple of young lawyers to work alongside him. One was a recent graduate of Howard Law School, Vernon Jordan.

Decades before Jordan would become head of the National Urban League and a Washington power player, he was Lonnie's high school classmate. At that time, a friend told Lonnie he should run for class president against him. Lonnie said, "Man, have you lost your mind? Vernon Jordan has a suit for every day of the week." Lonnie's mother started crying when he mentioned the contest. "I just feel so badly," she said, "that I only make five dollars a day and car fare, and you have to wear hand-me-down clothes . . . But you can beat him." She told him she would ask the white woman she worked for if Lonnie could borrow some of the suits that her son outgrew. Lonnie campaigned as he would later organize and won. The loss still stung Jordan years later, but weightier considerations made him eager to help out his former high school rival and Dr. King.

Hollowell had not known Dr. King long when he arrived at the court that day from his cramped office at 859½ Hunter Street (now Martin Luther King Drive). The young minister would sometimes pop into a beauty salon that belonged to Hollowell's wife, Louise, to charm her cosmeticians. The pastor and the lawyer would see each other at the Butler Street YMCA, and Hollowell had heard King give a sermon at Ebenezer.

Despite Hollowell's request for a brief postponement, Judge Webb ruled that he must begin the proceedings, leaving no time for the lawyer to speak with the students. Nevertheless, Hollowell had gathered enough information to point out that Rich's management never actually asked one of the student teams to leave but had left this job to the police; as a result, Judge Webb released at least that group.

Soon Dr. King and the students arrested alongside him were brought before the judge. Hollowell realized he had a big problem. Because of the new trespassing law that the Georgia legislature had passed to prevent sit-ins, King and the students conceivably faced months behind bars. Hollowell and Judge Webb knew that; some of Hollowell's clients did not.

Of all his thousands of notes, letters, memos, telegrams, sermons, speeches, and manuscripts, few are more evocative than a handwritten statement that Martin Luther King drafted in a blue-lined notebook he borrowed from a fellow arrestee. We do not know if he read the whole statement before Judge Webb that afternoon; United Press International quoted him as stating, "I will stay in jail a year if necessary. It is our sincere hope that the acceptance of suffering on our part will serve to awaken the dozing consciousness of our community."

King's written statement read, "Mayby [sic] it will take this type of self-suffering on the part of numerous Negroes to finally expose the moral defenses of ~~the~~ our white brother who happen to be misguided and therby [sic] awaken the doazing [sic] conscience of our community." Working under pressure, King made uncharacteristic mistakes. One of his gifts was an ability to exude calm in the midst of frenzy, a serenity that unnerved his opponents and steadied his followers, but even King was rattled by the events of the day.

And yet he maintained a lofty moral tone in his written statement, asserting, "If you find it necessary to set a bond, I cannot in good conscience have anyone go my bail." King added, "One of the glories of living in a democracy is that citizens have the right to protest for what they believe to be right." He continued, "I don't feel that I did anything wrong in going to Rich's and seeking to be served. We went peacefully, nonviolently and in a deep spirit of love." He asserted that they had broken no laws that day. He made clear, "We were there because we love Atlanta and the South." King laid down his terms, stating he would not offer any appeal because jail was "a way to bring the issue under the scrutiny of the conscience of the community." At last, he was putting Gandhi's jail principles into action and honoring James Lawson's dictum of not posting bail.

Whatever King said did not lighten Judge Webb's mood. Hollowell sensed that his earlier success was not likely to be repeated. Lonnie looked on; he loved watching Hollowell work. When it was his turn to speak for himself, he called segregation "a moral issue that needs to be solved," and he warned that the protests would continue until the status quo shifted; someone would have to give. Other students also said they would not post bail.

A court staffer interrupted to let Judge Webb know that more students had been arrested at Rich's and were on their way over. Webb considered allowing photographers into the courtroom, as was usually his custom, but then informed everyone, "This was a planned demonstration for the purpose of obtaining publicity . . . My courtroom is not going to be used for that purpose." His attitude toward the students left no doubt that he was not interested in helping their cause by letting them be photographed for national newspapers.

Outside, twenty students started picketing with signs reading, "We prefer jail to life in hell." Hearing this, Judge Webb ordered the band of protesters hauled into the courtroom so he could tell them that he found their actions to be a personal insult. The judge said, "If there is anywhere in the world that a Negro has received impartial treatment, it has been in the courts. It is clear in my mind that this act is contemptuous."

Hollowell interjected that the students' protest was aimed at their friends being held at the city jail, not their presence in his court. Judge Webb responded that perhaps they had not known they were in violation of his court, but they certainly did now, and if they went back outside to continue, he would punish them to the fullest extent of the law. He concluded his tongue-lashing with a warning: "If you persist in such vile acts, you will lose ground at every step."

Only one white sit-in participant went before Judge Webb, Richard Ramsay, an organizer with the American Friends Service Committee in North Carolina. While sleeping over at A.D.'s house during the previous week's SNCC conference, he was intrigued by the direct action being planned. "There was no question about what I was to do," Ramsay wrote. From his site at McCrory's five-and-dime on Whitehall Street, he and six students headed for the Magnolia Room at Rich's, joining students coming in waves from other sites. When Ramsay's group asked for a table, they were under arrest within seconds and steered to the elevator.

Once at the jail, when the police noticed that a white man was among the group, they pulled Ramsay out to question him as to why he was present. He stoutly maintained that he was with the others. After he was fingerprinted and photographed, an hour passed as he waited alone. Then Ramsay was taken to court with fifteen others, where all refused bond. While Ramsay's group was fully expecting to go to jail, Hollowell cross-examined the arresting officer to reveal that store officials had asked this group to leave the dining room, not the premises. Based on the judge's technical reading of the law, he had to dismiss the charges. When the students held a mass meeting at Morehouse later that night, they gave Ramsay a standing ovation for being arrested. He deflected the attention to instead praise all the students in jail that night and would later send a written account of the day's events to the Georgia Council on Human Relations.

Fifty-two protesters had appeared in Judge Webb's court by the end of the day. Lonnie was proud of the number of students arrested, with thirty-six ultimately heading to jail—nineteen women and seventeen men—and sixteen students released. Before they could be transported to the new Fulton County Jail, students were held near the courtroom downtown at Fulton Tower—the city jail known as Big Rock. It was a nineteenth-century Stone Mountain granite structure with a tall, narrow tower extending a hundred feet into the air. Beneath this were the cells, most in abysmal shape—dirt crusted so deep after decades of neglect that it could no longer be scrubbed away, not that this was any priority. This city jail was located across the street from the police department at Butler and Decatur Streets, in the shadow of Georgia's capitol dome. Only a few decades before, gallows stood on the roof.

In the reeking holding tanks, the students were held alongside drunks, addicts, and others hauled in for various offenses. Prisoners were curious about the bookish, innocent-looking young people who seemed completely unprepared for the environment in which they would have to sleep. The cell looked to have been designed for about twenty people, but they were packed in double that number. There was a toilet situated in the middle of the room, and it was difficult to adjust to using it without privacy. Guards left them sleeping pads that were so rancid that a student wondered if they had been there since the Civil War. One other prisoner wondered why they had volunteered to do this, asking, "You got a chance to bail out, and you don't bail out?" Their consensus about the activists, it seemed to the student Charles Person, was that "they're crazy."

Blondean Orbert described Fulton Tower as the "smallest, dirtiest, dankest jail." When the students were about to be moved, Donald Hollowell and King himself were allowed to visit the women. Though they were there to comfort and support them, they also had difficult news to share: their cases might take months more to go to trial, and an eighteen-month sentence for trespassing was possible. They needed to prepare themselves for this eventuality. Hearing this, Orbert fainted. When she regained consciousness, her roommate Marilyn Pryce and Dr. King were leaning over her, asking if she was all right. She remembered King as a "pleasant, jovial, unassuming man; kind and gentle." This would be borne out every time she saw him around campus in the years to come, when he would smile and ask, "How's my little fainting buddy?"

At five in the evening, King, Lonnie, and a portion of the students arrived at the two-month-old Fulton County Jail on Jefferson Street, just north of what is today the Donald Lee Hollowell Parkway. In contrast to the grimy, cold conditions at Fulton Tower, Lonnie could not believe the "brand-spanking-new" gleam their lockup displayed. So many students were arrested at Rich's that Fulton County needed to borrow beds from adjoining districts to prepare for the students.

King was allowed to call Coretta. He did not speak with his four-year-old daughter, Yolanda, or his two-year-old, Martin Luther King III, saying, "They're too young; explaining would get too involved."

■ ■ ■

The news of King's arrest came as a shock to Wofford. He and Louis Martin did not receive any further details until later in the day, and from an unlikely source. Although seldom remembered, the Kennedy campaign's involvement in the King case actually begins on the first day of King's incarceration: he received a jail cell visit from the Kennedy aide Frank Reeves, a staffer who normally traveled on the campaign plane.

When Louis Martin joined the campaign, he was struck by the testy rivalry between Reeves and Marjorie Lawson, the titular heads of the CRS. Lawson was affluent and well connected, and the Kennedys could talk with her and her husband, Belford, about New England private schools and summers on the Massachusetts coast (Martha's Vineyard for the Lawsons, Hyannis Port for the Kennedys). When the Kennedys first asked for their help, Belford Lawson said he would not give up his law practice, so despite Marjorie's warning that she had never worked in politics, the Kennedys hired her. The Lawsons were successful Washington lawyers, but by 1960, Bobby had begun to feel that they possessed little credibility with civil rights leaders nationally. In fact, Bobby said to Wofford that the two Lawsons were making his brother "look silly."

Lawson had tried to arrange a meeting with King, but she downplayed any eagerness on JFK's part, whereas Wofford stressed the urgency of bringing the two men together. With Wofford and Shriver supervising Black outreach and Frank Reeves having been hired in the summer of 1960, Lawson sensed that she was being edged out. Lawson said she felt doubly marginalized as a Black woman in the Kennedys' overwhelmingly white male circle, and she reacted with understandable frustration to two white men taking over issues related to the Black community. She also resented Frank Reeves, a lawyer she thought had gotten involved in the campaign only for the title and the status it conferred.

To ease the tension between Lawson and Reeves, Shriver decided in August that Reeves would henceforth travel with JFK, introducing the candidate to local Black leaders, while Lawson would retain the title of chair of the CRS back in D.C., though it was now Martin who was, in Wofford's eyes, "the heart organizing and directing the whole operation." Reeves sensed the shift, too, realizing that Louis Martin was "more and more the strong man in the national campaign staff operation."

The circumstances under which Reeves came to King's cell were convoluted. Earlier in the week, King tested the genuineness of Senator Kennedy's recent helpfulness by asking if the campaign would help investigate an incident that had happened during an SCLC gathering in Shreveport, Louisiana. Reeves immediately made plans to assist the Reverend Ralph Abernathy, who had been arrested and had several important SCLC documents stolen from him. On an even more troubling note, one of the SCLC's field secretaries had been shot at in his car on Saturday, the bullet just missing his head. No arrests were being made. The Kennedy campaign's plan was to have Reeves, a Howard law professor, speak with King to gather more information, though there was an ulterior motive: Reeves could also use this as an opportunity to secure an endorsement from King. Flying to Louisiana, Reeves took a detour to the Atlanta airport, where he was supposed to meet Dr. King Wednesday afternoon for this discussion.

Arriving at the airport, Reeves went to the lounge and waited, but King did not show. He called King's office and discovered that the minister would certainly not be making their meeting: he had just been arrested at Rich's department store. Now in Atlanta for no purpose, Reeves phoned Wofford to tell him King was jailed. Wofford and Reeves agreed that it was imperative for the campaign to respond, both for King's sake and for the campaign's own. Reeves agreed to stay in Atlanta for the time being.

Once Wofford received news of King's imprisonment from Reeves, he and Martin convened an emergency meeting. The last thing they wanted was some twist in the national narrative less than three weeks from Election Day, but none of the ideas they explored seemed quite right: either the downsides for Kennedy were too great, or the gestures themselves seemed half-hearted.

It was always difficult for the CRS to get anything approved, as Martin found out soon after he joined the campaign. Back in the first weeks of autumn, Martin had proposed that Kennedy telegram Nixon to demand a strong statement on integration. Shriver's question in response was, as always, "How many votes will this idea win or lose for us?" Martin insisted that such action would gain them more votes than it would cost, so Shriver determined that they would call Kennedy together from his room at the Mayflower Hotel. Around midnight, Shriver started to pitch the Nixon telegram but then stopped short, saying, "Wait a minute, Jack; let me put Louis on the phone. Maybe he can explain what he has in mind." Then, realizing Kennedy had no idea who he was talking about, Shriver added, "This is Louis Martin, a newspaper man from Chicago who is working with us."

Kennedy welcomed Martin to the campaign, and the latter began to describe his idea. Kennedy, however, quickly cut him off, saying, "You don't know that sonofabitch like I do." Kennedy explained, "Instead of answering directly, he will curve, and come back with another question. I don't think we can pin the bastard down that way." Far from being hurt by Kennedy's immediate dismissal of his idea, Martin loved the senator's decisiveness. After Martin put down the phone, Shriver said, "Now you see why he's a leader. His mind is sharp." Martin not only agreed but now saw that his telegram idea would have, in the hands of the cagey Nixon, rebounded on them.

On the first day of King's imprisonment, the only conclusion Martin and Wofford reached was that the CRS would have to keep abreast of the situation, because Kennedy's inner staff was not paying the slightest attention to events in Atlanta. At the Atlanta airport, Reeves phoned the SCLC's Wyatt Tee Walker. Walker, despite the fact that new sit-ins were breaking out all over the city, invited him to his home to talk about what was going on. Reeves rented a car and drove over. The two men decided it was not a bad idea for Reeves to talk to King in prison that night.

Reeves was older than King and had been born in Montreal. He attended Dunbar High School in D.C., followed by Howard University and Howard Law School, and then joined the NAACP's *Brown v. Board of Education* effort. Reeves had nothing but respect for King's courage, although his own tactics were closer to those of Thurgood Marshall: showing laws to be unconstitutional in the courts, instead of taking direct action to reveal their fundamental immorality.

When Reeves arrived at Fulton County Jail, he announced he was an attorney from Washington, which was true, leaving unsaid he was not actually King's appointed defender. He was surprised by the respectful reception he received, but he assumed that the Fulton County authorities believed him to be from the Justice Department. They did not want yet more federal officials poking into Georgia business.

King was busy being interviewed by reporters; Reeves waited his turn, eventually being taken in to see the prisoner. Reeves asked King, "What, if anything, could we do?" King replied that at this point his deepest concern was for his wife and that he would appreciate anything the Kennedy campaign could do to reassure her. King offered no specifics about what form this reassurance might take. They talked for a short time, with King's reluctance to side with either Kennedy or Nixon still holding firm. Soon, Reeves returned to the airport to head to New York City to rejoin the campaign, forgetting about helping Abernathy in Louisiana.

Speaking to Wofford that evening, Reeves suggested that Kennedy send a telegram to Coretta Scott King. Though this proposal would at first be ignored, it would later play an important role in events that followed.

Harris Wofford's sincere desire to protect King had first developed during a late-night car ride three years earlier. He offered to drive him and Coretta from an Omega Psi Phi conference in Baltimore to Washington, D.C., hoping to give his wife, Clare, an opportunity to meet a man he found fascinating. Their relationship would deepen in the coming years, and King later joked that Wofford was "the only lawyer who would help me go to jail instead of using all the tricks of the trade to get me out of jail."

Speeding south along a dark Maryland highway toward Washington, the four of them talked about the future. It was Coretta who said something that the Woffords never forgot. In an anguished tone, she suddenly unburdened herself from the back seat: "I've had this nightmare that keeps coming back that at the end of this road he has chosen, he is going to be killed." Coretta had a great-uncle who had been lynched. Growing up in Marion, Alabama, she knew that when it came to white bigots, "they will do anything."

King turned around from the front passenger seat and said, "Corrie, I told you to get that out of your head, and think what we can do while we're alive. I didn't choose this, they asked me to chair the bus boycott, and I said yes." King softly sang a spiritual that went, "And the Lord came by and asked and my soul said yes."

On October 19, however, King's predicament didn't yet seem especially dangerous to Wofford. King was jailed in a city controlled by a relatively sympathetic mayor, William Hartsfield, who deemed Atlanta "too busy to hate." King himself seemed confident, though he was steadying himself for the possibility of a long stay.

It turned out everyone was looking in the wrong direction.

■　■　■

Before being assigned to their cells in the segregated east wing, King and the students were stripped and searched, forced to surrender any valuables. Guards offered them their first meal: liver and onions, creamed potatoes, bread, salad, chocolate cake, and coffee without cream or sugar. The students figured that this relatively hospitable treatment must be on account of Dr. King's presence. When the guards pushed King's food to him, he declined. He told reporters who managed to interview him in prison that night that he was "fasting today in a spiritual act of self-purification, to prepare [himself] for what lies ahead." Other students who were moved with King to the Fulton County facility had no such reservations; as one exclaimed, "It's the first food I've had since breakfast. We couldn't eat the slop they gave us at noon at the City Jail." On the women's side of the jail, they were given beans, gruel, and other food they found terrible. Some barely ate at all over the next several days. Come morning, the women would be served spoiled buttermilk to drink; only pregnant women were served fresh milk.

King did a television interview with Atlanta's NBC affiliate, WSB-TV, his tie undone and suit jacket off, explaining how his fasting was different from a hunger strike, though he said he would consider one if it would help focus people on the plight of Black Americans and desegregate stores in the Deep South. He told reporters, "Maybe it takes some degree of suffering to change the attitudes of this very pressing national issue," and, "As Negroes, we must bear our crosses to save the soul of America."

King gave credit to the students, reiterating, "I did not initiate the thing. It came into being with the students discussing the issues involved." He said, "I felt a moral obligation to be in it with them. I had been in on this thing from the beginning, and I felt that when the actual moment came when somebody got arrested, I should be in on it." He was determined to reinforce to the students that they might have to endure more jail time than they had anticipated: "Whatever length of time it is, we'll stay. We have repeated that no one signs bond for us. We know it takes a good deal of struggle and sacrifice to attain any objective, and we are willing to do whatever is necessary."

The reporters departed, and King was ushered back to his cell. It would be a long night. As King's friends would learn over the years, he maintained a "war on sleep," particularly when imprisoned. He found excuses to talk for as long as his companions could stay awake, almost as an endurance contest. He would, when alone, pray and pace, as if surrendering to sleep would be a defeat. But for now at least, he had the company of four other students in his cell, including Lonnie King, who was impressed by how "convivial" King was. They had known each other long enough for King to drop his formal persona, and the minister sang and joshed along with his younger cellmates to pass the time.

As evening fell, reporters fanned out to solicit reactions to the day's events. On Hunter Street, a service station owner said of the arrests, "It is a means of showing the world that we intend to fight for our rights, even if it means sitting in jail. His [Dr. King's] taking part tends to inspire the students." There were rumors in the Black community that the Klan planned to hold marches. At city hall, Mayor Hartsfield knew these demonstrations would be waiting for him to deal with in the morning. Some two hundred college students had somehow paralyzed municipal courts, closed businesses, dominated newspapers, daunted city police, irritated local judges, and overfilled the jails. With the fourth presidential debate taking place in two days, Lonnie King seemed well on his way to achieving his goal of propelling the Atlanta sit-ins into the national news.

One county over, Judge Oscar Mitchell sent word to the authorities that King was a wanted man: he still had a suspended traffic sentence. King himself was unaware that he was under probation. As the lights went out that night, he had no idea that his arrest had now placed him in much greater danger than before.

DAY 2: THURSDAY, OCTOBER 20

Hundreds of students assembled with signs in hand to picket downtown Atlanta, their resolve seemingly strengthened by the arrests of the day before. At the helm of these protests was A. D. King. The students hit sixteen establishments, starting at 10:30 a.m. This time, those opposed to the sit-ins were waiting for them, with groups of Klansmen assembling at two dime stores to harass the students. The Klansmen wore their white robes without hoods, because the state had passed a ban in 1951 on masking faces in public with the Klan in mind. Police patrolled in greater numbers than they had the day before, their attention focused mostly on the students.

A.D. and twenty-four students went to the Terminal, Atlanta's railway station and one of the busiest hubs in the South. When the group arrived at the Terminal Station restaurant, three students entered and sat down at the lunch counter before the staff could close the door. A.D. and the others remained in protest outside the establishment.

Life as the younger brother of Martin Luther King Jr. and second son of the formidable Daddy King was not easy for A.D. He was less likely than his brother to stand up to his imposing father, lacking M.L.'s inner security and confidence.

A.D. struggled with alcoholism while attempting to complete his higher education and follow the family path into the ministry. Aware that he would likely always live in the shadow cast by his brother, he tried to live up to the family's expectations as best he could without jealousy. The two brothers genuinely understood each other's travails, and A.D. had a knack for lovingly piercing King's solemnity and prophetic poise.

As A.D. and the rest of the students waited outside the Terminal Station restaurant while the three students inside were denied service, Captain R. E. Little arrived to arrest yet another King. After Little told A.D. to move on because he and the students were creating a disturbance, they refused to do so and were willingly arrested. Soon they found themselves standing before Judge Webb.

A.D. announced that he was the spokesperson for his group of students and said that they "had no intentions of creating a disturbance . . . they just wanted to eat" at the station restaurant. Judge Webb sternly informed the students that they were "immature and unwise." Looking at the young King, barely older than the students he led, the judge went on to complain, "One of your troubles is you always have a spokesman. Maybe you're listening to the wrong persons."

Donald Hollowell raced to Judge Webb's courtroom for the second time in as many days despite being busy representing two Black students, Charlayne Hunter and Hamilton Holmes, whom the University of Georgia was refusing to enroll. Twenty-five more Black protesters ended up in jail that day (as well as a white counterprotester), with three taken to join Lonnie and company under the same Georgia trespassing law, and the other twenty-two being sent to the city's prison farm—where they would have to labor in the fields—for disorderly conduct under the city's statute. These students would be staying in what one described as "modern slave quarters." There was no natural light, only a few fluorescent bulbs, so it felt as if they were being housed deep underground. A pungent combination of urine, vomit, and perspiration overwhelmed the smell of disinfectant. The bench was showing little indulgence toward the students being sent there.

Even under such pressure, the students seemed to be holding firm; the real question now was who would break first: the mayor's office, the courts, or the city's increasingly tense business leaders?

More than half of the students waking up that Thursday morning in Atlanta's jails were women. Having heard stories of white guards raping Black female prisoners, Herschelle Sullivan and other leaders set up a rotation in advance so at least one student was always keeping watch during the night. Over at the Atlanta Prison Farm, the student Norma June Wilson listened as a white male guard set his gun down and raped a woman prisoner who was in the bunk bed under her.

What Atlanta women protesters endured is part of the story of sexual violence suffered by Black women at the hands of white men throughout the civil rights movement. In this terror, guards asserted power without accountability over women protesters who were left physically vulnerable. Before Rosa Parks resisted arrest on the Montgomery bus, she was a trained activist who investigated the systematic rape of area Black women for the NAACP.

In the Fulton County Jail, which felt much safer, the women started the morning by singing hymns and movement songs before praying together. Their prayers were not so much for themselves as for all those on the outside. To pass the time during the day, the women practiced dance steps, played games and did puzzles, read well-worn romance comics, exchanged jokes, and tried to study. A few had textbooks, but the jail mostly prevented books from being brought to them, making the tedium more unremitting and causing them to fall further behind in their studies. The students who had been held at the Tower the night before were relieved to be transferred to the Fulton County Jail, where they joined King and most of the students. When rumors that the famed NAACP lawyer Thurgood Marshall might be assisting with their defense began circulating—by coincidence, he was scheduled to speak in Atlanta that weekend—the students screamed for joy. It was, as Ann Ashmore recorded in her diary, "19 girls skipping and singing with all the gusto usually exemplified at a football game after a long sought after touchdown."

Women had been central to the movement from the start, and Spelman students in particular more than made up their share of the Committee on Appeal for Human Rights in Atlanta. Professor Howard Zinn observed that the expression used to be "You can always tell a Spelman girl by . . ." followed by a list of ladylike virtues. Now, given recent activism, the expression went, "You can always tell a Spelman girl—she's under arrest."

Back in the spring, when the presidents of the city's historically Black colleges advised the students to write and publish why they wanted to protest—in what Lonnie thought might have been an attempt to head off the first sit-in—Lonnie asked the Spelman student Roslyn Pope to compose a message on their behalf. Over a weekend, she prepared a statement expressing all that she had endured, all the daily indignities and frustrations of life under segregation. Professor Zinn gave her access to the campus's early version of a computer, and she wrote on a long legal pad as Julian Bond typed her words as fast as he could. She cited the Montgomery bus boycott as an inspiration.

> We do not intend to wait placidly for those rights which are already legally and morally ours to be meted out . . . We want to state clearly and unequivocally that we cannot tolerate in a nation professing democracy and among people professing democracy, and among people professing Christianity, the discriminatory conditions under which the Negro is living today in Atlanta Georgia—supposedly one of the most progressive cities in the South.

Atlanta University's president, Rufus Clement, secured the funds to publish "An Appeal for Human Rights" in not only the Black *Daily World* but the *Journal* and the *Constitution* as well. The students' declaration was soon picked up by *The New York Times* and *The Nation*, and New York's senator Jacob Javits put their words into the *Congressional Record*.

Knowing how central the women were to the movement, King wrote a message of gratitude and encouragement to them from his own jail cell. Beginning with the salutation "Hello girls," King thanked them for "your intrepid courage, your quiet dignity, and your undaunted faith in the power of nonviolence." He told them, "Never before have I been more proud to be a Negro. Never before have I had more faith in the future." He believed that "when young ladies are willing to accept this type of self-suffering for the cause of freedom it is both majestic and sublime."

Some students shared cells with the general jail population, while others were held with friends from the movement. The presence of young people whom King knew and appreciated, and who looked to him for leadership, helped King bear the tedium and stress of prison. Their morale was high, and he took the opportunity to do a little teaching and organizing. He also realized that conditions in the Fulton County Jail were far better than those that others were facing elsewhere. His own treatment seemed to reflect Atlanta's interest in avoiding bad publicity.

King had been incarcerated, briefly, only once before. In Montgomery, he had been driving a car full of fellow boycotters when he spied the police behind him. He let his passengers out and was instantly surrounded by the officers, one of whom commanded: "Get out, King; you are under arrest for speeding thirty miles an hour in a twenty-five-mile zone."

Police put King in the back of their car. He panicked, realizing they were headed in an unfamiliar direction, down roads leading out of town. As they turned down a "dark and dingy street . . . and headed under a desolate old bridge," King started to envision a waiting mob. Just then he saw the lights of the Montgomery jail come into view, and in this moment of possible deliverance he felt embarrassed that as a pastor to others he had not even known the jail's location. Kicking him, they threw King into a rank-smelling cell, where fellow prisoners crowded around him. The toilet was exposed, and men rested on torn-up mattresses and wooden planks. The minister was horrified that human beings were forced to live like this, no matter what they had done. They begged him to help them get out of jail. He told them, "Fellows, before I can assist in getting any of you out, I've got to get my own self out." A cash bail was quickly raised and posted, and before nightfall King was back home.

Now, at the Fulton County Jail, a student leader, Bernard Lee, slept in the bunk above Dr. King. Lee was, like most students, excited to spend time with a famous figure. Lonnie's perspective was different, as he had known Dr. King since childhood. Lonnie had always admired how talented M.L. was—his effortless grace with words, how he could cite complex philosophical ideas and Bible verses. Yet M.L. was cool, too: he could shoot pool, flirt with girls, tell a good joke. They shared childhood experiences, yet came from such different backgrounds. Lonnie grew up in an Atlanta alley behind a fish market, and until he arrived there, at age eight, he had lived in Calhoun County, near the Alabama border. He said, "I was born looking up at the bottom. I was not on the bottom, I was looking up at the bottom. The bottom was up there." Lonnie joined the Navy after his freshman year at Morehouse to earn GI Bill money for college. Despite his high score on an aptitude test, he was assigned to clean the bathroom for two hundred men on his ship. This position did not stop him from being perceived as a leader. Their tours took Lonnie around the world, beyond the segregated way of life he grew up with. When his period of enlistment concluded, he decided to return to the South. He sensed a revolution coming—it was at least possible—and he would regret missing it.

Lonnie appreciated the fact that M.L. never tried to dominate their movement. King had come to some of their tense meetings with Atlanta college presidents, rarely saying anything, whether out of loyalty to both sides or a wish to let the students speak for themselves. The student leaders appreciated that King's presence added weight to their cause in the eyes of older leaders.

King often felt unworthy of this admiration, once saying, "I am conscious of two Martin Luther Kings . . . somebody foreign to me . . . there's a kind of dualism in my life." His friend Stanley Levison called him "an intensely guilt-ridden man . . . And it could be said that he was tortured by the great appreciation that the public showed for him. If he had been less humble, he could have lived with this kind of acclaim, but because he was genuinely a man of humility, he really couldn't live with it." As a little boy, King's sense of guilt was so strong that he *twice* threw himself out of a second-floor window, once when he and A.D. accidently knocked his grandmother down, and again, later, when he had been out playing during her fatal heart attack. He paid little attention to earning money or garnering awards, believing he should not benefit from his ministry, to the more practical Coretta's dismay. He understood the power of his preaching, his ability to elevate his listeners, but these talents seemed to be separate from his inner self-doubt.

Jail time so far had felt like a movement retreat for the eleven students in the same cell block as King, complete with workshops. They would sing together, meditate, and find games to play. Lonnie saw a lighthearted King few ever witnessed. Yet Lonnie also observed an intense, searching side of King, who would spend hours talking about what the ministry of Jesus and the mission of Gandhi meant to this movement. King told them about Thoreau and about Joan Bondurant's *Conquest of Violence*; he shared stories of his Montgomery bus boycott experiences with them and joined in discussions about what the Atlanta student campaign should do next.

The long days in jail were, happily, punctuated by updates from the outside world, with Reverend Otis Moss and other representatives from the Committee on Appeal for Human Rights filling them in on the state of the ongoing actions happening across the city. They were cheered that more students were joining them; the more crowded the jails, the greater the pressure on the city. Hollowell or someone from his legal team would visit as well, but his news was discouraging, with no headway in negotiations with the city to report.

Julian Bond visited the students at Fulton County Jail on Thursday afternoon. He took in the modern design of the new building, its lobby far better lit than any place in Big Rock, its cell doors opened by new electronic technology—a "modernistic substitute for the dungeons of old." In the end, though, there was only cold comfort behind gray steel bars.

Bond had been Lonnie King's first recruit. After Lonnie read about the North Carolina sit-in back in February, he spotted a student he remembered from class registration in the Yates and Milton Drugstore, a student gathering place near the Morehouse campus. Recalling that the skinny kid had mentioned that he had interned for *Time* magazine in high school, Lonnie approached him. The fullback who busted through opposing lines was brandishing a newspaper. "Have you seen this?" he asked Bond.

At first thinking he meant newspapers in general, Bond was mildly insulted. But Lonnie pressed him. "What do you think about it?"

Now understanding that Lonnie meant the North Carolina sit-in, Bond said, "I think it's great."

"Don't you think it ought to happen here in Atlanta?"

"I'm sure it will happen here; surely someone here will do it."

"Don't you think we ought to make it happen here?" Bond was about to ask what, exactly, he meant by "we," when Lonnie said, "You take this side of the cafe, I'll take the other side. We'll call a meeting." Thus, the Atlanta Student Movement began, and Bond, whose life was changed that day, could not say no. They canvassed the store and got twenty students for their first meeting.

Bond understood that the civil rights movement was not about waiting for NAACP lawyers to arrive, but doing something yourself, forcing the issue, just like in Montgomery during the bus boycott. During their first citywide sit-ins in the spring, Bond's experience of jail revived fears he'd experienced in childhood after the murder of

Emmett Till (who, if he had not been murdered, would have been roughly the same age as the students in 1960). To Bond's relief, when the other prisoners heard about the student protest on the radio, they told him, "Good for you." With enough charges against him under various statutes to keep him in jail for ninety-nine years, Bond whipsawed between a panicked fear of dying in prison and the feeling those in the movement called a "freedom high." Hollowell got Bond out that spring, and now Bond's role was to remain on the outside cranking out communications. Because of their frustrations with the conservative (and determinedly Republican) *Daily World*, the students had started their own newspaper, *The Atlanta Inquirer*, in July.

Curious as to how the students were holding up after their first night in prison, Bond was reassured to find a confident group in high spirits. The students were undeterred, vowing to not accept bail until Atlanta desegregated its lunch counters. Some students regretted not having brought along cigarettes and toothbrushes, and others told him how bad the food was. He saw students reading and writing with the peace that came from their convictions. As Bond passed by, each of his friends asked for news. They begged for more books, which Bond thought their professors would be surprised to hear. As they faced hours of boredom, studying was looking better and better. Herschelle Sullivan told Bond, "The spirit is wonderful!" Bond's news of more arrests from the protests heartened her.

Lonnie said he was "extremely happy when I heard about the enthusiasm that was expressed by the students who were left behind. This type of follow up action will surely bring about the desired results that we all want." He wrote, "Those in jail feel they have already gained a larger measure of freedom by going to prison." The question posed by the *Inquirer* was not how long the students would remain behind bars but how long those on the outside "will be content with the comfortable jails they have been condemned to live in all their lives."

Lonnie cherished his hushed, late-night conversations with Dr. King, finding they were both in accord in their willingness to pay the ultimate price. Lonnie believed, "You gotta face the challenges, and if that means that some of us get killed in order to bring about liberation . . . then that's kind of the way it is."

King later wrote of how incarceration affected him:

> There is something inherently depressing about jail . . . It leaves one caught in the dull monotony of sameness. It is almost like being dead while one still lives . . . It is life without the singing of a bird, without the sight of the sun, moon, and stars, without the felt presence of the fresh air. In short, it is life without the beauties of life; it is bare existence—cold, cruel, and degenerating.

The only thing that really relieved King's intense dislike of prison were visits from his family and close staffers, which improved his state of mind. Luckily, Fulton County allowed daily visits by Coretta. Jail was a necessary evil he was willing to endure; it was isolation that really ground him down.

SNCC students, religious leaders from King's own denomination and from different faiths, and private citizens moved by his arrest sent supportive telegrams to the jail from around the country. While cautious about direct action such as the sit-ins, the NAACP leader and sometimes-rival Roy Wilkins wrote from New York, "It could be that your example will fire men and women everywhere of both races to end the discrimination that hurts both races."

Morning papers around the country printed the news from Atlanta. An AP story informed readers that a "highly organized, well-trained group of Bible-packing Negroes descended upon downtown Atlanta." Many, like the readers of *The Kansas City Times*, saw the wire photograph of King being led away by a stern plainclothes white police officer. Major papers nationally covered the story, though it made only page thirty-nine of *The New York Times*.

Atlanta's *Journal* and *Constitution* were both known as racially moderate papers, which meant they expressed vague sympathy for the students' cause while at the same time criticizing the sit-ins. The *Journal's* editorial on Thursday night was titled "There Are Better Ways" and maintained that the students had already made their point in the spring and should simply rely on the courts instead of increasing tensions through sit-ins. The editors wrote, "There are less provocative ways of seeking to achieve their aims than by pressure, bull-dozing and the risking of popular good will by dramatics." The *Constitution* agreed, focusing on store owners' rights and the uncertainty around school desegregation, believing the students "can only breed resentment, not reason, in this reasonable and sympathetic city." The paper also accurately noted that neither Kennedy nor Nixon had yet spoken up for them, which indicated to the editorial writers that the students' actions were unwise.

The *Constitution* also wondered why both Kennedy and Nixon were not questioning the new Georgia trespassing law, especially "at a time when both of them desperately need the Northern Negro vote." One *Journal* article asserted that King junior's participation was the students' greatest accomplishment, indicating his support for their approach over the NAACP's legal tactics. It was "a further strengthening of the position of Dr. Martin Luther King Jr. as the No. 1 leader of the Southern Negro."

King wrote a statement for the *Inquirer*: "Our decision to stay in jail rather than accept bail grows out of a deep moral and spiritual motivation. It is neither a publicity stunt nor an outer expression of rabble rousing." He noted that a thousand students had turned out at Mount Moriah Baptist Church the previous night to vow they would do what was needed to keep pressure on the city. King also dictated a letter for the SCLC to send out to the NAACP and other potential supporters for emergency funds. "It is difficult to prophesize what tomorrow will bring . . . we may remain in jail indefinitely."

Meanwhile, in New York, Kennedy was mobbed during a ride through Brooklyn, sitting in a convertible rolling past thousands of onlookers from Flatbush to Bedford-Stuyvesant. Nixon spoke on television from New York, and when the subject of King came up, he suggested that he would have a White House conference on civil rights if elected and that he was the candidate who would get civil rights legislation passed. Though he called his platform the strongest ever on civil rights, he said that civil rights was about "performance and not campaign promises." He sounded like the candidate more than willing to speak up for King.

This was the Nixon whom *Jet*'s political reporter Simeon Booker called "Mr. Civil Rights during the Eisenhower Administration" and a "civil-rights workhorse." This was the Nixon who was endorsed by the Black-owned *Los Angeles Sentinel* in 1950 when he declared that segregationists were as dangerous to how the world viewed America as communists were. Campaigning in 1956, Nixon said, "Segregation, discrimination and prejudice have no place in America," and to reinforce his message once moved his entourage out of a Missouri hotel because it would not let the Black journalists covering him stay there. This Nixon also said in 1956 that "most of us here will live to see the day when American boys and girls shall sit, side by side, at any school—public or private—with no regard paid to the color of their skin." Kennedy and southern Democrats voted for an amendment weakening the 1957 civil rights bill, allowing federal civil suits for voting rights violations to be judged by juries, which would inevitably be made up of white southerners. Nixon called it "one of the saddest days in the history of the Senate, because it was a vote against the right to vote."

Nixon's early sympathies might have been fueled by his sensitivity to the disadvantaged—perhaps because he felt that was exactly what he was. He was the boy who woke at 3:30 a.m. for the drive to Los Angeles to get stock for his family's modest store. Even after reaching the vice presidency, he still felt as if he could not measure up in the eyes of those who judged him, no matter what he did. He was nearly dropped from the ticket in 1952, in the wake of a campaign finance scandal, before saving himself with the famous Checkers speech, in which he highlighted his modest personal means. He had to listen as Eisenhower, whose approval he felt he could never quite fully attain, told him before the 1956 reelection campaign that he might want to take another role in the administration (he refused). Whether it was the media, liberals from elite colleges, or the wealthy who ruled his party, he had a sense that no matter how hard he worked, he was never seen as good enough. Nixon's Quaker values also encouraged him to combat racial prejudice. At Whittier College, he insisted the social club he founded accept Black members; he revered his Native American college football coach; he openly condemned segregation while in law school at Duke; and he even joined an NAACP chapter during his first congressional campaign.

Nixon himself said in the 1960 preelection issue of *Ebony*, "I am convinced that the future of the Republican party today lies in pressing forward on civil rights. In any one of the 'big six' states (New York, California, Pennsylvania, Michigan, Illinois and Ohio) our civil rights stand can make all the difference in the world. In the last election we lost the governorship of Pennsylvania by about 50,000 votes. A shift of just 5 percent of the Negro vote would have elected a Republican."

This was the Nixon that Martin Luther King knew, so the minister fully expected to hear from him. The vice president had spent many years building a reputation as a racial moderate, and now was the time to use it.

That evening, the Imperial Public Relationship Office, U.S. Klans, Knights of the KKK, released a statement that read, "Our God-given rights are being infringed upon. We are arising, showing we want our rights returned by the laws of God and the traditions of the Southland." They pressed Governor Vandiver to deploy the National Guard to protect white Georgians from "the advancing Negro race."

Vandiver announced state troops were ready to move if Atlanta store owners requested them.

DAY 3: FRIDAY, OCTOBER 21

Student protesters were back at Rich's by 10:40 a.m. for a third day of action. Yet when they heard Klansmen were about to arrive at the department store, their leaders decided it was too risky to continue the sit-ins. Students jumped into station wagons to head to smaller stores not staked out by the Klan. Mostly female students picketed outside Walgreens, Kress, McCrory, and other stores. Seemingly every downtown block was full of uniformed and plainclothes police patrolling the streets, more interested in the protesters than the agitators intent on intimidating the students. Officers buzzed by on motorcycles, and police wagons circled the blocks, as if impatient to be filled. Tension increased in the city, with law enforcement leadership warning that a hundred more officers were in reserve, ready for deployment.

Most downtown lunch counters had closed in order to avoid becoming the sites of sit-ins. Central Atlanta was so tightly wound that only two students managed to get themselves arrested that day. When asked how long his lunch counter might be closed, a business owner replied, "Indefinitely." With stenciled signs, fifty students returned to picket outside Rich's at 1:00 p.m., undeterred by the threat of the Klan's presence.

Students also kept up a twenty-four-hour prayer vigil near the entrance to the county jail. Ministers from the Atlanta University Center asked to give Communion to the jailed students but were refused. They also asked if they could gather the students for a jail chapel service, but were again told no, on the basis that spiritual counsel must be offered to individuals only—no mass meetings.

In Chicago, the *Daily Tribune* read, "Flying squads of Negroes attempted to desegregate at least 11 downtown Atlanta eating places today but their efforts were thwarted by several closings."

Both SNCC and SCLC sent out increasing numbers of messages to sympathetic supporters like Harry Belafonte, Adam Clayton Powell, Eleanor Roosevelt, and numerous religious leaders. The students were mostly pleased by the response, especially when New York City's mayor, Robert F. Wagner Jr., told reporters, "I know I speak for the people of our city when I say they are appalled at the news of the arrest of Dr. Martin Luther King Jr. and a number of students who are doing nothing more than seeking to extend democracy." On the other hand, a longtime rival of King's within the Black Baptist world, the Reverend J. H. Jackson of Chicago, said while preaching in Jackson, Mississippi, "You can't get anywhere just by sitting down." He wanted less discussion of "racial integration" and more discussion of "racial elevation." He felt integration would never happen "until we admit our shortcomings." In years to come, Jackson would continue to be a thorn in King's side.

King's fellow Baptist minister Wyatt Tee Walker quickly assumed an important role. King was the widely hailed saint, Walker the hidden enforcer, and his style, as he said, was to "run smack dab over you." No one took Walker's deference to King as a measure of his own lesser sense of worth; he often said the best way to know King's greatness was to observe a man with an ego like his taking second place. While King's friend Ralph Abernathy gave him comfort, Walker offered effectiveness on the street. He demanded, on day 3 of the sit-ins, that the U.S. secretary of state, Christian Herter, intervene in King's case, while the

NAACP asked Hartsfield to appoint a citywide biracial committee to address lunch counter segregation.

Mayor Hartsfield had seen enough of the growing commotion; it was time for him to step in. In his office at city hall, Hartsfield leafed with increasing irritation through a growing stack of telephone messages, letters, and telegrams from around the country imploring him to get King out.

He had never felt so besieged by an issue, not even the bombing of a synagogue two years earlier. Everyone except the presidential candidates seemed to be offering him advice. Roy Wilkins of the NAACP called on him to "provide now the moral leadership necessary to bring about conversation between all affected to the end that justice shall reign in the city." The mayor most definitely wanted to avoid any such public "conversation," but in his usual sly way he concluded he needed to assemble a core of city fathers to gather around him the next morning.

Hartsfield, of course, had no ability to release King, because the minister had been charged under a state, not a city, statute. Calls to Atlanta university presidents weren't going anywhere; they felt as powerless as Mayor Hartsfield did. Dick Rich was having a small nervous breakdown, upset and anxious, still refusing to drop the charges against King and the students. Hartsfield was tired of looking impotent in this matter.

Late Friday afternoon, Mayor Hartsfield sent messages to Black leaders that he wanted them around his table the next day to negotiate a halt to the protests while he brokered with downtown business leaders a desegregation agreement. Perhaps getting ahead of himself, he stated that a sixty- to ninety-day cessation of protests would be agreed to by all, and he offered himself as "an unofficial mediator." He had such faith in his long-standing relationships with older Black leaders like John Wesley Dobbs, John Calhoun, and Daddy King himself that he thought he might manage to corral the crisis then and there. The old guard hardly supported these sit-ins any more than he did, and he figured the students might be growing increasingly eager to get back to their dorms and normalcy.

What the mayor overlooked was that his "leaders on both sides" did not include the students leading the movement, none of whom had heard from him. Lonnie King, behind bars, was incredulous at the mayor's proposal and the fact that he and Herschelle had not been consulted. He told a *Journal* reporter that Hartsfield was being "absolutely inauthentic. The mayor has talked to no student leaders. He cannot speak for us." When the reporter talked to King, he said he would make no statement until the students had decided what they wanted to do. Lonnie said he needed to speak with the leader he left in charge on the outside, Otis Moss, but made clear that the protests would go on, "all day, every day, if necessary to achieve their ends."

The Reverend Otis Moss was, like Lonnie, older than most of the students, and this was apparent in the brotherly style in which he cared for them. Moss had earned his master of divinity degree from Morehouse the year before. Lonnie favored military efficiency, whereas Moss was more pastoral. Already beloved at the Atlanta church where he preached, Moss helped students through anguished late-night conversations where, in tears, they told him how their parents said to never come home again if they got arrested. He counseled them, "One day your parents will talk about this with the greatest pride and the greatest depth of appreciation you could ever hear." The elegant, steady rhythm of his voice soothed them. Along with Bond, Moss sent telegrams to both presidential campaigns about King's imprisonment but heard nothing back from either.

Yet the Georgia Republican district chairman C. J. Broome linked one candidate to the students anyway, saying in the *Constitution*, "The actions of these unlawful demonstrators in Atlanta was inspired, motivated, encouraged and urged by Sen. John F. Kennedy." The election was close in Georgia, and Republicans had a card to play. King was in prison, and the governor, mayor, and local judges holding sway just all happened to be southern Democrats.

Moss felt the weight of responsibility on his shoulders as he directed telegrams to potential allies outside Atlanta. The next day, invited or not, he was going to city hall for negotiations with a mayor and an old guard who had been in power since before he was born. He was determined the student voice would be heard.

Trezzvant Anderson, a journalist for *The Pittsburgh Courier*—*The Chicago Defender*'s chief rival among Black papers—came to see King on Friday afternoon. Before joining the *Courier*, Anderson wrote a book about his World War II tank battalion, the 761st, and its journey from Omaha Beach across Europe. He had spent the past three years on an assignment hardly less perilous, roving the rural back roads of the South to places others would not dare go, tracking the growing civil rights movement.

In jail, Anderson found a King unfamiliar to him, in short sleeves with no tie, rough stubble on his face. Though the minister struck a casual tone, he was far from at ease. When asked how long he expected to be in jail, King stated that he would stay "ten years if necessary." King talked of threatening slurs he heard from guards, though a few were courteous. "On the whole, it's as comfortable as jail can be."

Anderson wondered, "Do you actually intend to remain here in jail?" This new strategy still shocked the reporter; no sane Black person would willingly sacrifice themselves before a white judge and jailer. (Today, photographs of civil rights activists sitting in prison cells are so ingrained in the culture that the novelty of this tactic can be hard to appreciate.) King replied, "We will positively stay in jail unless the lunch counters are desegregated before our trial. If that should take place, then we will reconsider coming out. This is our self-suffering to arouse the community conscience."

"Won't your being in jail work hardship on you, with regard to your speaking engagements and other activities?"

"Yes, indeed, it will be a hardship on me and the organization. I was to have been in Cleveland on Sunday for a big fundraising meeting sponsored by the Ministers' Alliance, which had guaranteed us from $7,000 to $10,000. I had looked forward to it, but when the students called me at the last minute to go with them, I felt I had a moral obligation to take part, since this was what I had been preaching." King said, "I had to practice what I preached." He added, "But this was the great cause, and something had to be done about it, now."

King brightened when he started talking about the students there with him, saying, "It's a great and inspiring experience. I have never seen such willingness and cooperation from students like this. Why, do you realize that presidents of five college student bodies are in jail here, and two college queens. There are many honor students, too." King had the reporter talk to these students, giving them full credit for initiating and leading the sit-in.

Lonnie offered a flattering portrait of King by saying, "When we called him and asked him to go with us, he didn't hesitate a moment. He is a truly great man." The message might have been for the greater good of the movement, if not entirely accurate. In the end, King had indeed said yes; there he was, in the same predicament they all found themselves in.

■   ■   ■

The candidates were face-to-face in New York for their fourth and final debate. Each knew his opponent well; they first shared a stage together as freshmen congressmen in McKeesport, Pennsylvania, in 1947, eating hamburgers at a diner afterward and riding the train back to D.C. while talking of baseball and defeating communism. Kennedy even gave Nixon a thousand-dollar contribution from his father for his Senate race, and later an invitation to his wedding, which the vice president missed only because of a rare opportunity to golf with the president. Nixon went to see Kennedy in the hospital when he was near death following back surgery and was heard to say, with tears in his eyes, "Oh, God, don't let him die." Kennedy thought less of the friendship with the socially inept Nixon, while Nixon genuinely imagined Kennedy was his friend, though JFK did respect Nixon's considerable mind. The most powerful prize stood between them, and as Kennedy predicted, their relationship would not survive the competition. Nixon held on to a residual sense of camaraderie, telling himself they were still friends. It would take a while for him to realize how badly the campaign's stresses had damaged their bond.

Students like John Lewis and Lonnie King had seen nothing in earlier debates to suggest that either man was bold enough to stand up for them. There would be nothing tonight to change that for any student watching from outside jail—no recognition at all from either candidate of the sit-ins. The focus that night was foreign policy, and Castro, Cuba, and communism dominated the discussion. But in this last debate, a Nixon who seemed far more assertive did say, "Let's talk about civil rights; more progress in the past 8 years than in the whole 80 years before." If he became president, Nixon declared the nation would be "a splendid example for all the world to see of democracy in action at its best." Still, the student activists found very little in either man to sway them.

John Lewis said of the election, "I didn't care for either man, nor did most of my friends. In fact, none of us cared much about the presidential race at all."

DAY 4: SATURDAY, OCTOBER 22

Harris Wofford watched his children, Daniel and Susanne, run in the fall morning sunlight in his garden. That Saturday was a time for much-needed play with his kids, especially because there might not be much more family time until after the election, a little over two weeks away. He and Louis Martin were working frantically, especially now that Shriver had decamped to Chicago to help ensure victory in excruciatingly close Illinois.

The Woffords had moved to Hollin Hills, a model development community off the parkway near Alexandria, Virginia, where other young, highly educated, liberal families lived on the edge of woods. He planted his own willow trees in the yard, but the house was a rental, and he did not know if he would see them grow. The point of the morning was to get away from the office, and Wofford loved being with his children, yet his mind kept racing back to work, especially having heard on the radio that morning of Klansmen parading openly in Atlanta. He felt guilty: "What the hell? Martin's been in jail for three days, and I'm the civil rights guy, and I haven't done a thing."

As his children played next to him, Wofford sat confounded. Why was he working at the CRS if not to help people like King, who, more-over, was a friend? What were he and Louis Martin thinking?

Wofford would appear as a perplexing figure in the eyes of many over the years. Seemingly born on a path to conventional success, he instead developed an uncanny sense of when and where the door of history might crack open. Of all the causes that Wofford gave his heart to, King's mission was most essential to him. A fascination with Gandhi was the foundation of their bond, though they had both come to his teachings on their own. When they finally met at an event in New York, Wofford proposed raising funds to help King visit India, which eventually happened in 1959. Wofford was drawn into the tight world of King advisers, a rare white voice in their midst. The fact that Kennedy had hired a member of his brain trust raised King's estima-tion of the Democrat's campaign.

Wofford's admiration for Gandhi exemplified his engagement with the idea of internationalism, a long-standing interest of his. When he was eleven, his Johnson City, Tennessee, grandmother took him on a yearlong world tour. With World War II about to erupt, they wit-nessed Mussolini shouting from a balcony over a torchlight parade through Rome and later hid in Bethlehem's Church of the Nativity to escape nearby gunfire. But it was seeing Gandhi walking down a street in Bombay, surrounded by his followers, that inspired Wofford's lifelong devotion to the Mahatma's teachings. He and Clare would re-turn to India in 1951, publishing a book together called *India Afire*. Just after Gandhi's assassination, they traveled in his steps throughout India, and Wofford was struck by how many people posed the question of how Gandhi's teachings might be applied to America's own problem of racial discrimination. Back home, Wofford pondered the potential of this idea. When he did succeed in raising money for King and Coretta to visit India in 1959, he did not join them, instead remaining at the U.S. Commis-sion on Civil Rights.

While he was immediately drawn to King, the same could not be said of his first encounter with John F. Kennedy. They met after World War II at a party in Greenwich, Connecticut, the host thinking

Wofford might hit it off with the congressional candidate. She informed Wofford, "If old Joe has his way, Jack will be President of the United States." About to enroll as an undergraduate at the University of Chicago, Wofford tried throughout the afternoon to engage the Navy captain almost nine years his senior, while Jack ravaged the spread of food, accompanied by two young women. When Wofford thought he had Kennedy's attention, he, in his earnest way, put forward several minutes of political insight (Wofford's speaking style gave one the impression of a romantic radical from the nineteenth century, replete with classical allusions). Jack replied to Wofford's speech by saying, "Right now, I've got my eyes on tennis," and wandered off toward the courts with the two women.

A decade later, Wofford began to reevaluate his initial impression of Jack Kennedy. After reading the senator's impressive speeches on new approaches to Poland and Algeria, Wofford wrote him a letter from his corporate law firm praising the senator's worldview. Wofford's overture was successful, and he ended up editing Kennedy's speeches on international affairs for a book, *The Strategy of Peace*. Kennedy and his speechwriter Ted Sorensen tried to get Wofford to join the campaign in the summer of 1959, seeing Wofford as someone who understood international affairs and might be able to help Kennedy with the liberals who were wary of his nomination. But Wofford had promised the president of the University of Notre Dame, Father Ted Hesburgh (whom he had worked under at the U.S. Commission on Civil Rights), that he would teach there for a year. At Notre Dame, Wofford got an unexpected call from the university's former president—and Ambassador Joseph Kennedy's confessor—Father John Cavanaugh. Cavanaugh relayed Joe Kennedy's message to him: "I understand my boy wants to get somebody that you've got in your law school teaching, Wofford, or Wufford or something. Would you tell Father Hesburgh that moral teachings be damned—that my boy needs him, so put him on the next plane back to Washington."

Wofford declined again, saying, "I'm here, and I'm doing this book for Kennedy, and I will go at the end of the year." In April 1960, JFK came to South Bend for a campaign speech, and he spotted Wofford at the reception. He stated, "We need you now. When is your last class?" Wofford said he still had another few weeks; Kennedy responded, "Could you miss it? Could you get on the plane and come?"

Wofford replied, "My wife is nine months pregnant, and I couldn't go until the baby's born."

"Let me talk to her."

JFK took Clare aside, and when they returned, they were laughing. Clare said, "Look, if he wants you this badly, go ahead now. We'll be fine." That night at home the conversation continued, and around midnight Clare realized she was going into labor. Wofford would say of Kennedy, "If he can turn the womb of my wife, he can win the women's vote."

Kennedy eventually decided to put him to work on Black outreach, for as he told Wofford in his Senate office early in the spring, "You know I'm way behind on this, because I've hardly known any Blacks in my life. It isn't an issue that I've thought about a lot."

This push to help Kennedy close the gap with Black voters had so consumed Wofford over the past months that it had distracted him from his involvement with King's movement. Wofford remembered meeting an attorney in Atlanta during his Civil Rights Commission days who seemed well connected. Why not give that man—Morris Abram—a call, he thought. Scooping up his children, Wofford went back inside, found Abram's number, and dialed it.

Abram was also spending the morning at home and was about to take his nine-year-old daughter out to play. Wofford said, "Morris, Martin Luther King, Jr., is in jail in Atlanta."

He replied, "Harris, surely you don't have to call long distance to tell me. Everybody knows that."

"I'm supposed to be a civil-rights man for John Kennedy—and King's old friend—and I haven't been able to do a thing." Wofford asked, "Can't you do anything? Can't the mayor really do something to get him out?" He added, "Atlanta's supposed to be the enlightened leader of a New South; Hartsfield's the best mayor in the country; and you're a lawyer who can do anything. So why is Martin still in jail?" He concluded, "This is a scandal."

Abram retorted, "How in the hell do you think I'm going to spring him?"

"Go see Mayor Hartsfield, since he was arrested by Atlanta police."

Abram protested that he was just about to spend time with his daughter, but Wofford insisted, saying, "Take her with you."

Amazingly, Abram agreed to do just that. But when Abram said he would let the mayor know of Senator Kennedy's interest in King's case, Wofford immediately put the lid on that idea. He stressed to Abram that Kennedy knew nothing of his call; while the candidate would surely want to see King released from prison, their communication was not authorized by the senator.

When Abram called Hartsfield, with local and national coverage swirling around the events at city hall, the mayor said, "Yeah, come down at once. We're negotiating right now with every important Negro in town. They're all sixty of them in the council chamber."

With his daughter in tow, Abram rushed to city hall. He was excited at the possibility of being helpful to the mayor in a crisis like this. Raised in Fitzgerald, Georgia, Abram had not only longed to escape his rural roots—his Jewish faith and bookishness making him feel like an outsider—but also aspired to become a popular southern politician. The anti-Semitic lynching of Leo Frank in Marietta, Georgia, in 1915 left him with a fear of being defenseless. In his college years, Abram came to believe Black people suffered under a system of segregation that was fundamentally wrong and kindred to the discrimination Jews faced. After attending law school at the University of Chicago and serving as part of the Nuremberg prosecution team, he began a long quest to reform the Georgia electoral system. Abram then ran for Congress, but as a Jewish racial progressive running after the *Brown* decision, he did not win.

Abram headed downtown, where police were posted everywhere. Many stores were closed. In front of Rich's, whose restaurants were all shut, the Klan was back, hoisting signs proclaiming, "We will not accept race mixing in Georgia." Abram and his daughter arrived at the cream-colored city hall tower, across from the Georgia capitol, late in the morning. Inside, Abram found a chaotic scene, with Hartsfield presiding as ringleader. Hartsfield shooed the media out, saying their presence didn't allow his Black constituents "to say what they really think and to let us get right to the heart of the problem." The mayor had planned to hold the meeting in his office, but with so many older leaders showing up, including Daddy King, Dr. Benjamin Mays, and Dr. Rufus Clement, they had relocated to the Gothic-style aldermen's chamber on the second floor.

Mayor Hartsfield was selling a simple proposal: "If you will give me a thirty day truce, I will promise to try to get a settlement for you. I will be your advocate to try to get these merchants to agree to a general custom in this city to admit Negroes to their lunch room, and I will also see that Dr. King is turned out of jail." He had talked with business leaders the day before, and he said they were willing to negotiate. Watching Hartsfield interact with citizens the rest of the Georgia political establishment ignored (when not actively oppressing them), Abram was impressed. He found Mayor Hartsfield to be a "distinct and marvelous southern prototype, the rough-hewn, even comical character who knows the difference between right and wrong, and has the guts to act accordingly and the wits to survive." When an Atlanta synagogue was bombed in 1958, it was Hartsfield who showed up to denounce the act of terror and to promise to find the perpetrators.

At seventy, Mayor Hartsfield was, at last, starting to see the finish line of his career as a politician coming into view, and he wanted to solidify Atlanta's reputation as a major, desirable American city, which required harmony between its white and its Black residents. Martin Luther King's arrest at a sit-in threatened to upend all of this. The peril this posed for his legacy roused the old municipal battler for one last fight before stepping down after a quarter century as mayor.

Hartsfield had amazed Daddy King when he was photographed shaking hands with Black Atlantans in the 1940s, and the pastor believed he was "an unusually effective leader during an especially difficult time. He tried to walk a line between two opposing forces." In fact, Daddy King added, "I believe William Hartsfield may have been alone in his desire to make Atlanta into one city instead of two." When Daddy King called Hartsfield to say that his daughter, Christine, was not being hired as a teacher because of her race, she had a job offer within minutes.

The meeting that day went on for almost three hours, with Hartsfield in the room for more than two-thirds of it, occasionally taking refuge in his office to let the city fathers discuss how they would proceed. Back at his desk, telegrams continued to pour in demanding King's release. Flipping through them, he saw that they came from everywhere from Maine to California. All eyes were on him, which was as he liked it.

After talking with Abram in his office, Hartsfield started making calls to the Kennedy campaign, which was sweeping through Kansas that Saturday. He later said that every time he tried to reach JFK, all he could hear was "hoopin and a hollerin." Because he imagined that the announcement he planned to make that afternoon would be in Kennedy's interest—it was certainly in his own—he figured that he might as well get on with it. After being told of Wofford's call to Abram two hours prior, he thought that he might now have the cover he needed.

Hartsfield rose and signaled for Abram to follow, and he walked confidently back into the chamber to tell the Black leaders, "I will turn Martin Luther King loose, and I want you to know that Senator Kennedy has evidenced his interest in this thing. He has phoned me to help get a peaceful settlement, and he has also asked me to turn Martin Luther King loose." Though it would soon become clear that the mayor alone did not possess the power to free King, Hartsfield wanted this problem solved, and he felt he could gamble on Kennedy carrying his state even after being thrust into the middle of King's predicament. The mayor had a lifetime's worth of experience in determining how far he could push racial progress without risking too much electoral backlash.

The reaction to Hartsfield's announcement was explosive, and reporters who had filtered back into the meeting ran to break the story. It was immediate national news.

■ ■ ■

John Calhoun heard the mayor's announcement and hastily begged to be excused. He was desperate to get someone from the Nixon campaign on the phone. But even before the mayor's announcement, Calhoun had been trying to reach the vice president's campaign to urge him to act. As a Black Republican leader in such a crucial city, Calhoun hoped he might have the influence to reach Nixon himself. It looked as if he did not.

Calhoun, then in his early sixties, was a powerful man in Atlanta—not someone a campaign should ignore. Vernon Jordan never forgot as a child seeing the Republican Calhoun lead a voter registration drive, an especially brave thing to do. Lonnie, for one, while he had doubts about the previous generation of leaders, found he couldn't help but admire the affable Calhoun's organizing skills. Lonnie regularly had breakfast with the Republican elder, to learn more about the NAACP tactics that Calhoun had perfected.

Hartsfield generously offered a phone to Calhoun, in deference to an honorable opponent. Calhoun foresaw that there would be a price to pay with Black voters if the Kennedy campaign got credit for springing King from jail. Little did he know that Kennedy was completely unaware of this development and would not be happy at all to learn of Hartsfield's announcement.

Calhoun dove into more calls. Though they belonged to different political parties, his friend Morris Abram watched him sympathetically, overhearing Calhoun say to someone at the Republican National Committee (RNC), "A report! We don't have time to write a report; you've got to get through to the vice-president at once." Calhoun looked indignant as he hung up the phone.

Abram asked, "What did they tell you?"

"They told me to send in a report air mail, special delivery." He shook his head at the foolishness of it all. Calhoun later told Hartsfield that he had been informed over the phone that "the race was very close and Mr. Nixon didn't want to upset the apple cart." Hartsfield, for one, took secret pleasure in the thought that the Republicans were asking Calhoun to send them a registered letter while the Democrats were hot on the phone with each other.

Calhoun had tried to reach Val Washington, the Republican National Committee's director of minorities, and Washington returned his call while the mayor was talking to the press. Washington was a determined party operative who rose to the rank of assistant to the chairman of the Republican Party on the proposition that minority voters mattered. He thought it was important to reclaim Black Roosevelt Republicans—voters who appreciated New Deal economic programs but knew that southern Democrats were still resisting *Brown* and civil rights legislation. Washington's vision that these Black voters could become faithful Republicans once again had paid off during President Eisenhower's reelection campaign. Yet Washington lamented having a budget of only thirty thousand dollars and a team of five staffers to aid him in his quest of reaching eighteen million Black people.

Calhoun filled Washington in over the phone: "Val, this is going to have some terrific repercussions, and you oughta get ahold of Nixon to get him to say something." As he spoke, Calhoun realized this was a stretch, not because Val Washington happened to be Black, but because Nixon ignored *everyone* at the national committee. Calhoun had previously offered Washington the use of his Georgia Republican campaign literature targeted at Black voters so the RNC could deploy it around the country. Washington told him that he knew he would never get approval from Nixon, given his micromanaging tendencies. Nixon was committing a fundamental sin of politics—trying to be both candidate and campaign manager.

Washington also said, "John, I don't know whether I'll be able to do that because Nixon doesn't deal with the Republican committee. He's got these other organizations he's dealing with, the Democrats for Nixon . . . I don't know whether I can talk to him or not." Democrats for Nixon were white southerners primed to leave a party inching toward support for civil rights. Calhoun vowed to keep trying to get his message across to Nixon, but the candidate was listening to people with a different agenda.

Hartsfield had started with a three-month "peace and quiet" offer, but he always began negotiations with a target he could bargain down from. Black leaders agreed to Hartsfield's deal of a truce of at least thirty days, which would hopefully allow him to persuade stores to desegregate. As part of the deal, Hartsfield would release the twenty-two students charged by the city and then work with county and state officials to get the other thirty-nine activists who would still be in jail—including King—freed, too. Peace and quiet for Hartsfield meant no protests on the street or by those wanting to stay behind bars—especially the minister eliciting calls of concern from a presidential campaign. From his desk, Hartsfield spoke to the press—twinkling blue eyes betraying no guile behind thick glasses. An uneasy Otis Moss, with a narrow mustache and tie, stood behind him. Hartsfield announced, "I will give the Negro leadership weekly reports on the progress being made if they want. I think they are justified in wanting to know that real progress is being made and that this is not just a stalling tactic."

His message to the students was blunt: "I can't negotiate at gunpoint—with picketers out there."

Moss felt that this was the right deal to make: trusting Hartsfield to broker a solution within a defined window of time. The young minister added, however, "At the end of that time we will review progress made and decide our future of action." There were still hard negotiations in store, and suddenly a raging storm in the form of Kennedy's friend Bobby Troutman sweeping into city hall.

Like Wofford and Abram, Troutman had been spending a pleasant day with his kids, driving across Atlanta to a baseball game, when, on the radio, he heard a report about Hartsfield's announcement. He almost swerved off the road in disbelief; it seemed impossible that Kennedy was involving himself in Georgia's affairs, and on behalf of the controversial Martin Luther King, no less. Troutman served as Kennedy's eyes, ears, and advocate in the South and had been a trusted law school roommate of John F. Kennedy's older brother, Joe junior (whose death in World War II cleared the way for Jack to enter politics—with some reluctance). Bobby Troutman was something of a southern aristocrat, and his wealthy family had sometimes stepped in to help out a college friend of his—none other than Morris Abram. Now this friendship was about to be tested.

Troutman pulled over and found a pay phone from which he called Bobby Kennedy, who was as shocked as he was. Wofford later learned that Troutman told Bobby he "suspected the dark hand of Harris Wofford in this."

When Troutman got to Hartsfield's office, he was apoplectic. Staring at his friends, he said, "Who is this representative of Senator Kennedy who is trying to get this King fellow out of jail?"

"Well, I don't know," said Hartsfield, feigning befuddled innocence.

"I do know. You two have just blown the election. Do you understand that?"

Abram had never in twenty years seen his friend this angry. The prize Troutman had long hoped for—seeing Kennedy elected president—had potentially been lost because of something fishy happening in his pond: "We had it sewed up, but now you're going to lose the South. These southern politicians are going to turn against us. They'll never accept Kennedyism with Martin Luther King tied to its tail. I have already heard from Fritz Hollings. He called me from the governor's mansion in South Carolina. What do you think he said? He said that if Kennedy is trying to help that rabble-rouser, he's off the team."

Troutman reached for a phone, but then looked around. "Ah, forget it." There were too many people in the room for the call he wanted to make.

■ ■ ■

Harris Wofford waited at home for a call to see if anything positive had come of his request. When it arrived, Abram's voice was hesitant:

"I know this might lose you your job, and I didn't intend to do any harm to you." This was not how a call should begin. "Sit down and hold on to your seat. I realize you didn't mean anything like this. The Mayor wants to talk to you in just a minute. Let me tell you that he has just gone on the television and radio networks and announced, that in response to Senator Kennedy's direct personal intervention, he has ordered the release of Martin Luther King and the other sit-in prisoners."

"He said what, Morris?" After Abram repeated himself, an aghast Wofford sputtered, "But Kennedy knows nothing about my call—I told you I was acting on my own." His job, his reputation, had been placed in jeopardy. "I hadn't checked with the campaign in asking you that."

Abram said, "The Mayor knows that, but it is a good agreement, and he wants to talk to you." Abram handed the phone over.

"This is Bill Hartsfield. Now I know that I ran with the ball farther than you expected, Harris, my boy, but I needed a peg to swing on and you gave it to me, and I've swung on it. You tell our Senator that he and I are out on the limb together, so don't saw it off. I'm giving him the election on a silver platter, so don't pull the rug out from under me."

"Well, you know, the Senator still doesn't know anything about this." Linking Kennedy to King without the candidate's permission was a huge gamble. They were all playing with fire.

"I'd guessed that, but you can get through to him before the press does. Okay? I've only *just* announced it to the radio and television."

Wofford pleaded with him; how could such an announcement be made so blithely, and this close to an election to boot? He rang off in disbelief. How was he going to tell the Kennedy brothers that he had inadvertently set in motion something so controversial, with absolutely no approval?

He tried to recall any campaign radiophone numbers he had at his disposal; there was no time to go through Shriver. He knew Kennedy was somewhere in either Kansas or Missouri, and he eventually got through to Kenny O'Donnell in Kansas City on a walkie-talkie in a noisy parade car. Wofford stumbled through an explanation, and the aide barked, "Hartsfield said *what*? You did *what*?" over the noise of the crowd. It was the last thing they needed on a day when Nixon was accusing Kennedy of risking world war with proposals supporting the overthrow of Castro.

Wofford was bombarded with a slew of profanities. They argued back and forth about how disastrous the idea of Kennedy's being tagged as King's liberator was, how badly Wofford had screwed up, and what to do next. Then the press secretary, Pierre Salinger, came on the line. They were losing time; their campaign would soon be inundated with reporters asking who had reached out to the mayor, who had told him that King should be released. Wofford urged a calm response, something bland and soothing—that of course Kennedy wanted the students safely released. Salinger rang off, almost too angry to respond.

Abram was also on the phone trying to head off Troutman. Over the roar of Kennedy's plane on the tarmac in Joplin, Missouri, he eventually got through to an aide and shouted, "If Senator Kennedy is asked anything about Martin Luther King, Jr., let him say *nothing*. Do not let him say that he has encouraged what has been going on in Atlanta, but for God's sake, do not let him say he *didn't* encourage it."

The campaign ultimately took Wofford's and Abram's advice, and after Salinger had consulted with Kennedy, the campaign released a quickly worded statement, saying almost exactly that. The mayor was right; he did indeed have a peg to swing on, and no one, not even JFK, could afford to whittle it down. News came over the wire from the campaign: "As a result of having many calls from all over the country regarding the incident in Atlanta, Sen. Kennedy directed that an inquiry be made to give him all the facts on that situation and a report on what properly should be done. The senator is hopeful that a satisfactory outcome can be worked out."

King's name was absent from the carefully crafted understatement. Considering the pressure, it was a masterful job of some sort.

■ ■ ■

Hartsfield and Abram had their truce, and now they wanted the students out of jail. They worked toward this outcome until eight that night, calling Judge Webb and the prosecutor, securing the release of the twenty-two Black students held at the Atlanta Prison Farm, who had been charged under the city's disorderly conduct statute, and finessing the day's deal with the police department to avoid hurting morale. But King and thirty-eight students were still at the Fulton County Jail, having been charged under the state's "leave the premises" law—making their release more complicated for the mayor.

Just when they thought they could call it a day, they got word that King would not entertain leaving jail on bail—Hartsfield's initial proposal—unless all charges were dropped. As Abram wrote, the minister would otherwise not be "legally vindicated, that the charge, under an unjust and unconstitutional law, would still be hanging over his head."

Hartsfield and Abram looked at each other. They should have anticipated that King would stubbornly refuse to do the one thing they needed him to do, something people were usually quite pleased to do—go home. Mayor Hartsfield arranged for Morehouse's president, Dr. Benjamin Mays, to go to the jail to plead with King to take the deal that Hartsfield was working to make possible. Even when encouraged by his beloved mentor, King said he would not leave jail unless the charges were dismissed.

Hartsfield and Abram realized they needed to speak with Dick Rich, to persuade him to drop the charges against King and the students who had been arrested at his store. Abram's daughter had gone without lunch or dinner, but he reassured himself that she was learning a lot about politics that day.

Together, Hartsfield and Abram drove north to Rich's Buckhead home, situated atop a hill at the end of a long, winding driveway that cut across a well-manicured lawn. They walked up to the mansion, rang the doorbell, and were greeted by a truculent businessman in a dressing gown and slippers. It was late, and Hartsfield launched into the deal, telling his usually firm supporter that "Atlanta is getting a horrible image, a horrible image!"

Rich nodded in a way that suggested this was Hartsfield's problem to fix, not his.

"Look, I've agreed to release the Klansmen." No Klan members had actually been arrested, however—only a white counterprotester. "Their supporters are delighted. If you drop the charges against King, those happy rednecks will barely notice."

Rich was reluctant to budge, and they argued back and forth over whether he would be perceived as too lenient. Abram felt Rich was "in terror that his company would be charged with caving in to Black pressure, a public relations gaffe that could cost him millions of dollars." Rich felt Abram and Hartsfield were pressuring him to do something that his competitors were not having to do, leaving him exposed. Abram found that Rich seemed to be missing the issue of racial injustice at the heart of the matter. At that moment—feeling hurt and offended that King had singled out his store—Rich was unmoved because, in Abram's words, "he just wanted to sell shoes, furniture, and perfume."

Finally, Rich acquiesced. He said if the prosecutor would sanction dropping all charges, then Rich's would have the cover it needed from the legal establishment. Rich would then tell others that he had dropped the charges because he did not want to "make martyrs out of them and King."

Hartsfield and Abram walked out of the mansion, exhausted and relieved. It was too late to go see the prosecutor, so they would regroup the next day.

DAY 5: SUNDAY, OCTOBER 23

As he returned from church in the morning, the prosecutor John Kelley—whom Abram called "a pleasant, rotund little man"—was amazed to find the mayor standing at his doorstep, along with Morris Abram and Dick Rich. It was quickly apparent that they were there to ask a favor—a large one, in fact. As it turned out, Kelley needed little convincing with such people on his porch.

In Atlanta, a Sunday headline read, "Did Kennedy Man Ask King Release?" It described "small tempests in Atlanta and Washington over who was the 'local representative' and whether he in fact spoke for Sen. Kennedy." Abram and Troutman both denied being the initiator of Kennedy's supposed intervention, and Hartsfield would say only that the call came from Washington. Kennedy's Georgia co-chair Griffin Bell said that none of the Kennedy campaign leaders in Georgia had ever been contacted about the matter, emphasizing, "We know that Sen. Kennedy would never interfere in the affairs of a sovereign state." The Democrats had long assumed they would hold Georgia, but could Nixon steal the prize at the last moment because of the backlash against the mysterious call? Bell, who later served as Jimmy Carter's attorney general, tossed red meat to their Democratic white voters, adding, "King has violated a state law. He is charged with trespassing on private premises, has been offered bail, and refused it because he wants to be a martyr. He must stand trial and he will get equal treatment just as any other common law violator."

The identity of the person who had reportedly spoken for the Kennedy campaign remained a mystery, but the larger question of what effect this intervention would have on voters in less than three weeks persisted. Might it serve to inspire Black voters? A *New York Times* story that morning reported on a series of conversations from the previous week in which these voters expressed a lack of excitement about the choice they faced. One Baltimore lawyer said, "A lot of people I know wouldn't care if both Nixon and Kennedy lost . . . [W]hat have the two parties really done on civil rights for the Negro? They both seem more interested in grabbing off the Southern white vote than the Negro vote."

Despite the vice president's silence on King, not everyone was silent within the Republican ranks. At four packed Bedford-Stuyvesant church services, New York's governor, Nelson Rockefeller, and Jackie Robinson exemplified the sorts of promises that Republicans could make if they were bold enough. Rockefeller said, "When the great spiritual leader, the Rev. Martin King, finds himself in jail because he had the courage to love . . . we still have a long way to go in America."

■ ■ ■

Troutman called Wofford, ostensibly to reassure him that his Georgia crew had things back under control. He began by saying, "Harris, you're just fucking everything up—you're screwing up my life." Still, Troutman reassured him, "We're gonna work it all out, don't you worry anymore. But don't interrupt my weekends anymore after this."

Wofford was glad to still have a position on the campaign. Sunday's *Journal-Constitution* reported that Senator Kennedy had made a call from Kansas City the day before to Governor Vandiver, who was livid about King's potential release. Vandiver later said that no such call had taken place. Regardless of whether contact ever occurred, it was made clear to Wofford that the CRS was to offer no further statements on the matter, nor do anything else for King. Wofford thought such silence was a fair trade for King's release from jail.

This understanding lasted barely forty-eight hours.

■ ■ ■

Almost no one seemed to notice an ominous cloud gathering just one county over. DeKalb's judge Oscar Mitchell believed King's sit-in arrest violated the terms of his suspended sentence and that his county had the right to take King into custody before Fulton County freed him.

Perhaps only Daddy King, with his instinct for protecting his son, could have sniffed out future trouble. Daddy King understood the depravity people were capable of from his Stockbridge, Georgia, childhood. He witnessed the lynching of a Black man at the local mill by whites; he himself was beaten by a mill owner, and he had fought back against his alcoholic father's abuse of his mother. He had escaped to Atlanta, where he set his sights on marrying Alberta Williams, daughter of the minister of Ebenezer Baptist Church. Becoming her husband and earning a theological degree first required a secondary education, so at twenty-one he endured the humiliation of restarting his studies at a fifth-grade level at Bryant Preparatory School. He willed himself through those classes, eventually making it to Morehouse and assuming the pulpit of Ebenezer Baptist Church. He understood that his family could be taken from him by the Georgia authorities on the flimsiest of pretexts, but in this case his attention was diverted elsewhere.

Daddy King had flown to Cleveland to fill in for his son at a preaching engagement. He spoke to hundreds about his son's predicament, raising two thousand dollars for the imprisoned students and telling the crowd, "We must awaken the conscience of the white man. Our

students are not afraid—they'll fill the jails if they have to." He said
that his son told the students when they asked him to join them, "I
have no choice since I believe in what you are doing." He added that
soon enough "we can sign our own Emancipation Proclamation at the
ballot box, Nov. 8, by a wise vote."

DeKalb's judge Mitchell had not seemed particularly interested in
King when he appeared before him on the traffic charge, but he was
now fully alert to recent events. The day after King's arrest, he had
issued an order that, on the coming Tuesday, King would need to convince him why his suspended driver's license sentence should not be revoked. A news item Friday in the *Constitution* was headlined "DeKalb
Seeks to Jail Rev. King," and the *Journal* ran with "King Faces Year in
Jail on Old Count." But no one seemed to pay much attention to this
new risk to King, including King himself, as if Hartsfield's deal had
resolved his legal troubles for good. Even Hollowell was not focused
on such a threat.

■ ■ ■

At the Wheat Street Baptist Church in Sweet Auburn, the congregation celebrated Men's Day. It was something of a coup to feature
the famed civil rights lawyer Thurgood Marshall as their speaker.
Burly and charismatic, Marshall was already a legend within the
Black community nationwide. He was an NAACP man and believed
in the power of the courts. Still, he was in Atlanta, so on that Sunday
he avoided creating the appearance of a gulf between his courtroom
strategy and the students' activism in the streets. He had just returned
from Kenya, where he had helped draft the future country's new constitution, and he noted how much the American sit-ins inspired young
Africans.

In front of more than three thousand Black Atlantans, he boomed,
"Stop spending your money where you are being insulted." He called
for something he termed "do it yourself integration." The students
promoted the event, and Marshall's NAACP Legal Defense Fund

worked behind the scenes to assist Hollowell's efforts on the students' behalf.

■　■　■

Later that Sunday, Coretta dressed and headed to Paschal's to wait for her husband, where supporters of King and the imprisoned students had decided to celebrate their release—not knowing that King would not be joining them. Years before her frenetic life in Atlanta with a famous husband, she had first waited for Martin Luther King in the January rain on Boston's Huntington Avenue. It had been a long journey from a rural Alabama childhood to the New England Conservatory of Music. White men burned the house she was born in to the ground when she was fifteen, and she had lived in constant fear that her father might be murdered after opening his own lumber mill. He lost the savings he poured into the mill when white men set that on fire, too. She left Alabama for Antioch College in Ohio before transferring to the New England Conservatory in Boston. Coretta was drawn to music and progressive politics and revered the radical singer Paul Robeson. She looked confidently to a life in music, until that first date.

The theology student had confidently called her out of the blue, saying she had been recommended to him. She was initially unimpressed by her suitor's small frame, but as they ate at a Massachusetts Avenue restaurant, "he grew in stature . . . his eloquence, his sincerity, and his *moral* stature." From their first date, King believed she possessed everything he wanted in a wife, though Daddy King, having already singled out a different woman from their Atlanta milieu, took some persuading. For her, the decision to give up the independence of a career and return to the South, far from Boston's relative liberties, to be a minister's wife was not an easy one. Yet she loved King and believed in him.

Their children, Yoki and Marty, as they called Martin III, were now just old enough to understand what was going on. On the way home from nursery school, the car radio broadcast a story about King going to jail. Yoki was in tears when they got home, and the two children asked their mother, "Why did Daddy go to jail?" Coretta had known this day would eventually come—one of the painful inevitabilities of their lives. It was difficult to explain that counter to what most children learn, going to jail could be an honorable thing. She simply said, "Your daddy is a brave and kind man. He went to jail to help people. Some people don't have enough to eat, nor do they have comfortable homes in which to live, or enough clothing to wear. Daddy went to jail to make it possible for all people to have these things. Don't worry, your daddy will be coming back."

Marty had an interest in airplanes. He asked, "Did Daddy go to jail on the airplane?" Hoping it would help soothe her son, Coretta answered, "Yes."

When Yoki was at Atlanta's Quaker House, where the Kings had enrolled her in a children's literature class, a white girl observed, "Oh, your daddy is always going to jail."

Yoki replied, "Yes, he goes to jail to help people."

Driving the author Lillian Smith to Emory University Hospital for breast cancer treatment in May was a favor that changed King's life—a dangerous act, in retrospect, because any Black man put himself at risk by being in the same car as a white woman.

King had known Smith for years and found their friendship to be useful to the movement. Her books *Strange Fruit* and *Killers of the Dream* explored interracial romance and the immorality of segregation, earning literary bans throughout the South and even in cities like Boston. The postal service refused to accept her radical books as mail. Like Wofford, she was the rare white person who wrote to King during the Montgomery boycott to offer heartfelt support, inaugurating their friendship. Although she felt King was a bit overly influenced by his father, she said of him, "He is one of my friends and a most wonderful guy; if you only knew him you'd be sure the man is good, honest, sincere, sensitive and full of compassion and also well stocked with brains." She predicted in a *Saturday Review* article that King's Montgomery struggle would go down in history with Gandhi's Salt March. After King's Magnolia Room arrest, she wrote Dick Rich a letter threatening to cancel her account with him if he did not open his lunch counters to all.

During his tax trial back in mid-May, when it appeared all too likely that King would face jail time in Alabama as a result of trumped-up charges, the traffic ticket had seemed like a minor annoyance at worst. King had difficulty even recalling the uneventful September 23 hearing in front of DeKalb's judge Oscar Mitchell. But there had been some confusion between King and the elderly Black lawyer Daddy King had selected for him, Charles Clayton. King was sitting at the defendant's table as Clayton was consulting with Judge Mitchell at the bench. Clayton motioned for King to come up and told him, "I've worked everything out." It seemed to King that the old lawyer knew how to get things done in the county in which he had long practiced.

King heard the judge say that because King had shown that the car he was driving's tags had been updated, the improper registration charge was dropped. Mitchell then added, "But I would have to fine you for the charge on the driver's license twenty-five dollars." King was hardly listening, having been told by a longtime resident of the county that he had never heard of anyone being fined for driving with an out-of-state license. It was not even clear how long one had to live in the state before acquiring a Georgia license. When Daddy King interjected to ask Judge Mitchell, as he was on his way out, for a full hearing to completely clear his son and straighten out the license issue, the judge laughed and said, "I don't have time, I'm going fishing."

After paying the fine for driving without a Georgia license, King considered the matter closed. He did not understand that with his lawyer's instructing him to plead guilty, he was now on a year's probation. This inattentiveness was unusual for King. The sentencing form read that King could "be put to work and labor in the public work camp . . . for the space of 12 months" if he violated the statutes of any municipality of Georgia. Since the end of slavery, work camps were a common form of imprisonment in the South for Black men found guilty of even trivial offenses.

The look of surprise Lonnie saw on King's face revealed to him that being transferred to DeKalb County was simply beyond his imagining. The pastor had profoundly misjudged the judge. It seemed Oscar Mitchell possessed a lively and deep sense of the finer uses of the law, and he was looking forward to having Martin Luther King pay a return visit to his Decatur courtroom.

And now the energy that the students' high spirits had provided King for five days was gone. He would have to face another long night in jail with no friends to lessen the sense of isolation. He also sensed the mood among the guards shifting, and they allowed themselves to show more animosity without the students there as witnesses. His visitors were cut off.

On the outside, Daddy King was frightened. As he told a reporter, he was "worried about what they might do to [his] child when they got him in there by himself."

DAY 6: MONDAY, OCTOBER 24

The deputy sheriff of DeKalb County showed up shortly after dawn and instructed the Fulton County Jail desk clerk to release King to him. But after King's supporters informed Hollowell of the previous night's shocking events, he had asked the Fulton County sheriff not to release King to DeKalb County. Hollowell, along with the attorney Horace Ward, was playing catch-up, struggling to figure out what exactly was going on.

The deputy said he would be back the next day to claim King. Hollowell had no reason not to believe him, though he was still mystified as to why King was on a year's probation over a minor traffic ticket. The word spread quickly that while the students were back in their classes that morning, King was still in jail—to the considerable frustration of Mayor Hartsfield, who feared the thirty-day truce would unravel through no fault of his own.

For his part, while talking to reporters, King praised Mayor Hartsfield's effort to broker a solution to the standoff over segregation. He thanked the mayor for getting the students freed, explaining that Atlanta was "a community trying honestly and desperately to adjust to inevitable change." King even commended his jailers in Fulton County for how they had treated him, even if he let Black reporters know that some guards had been verbally hostile.

Mayor Hartsfield appeared on WSB in Atlanta, interviewed in his darkened office with the shades drawn behind him, half his face in shadow, microphones held in front of him. He emphasized that "the officials of the downtown store where [King] was apprehended . . . have indicated that they do not wish to prosecute in the state courts Dr. King or any of the other students." Rich didn't want his store being the reason King was sent to state prison. Fear of an impending crisis was much ado about nothing, according to Hartsfield, because "we are of the opinion that [DeKalb] will accordingly in a spirit of cooperation with us withdraw the charges enabling Dr. King to go free of any charges in Atlanta or this county."

A reporter asked, "Mayor, did you receive a call from Martin Luther King's brother saying in effect that if Mr. King is turned over to the DeKalb authorities that that would be a breach of the compromise reached with you regarding the sit-ins?"

"No, sir, I have not received any such call, and I am quite sure that the Negro participants in this realize that we have done everything that we promised them and the existence or complications caused by an outside traffic case have nothing to do with this matter. We hope it is settled in a friendly way, however."

Another reporter spoke of Governor Vandiver saying that Kennedy told him over the phone that he did not wish to inject himself into the affairs of any state. "Have any further inquiries been made to you, sir, and who did make the inquiry to begin with?"

"Well, I would not want to say who I talked to, talked with, in the Kennedy headquarters, but I did talk with them and they transmitted to me the friendly interest of Senator Kennedy, in a friendly solution of this matter, coupled with the statement that neither they, nor Senator Kennedy, had any desire to be put in the position of interfering. I told them that I understood that, and I considered their interest in this matter to be in perfectly good taste and good order, and such as

I would expect from a friendly person towards Atlanta in any walk of life or any political party."

"Was that local or a national inquiry, sir?"

"Uh, the, uh, conversations I had were over the long distance in Washington."

Hartsfield was primarily hoping to keep his city calm, even as he also communicated that he shared the concerns of King's family and staff regarding the strange delay in the minister's release. He believed, incorrectly, that Governor Vandiver had directly influenced Mitchell's actions, but he put on a hopeful face. This was a little traffic charge, he argued; nothing bad was going to happen to King. But the gears of what passed for justice were grinding, no matter what Hartsfield said on camera.

■ ■ ■

All day Monday, an increasingly frustrated E. Frederic Morrow tried to get Nixon's campaign director, Robert Finch, on the phone at his Nineteenth Street D.C. law office. After the gestures of friendship, the private conversations, and all the hard work he had done for Nixon, the Black adviser now felt locked out.

His phone calls to Nixon weren't going through, which was why he was reaching out to Finch, the man rumored to be Nixon's best friend, if he had any friends at all. To Fred Morrow, it seemed urgently important to convey that the chance had arrived to turn around their insufficient Black outreach thus far and that it was Kennedy who seemed to be seizing the opportunity. If Nixon would act—and there was still time—the future that Morrow imagined for the GOP could still be realized.

Morrow's involvement with national Republican politics began in 1952 when the RNC's Val Washington decided he needed a cadre of able Black operatives to realize his vision of bringing Black voters back to the GOP after the New Deal. He recruited Morrow, who was soon riding on Eisenhower's campaign plane. Morrow acquitted himself well in the role, believing the GOP was simply a better vehicle than the Democratic Party for the aspirations of Black Americans—far from perfect, but not infected by southern leaders who made a mockery of that party's appeal for Black support.

Eisenhower's team told Morrow there would be an opportunity in Washington for him after the campaign was over, so Morrow let his previous employer, CBS, know that he would not be coming back. Morrow came to D.C. with great anticipation. However, a White House job offer did not appear after he relocated to the capital, and he watched the inauguration in the cold. Eventually, Republican friends found him a job at the Department of Commerce. Two years later, Morrow was summoned to the office of the White House chief of staff, Sherman Adams. Morrow reported to the west gate at the White House, wondering what he had done wrong. Unapologetic about the broken promise of two years earlier, Adams offered him a newly created position at the White House: administrative officer for special projects. Morrow was in shock. Riding in a cab later in the evening, he heard his staff appointment mentioned in a radio news report, and he teared up with emotion, having achieved the breakthrough of becoming the first Black person to receive an executive position at the White House.

The burdens of being a pioneer, its isolation and indignities, began to reveal themselves. Once Morrow moved into a room in the Executive Office Building, no secretary would accept the assignment of working for a Black man at first. It took five years for Morrow to get his formal commission, and though Eisenhower often attended the swearing in of his staffers, he did not come for this one. Morrow wrote in his diary, "The White House is a little embarrassed about me." He loved Eisenhower nonetheless; the president was capable of small kindnesses such as sending Morrow a note after he had referred to himself at a meeting as a "guinea pig," writing, "We are proud of you—and I assure you that never for one minute did any one of us consider you a 'guinea pig.' From the beginning you have merited and won our respect and admiration." Morrow hung on through the 1956 election, pleased with the increase of Black support for the president, which suggested that his advocacy for civil rights within the White House was having an effect.

Outside work, he was apprehensive of doing anything that could imperil the progress he was making. He did little socially, fearing that even an accidental stumble would allow people to gossip about his being a drunk. He and Jackie Robinson became friends, each understanding the pressure of being the first. Both summoned restraint when racist taunts came their way, and they accepted the loneliness that made their positions especially difficult. Instead of being asked for advice on how the administration could move toward equality, Morrow more often had to deal with the president's belief that Black voters were not grateful enough for all that Eisenhower was doing for them. It was a conflicting position to be in, with many seeing him merely as window dressing—or worse, as a traitor for not pushing the administration hard enough. As much as Morrow resisted becoming the administration's point man in handling the emerging civil rights movement, with the 1954 *Brown v. Board of Education* decision and the brutal murder of Emmett Till the following year, Morrow faced an avalanche of letters accusing the president of indifference and he himself of being an Uncle Tom. Morrow struggled to awaken his fellow Republicans to this wave of change sweeping toward them, but it was even more difficult to tell them that they probably deserved the criticism—that the president was missing a chance to lead.

Morrow believed Eisenhower was a good man, but when it came to the issue of race, Eisenhower made him "heartsick . . . the greatest cross I had to bear." Something in Eisenhower usually resisted endorsing full civil rights action—his belief being that improvement came only with a change in the individual heart, something that no government could effect. (King disagreed, acknowledging once that a law could not make someone love him, yet "it can keep him from lynching me, and I think that's pretty important also.") Briefing Eisenhower before a speech to the National Newspaper Publishers Association, an organization of Black papers, Morrow prepped Eisenhower on talking points to avoid, but Eisenhower departed from his script onstage to talk about how "you people" needed "patience and forbearance" because there were "no revolutionary cures." As he sat watching, Morrow recalled, "I could feel life draining from me." Jackie Robinson, also in attendance, nearly jumped out of his seat in outrage but thought better of making a public rebuke.

After Nixon met with Dr. King in 1957 and told President Eisenhower how impressed he was with the minister, a presidential meeting was arranged the following year with King, Roy Wilkins, A. Philip Randolph, and the Urban League's Lester Granger. Despite the smiling photographs, Eisenhower was upset that the passing of the 1957 Civil Rights Act and his decision to enforce school integration in Little Rock, Arkansas, had not seemed to satisfy them. It was reported that the president "wondered if further constructive action in this field would only result in more bitterness." For King, it had not been a disaster, because he did not expect the old man to be a "crusader," but it certainly made the openness of Vice President Nixon look even better.

Morrow implored senior staff, "Some kind of gesture must be made by the White House to assure Negro citizens they have not been forsaken by their President." Morrow tried to explain to Chief of Staff Adams that people could not be expected to be grateful for progress on attaining rights that should have always belonged to them. When Republicans did poorly in the 1958 midterms, Morrow told his party that they had not been doing enough work to turn out their Black supporters from the previous presidential election. He wrote in a memo, "In most of the states where the Republican Party took a drubbing, Negros hold the balance of power in any close election." In none of these vital electoral states "has an earnest and sincere effort been made by Republican officials to appeal to the Negro voter or to offer these persons an opportunity to become an integral, vital part of the party." In a 1958 survey, the two parties were viewed as being equal in caring about the welfare of Black people. Morrow said they had two more years to figure out a solution, and he was eager to do anything to help. He wrote, "I say emphatically and categorically there cannot be a Republican victory in 1960 until this situation is faced squarely and honestly."

To his mounting horror, Morrow's frustrations with Eisenhower now seemed minimal compared with his being kept at a distance from Nixon during the campaign. He sensed Nixon was weighing an election-defining decision: whether to build on Eisenhower's progress with Black voters or to fully commit to winning over white Democrats in the South. Morrow hoped Robert Finch could help him sway Nixon toward speaking out for King, which might in turn decide the larger question.

Finch was a genial Californian with Hollywood good looks who had everything he needed to be president himself—except an instinct for the jugular. Perhaps that is why he had gravitated into the orbit of Nixon over the previous eight years, rising to the status of adviser, counselor, and eventually campaign manager, serving faithfully in multiple roles to further the political ends of his far more ambitious friend. But Finch's unwillingness to bring out the knife was finally starting to affect his old bond with Nixon; he lost influence and status as the campaign went on, with Nixon increasingly serving as his own adviser.

Even though he sensed that his ability to help was being ignored, Morrow felt that Finch was still worth a try. He dashed off a confidential letter to the campaign manager. He wanted to make sure Finch understood a simple fact: "Dr. Martin Luther King, leader of the student sit-in movement and idol of millions of Negros, is languishing in an Atlanta jail." Though he was seeing something others were missing, Morrow was overestimating the complexity of the strategy guiding Hartsfield's moves and, by extension, those of the Kennedy campaign. Not knowing the somewhat accidental fashion in which Wofford had intervened, Morrow warned, "The Kennedy forces have seized upon this unfortunate incident and have sent telegrams to the Mayor of Atlanta."

Anticipating what his opposite number on the Kennedy campaign, Louis Martin, was now realizing, Morrow saw that this situation could shift the election, writing, "This is a very smart move and the Kennedy forces are going to release this to the Negro press and other media so as to get credit for his humaneness and sympathetic understanding of Negro problems." Morrow had fielded plenty of calls over the previous couple of days from Black Atlanta Republicans, from Calhoun on down, begging him to get Nixon to send a telegram of support to King or the King family. The White House staffer thought this move was an easy one, posing only a slight risk to the campaign. Such a visible gesture would balance out Kennedy's supposed interest in the case and would confirm in the eyes of Black voters that Nixon was indeed King's friend. Morrow saw the threat they faced from the other side if they did not act. In closing, he wrote that he hoped "a determination can be made at once."

Had Nixon acted within twenty-four hours of Morrow's sending this letter, it would likely have been enough to blunt the later impact of Kennedy's intervention in King's case.

It cannot be said that Nixon did not receive sufficient advice: George W. Lee, a Black Republican leader in Memphis, also begged Finch and others on the campaign to help King, writing, "It was Democrats who arrested Mr. King, and put him in jail . . . He is a martyr, a hero to Negroes." The Nixon campaign was receiving telegrams from private citizens and NAACP chapters across the country begging him to act to save King. Both candidates resisted such pleas for nearly a week, but the difference would soon be that Wofford, Martin, and Shriver were daring enough to gamble the election itself.

Earlier in the year, while the CRS was pushing Kennedy to meet with King, a civil rights group (which included King himself) had requested a meeting with the vice president. Nixon wrote to an aide, "Tell them that I would like to see them but that I am completely booked this week—or whenever they asked for." Nixon's calculated indifference—if not hostility—was but a sign of things to come.

■　■　■

The picture of Lonnie King's arrest alongside Martin Luther King had made national news, but now that he was out of jail, Lonnie headed back to his night-shift job at the U.S. Post Office. He worried about his friend M.L.'s predicament, particularly because he had no idea what he could do to help him now, but worrying didn't feed his family.

As Lonnie walked downstairs for a snack during his first shift back, a question occurred to him: After all he had been through in these last few days, how could he abide by Atlanta's tradition of segregated break rooms? He resolved to himself, "Let me be consistent. If I'm gonna challenge segregation outside, I should not be afraid to challenge it inside, where I work." So instead of going left, Lonnie turned right, into the room where white employees ate. The look of shock on white workers' faces as he sat down with his food was almost worth what was about to hit him. Rumors flew through the mail room: "Lonnie King pulled a sit-in downstairs." When he was about to do it again the next night, one of his Black friends said, "Well, I don't want you to get killed by yourself; I'm going with you," and then a third colleague joined them, too.

Within two weeks, Lonnie received notice that he might be fired for having been absent without permission, though he figured it was really a result of his break-room sit-ins. He appealed and kept the job.

■   ■   ■

Now that Wofford was back in the CRS office after the weekend, Louis Martin helped him start looking at the near disaster differently. What if, instead of initiating damage control measures, they proceeded under the assumption that they should actually be pressing their advantage? Side by side, they started testing ideas and the bounds of what they could do to champion Kennedy's intervention for King as opposed to Nixon's doing nothing.

A release they drafted, written in Martin's style, quoted Frank Reeves as saying, "Congratulations are pouring in to Senator John F. Kennedy for his efforts on behalf of Dr. Martin Luther King and the sit-in demonstrators in Atlanta." They noted that Kennedy's inquiry into King's jailing (though it was no such thing) was "in marked contrast to the silence of Vice President Nixon . . . The Republicans talk a lot but when it comes to any positive steps to assist anyone they alwasy [*sic*] miss the bus." The draft, however, was never released.

The stakes were getting exponentially higher with each passing day. Martin and Wofford would have to figure out a way to be bolder.

■ ■ ■

The DeKalb County solicitor Jack Smith was asked if Rich's decision to drop all charges against King would affect his suspended sentence, and he answered, "It doesn't matter if they drop the charges or not." Judge Mitchell scheduled King's hearing for the next day, Tuesday, at 11:00 a.m., and ordered that King be transferred to the DeKalb County Jail.

DAY 7: TUESDAY, OCTOBER 25

On Tuesday morning, King was allowed to shave and don his solemn dark suit and green tie for the court hearing. Though he was obviously not a flight risk, he was placed in handcuffs. Two fedora-clad officers in suits—a younger man smoking a cigarette, an older guard chewing a cigar—led him past waiting photographers. Reverend Otis Moss was told King was in handcuffs for his own protection, to which Moss could only wonder, "Protect him from what and whom?" That day, there would be no big-city niceties for the activist.

Images of King as a "criminal" would run in newspapers around the country, even on the front page of *The New York Times*. Seeing her husband emerge, his facial expression far away and absent, Coretta wrote that the DeKalb County sheriff "walked arrogantly out with his prisoner."

Coretta, Daddy King, A.D., Martin's sister, Christine, and Christine's husband, Isaac Farris, got in their car to follow behind King and his captors, driving out to the hearing in Decatur. Coretta had a sense of foreboding about this place she called "a well-known stronghold of the Klan." Passing roadside gas stations, they neared the courthouse in Decatur, which looked like a small town compared with their city. A

Confederate statue stood in the middle of the town square. Few Black people lived in Decatur, and Black Atlantans did not travel through DeKalb if they could help it.

Students had wanted to protest outside the courtroom, but Wyatt Tee Walker counseled them against it; it would be far too risky in this unfamiliar area where the KKK had held a demonstration just weeks before. Still, a stream of familiar faces emerged from the line of cars, and the Kings realized with relief that Martin would not be alone in Judge Mitchell's courtroom. They saw Dr. Mays and other Black leaders, including the elderly John Wesley Dobbs.

The Kings squeezed into the courtroom, overflowing with 250 people. About a third of those present were Black, and they sat on the left side. Individuals of both races stood toward the back, abuzz, shoving to get a view. Even the lanky form of Roy Wilkins of the NAACP could be seen slipping in ten minutes before the session began; he had hopped a plane from New York early that morning.

When Dr. King was brought down the hallway, now uncuffed, flashbulbs popped all around him. Fellow Baptist ministers and staffers filled several rows, and a group of supportive white seminary students prayed together as he entered. King sat at the end of the defendant's table beside Hollowell and his team. Next to Hollowell was his firm's second lawyer, Horace Ward, a Morehouse man. After several years attempting to be the first African American to enter the University of Georgia Law School, Ward finally went ahead and earned a law degree at Northwestern University before choosing to come back to Atlanta to take on discrimination in Georgia.

Judge Oscar Mitchell emerged from his quarters, taking his perch center stage, surveying the crowd, looking down at King and Hollowell. He settled in and said, "Ladies and gentlemen, the Court will expect no demonstrations. There will be no picture taking in the courtroom." Hollowell's young clerk, Vernon Jordan, sensed that Mitchell was relishing the attention. King's future was in his hands. The national limelight had unexpectedly shifted from Atlanta to his courtroom, and he was going to savor it.

Mitchell was from nearby Panthersville in DeKalb County, where he lived on land his family won by lottery following the forced removal of members of the Creek and Cherokee tribes in the 1820s. In his late forties, Mitchell was a broad man, with saggy cheeks, small eyes, tight lips that smiled without warmth, and large ears. From the bench, his good-ol'-boy mannerisms belied his need to tightly control his cases and his wily political sense. He maintained a brisk pace in his courtroom so he could retreat to ride his tractor on his farm. Morris Abram described Mitchell as "a shrewd, bitter-end segregationist who would relish holding a tether around the neck of the nation's foremost practitioner of civil disobedience."

Mitchell asked Solicitor Jack Smith, a thirty-six-year-old native of Decatur, if he was ready to proceed. As a World War II pilot, Smith had flown bombing missions over Berlin unaware that his future wife, who would immigrate to Georgia after the war, was living below his sights in the German capital. The balding lawyer with close-set eyes and a slightly receding chin rose to reply, "The State is ready."

Hollowell jumped in: "May it please the Court, we are ready for the defendant, and we would like to offer a motion to dismiss the Show Cause petition." He asserted that because King's suspended sentence of twelve months in a work camp was twice as long as the state statute allowed, the entire exercise today should be dismissed. Thus, "inasmuch as said sentence is a nullity, there could not be any violation thereof." Hollowell proceeded to his second basis for releasing King: documentation from Chief Herbert Jenkins showed that there were no charges pending against King in Fulton County. Thanks to Hartsfield and Abram's late Saturday night visit, it was true that there were now no charges in existence; Rich had grudgingly dropped them.

Prosecutor Smith objected, saying just because there was no longer a current charge did not mean King had not broken the law last week when he was arrested.

Hollowell argued Mitchell would be well within his powers now to dismiss. But the cat never gives up the mouse until having played with it. Judge Mitchell said of the documents attesting to the lack of charges against King, "I will admit them for what they are worth." Hollowell did not expect these defense probes to succeed, but they allowed him to gauge the judge and his receptiveness to different lines of reasoning. Everyone was just warming up.

With his imposing posture, Hollowell drew the eyes of the courtroom to him. He had an elegant, trim mustache, a slight widow's peak, deeply lined cheeks, and a baritone voice; Andrew Young compared him to a Shakespearean actor in lawyerly guise. Whereas Thurgood Marshall had a talent for earthy folksiness that served to forge a connection with a jury, Hollowell gave you no choice but to accept his impressiveness. This was no mere posturing; when a judge asked a clerk to find something in a document, Hollowell would call out exactly what page it could be found on from memory.

Smith rebutted the motion to dismiss by saying the judge's sentencing mistake had been meaningless. Reduce the sentence to the six-month maximum if you must, but King had still violated his probation. Smith cited a Georgia law that stated, "There does not have to be an accusation pending." Judge Mitchell was not about to assent to Hollowell's request for King to walk out of his courtroom. He announced, "Gentlemen, I will reserve my ruling on the motion to dismiss at the present time. And we will proceed with the hearing."

Bennett Tuck, the general superintendent of Rich's, was called to the witness stand, where he testified about King's participation in the sit-in on October 19. Smith guided Tuck through King's arrival at the Magnolia Room, how Tuck had informed him of the basement facilities for Black people and that what they were doing was unlawful. Hollowell took up his cross-examination, asking if there were other people that afternoon eating lunch. "Did you ask them to leave?" Tuck, of course, had not. So Hollowell asked about King and the students: "Were they clean?"

"Yes."

"Were they properly dressed?"

"Yes."

"Were they respectful in their manner at all times?"

"Yes."

Smith jumped in: "Your Honor, I am going to object to whether or not they were clean dressed or respectful. That is not the point. The point here is whether they refused to leave the premises when asked to do so."

Hollowell said, "I submit to Your Honor here again, this is a matter that incorporates all the aspects in dealing with any conversation or any action which took place between this gentleman and defendant."

Mitchell said, "All right. Go ahead."

"And they were clean and courteous, Mr. Tuck? Did they indicate that they wanted to do anything other than eat?"

"No."

"This was an establishment which caters to persons wanting to eat, is that not true?"

"That's right."

"Was there any disorderliness about Mr. King or anyone who may have happened to be with him?"

"No."

Hollowell asked if the female student standing next to King had been of the same race. Tuck said yes. Hollowell went on, "Then it is your testimony that there was no one asked to leave other than those of the same ethnic extraction."

Smith said, "I am going to object to any ethnic extraction in this case."

Judge Mitchell said, "I will sustain."

Hollowell disagreed, turning to the judge and saying, "I think it would be proper to indicate why he asked those persons to leave, since it appears from his own testimony that their actions, dress, demeanor was consistent with that of the other persons who were eating." Along with the necessary technical arguments, Hollowell was putting segregation on trial. Mitchell might not have been interested in this line of argument, but Hollowell would not let the proceeding end without stating the fundamental issue at hand.

Judge Mitchell interrupted: "In my construction of the statute, it does not have to show any reason why you ask someone to leave the premises. It just provides that if you ask them to leave and they refused, then at that time the law is violated irrespective of the law, race or religion."

Hollowell conceded the statute could be read this way, but he had the right to ask Tuck if race was the reason Tuck said they could not eat at the Magnolia Room. The judge sustained Smith's objection, and the department store manager was dismissed. Next up was Captain R. E. Little, who relayed the circumstances of the arrest. In his cross-examination, Hollowell asked, "There was no loud talking?"

"No."

"No boisterousness?"

"No."

"They were dressed in an exemplary fashion?"

"Yes."

"No fisticuffs?"

"No."

"When you told them to leave because they were breaking the law, this was your interpretation of what the law was? This is what you thought to be the law?"

"At any time we make an arrest, we book the cases on our interpretation of what the law is. The Court decides after we take them into Court."

Cecil Semple, the vice president of operations at Rich's, was called to the stand next. After a similar exchange, Hollowell asked him "whether or not there have been any accusations filed by your store pertaining to this defendant." Quickly butting in, Solicitor Smith insisted that he would object to any questions about previous accusations. Mitchell quickly sustained that, prompting Hollowell to complain, "Without counsel having opportunity to give his argument on it, sir?" It was like playing chess against two opponents simultaneously.

Smith now entered into evidence King's guilty plea from September. Hollowell had no objection, but renewed the motion to dismiss because the statute, "though constitutional on its face, is unconstitutional in the application, in that it is an abridgement of the rights and privileges of this defendant." Hollowell added that the department store had violated King's First Amendment rights to freedom of assembly and the equal protection clause of the Fourteenth Amendment.

All this fell on deaf ears, which Hollowell likely knew it would, but he thought it must be said anyhow. Hollowell asserted in his almost Elizabethan tone, "This defendant was in a place where he had a right to be; this is a public place. This is a privately owned store, yes. But this is a store that has to be licensed by the State, the City. They are representatives of the public . . . And it was very evident that only persons of his extraction were those who were being denied the utilization of this particular facility." Hollowell offered to submit cases to substantiate his assertion that "there is no basis for . . . any arrest in this particular situation."

"You want me to rule on that point, now?" Mitchell did not want to have a constitutional law debate over segregation.

Hollowell said, "I would like for Your Honor to rule on the renewed motion, which is a motion to dismiss."

Smith attempted now to steer things away from these larger questions back to motor vehicle codes. Judge Mitchell liked that, saying, "I am concerned with the one dealing with the driver's license." Hollowell swerved back to motor vehicle rules, saying how King's suspended sentence exceeded the limits of the statute. Judge Mitchell told Hollowell, "I am overruling your motion as made. But I am inclined to agree with counsel that six months is a limitation upon this offense." This was a small victory—Mitchell conceding that he could not sentence King to a year. Yet six months was still in play, time enough in a dangerous state prison.

Hollowell rose and said, "The defense calls defendant Martin Luther King." King went forward, was sworn in, and stoically sat facing the crowded courtroom. The minister's shield of dignity sometimes seemed impenetrable, but close allies and friends knew the vulnerability, the self-doubt, and, at other times, the humor were there. You could see it in his soft eyes; however majestic his voice might be, however large he would appear to grow in the pulpit (rising to the balls of his feet from his five feet seven inches), however extraordinary his words, this wounded sensitivity was there.

Regarding the May arrest, Hollowell asked King, "Did you have any license at all?"

"Yes sir, I did, I had Alabama."

Smith objected that this was about an already decided case, and Mitchell sustained. Hollowell asked, "At the time that you paid the twenty five dollar fine, did you know that a plea of guilty had been entered?"

"No." Seated in the crowded courtroom was the elderly lawyer who had represented King a month earlier in front of this judge. Charles Clayton told the press the day before this hearing that he did not know how King missed what went on during the proceeding the previous month, with both of them standing at the bench looking up at Judge Mitchell. In defending himself for not having better informed his client, Clayton maintained King was right next to him in September as Judge Mitchell announced the probated sentence.

Smith objected again, saying, "The record speaks for itself."

Hollowell replied it would be incumbent on the court to ascertain whether King had understood the extent of the sentence. Judge Mitchell was not pleased to hear one lawyer seeming to question the veracity of King's first counsel, much less his own word, and said so. Hollowell clarified, "We are merely attempting to show what his knowledge was relative to the situation, so Your Honor can be apprised to at least his mental satisfaction."

"All right. I will let you get into that."

"Dr. King, did you know that a plea of guilty had been entered as such?"

"No sir, I did not know that." Sensing Hollowell gaining traction, Smith objected that whether or not a defendant understood he had pleaded guilty should have no bearing on if he went out and violated the law again.

Now the judge turned himself into a witness of sorts by saying, "I might state that when the plea of guilty was entered, Dr. King and his counsel stood right there and he signed the plea, and when he signed the plea, I told his counsel again I would do exactly as I told him I would do—let him pay the twenty five dollar fine on one count and give him twelve months probated sentence. I asked his counsel in the presence of Rev. King, 'Have you explained to your client concerning this sentence?' Rev. was standing there—"

Hollowell interjected, "We are not trying to show that was not said, Your Honor. We are not in any way seeking to impeach—"

"I want it clear in the record. Because I am stating that now in the presence of his counsel. If he wants to deny that, he is standing here now before the Court. He—I might like to inquire of him now standing in his place as an attorney if that is not what happened."

Though seated far back in the crowded courtroom, King's former attorney, hearing this question from the bench, shouted out (although he had not been sworn in, or even seated with the defense), "That did happen."

Hearing Clayton, Mitchell asked, "You are stating that in your place as an attorney at bar?"

The elder lawyer assented. Hollowell backtracked. "Dr. King, do you have any recollection of having heard anything about the probation?"

Still calm, the minister denied any recollection of that aspect of his suspended sentence. Hollowell asked King what exactly he had heard that day, and King told Judge Mitchell that he remembered him saying the tag charge was dismissed and he would just have to pay a small fine concerning the license. Hollowell said, "I will ask you whether or not you at any time have ever talked with the Probation Officer of this Court?"

"No sir."

Standing crowd members were moving closer to the proceedings, leaning into the escalating intrigue over what exactly had happened in King's earlier hearing. The sheriff halted things in order to move eager listeners back, with Mitchell saying they were pushing the counsel too close to the bench.

When he was given the go-ahead to continue, Hollowell asked if King had ever been directed to the probation officer's office. King replied, "I don't recall being directed to his office."

"Has the Probation Officer ever contacted you in any way whatsoever?"

"No sir, I have not been contacted by a Probation Officer." His defense lawyer asked King one more time to emphasize this key point. King answered, "Yes sir, that's correct. I am not saying it was not said. I only said I didn't hear it, and never knew until three days ago, or whenever they served me at the Fulton County Jail." As King stepped down, Hollowell pressed his momentary advantage by questioning the DeKalb County probation officer, Ernest Johnson, who testified that he indeed had never spoken with King.

Smith cross-examined him, asking how many staff members Johnson had—the answer was one person—and how many cases he handled. "I imagine around 2,000." Smith asked if it was customary to talk to everyone on probation, and Johnson replied that there were hundreds of cases placed on probation never referred to him.

Hollowell had kept Mitchell's exposure to King to a minimum, because all he had to do was prevent the judge from doing something verging on the outrageous. Perhaps this judge could be persuaded to simply be rational, to let King go home after five days already spent in jail. Hollowell also had a secret weapon: a slate of character witnesses, including four of the five Atlanta University Center college presidents, all of whom admired King and saw him as an exemplar of Black Atlanta—especially Dr. Mays of Morehouse, who had remained extremely close with King since he graduated.

Hollowell then presented John Wesley Dobbs, for decades the most renowned Black leader in Atlanta and a prominent Republican, a man who had known King since he was born. Dobbs had listened to one of King's first sermons. The elder gentleman summed up the young minister as a good man—profoundly "idealistic." F. M. Martin of the Atlanta Life Insurance Company (among the most successful Black businesses in America) said King's reputation was "one of the best I know of anywhere in the country." The defense then rested, only renewing the motion to dismiss "on the grounds that there has been insufficient evidence to establish any conduct on the part of this defendant which would justify this Court in revoking any sentence which has been previously imposed."

Jack Smith rose to make his closing statement by saying, "I'm going to indulge in a few moments of plain talk, your honor. This defendant pleaded guilty to violating the law on May 4. On October 19, he violated the law again. He has not said he is sorry he violated the law. He has stated the law is not what he thinks it ought to be." Mocking the character witnesses Hollowell had produced, Smith said, "If a kissing bandit kisses the ladies and robs the men in a group, he is guilty of robbery all the same."

They had come to a close. All eyes were on Judge Mitchell. He paused and then sternly signaled where he was going: "We expect no demonstrations." He paused again. "However, it is the judgment of this Court that four months of the defendant's probated sentence is revoked."

The judge's pronouncement and its convoluted phrasing took a moment to sink in. Then, seeing the evident distress of King's lawyers, it dawned on the crowded courtroom that the minister had just been ordered to a labor camp for four months.

Gasps of dismay filled the room. King's friends knew this outrageous pronouncement could prove lethal, as similar sentences had for Black men for generations throughout the South, from Mississippi's infamous Parchman Farm to Louisiana's Angola. Despite anguished exclamations around him, King sat composed as he absorbed the brutal sentence. He thought Hollowell had argued the case brilliantly and that the outcome was just another example of the persecution he faced.

Hollowell shouted an interjection: "Prior to the time the Court was adjourned, I would like to ask the Court whether or not the Court will set a bond in connection with this matter."

"It is the opinion of the Court that the defendant is not entitled to bond on revocation of a probated sentence."

Hollowell pressed, "I submit Your Honor, wondering if that judgment might not be reserved until such time as Your Honor has considered the matter of the Bill of Exceptions."

"I will be glad to hear you on that Bill of Exceptions. You and the Solicitor get together. Court is now adjourned."

King's sister, Christine, started sobbing. Watching her, Coretta was overwhelmed. For the first time since the Montgomery bus boycott had begun, she could not publicly hold back her tears. The sentence meant her husband would not be with her as she gave birth to their third child. Watching her crumple, Daddy King glared, shocked by her response. He snapped at her to stop this; people could see them, which only made her cry more.

In the chaos of the moment, the president of the Atlanta NAACP, the Reverend Samuel W. Williams (who was also a classical philosophy professor at Morehouse), was so upset that he stepped forward to object, ignoring the deputy sheriff's warnings to step back. They wrestled him into custody and placed him under arrest. King himself was taken away in custody to a jail cell upstairs, past more blinding photo flashes in the hallway. Daddy King managed to get Mitchell's attention as he called out, "Judge, you're killing me because you're killing my son." Mitchell shuffled away, looking unsettled, as Daddy King continued, "But you've got to go to church on Sunday and see your God."

Daddy King avoided arrest and, with Coretta, was permitted a short visit with King in the cell above the courtroom. Coretta was still trying to stifle her tears. Her husband, like his father, seemed unnerved by her weeping. King said, "Corrie, dear, you have to be strong. I've never seen you like this before. You have to be strong for me."

Coretta later wrote, "Martin had been weakened by his days in jail, and was greatly depressed by this unexpected shock." He was looking to her for strength, but she, too, was "totally unprepared."

Daddy King said in turn, "You don't see me crying; I am ready to fight. When you see Daddy crying, Coretta, then you can start crying. I'm not taking this lying down." All of Daddy King's fears were proving well-founded, but seeing his resolve, Coretta was able to collect herself.

King looked at the two of them, saying softly, "I think we must prepare ourselves for the fact that I am going to have to serve this time."

Coretta answered, "Yes, I think we must prepare ourselves for that."

He asked her to see if she could get him writing materials, in addition to some books, newspapers, and magazines, as well as a little money. Wyatt Tee Walker spoke to him briefly as well, and King told him, "As bad as this may seem for me, this is all a part of the redemptive process by which the soul of America will be redeemed. I hold no bitterness toward anyone." Walker relayed this sentiment to the press.

After the hearing, Roy Wilkins tried to see King but was not allowed near the holding cell. Having said he was from New York, he immediately thought to himself, "I made a boo-boo there." Wilkins had George Orwell's *1984* to give to King, thinking it appropriate to the situation King now found himself in. When reporters asked Wilkins what the NAACP would do to help King, he said they would provide moral, financial, and legal support (though he praised the counsel King already had in Hollowell). This was no small promise, given the sometimes heated rivalry he had with King. Wilkins felt the NAACP had been doing the work of racial justice for years and that the upstart SCLC was undermining his organization's fundraising. Still, despite his concerns regarding the hazards of direct action in the streets, Wilkins showed up, and King never forgot the gesture. Wilkins called Judge Mitchell's actions a shocking decision that would shake Black people, along with "a great many white people as well, who will not be able to understand how the lack of a driver's license on the part of a man transferring from one state to another could be parlayed into this kind of sentence." Wilkins admitted, "I don't know that our people are not completely sold on the go to jail, stay in jail business," but he added that the sit-ins showed how "you have 18 million people in this country who are through with discriminatory treatment." Within an hour, Wilkins was leaving Decatur to get on a plane back to New York.

The crowds quickly dispersed; Black Atlantans had little reason to linger in Decatur Square. Hollowell was already working on a comprehensive bill of exceptions for their appeal. Coretta understood that the judge had promised King would not be taken to Reidsville until that appeal had been heard. She tried to focus on getting her husband the things he requested, but she was soon thinking of someone who might be able to help get him out: their friend on the Kennedy campaign, Harris Wofford.

■ ■ ■

When word of the sentence made its way over the wires to the Justice Department in D.C., a meeting was called. Top Republican department officials gathered to debate what they could do for King; it was clear that this local judge was out of control in his sentencing. One idea was to go to the federal courts with their own writ of habeas corpus, to get King out of jail immediately. Someone else suggested a DOJ official be sent to appear before Judge Mitchell as a friend of the court, asking him to release King; maybe a little federal pressure would make the judge back down. But there were drawbacks to both options in an administration so loath to interfere in state affairs. Furthermore, they knew the president did not like entangling himself in racial issues, with his belief that moral progress would be more likely without government interference. Yet he had sent troops into Little Rock three years earlier, showing that his sense of justice could prod him into action.

The idea that emerged was to have President Eisenhower make a brief statement before the cameras: their well-loved, moderate (and nearly out of office) leader calling on common sense to secure justice for King or, at a minimum, access to bail. The minutes of the meeting have been lost, but the participants tasked Deputy Attorney General Lawrence Walsh with drafting a statement.

Walsh's boss, Attorney General William Rogers, was on the campaign trail with Nixon in Ohio that day, so Walsh's draft should have gotten to both men together. One telegram the Nixon campaign received that day came from Hartford's NAACP, asking that Nixon "USE EVERY METHOD TO SEEK RELEASE OF REV KING." Rogers would later say he supported getting a statement to the president for him to use. Nixon claimed he asked Rogers if this were not a situation in which King's constitutional rights had been infringed, "thus paving the way for Federal action."

What Walsh came up with was a simple, almost heartfelt, statement that would likely have been effective in altering the course of the election: "It seems to me fundamentally unjust that a man who has peacefully attempted to establish his right to equal treatment, free from racial discrimination, should be imprisoned on an unrelated charge, in itself insignificant. Accordingly, I have asked the Attorney General to take proper steps to join with Dr. Martin Luther King in an appropriate application for his release."

Eisenhower never spoke these words. The date on the existing memo reads October 31, six days later, and four days after it would have even been relevant. When the memo was actually completed, and what happened in the interim, remain unknown. Perhaps the statement was never delivered by President Eisenhower because it never got past Nixon.

■   ■   ■

Whatever Wofford had done over the previous weekend—risky as it might have been for his own position on the campaign—it had not been enough. He and Louis Martin agreed that they needed to call their higher-ups once more. Despite firm admonitions from top staffers to drop the whole King matter, the two of them, backed by Shriver, argued that the Kennedy campaign needed to put out a strong statement on King's behalf. The two men were savvy enough to understand that this segregationist judge would not be shamed into reason, but they wanted to start a drumbeat to free King.

Martin had another worry—that Nixon would finally speak out on behalf of Dr. King. They couldn't figure out why he hadn't said anything yet, or at least quietly prodded the Department of Justice to issue some statement of protest. Attorney General William Rogers was supposed to be a decent man and Nixon's close friend—what were their opponents waiting for?

Georgia Democratic leaders had told Kennedy, predictably, that the state would be lost if his campaign made any statement even remotely resembling a rebuke of the Georgia judge. Wofford believed that the Georgia co-chair Griffin Bell, who privately acknowledged that King's sentence was unreasonable, might be willing to produce a more moderate draft so they could release something. Even that hope was stymied when Wofford got the message from Kennedy that Vandiver had just told him, "Don't issue it and I'll get the son of a bitch out." Vandiver later maintained that no such conversation happened at that point in the crisis.

Kennedy reassured Wofford that King would get more effective help if they quietly worked behind the scenes with Georgia officials; no more controversial statements could appear in the media. With a touch of exasperation, Kennedy asked Wofford a simple question: Wasn't getting King freed what he wanted? He added, "After all, we're interested in getting him out, not in making publicity." At this point, Kennedy might have been as interested in getting the chess piece off the board (or out of jail) as he was in getting Wofford off his back.

Wofford could not argue with that, but after hanging up, he was left to think about how foolish it was to trust any southern Democrat with his friend's life. Was Kennedy just placating him—or worse, deceiving him to get him to drop the issue? Maybe Kennedy would do nothing. The stalemate over issuing a statement was an unsettling reminder that the Massachusetts politician hardly shared the extent of Wofford's sympathies.

On a hot August morning two months earlier, Wofford was standing on a Georgetown street corner hoping for a taxi when a red convertible swerved to a halt in front of him. It was JFK, the newly nominated candidate, calling out to him, "Jump in."

As they drove to the Capitol, Kennedy impatiently tapped the car window with his left hand, saying, "Now, in five minutes, tick off the ten things a President ought to do to clean up this goddamn civil rights mess." Wofford told Kennedy that he could stop discrimination in federally assisted housing with "one stroke of a pen," and then listed other opportunities for executive action that had been ignored in the Eisenhower years. Kennedy vowed he would enact his platform promises if he were elected, but there was no avoiding the blitheness of Kennedy's five-minute request, which suggested that to him civil rights was a problem that needed to be managed in order to win, not a moral undertaking requiring empathy with others' suffering.

Earlier in the year, Kennedy mused with Wofford that as a result of the discrimination his own Irish family had endured, he had developed an innate dislike of any sort of prejudice. He viewed racism as shameful, though he saw it more as illogical than as cause for outrage. Despite the Kennedys' privileged childhood, the family could not help but be aware of poverty in the Depression. Yet understanding racism was, as Bobby said, "not a particular issue in our house." Now, on the cusp of power, fear of speaking out on civil rights weighed heavier in the pragmatic candidate's thinking than any urgency about advocating for those facing persecution.

Still, that summertime car ride also demonstrated to Wofford that Kennedy, momentarily freed from his cautious advisers, might be persuaded to take real action.

On Tuesday afternoon, with word of King's sentence just beginning to make its way over the wire, Wofford received a call at the CRS office. He recognized the voice of Coretta King, and although he did not know her well, he was still startled to hear her like this. She sounded panicked.

"They are going to kill him, I know they are going to kill him," Coretta cried, without introduction, in a breathless rush.

Wofford tried to comfort her, to slow her down so he could catch up. She relayed a conversation she had just had with Harry Belafonte about the threat her husband was now facing. Belafonte later wrote that his opinion was, "Every hour that Martin spent on that chain gang, we knew his life was in danger. What was there to keep some white supremacist on the gang from killing him with a blow of his pickax? Not the police guards, that was for sure."

Wofford absorbed the details of the DeKalb disaster, and though he tried to reassure Coretta, he had no real comfort to offer. Her assertion that King was in mortal jeopardy meant that the stakes were now too high for playing political games. They would have to do something, whether the Irish Mafia on the *Caroline* was on board or not.

Wofford wished he could say more to her, believing JFK was now working Georgia contacts on her husband's behalf, but any public revelation of southern white Democrats helping Martin Luther King behind the scenes would harm the best chance they had for freeing him. Wofford simply said that they were "doing everything possible." He knew it was insufficient. They had not begun to explore what was possible.

After putting down the phone, Wofford turned to Martin. He briefed him on Mrs. King's conversation with Belafonte and what was going on in Atlanta. His partner was equally disturbed and needed no persuading that King was indeed in serious trouble. When Martin had heard a younger King speak at the University of Chicago's Rockefeller Chapel in 1956, the editor wrote, "Can civil rights in some form become a world issue? How I wish I could take a peep at the future." That future was now at risk of being foreclosed.

The two struggled again to draft a statement Kennedy could make. But they realized they were hitting the same old wall. For two workaholics, Wofford made a startling suggestion: Would Martin like to go get a late afternoon beer to clear their heads? Martin took him up on the offer. Escaping the office, they went over to their nearby mainstay, Harvey's Restaurant, the bright red sign of the D.C. fixture beckoning them. Harvey's was next door to the Mayflower Hotel, where Shriver had stayed before heading back to Illinois, and the three of them had often convened there after twelve-hour workdays, staying until the

Martin Luther King Jr. speaks with student sit-in organizers in his office on September 1, 1960. Lonnie King is to Dr. King's left. Julian Bond is facing Dr. King in a white shirt, fourth on the right. (DONALD UHRBROCK / THE LIFE IMAGES COLLECTION / GETTY IMAGES)

LEFT: Police take Martin Luther King Jr. out of Rich's department store in Atlanta. Behind him are Atlanta Student Movement leader Lonnie King and Spelman College students Blondean Orbert and Marilyn Pryce. (ASSOCIATED PRESS)

RIGHT: Lonnie King, Marilyn Pryce, and Martin Luther King Jr. under arrest in downtown Atlanta (CHARLES JACKSON / *THE ATLANTA JOURNAL-CONSTITUTION* VIA ASSOCIATED PRESS)

King and Blondean Orbert being taken to jail following their arrest. Driving the car is the Atlanta police captain, R. E. Little. (ASSOCIATED PRESS)

LEFT: Two officers escort King from Fulton County Jail on the way to the DeKalb County courthouse. (HORACE CORT / ASSOCIATED PRESS)

RIGHT: King prior to his appearance before Judge Oscar Mitchell at DeKalb County Civil and Criminal Court (DONALD UHRBROCK / THE LIFE IMAGES COLLECTION / GETTY IMAGES)

Martin Luther King Jr. and Coretta Scott King with their children Yolanda and Martin, King's sister Christine King Farris, and student activists at Peachtree-DeKalb Airport after King's return from the Georgia State Prison in Reidsville (AFRO AMERICAN NEWSPAPERS / GADO / GETTY IMAGES)

Louis E. Martin with President John F. Kennedy at a 1963 White House reception celebrating the centennial of the Emancipation Proclamation (COURTESY OF THE JOHN F. KENNEDY PRESIDENTIAL LIBRARY AND MUSEUM)

Harris Wofford and President Kennedy on the South Lawn of the White House (COURTESY OF THE JOHN F. KENNEDY PRESIDENTIAL LIBRARY AND MUSEUM)

Sargent Shriver with Peace Corps members on the South Lawn (COURTESY OF
THE JOHN F. KENNEDY PRESIDENTIAL LIBRARY AND MUSEUM)

Donald Hollowell and student activist Prathia Hall leaving federal court early in the sit-in
movement (BETTMANN / GETTY IMAGES)

Lonnie King leads demonstrators in prayer before a protest against segregated retail shops in Atlanta on December 12, 1960. (ASSOCIATED PRESS)

E. Frederic Morrow and Richard Nixon sometime in the 1950s (E. FREDERIC MORROW PAPERS [BOX 11, PHOTO 007], VIVIAN G. HARSH RESEARCH COLLECTION OF AFRO-AMERICAN HISTORY AND LITERATURE, CHICAGO PUBLIC LIBRARY)

LEFT: E. Frederic Morrow, left, and Jackie Robinson, center (CECIL LAYNE / E. FREDERIC MORROW PAPERS [BOX 12, PHOTO 088], VIVIAN G. HARSH RESEARCH COLLECTION OF AFRO-AMERICAN HISTORY AND LITERATURE, CHICAGO PUBLIC LIBRARY)

RIGHT: Louis E. Martin and President Lyndon B. Johnson in the White House colonnade (YOICHI OKAMOTO / LYNDON B. JOHNSON LIBRARY)

Harris Wofford and Sargent Shriver on a Peace Corps trip in Africa (COURTESY OF HARRIS WOFFORD)

Robert Kennedy and his wife, Ethel, pay their respects to Coretta Scott King in her home after the assassination of Martin Luther King Jr. in 1968. (FLIP SCHULKE ARCHIVES / GETTY IMAGES)

staff turned out the lights. Then they would either head back to the office or just collapse in Shriver's room. It was during such long nights that Martin and Wofford saw another side of their driven boss, watching Shriver meditate, kneel in prayer, read radical Catholic theology on his hotel bed, and quote Gerard Manley Hopkins before finally falling asleep.

Over their beers, Martin pondered, "What do we do now? What do we do to help get King out?" Was there something that they were not considering?

Wofford said, "Who cares about public statements? What Kennedy ought to do is something direct and personal, like picking up the telephone and calling Coretta. Just giving his sympathy but doing it himself." He said, "If these beautiful and passionate Kennedys would just lose their cool for once and show their passion, maybe Jack would do something like just calling her."

"That's it, that's it! That would be perfect," Martin responded. "That would really make 'em, if he would call them on the phone it would make a huge impact." He said, "That's the most beautiful thought I've heard. You don't know what that would do for her, and people like me." They decided to find a way to get this idea to Kennedy.

Martin's sudden enthusiasm was galvanizing after days of restraint. They talked into the evening, imagining such a call from different angles—how and when best to do it, the risks involved, what strategy would be required. Getting through to Kennedy would not be easy, however, given how skeptically Wofford was viewed within the campaign. They phoned Shriver, intending to ask who the best person to present the idea to Kennedy might be, but they did not reach him. Their boss was busy arranging Kennedy's tour of the Chicago suburbs, scheduled for the next day. Impatient, Wofford tried calling Kennedy himself, then other aides. He waited, but received no reply. The last few days had confirmed to the rest of the campaign that Wofford and the CRS were a nuisance to be ignored.

It was getting late, and Wofford was still worried about Coretta. The idea came to him that a temporary proxy for Kennedy could be the former Connecticut governor Chester Bowles, Wofford's partner in writing the civil rights plank of the Democratic Party platform at the convention and a fellow liberal whom he could count on. Getting Bowles on the line, Wofford explained the situation and asked, "Mrs. King really needs some word from afar that would encourage her. Why don't you call her?"

Bowles, though barely on the edge of the Kennedy circle, had gravitas. He responded, "Wonderful. I'll call her, and as a matter of fact, I'll have Adlai Stevenson call her. He's here for dinner, and we'll both talk to her."

"That'll be wonderful; that'll help."

Wofford had at least gotten something done. He would keep trying to get their idea to JFK in the morning. Everything was moving fast.

DAY 8: WEDNESDAY, OCTOBER 26

It was around 3:30 a.m. In the pitch-black, no sign yet of dawn, Martin Luther King was, for once, deep in slumber, having at some point that night lost his battle against sleep.

There was the metallic grating of keys, and then his cell door opened.

Guttural shouts: "King! King! Wake up!" He thought he was still dreaming. "King, get up, put on your clothes." He was slow to move, and the guards insisted, "Did ya' hear me, King? Get up and come on out here. And bring all your things with you."

His jailers kept their flashlights in his face. They told him to stand up and dress, and they grabbed his wrists and handcuffed them. Then the guards pushed him out into the dark corridor.

It was hard not to succumb to the panic. King knew all too well the long history of Black people being led toward an extrajudicial death in the dark of night, the fiction of their resistance an easy excuse. If they could toss the mangled body of a child as young as Emmett Till in a river, what were they about to do to him? His lawyer Hollowell represented the widow of James Brazier, a Black man who was pulled over by the police in Dawson, Georgia, without cause; when Brazier continued to protest this, he was taken from his prison cell and fatally beaten.

As they emerged into the parking lot, King saw a police car waiting for him. Exhaust fumes trailed into the chilly Georgia night. The guards knelt to bind iron shackles around King's legs that could be attached to the floor of the car. When the shackles were clicked shut, he now had chains on both his ankles and trailing from the manacles on his wrists. The guards were treating him like a dangerous criminal.

As he tried to find a comfortable position in the back of the car, the next threat he had to deal with was a German shepherd in the back seat. These dogs were trained to lunge, but luckily King's back-seat companion did not do so. King was raised with dogs and liked them. Maybe this huge animal somehow sensed that.

The two white men settled into the front seat, and within five minutes of his being awakened, they pulled away from the jail into the darkness beyond Decatur. He did not know it then, but the two officers were from the Georgia State Board of Corrections.

Every time King shifted in discomfort as they drove along the bumpy Georgia roads—wherever they were going, there were no expressways—the dog growled. As the night wore on, King heard the officers muttering to each other. They never spoke to him about where they were headed.

With the guards not speaking to him, King was hit by the desperate feeling that he might never see anyone he loved again. His family might never know which roads he was driven along that night, nor the truth about his eventual fate. King said later, "That kind of mental anguish is worse than dying." He described it as "hell on earth."

With each mile they traveled, King grew hungrier and thirstier, and he silently prayed. After some hours, he figured that if they were not going to kill him, then they must be heading for the infamous state prison where he was to serve his four-month sentence. He had never been to Reidsville, had no sense of how one could get there or how far away it was. He knew only that it was in the piney backwoods very far from the comforts of Atlanta. He had a dim idea that the distance to Reidsville must be more than two hundred miles, so he simply held on.

King's first clue as to where they were heading came near the three-hour mark, when they were around Dublin, Georgia, and he heard the officers make a remark that led him to believe Reidsville was indeed the intended destination. On that long night, the sun did not rise until the last half hour of the ride. Just after it did, some four hours into the journey, they arrived in Tattnall County—finally in sight of the long, austere, WPA-era Georgia State Prison building, an incongruous sight amid the endless miles of rural farms that surrounded it. The looming jail was built here for a reason; it was far from all but the most desolate towns. Above its entrance was a frieze of muscular men engaged in hard labor, a not-so-subtle evocation of the fate of those imprisoned inside. When they finally arrived, King did not feel any particular relief, such as he had experienced when he had reached the Montgomery jail years earlier. This time he was, as he later told Coretta, "exhausted and humiliated."

Unshackled to finally stretch his muscles after the long ride, he was put through fingerprinting, a review of his criminal record, a medical exam, and a short meeting with the chaplain. King stayed silent as guards led him into a narrow cell and had him dress in the prison uniform: white with dark stripes down the legs. Guards gave him two pairs and instructed him to put on the older one. R. P. Balkcom, the forty-five-year-old hard-nosed warden who had worked at Reidsville for nearly two decades, informed King that he would be held in solitary confinement for between ten and twenty-one days while the prison determined what duties he would be assigned. Balkcom told the minister that he did not yet know whether he would labor on a prison farm or perform road work.

Meanwhile, whispers went between cells: "King's here."

■ ■ ■

Governor Ernest Vandiver had achieved his lifelong dream of leading Georgia and was not enjoying it nearly as much as he imagined he would.

He had suffered a heart attack in March, at age forty-one. Nineteen sixty had been the most difficult year of Vandiver's life. He had worked (and schemed) his way to the Georgia governor's mansion, and once he got there, it appeared that the federal courts' willingness to indulge Georgia's resistance to *Brown v. Board of Education* was finally coming to an end. Not that his white voters would accept such an explanation, hostile as they were to *Brown*. They expected him to keep stalling, as his predecessors had.

Vandiver wanted to tinker with the state budget, enact government reforms, and improve the treatment of the mentally ill, all while keeping matters of race hidden away as they were in the rural world of Lavonia, Georgia, where he'd grown up. The times would not cooperate. Emboldened Georgians like Lonnie King would not allow the old racial hierarchy that Vandiver believed in to endure.

He had no one to blame but himself for his predicament in relation to white expectations, given his promise that integration—in the schools, especially—would never happen. That traditional political ploy now looked like an impossible promise, unless he shut down the entire school system of the state of Georgia. That is what he had said he would do if forced to, before ever allowing mixed schools. Parents were on edge, not knowing whether their children would be going to school. The white response to potential integration was likely to be violent. Vandiver felt besieged by both Black student activists and the KKK, failing to distinguish morally between the two. It was a dilemma for an ambitious southern politician who preferred stability over civil rights. The possibility of a foreshortened political career loomed.

Vandiver thought of himself as a good and moderate man. By nature, he was not a demagogue like gubernatorial peers such as Alabama's John Patterson and George Wallace, though he was no more sympathetic to King than they were. When King moved back to Atlanta, Vandiver announced, "Wherever M. L. King, Jr., has been there has followed in his wake a wave of crimes including stabbing, bombings, and inciting of riots . . . He is not welcome to Georgia." Vandiver believed, "Until now, we have had good relations between the races."

King was costing Vandiver sleep—quite literally on that Wednesday morning. The state patrol would ordinarily not put calls through to him until after 7:00 a.m., so Vandiver was startled by the jangle of his bedside phone, his wife, Betty, still asleep next to him. Why was a call being put through at 6:30 a.m.?

John F. Kennedy was on the line. Without early morning apologies or political pleasantries, Kennedy stated his request: "Martin Luther King is in jail. Is there anything you can do to get him out of jail? I think if you could work it out, and we could get him out of jail it would help tremendously in this campaign." Kennedy was eager to solve a problem for their party.

It was at the Democratic National Convention earlier in the summer that Vandiver first met the candidate, and the two had a productive private conversation as Vandiver implored him to let Georgia handle its own affairs. Kennedy promised never to send federal troops into Georgia to enforce school desegregation; for the prize of Georgia's twelve electoral votes, it seemed to Kennedy a bargain worth making.

Suddenly Vandiver was faced with an unthinkable request from his presidential candidate: "It's important to me if Martin Luther King is free."

Vandiver answered, "Well, he was driving a car without a license; he's obviously guilty, it's gonna be a difficult thing to do to try to get a man out."

"Well, just get him out."

Vandiver said, "If I did anything to help get Martin Luther King out of jail, they'd probably throw me out of the state, or run me out on the rail." He added, "Senator, I don't know. It would be political suicide for me to do it overtly. And I don't know whether I can or not. I don't—I couldn't make any promises."

Kennedy replied, "Yeah I know that, but see if there is anything you could do behind the scenes maybe to get him released."

"I'll do what I can undercover, and we'll see what we can do."

"Well, I'm going to be busy today, but here's a number where you can reach Bobby." Jack read out the number and added, "If you are successful, call Bobby and let him know."

The candidate hung up, leaving Vandiver shaken. JFK was someone to whom he wanted to say yes—his party's nominee and a man who, if he won, could be quite helpful to Vandiver in the future. And so the Georgia governor did what he always did at difficult moments: he called his best friend, Bob Russell, brother of his wife, Betty, and nephew of the Georgia senator Richard Russell, American segregation's arch legislative tactician. Besides that of Betty, it was Bob Russell's judgment that Vandiver trusted most in this world—even if he was starting to wonder if Russell had been wise during the campaign in pushing Vandiver to make his "No, not one" promise against Black students ever being allowed into schools with white children.

Still, Bob Russell was a man who thought quickly, and Vandiver needed to make a swift decision that morning. He sat down in the den as Betty hurried to get the kids off to their nearby public school. The governor had short, wavy black hair, a thick bottom lip, and placid blue eyes behind thick glasses. He got his brother-in-law on the phone and related Kennedy's request. Bob Russell's instincts were the same as his own. Russell wondered just how much this maneuver would cost them if it ever became public knowledge; still, political patronage might flow back to Georgia if they somehow pulled it off, completely sub rosa. Vandiver assured Russell that only Betty knew about Kennedy's call.

Getting King freed would solve an uncomfortable problem for the Democrats. It would help not only Kennedy but also the best friend of Bob's uncle, Senator Lyndon Johnson. Senator Russell wanted his friend Johnson in the White House, and having Democrats in control would be good for all of them at such a tenuous time. Though Vandiver and his fellow southern Democratic governors hated Kennedy's liberal civil rights plank, they concluded that their best shot at warding off the implementation of these policies was to be owed favors by D.C. politicians, and they were piling up. These promises could lock Kennedy into the deal he made with Vandiver at the convention to keep federal troops out. Nixon still seemed more aggressive on civil rights enforcement than Kennedy, so they certainly did not want the Republican in the White House.

Still, intervening to secure Martin Luther King's release posed an existential threat to their political futures. Bob Russell, though, just happened to have a clever idea about whom to call to help them get the job done: George Stewart, the secretary of the state senate. Not long ago, police had found Stewart drunk in his parked car and arrested him. This embarrassment could have ended his career, but Vandiver, who was the lieutenant governor at the time, told him, "Our friendship goes way beyond that, George." A couple of days after the arrest, Vandiver walked with Stewart through the senate chamber, sending the message that Vandiver would not abandon him, and that no one else should, either. George Stewart therefore owed Vandiver a favor, and he just so happened to be a close friend of Judge Mitchell's. Given how they all felt about King, asking Mitchell to release the minister was a request that could come only from a friend.

Though Stewart's leadership role in the States' Rights Council of Georgia—a group formed to defend segregation against federal intervention—made him among the least likely people in the Peach State to want to aid Martin Luther King, these were not normal circumstances. They were not asking Stewart to do it for King's sake, after all.

So Vandiver picked up the phone and invited Stewart to the governor's mansion. They were close enough that even if he refused the request, Stewart could at least be trusted to keep his mouth shut.

When Stewart arrived later that morning, Vandiver and Russell, who had also come to the governor's mansion, described their predicament and asked him if he could do anything to persuade Judge Mitchell to release King. They all knew Mitchell was a stubborn man. He would not have exposed DeKalb County to the scorn of the nation without some personal desire to sentence King.

Stewart said, "I don't know. I don't know whether I can or not. I'll try." Vandiver was his friend, and he would do what the governor asked of him. Stewart told them he would head to Decatur and report back.

Vandiver concluded, "Well, that's all we can do. That's the only thing we can do."

■   ■   ■

A. D. King was up early that morning to drive to Decatur to see his brother. When he arrived, he was told that Dr. King was on his way to Reidsville. Furious, A.D. dialed Coretta at 8:30 a.m. to tell her that Martin had been taken away during the night. It was sickening; with Reidsville well over two hundred miles away, how would she be able to go see him? She was both deathly afraid for his safety and worried about how he would withstand the emotional toll of the months ahead.

Coretta was supposed to be a pillar of support for her husband, but who was there to support her? When she called Daddy King with the news, she struggled to contain her emotions. Coretta said, "Dad, what's going to happen to him down there?"

His reaction upset her even more. Daddy King knew Reidsville was home to sadistic guards and—perhaps worse—the state's most menacing, unstable prisoners. It was hard to say which of the two would prove more dangerous to his son.

When King junior was in Montgomery, Daddy King had received calls from well-connected men he trusted who warned him that his son's life was at risk. With his son now at Reidsville, Daddy King ascertained from his contacts that certain authorities wished to stage a fight between his son and a convict that would result in King's death. Regret would be expressed afterward; hands would appear clean enough that no one could be held responsible; it would be just one of those unfortunate things that happened all the time in prisons across the South. Little over a decade before, eight Black men on an Anguilla, Georgia, prison work gang were shot and killed after dubious claims that they had made a run to escape.

By sheer coincidence, a shocking series of articles had appeared that same week in the Atlanta papers, testifying to the perils King now faced. On the previous Friday morning, when King was still being held at the Fulton County Jail, there was a story in the *Constitution* about a predawn stabbing at Reidsville earlier in the month that left two prisoners dead and two others critically injured, perpetrated with weapons made on-site. This was exactly the kind of cover story Daddy King feared. Furthermore, three handwritten pleas for public attention had been smuggled out of Reidsville and reported in the *Journal*. The prisoners documented constant rapes, most often of young inmates by longtime prisoners; brutality from the guards, who goaded those on work details to fight until they could no longer stand and then encouraged the battles to continue once they returned to the prison for the night; beatings of prisoners in solitary confinement; and, on top of these abuses, a simple lack of adequate medical care. The pleas, which were signed, "Inmates of Georgia State Prison," noted, "We are in prison for our crimes, that we know. But do we have to be beat, cussed at, starved of food and made to submit to sadistic . . . guards?"

The Southern Regional Council would later write that Reidsville hired guards who it believed were hostile to Black prisoners. Worse, these guards allowed white prisoners to possess illegal weapons. Long-standing issues would eventually boil over in a 1976 riot, started by a white gang whose members attacked Black inmates with shanks, resulting in five deaths and forty-seven injuries. In subsequent court proceedings, a Georgia ACLU official stated, "The conditions at Reidsville, which concern overcrowding and the way inmates are treated, go back 40 years."

One hardly had to be a well-known agitator to receive such treatment. James Baldwin wrote, "It was on the outskirts of Atlanta that I first felt how the Southern landscape . . . seems designed for violence, seems, almost, to demand it. What passions cannot be unleashed on a dark road in a Southern night!"

Hollowell phoned the DeKalb County authorities at 8:00 a.m., asking for the sheriff so that he could explain that he had a writ of habeas corpus. He thought that King should get bail for this misdemeanor and said that he wanted to "get King out this morning."

There was a pause, and then the man on the phone replied, "Well, he ain't here."

"What do you mean, 'he ain't here'?"

"Well, they took him away this morning sometime." The man was clear: "Martin Luther King is no longer here in DeKalb County." Hollowell, knowing what this could mean, pressed him until he was told that King had been taken to Reidsville: "That's where he is and you can't get him."

Hollowell, however, was able to get Reidsville's warden, Balkcom, on the phone to reassure himself that King was still alive. He told the DeKalb County officials how difficult this made his job as an attorney, transferring a client across the state without informing him. On camera later, he said that King was transferred with "astonishing swiftness and unnecessary swiftness."

One of Hollowell's former clients, Nathaniel Johnson, was convicted of raping a white woman and put to death in Reidsville despite Johnson's maintaining that it was a consensual affair. After he was sent to death row at Reidsville, Hollowell and Vernon Jordan struggled to save him. They were standing in the office of Governor Vandiver's counsel to plead for a delay when they learned that Reidsville had already sent Johnson to the electric chair. Their helplessness as a client was being killed was what Reidsville meant to them.

When Hollowell learned of King's transfer, he dispatched Jordan to begin researching new angles for the defense. Jordan tore into the task. King was in solitary now. Who knew how long they had?

Word of King's predicament spread with amazing speed. Telegrams poured in to Mayor Hartsfield's office from people in nearly every state, including one from Eleanor Roosevelt asking Hartsfield to correct the injustice Georgia was inflicting on King. Most of the messages coming from out of state were critical of King's sentence, while a good amount of mail from white Georgians seemed all for it. Hartsfield complained to reporters, "They all think this thing happened in Atlanta." There was nothing he could think of to do but to call national news outlets and declare, "We wish the world to know that the City of Atlanta had no part in the trial and sentencing of Dr. Martin Luther King for a minor traffic offense." He wanted it made clear that "the responsibility for this belongs to DeKalb County and the State of Georgia."

Organizations from all over the nation quickly weighed in. The chairman of the Jewish Labor Committee, Jacob Siegel, proclaimed, "Khrushchev told the U.N. . . . that America was a land of discrimination and bigotry. The arrest and imprisonment of Dr. King will be played up in the Soviet and stooge press in order to buttress Khrushchev's contentions." The Congress of Racial Equality appealed to President Eisenhower and Attorney General William Rogers for help, asking, "Does this not constitute a violation of the civil rights laws of the United States?"

But in Georgia, the reaction was mixed, at best. The governor's office seemed pleased with the sentence for King, with Vandiver's executive secretary saying, "I think the maximum sentence for Martin Luther King might do him good, might make a law-abiding citizen out of him and teach him to respect the law of Georgia." The *Constitution* suggested leniency toward King was the wisest course. It urged the state to pardon him, which of course Vandiver was not likely to do. The paper asserted that applying the strictest possible legal interpretation was not worth "the wreckage of this community's reputation for racial restraint and forbearance." It advised Georgia against "placing [King] in the martyr's pillory."

In the midst of the growing unrest, Wyatt Tee Walker sent Nigeria's government a cablegram regretting that King could no longer attend the swearing-in ceremony for the newly independent government's officials "because he is presently serving a four-months prison sentence due to his leadership role in the freedom struggle in America."

■ ■ ■

Wofford's morning at home began with another alarmed call from Coretta, and the news she relayed of her husband's late-night transfer shocked him. He was pleased, however, that she had correctly guessed he was behind Chester Bowles's call to her the night before. Coretta said it was good to hear from Bowles, who had offered hope for her husband. Wofford was puzzled that she did not mention having talked with Adlai Stevenson, and when he later called Bowles, he said, "I tried my best to get Adlai to talk to her, but Adlai said he had never been introduced to her, and so it wouldn't be proper." To Wofford, this sort of aloofness explained why Stevenson had lost two presidential elections.

Wofford immediately called his friend in Atlanta Morris Abram. Unexpectedly calm, Abram told him that King would likely be safer in the state system than in DeKalb County. Furthermore, the lawyer thought well of the superintendent there, and getting King out of Mitchell's clutches was no bad thing. Over the decades, the wide gap in perceptions of Reidsville between whites like Abram and those closest to the King family came to be a puzzle. King's staff was convinced that their leader was in danger, and Daddy King made no secret, then or decades later when writing his autobiography, that Reidsville was a death trap for Black men.

Wofford was still distressed, wishing Kennedy had spoken with Coretta the night before. He realized that the CRS might have a momentary advantage, a small window of access to the candidate. After being constantly blocked by Kennedy's inner circle, Wofford remembered that this very morning Sargent Shriver was near Kennedy in Chicago. Perhaps he could reach him to make good use of this moment.

When they finally connected by phone around 9:00 a.m., Wofford was thrilled to hear Shriver's voice from Chicago. Wofford spit out, "Sarge, I have been thinking about the situation involving Martin Luther King Jr., who is in jail in Georgia. I think it would be a marvelous idea if we could get the candidate to call Mrs. King and express his sympathy. He doesn't have to do anything more than that; he doesn't have to make any kind of political commitment."

Wofford conceded, "Look, nobody wants to hear from the Civil Rights Section right now." Believing Shriver would support them, Wofford dared to repeat the phrase that Louis Martin had responded to so well the previous night: "The trouble with your beautiful, passionate Kennedys is that they never show their passion. They don't understand symbolic action. Last night, Louis and I suddenly knew what Kennedy should do, but we couldn't get through to him and you weren't home, so Chester Bowles did it." Wofford suggested, "If Jack would just call Mrs. King down in Atlanta, and tell her he's very sorry about what has befallen her husband, that gesture will be incredibly important to Negro voters." He then added, "All he's got to do is say he's thinking about her and he hopes everything will be all right. All he's got to do is show a little heart. He can even say he doesn't have all the facts in the case."

Shriver answered, "It's not too late. Jack doesn't leave O'Hare for another forty minutes, I'm going to get to him. Give me her number, and get me out of jail if I'm arrested for speeding."

Wofford started to give him Hartsfield's and Abram's numbers, thinking he would want to clear it with them first and get more background, but his boss was ready to—as people who worked with him said—"Shriverize." "Shriverize" was a verb, meaning to go big, bold, and fast. He cut Wofford off. "No, no. Where is she? Give me *her* number."

Wofford was surprised that Shriver was not going to at least run the plan by Bobby. Their crazy idea might happen after all. All he could do now was wait and watch the clock. If the speeding Shriver did not make it to the airport before Kennedy got on that plane, chances were it would never happen.

■ ■ ■

With the election two weeks away, Shriver was spending the night once more in his apartment overlooking Chicago's Lincoln Park and Lake Shore

Drive. The Kennedy campaign needed Illinois for its Electoral College math. Shriver might have been running for governor there if he were not such a dutiful son-in-law and employee. Joe Kennedy had made clear that he needed Shriver's help in order to see his son elected president. Shriver would have never lived in Chicago if not for the ambassador, either.

Like his brother-in-law, Shriver had demonstrated his bravery in the South Pacific during World War II. During the Battle of Guadalcanal in 1942, Lieutenant Shriver commanded his ship's starboard guns through a hellish night of relentless Japanese shelling, slipping on the blood of friends and praying that he would live to see a new day. His ship survived the night and so did Shriver, though he took shrapnel to the shoulder, for which he earned a Purple Heart. Having found a new sense of purpose in a life that had been spared, Shriver tried journalism in New York City, but when he met Eunice Kennedy at a party, his life took a new direction. It would be another five years before he would finally marry her, but even before that her father took him under his capacious wings. Joe Kennedy saw ability in Shriver and, despite his lack of business experience, offered him a job. He was to turn around an investment Kennedy had just made, the gargantuan Merchandise Mart building on the Chicago River. Shriver not only succeeded in filling the building's showrooms and offices with businesses, but one morning at Mass, Eunice said to him, "Sargent Shriver, I think I'd like to marry you."

Grounded in his Catholic faith, with a fire for social justice, he became civically involved, both with the Catholic Interracial Council and then by heading the Chicago School Board. At a Catholic conference, he told attendees that even if they succeeded in ending legal discrimination, they must also "treat the disease of racism itself." Shriver pressed the church to speak out against discrimination, helped create scholarships for Black students to attend Catholic schools, and introduced King before a speech in Chicago. The great irony of Shriver's effectiveness was that both Jack and Bobby had misgivings about their brother-in-law because of his liberal idealism, calling him "the house Communist" and joking about his earnest Boy Scout manner. In a family of Catholics, he seemed to be the only one to rival their mother, Rose, in religious devotion, and that was not a compliment. Shriver was, however, more than a meek choirboy; he was tough and determined and demanded much of all who worked for him. He was from a Maryland Catholic family that had fought on both sides of the Civil War generations before the Kennedys began their climb, and he maintained a sure sense of himself. He was, his friends and admirers believed, nothing less than a secular priest in politics, and that would define both his successes and his failures in public life.

The bond between Wofford and Shriver was forged when Wofford was delivering a speech in Chicago a year before the start of the campaign. A man Wofford did not recognize, but who he would soon learn was Shriver, rose and asked, "You said you're supporting Gandhi's strategy in applying it to the civil rights movement. What would be your advice for the school system of Chicago that has a terrible problem of discrimination and race?" Shriver came up afterward and gave him his card, saying, "I don't think you gave me an adequate answer for what Gandhi could do."

Wofford confessed, "No, I didn't." Shriver asked him to write him with a response. Back at Notre Dame, Wofford—who was unaware of Shriver's ties to the Kennedys—still had not done so when a week later a letter and then a call came from the intrepid Chicagoan saying, "I'm coming up for the football game, could you and your wife come?" The two spent the whole game talking about addressing racial inequalities in Chicago's schools, and Wofford was impressed by Shriver's thoughtfulness. Their plans to work together on segregation in Chicago, however, were soon put on hold—along with everything else in Shriver's life—when his father-in-law commanded him to go work for Jack. When Bobby Kennedy directed Wofford to begin working with Shriver, the campaign manager was unaware that Wofford not only knew Shriver but was more impressed by him than by anyone else in the Kennedy family.

Now, racing toward O'Hare, Shriver made his way through rush-hour traffic with good luck playing a part. On Mannheim and Higgins

Roads, minutes from the airport, he saw the bright orange letters of the O'Hare Inn sign. The recently opened air-conditioned hotel, with TVs and ice machines, was the embodiment of jet-age luxury, with pools and a par-three golf course spread over the grounds of the long, two-story hotel.

Since the beginning of October, when Kennedy's staff had last fine-tuned the campaign schedule, the candidate had rarely had more than four hours of sleep a night, committed as he was to the marathon. Each day seemed numbingly, relentlessly, just like all the others: a hurried solo breakfast of eggs, toast, and coffee; then rushed conversation with the campaign staff crowding into an anonymous hotel room while Kennedy shaved and personally packed his bag; then a public breakfast with local officials, donors, and businesspeople, followed by a sprint to the local airport to Kennedy's real home, the *Caroline*.

Then, by bus or motorcade, the staff managed somehow to escort Kennedy to up to nine events a day, testing the candidate's endurance and his voice. By Election Day, Kennedy's advance team had planned and executed rallies in 237 cities, compared with Nixon's total of 168. To preserve Kennedy's voice, his staff learned early to write and receive handwritten notes during hops on his noisy plane, especially because rallies were being scheduled until one in the morning. Occasionally, Kennedy could relax for an hour in another nondescript motel room, take off his back brace, and sink into a scalding bath with a sigh of relief, the only indication his staff ever had of his chronic pain. Oftentimes, if he ate lunch at all, he consumed a chicken sandwich with two glasses of milk at the head of the plane. For a man who didn't much like being touched, he learned to endure hours of handshakes, until, on a stop in Pennsylvania coal country, his calloused hands began to bleed, but he was back at it the next day.

Kennedy's staff, though exhausted, were quietly confident by late October 1960. They would concentrate on only nine states, spending two days in each, and visit suburban towns ringing larger cities. Illinois was at the top of the list. Unless he carried Texas and Illinois, Kennedy would not become president. The campaign could rely on LBJ to carry his home state, but Illinois was seen as more of a challenge. Mayor Richard Daley of Chicago promised all would go well on Election Day, but there was a reason this whirlwind through the Chicago area was being conducted under Shriver's guidance. Daley's political resourcefulness might not be enough to counter Nixon's rural downstate strengths, so Shriver's business connections and local popularity made him a crucial endgame asset.

The day before King's transfer to Reidsville, Kennedy had made brief stops in Des Plaines, Libertyville, Barrington, Carpentersville, Dundee, Elgin, St. Charles, Geneva, Batavia, North Aurora, Aurora, Plainfield, Joliet, and Elmhurst. Gallup's daily poll gave Kennedy a lead of 49 percent to 45 percent, with 6 percent of voters still undecided. Now Kennedy was bound for Michigan. Advance men were waiting for him in Detroit, with rallies planned for Mount Clemens, Warren, Roseville, Hamtramck, and the Detroit Coliseum, after which Kennedy would end the day in New York, past midnight, in another motel suite near LaGuardia Airport. Thirteen days to go.

Kennedy complained he wasn't feeling well, with a cold or flu coming on, not that this would affect the day's grueling schedule in the slightest. JFK had survived a childhood punctuated by so many illnesses that Bobby joked that if a mosquito had bitten him, the bug would have died. He later said his brother spent at least half his days on earth in "intense physical pain." His litany of ailments—Addison's and Crohn's diseases, a disintegrating back (exacerbated by his dragging men to safety through shark-infested waters during World War II)—was a reality his tanned, confident, oft-invoked "vigor" tried to obscure. He received last rites twice, most recently after life-threatening surgery aimed at easing his back pain in 1954. There was no doubt about his physical courage; the question was if he had the moral and political kind.

Shriver arrived at Kennedy's suite to join a crowd around the candidate. He felt uneasy at the looks he was receiving, particularly from Ken O'Donnell, the scheduler, a lean and wiry man whom Jackie Kennedy called "the Wolfhound." Pierre Salinger described the taciturn

O'Donnell as a man who loved using one word when others would use five, "and that word was very often a flat 'no.'" O'Donnell knew there was no need for Shriver to be with them at this stage, so why was he here—what might he be up to?

Shriver hung back and kept quiet, hoping the advisers would leave. He knew that if he brought up the possibility of a call to Coretta with these advisers around, things would descend into a debate over pros and cons, which Shriver would lose.

There came an announcement from someone: "The plane leaves at about ten o'clock; we have to pack." Sorensen went off to polish the next speech; Salinger went to brief the press; that left only the Wolfhound, O'Donnell, in the room. Shriver kept silent as O'Donnell looked at him suspiciously. Reluctantly, O'Donnell left the room to go to the bathroom. Shriver had his brother-in-law alone, but likely not for long.

After getting into his suit, Kennedy folded his remaining clothes and placed them in his suitcase. Shriver said, "Jack, I have an idea that might help you in the campaign: Mrs. Martin Luther King is sitting down there in Atlanta, and she is terribly worried about what is going to happen to her husband." Shriver told him about the injustice facing Dr. King and said, "I know you can't issue a public statement, but Mrs. King is very upset and very pregnant, what about telephoning her?" He went on, "Jack, you just need to convey to Mrs. King that you believe what happened to her husband was wrong and that you will do what you can to see the situation rectified and that in general you stand behind him."

JFK had not been paying close attention to Shriver's plea at the start, but something about it caught his attention. Understanding that his brother-in-law, though far from a sentimental man, could be personally kind, Shriver said, "Negroes don't expect everything will change tomorrow, no matter who's elected. But they do want to know whether you care. If you telephone Mrs. King, they will know you understand and will help. You will reach their hearts and give support to a pregnant woman who is afraid her husband will be killed."

There was a long pause. Zipping his suitcase, Kennedy turned to him and said, "That's a good idea; can you get her on the phone?" Shriver whipped the scribbled number out of his jacket and thrust it forward. Kennedy said, "Dial it for me, will you? I've got to pack up my papers," as he placed them in his briefcase. With precious seconds ticking by, Shriver took a seat on the bed and dialed the number.

Coretta was getting dressed in Atlanta to go with her father-in-law to meet Morris Abram when her phone rang. Daddy King had a practical streak, and he had decided that King needed a white lawyer to get anywhere in the state of Georgia, in spite of Hollowell's apparent talent.

When Coretta picked up the phone, she heard Shriver say, "May I speak to Mrs. Martin Luther King, Jr.?" Shriver said, "Mrs. King, this is Sargent Shriver, and I am here with Senator Kennedy. He would like to speak with you; is that okay?"

"Fine."

"Just a minute, Mrs. King, for Senator Kennedy."

Shriver handed over the receiver to Kennedy. Kennedy said, "I want to express to you my concern about your husband. I know this must be very hard for you. I understand you are expecting a baby, and I just wanted you to know that I was thinking about you and Dr. King." This was a deft touch; like Coretta's, his wife Jackie's due date was fast approaching. "If there is anything I can do to help, please feel free to call me."

Coretta said, "I certainly appreciate your concern. I would appreciate anything you could do to help."

JFK listened to her brief reply and then said goodbye. The entire call lasted less than a minute and a half, but Shriver was impressed, as he often was, with Jack's genuine warmth.

"Thanks, Jack," said Shriver, relieved that no staff member had barged in during the brief call. "I think that will make a big difference to a lot of people." Shriver mostly thought it was the right thing to do—it was far from an act of history-changing magnitude—but he was glad they had done it. What Shriver did not know was that Kennedy had already called Vandiver at 6:30 that morning about King and that he had been on the case for some hours by then. Just as Shriver spoke, O'Donnell swept back in, looking quizzically at Kennedy and Shriver standing by the bed, Kennedy putting down the phone. Shriver got out as quickly and unobtrusively as he could before an argument could occur.

Minutes later, the candidate left to board his short flight to Detroit.

The staff only began to realize what had transpired under their noses during those last moments near O'Hare, when, on the flight, Kennedy mentioned casually to Salinger what Shriver had asked him to do, a small call of concern, nothing major. Salinger looked at him, sensing possible implications. Walking down the narrow aisle of the *Caroline*, Salinger told the staff member carrying the heavy case containing the mobile radiophone to get Bobby on the line, now.

■ ■ ■

In Decatur, a hundred people waited in the courtroom for that day's hearing. Suddenly sheriff's deputies burst in, loudly announcing that all of them had to get out. Two anonymous callers said they were "going to blow up the courthouse." Officials emptied the large courtroom where the previous day's theatrics had occurred. Judge Mitchell decided the hearing would go on, but with increased security measures and without a public audience. Along with some reporters, Hollowell and the defense attorneys trooped to a smaller nearby courtroom and were searched before entering. Judge Mitchell said at the start, "We all like our Master, but don't many of us want to hasten our visit."

Lonnie King had not been present the day before, catching up on his job, family, and schoolwork, but he came out to Decatur that day. DeKalb County made him uneasy. When Lonnie's wife, Alice, and their baby were alone at home one night during the summer, a carload of white men with license plates from DeKalb—off-duty police, they would learn—pulled up in front of their house and shined their flashlights inside. A neighbor eventually approached the car to ask what they were doing, and an armed man replied, "We're waiting on a fellow to come home. We're going to lock him up." The neighbor went to call the Fulton police, but the men drove off. Another night, Alice heard banging at her door around 4:00 a.m. Though his family was unharmed, these experiences reminded Lonnie that he might not survive his participation in the civil rights movement, because "this was an idea that was so powerful . . . you're a dangerous person." His friend Dr. King had been seen as so threatening that DeKalb County sent him off to state prison. Lonnie would not abandon his friend now, and he was there to see if Hollowell could persuade Judge Mitchell to undo that decision. Hollowell was also able to get Dr. Mays, King's brother, A.D., and Wyatt Tee Walker into the proceedings.

Hollowell was frustrated, having prepared a writ of habeas corpus to stop King's transfer to state prison. These documents had to be presented in the county where the prisoner was held, but now Hollowell had a client half a day's drive away. Hollowell adopted a more personal, raw tone before the court that day. He sought to put Mitchell on the defensive, saying in effect that as a result of his resentment toward King, Mitchell was not grappling with the mistake he made in September, which now invalidated the sentence he was seeking to impose. He kept digging in, stating, "I don't think the Solicitor could bring in one case, one, our searching hasn't found one, which shows that there has ever in the history of the State of Georgia, from the time of its inception, been an individual who was sentenced to serve four months on the public works for failing to have a driver's license. Particularly, particularly, when the man was new in town." Trying to appeal to Mitchell's conscience, he said, "Here is an opportunity Your Honor, for you to correct this situation."

Solicitor Jack Smith followed, arguing that even if Mitchell got the maximum punishment wrong, what Hollowell was asking for was premature: "At the moment no right of the defendant has been violated. No right of the defendant would be violated until one day after or one minute after six months has elapsed." Hollowell had earlier criticized his comparison of Dr. King to a kissing bandit, so Smith also clarified that all he had meant to say was that a thief possessing a "nice, courteous and apologetic attitude" was still a criminal.

Hollowell snapped back, "I can't think of a more strained and tortuous hypothetical."

"Of course I am not considering any hypothetical matters anyway," Mitchell assured him. "The hearing here is strictly from a point of law."

Good, because Hollowell reminded the court that King was not a thief, but a man of the cloth. He made one more try: all for a minor traffic violation, "a man is at the State Prison serving time. I would submit to you that this is too harsh, this is too hard, Your Honor. That this is not in the best of conscience, even though it might have been done with all good intent."

Mitchell said, "I am not going to rule on this immediately. I will have to go into the office and do some study on this, and it will be approximately 3 o'clock this afternoon before I sign the order."

Of course, King's legal team had no idea that George Stewart, an emissary from the anxious governor, was waiting to talk with Judge Mitchell. The hearing ended by noon, with another one set for 9:00 the next morning on Hollowell's bill of exceptions, with the aim of getting King out on bond while an appeal took place.

Hollowell left the courtroom and told reporters and the assembled television cameras that he had planned to present a writ of habeas corpus that morning when he discovered King's 4:00 a.m. transfer. Wyatt Tee Walker went out to talk to reporters, too, concluding, "This is a dark day in our State of Georgia, the southland and America. I am fearful of the international implications involved in such an unwise notion by the court of DeKalb County." He asked every church to pray for a softening of the hearts of those who were allowing this miscarriage of justice to continue.

■ ■ ■

Waiting to find out from Shriver if Kennedy had indeed called Coretta, an impatient Wofford learned the news from a different source. Picking up his phone, he heard Coretta's own voice over the line. The lawyer was moved, hearing how appreciative she was of the call from JFK.

Wofford immediately called Abram, who nearly shouted into the line, "It's happened, man; it's happened."

"What's happened?"

Abram reported that Daddy King had just come to his office, and the old man was nearly in tears at the thought of this sudden new hope. Abram was in awe that Daddy King was so moved: "Kennedy's done it, he's touched the heartstrings. Daddy King says if Kennedy has the courage to wipe the tears from Coretta's eyes, he will vote for him whatever his religion." Daddy King had told him, "I'll vote for him, even though I don't want a Catholic. But I'll take a Catholic or the Devil himself if he'll wipe the tears from my daughter-in-law's eyes."

This was a remarkable development. Excited, Wofford asked if Abram could persuade King senior to say this publicly, and perhaps include an endorsement from his son, too. Abram calmed Wofford down, saying King junior was not likely to budge from his commitment to nonpartisanship no matter what Kennedy had done that morning, though they might be able to secure an endorsement from the more impulsively emotional Daddy King.

Wofford responded, half jokingly, "That's great, a Martin Luther King is a Martin Luther King: the public will never know the difference." Abram said he would ask Daddy King to issue a statement. Both were so thrilled that they were momentarily distracted from the reality that King junior was still very much in danger—that a call, no matter how well-intentioned, was just a call.

The next call to reach Wofford was from *The New York Times*; the reporter Anthony Lewis was on the line, asking why Kennedy was not doing anything about King's imprisonment. Wofford knew he could not tell Lewis what had just happened, but hoped the reporter would soon learn more. He guided Lewis toward the story he couldn't offer, saying that there was action happening in Atlanta, not Washington, and the reporter should be in contact with Coretta King. A few minutes later, Lewis called back to say their Atlanta correspondent had just talked to Mrs. King, but she could not speak further without Harris Wofford's approval. The onus was now back on Wofford, so he quickly called Coretta to ask if his candidate had told her whether to disclose their conversation.

She said Kennedy mentioned nothing of that sort. Wofford figured it was fair game, then, to get the news out there; one more nudge should do it. While he imagined the campaign would not be releasing any information about the call, he told her that she was certainly free to say anything about it she wished.

As he hung up, he and Louis Martin waited to see the results of what they had set in motion. A big story was about to break, yet they had not talked to Shriver since that morning, nor sought guidance from Bobby or anyone else on the campaign. The CRS had been dismissed as idealistic and impractical, but now its leaders were becoming something else entirely: mavericks.

Louis Martin decided it was time to do something he knew how to do well: utilize his contacts in the Black media. He called the *New York Amsterdam News*. Its story would detail how it had learned from an "unimpeachable source" that "Kennedy made a series of last ditch efforts to save Dr. Martin Luther King, Jr. from going to the chain gang."

Not for the last time, Martin and Wofford had ignored the chain of command. The same article explained that its source revealed that Senator Kennedy had spoken with Vandiver about the King case (an assertion likely based on what Martin had heard earlier in the week), and this just as George Stewart was making his delicate ask to Judge Mitchell in DeKalb County. The story would find its way to the national newspapers before the *Amsterdam News* could break it in its weekly edition three days later, but for now Martin was using the separation of Black and white media to tell the story he wanted to tell without white voters knowing what was going on.

■ ■ ■

Back in Atlanta, John Calhoun was still trying to get Nixon to speak out. The RNC's Val Washington told him, referring to Nixon, "I can't get to him." Another operative told Calhoun, "All of this thing is emotional. In three or four days it's going to die down. Then hit them with whatever you got."

Calhoun called the office of Peter Flanigan, national director of Volunteers for Nixon-Lodge, and told an aide who answered, "Look, we have been trying to get Mr. Nixon to do something or say something . . . just make some kind of statement." Calhoun reminded the staffer, "[Nixon] knows King. Kennedy doesn't know [King]." Staying silent would mean that "they are going to kill us." Calhoun explained that both sides would quickly use whatever they did or did not do for King, either for or against them, so he needed something concrete from Nixon: "I'm going to use it and they are going to do the same thing."

The aide said he would get the message to Nixon.

■ ■ ■

Meanwhile, as the Nixon campaign was traveling across the Midwest, E. Frederic Morrow readied himself for one last effort to get Nixon to act on the King affair. During eight years in Washington, Morrow had largely been ignored, but if he could persuade Nixon to finally move on this one issue, it might be enough to tilt the election. After two months of feeling sidelined, however, he had trouble remaining optimistic.

All that day, Morrow also kept receiving messages from Black Republicans around the country asking for money to help the campaign, and yet he had nothing to give them—even as Shriver was making a seemingly limitless budget available to Louis Martin for his appeal to Black voters. Nixon's campaign had resisted spending money on pamphlets for Black voters or doing a telecast for them. And now, with

King in the news, the Nixon campaign was receiving more telegrams than ever, including one from Clarence Mitchell, the director of the NAACP's Washington Bureau, who wrote, "IT CALLS FOR THE STRONGEST CONDEMNATION ON YOUR PART URGE THAT YOU DO SO TODAY." An NAACP field secretary warned, "AN EXPRESSION FROM YOUR OFFICE IS NECESSARY."

Morrow had done his part in speeches, linking Kennedy to racist Georgia Democrats and declaring, "You must laugh heartily at how Senator Kennedy and Senator Johnson have suddenly become bleeding hearts for the rights and advancement of Negroes." The one asset Morrow still had was Jackie Robinson, who, like him, was taking time off work to campaign nationally on Nixon's behalf. Unfortunately, Robinson's disillusionment was growing, too. An unnamed Nixon adviser told Robinson that Nixon would be avoiding Harlem because it could cost him South Carolina and Georgia. During Eisenhower's presidential campaign, at least Morrow had been seen with the candidate. The midnight meeting at the convention was a distant memory at this point.

Still, with one forceful remark, all these lost opportunities could be redeemed. And yet Morrow kept finding himself being blocked by aides. When he got any response at all, he was told by those close to the candidate that making a statement would be "bad strategy." One person told him, "You're always thinking up things to get us into difficulty, so forget it." Morrow believed that if he could just sit down one-on-one with the candidate, the old Nixon could be persuaded to do the right thing. His message to advisers was, "Send a telegram to the governor, or to the mayor, or to Martin Luther King's family expressing regret . . . asking if there was anything he could do."

On the vice president's campaign train, Morrow settled for talking to Nixon's press secretary, Herb Klein, cornering him to make his case. Morrow was nearly begging; he even handed Klein a statement he had drafted, directed at the mayor of Atlanta and requesting his help in freeing King. While Louis Martin spent hours on the phone with Black editors, the Nixon camp was now shunning Black journalists to the degree that Simeon Booker of *Jet* asked to be moved to the Kennedy campaign so he might be more effective in his reporting on the election.

Klein accepted Morrow's statement and slipped it into his pocket. Morrow feared it would never be used. Klein said he would "think about it." However, Klein did show the note to Nixon, who read it, apparently wrestling with the decision. Finally, Nixon looked up and briskly told Klein that issuing such a statement would "look like he was pandering."

Morrow thought back to Nixon's superb convention acceptance speech, wondering what had happened to that man. He had thought that moment would be a jumping-off point for a leader he believed in, a new kind of Republican campaign championing racial equality. Leaving the campaign train, Morrow headed back to the White House. He would await the outcome of the election in room 224 of the Executive Office Building. He had tried to save his party.

Jackie Robinson kept on barnstorming for the GOP. This Wednesday in Memphis, Robinson told an adoring audience of five thousand, Nixon would indeed appoint a Black cabinet member. He reminded them of the violently racist Democratic governors Kennedy was so closely allied with; Robinson's instinct that Kennedy would strike bargains with them would turn out to be accurate. He warned them, "Kennedy goes the way the wind blows." The old ballplayer was used to losing streaks; the only way through was to keep swinging.

■   ■   ■

Pacing in his suite at campaign headquarters, Bobby interrogated his assistant John Seigenthaler, "Did you know about that call?" Bobby had been campaigning in Pittsburgh the day before, so maybe he'd missed something. Seigenthaler wondered if Wofford and Shriver had kept their scheme from Louis Martin, because he thought Martin would have informed Bobby about it.

"No, I didn't."

"Well, get every Southern chairman of the Democratic Party. Find out how this is going down."

Seigenthaler called Georgia's Griffin Bell, who responded, "Well, I was a little surprised to read it, but tell Bobby not to worry about it. We're gonna carry Georgia, big. But tell him I could use a little more advance notice on something like this." *So could Bobby*, Seigenthaler thought to himself. Mississippi's chairman was more upset. Though most southern politicos were still feeling all right about their chances, Seigenthaler knew the campaign's director of organization, Lawrence O'Brien, would also be irritated that he had not been part of the decision as to whether a call to Coretta should have been made.

Bobby Kennedy called his brother-in-law, and in Shriver's recollection Bobby "landed on me like a ton of bricks . . . He scorched my ass." Bobby sputtered, "Who in the hell do you think you are, screwing up the whole campaign?" Shriver just listened, knowing how hot Bobby's temper could be. "You've gotten Senator Kennedy exposed on this highly volatile issue and you should never have brought it up without clearing it. You've wrecked the campaign. Who the hell do you think you are?"

Shriver said, "I didn't think I was anybody, except I thought it was a decent idea." He added, "Jack is a decent man, and people will read the call as an indication of the kind of character that he has."

Bobby replied that his brother "was going to get defeated because of this stupid call to Martin Luther King, and for Christ Sake, who had given [you] permission to do this."

After the smoldering phone was slammed down, Bobby instructed Seigenthaler to call the CRS office. Seigenthaler simply said, ominously, "Bob wants to see you bomb throwers right away."

Wofford suggested that Martin go over first, and then he would join him later. Martin understood the logic: Bobby simply liked him better, and he might be able to calm the campaign manager down before Wofford arrived. Martin rushed out of the CRS's office, thinking about how to handle the conversation. As he headed to meet Bobby, the view opened up on Sixteenth Street, all the way down to the White

House. Winning over Bobby would determine whether they could all now seize this unexpected opportunity in the campaign. If he were advising Nixon, he would tell him to act, now, and Martin guessed there were people on the other side just as smart as he was. At this very moment, someone like Jackie Robinson was out there as the critical piece on the chessboard, and Robinson and Nixon could checkmate Kennedy simply by speaking up for King. No matter how angry Bobby was, Martin resolved not to just sit there and take it; he had to make it clear to his boss that Nixon was going to help King. While Martin did not know this to be true, it could well be, and thus they should operate as if it were.

Bobby was furious, but Martin leaped in before he had a chance to unload, informing him of King's transfer to Reidsville over a traffic citation. Then Martin pretended as if the scenario he imagined coming to pass were in fact happening: "You know, Jackie Robinson is trying to get Nixon to call a press conference." He said Nixon was going to blast the Democrats for jailing King. Growing more animated about the (imagined) imminent threat, Martin said that Nixon "would charge that King had been arrested and jailed by the minions of the Georgia Democratic-controlled state and blame racist Democrats for persecuting the black hero." He wanted Bobby to understand that "they're going to blame the jailing of King on Democrats because the judiciary and everybody down there are Democrats and I think you've got to do something about it."

When his speech was over, Bobby surprised him by saying, "What the hell do you mean, four months for a goddamn license?"

"Wait a minute, don't talk about that. He's black, this is what I'm talking about." It was as if the black-and-white Bobby at his most lawyerly were outraged at the improper sentencing procedure and unable to respond to the larger racial injustice at hand. Bobby indeed looked aghast, but Martin could not tell if it was for the right reasons. Martin realized he needed to situate what had happened in a moral framework Bobby would understand.

Before Martin could determine if his line of argument had

succeeded, however, Wofford walked in, hoping that Martin had gotten Bobby to calm down. No such luck. Wofford's arrival sent Kennedy spiraling back into his earlier outrage. Bobby was white with anger, pacing back and forth, but he also seemed frightened. By this point in the campaign, Bobby's already slim frame was gaunt, dark circles had formed under his eyes, and exhaustion was visible in every movement. Bobby glared at the two of them, saying, "Do you know that three Southern governors told us that if Jack supported Jimmy Hoffa, Nikita Khrushchev, or Martin Luther King, they would throw their states to Nixon? Do you know that this election may be razor close, and you have probably lost it for us?" He reminded them, almost in pain, "We said we wouldn't support King," and now it looked as if that were exactly what they were doing.

Before they could reply, Bobby laid down a command—not firing them, exactly, but instructing them that they must do nothing further to generate publicity.

Wofford protested that nothing was going to stop the story in Atlanta (he wrestled with whether to inform him that *The New York Times* was already on the trail, while Martin knew the *New York Post* was on it as well). Bobby concluded his tirade by saying, "You bomb throwers probably lost the election. You've probably lost three states. From now on in, the Civil Rights Section isn't going to do another damn thing in this campaign."

Bobby had left Martin and Wofford with the unequivocal message that their shop was shut down. He gave them no sense of whether he personally would do anything to aid King, but they had better not. With their morale at its lowest point, Martin and Wofford shuffled out. Their window of opportunity to swing the election and help King appeared to have closed. Perhaps their careers in politics were over as well.

■   ■   ■

George Stewart came and went in Georgia politics like a ghost, a shadowy presence wafting through judges' chambers and the state capitol. He had receding dark hair sharply parted to the side and a full, jowly face. After his unexpected conversation with the governor that morning, he pondered what to do next. If he could get King released on solid legal grounds, the Democrats might as well get credit for it. But how to smooth down his friend's grit?

The day before, a more liberal-minded Decatur attorney, James Mackay, went to Judge Mitchell's office, pleading with him, "You can't do this. You can't deny a man bail on a misdemeanor pending appeal." But Mitchell was resolute: "I'm committed to it. I'm going to do it." Stewart needed to soften his friend's resolve to keep King in prison.

Once the two were together, Stewart drew on his own legal degree to tell Mitchell to just follow the law by offering King bail while his case went through appeal. Mitchell said that was not possible: the thirty-day window had expired for King's appeal on the traffic case. Always resourceful, Stewart had an idea: a holiday, Columbus Day, fell during that period, and that day should not count. Add that extra day, and the appeal was still possible in the thirty-day window since King's original legal paperwork was filed. With this legal angle accounted for, Stewart stressed the political necessity of doing this for their party. Vandiver later claimed that Stewart told Mitchell a federal judgeship might just be in the cards if the Kennedys won.

Mitchell knew he would not have his position on the bench if not for his friend Stewart, a political insider, who was asking for this favor. But there were two problems: Governor Vandiver's fingerprints had to be effaced, and Mitchell needed political cover in order to reverse course so abruptly. They decided on a surprising plan: Bobby Kennedy would have to call Mitchell personally. Vandiver would be left out of the affair, his reputation intact. It could hurt the Democrats in Georgia, but if the Kennedys wanted it done because they thought it could help them overall, then the Georgians were more than happy to let them deal with the fallout. Vandiver and Mitchell were not going to take the blame on their behalf, no matter how the election turned out.

■　■　■

Governor Vandiver was pleased when, at last, Stewart called him to report on his promising conversation with Judge Mitchell. The governor called Mitchell as well to reinforce that this request was coming straight from the Kennedys. Vandiver then phoned Bobby, who seemed to be expecting to hear from him. He told Bobby what he needed to do: call the judge. Vandiver pleaded with Bobby that this "would affect my political future if I get involved in it. Please don't involve me in it . . . they'd run me out of Georgia."

Bobby understood. Not only did he have a sense of how southern politics worked from attending law school at the University of Virginia, but he had personally been to the governor's mansion and been introduced to Vandiver's children.

Bobby had told Wofford and Martin that they were to do nothing, but that did not preclude him from taking action, in secret, on his own.

■   ■   ■

There were no special privileges that came with being a famous prisoner. A few guards took it upon themselves to remind King that he was just another Black man, threatening and harassing him with epithets he refused to repeat later. Every meal was cold—greens and black-eyed peas. The breakfast eggs were speckled with pieces of shell. There was at least bread to ease his hunger: a light corn bread for breakfast and again later in the day. It made him miss the Fulton County prison meals.

King began a letter to his wife: "Hello darling." Not knowing if she knew what had befallen him, he wrote, "Today I find myself a long way from you and the children." He understood it was a burden on her for him to be so many miles away: "This whole experience is very difficult for you to adjust to, especially in your condition of pregnancy, but as I said to you yesterday this is the cross that we must bear for the freedom of our people." Asking her to be strong in faith, he told her that her strength would uphold him. "I can assure you that it is extremely difficult for me to think of being away from you and my Yoki and Marty for four months, but I am asking God hourly to give me the power of endurance. I have faith to believe that this excessive suffering that is now coming to our family will in some little way serve to make Atlanta a better city, Georgia a better state, and America a better country." Because he thought himself a man, not a prophet, he added, "Just how I do not yet know, but I have faith to believe it will. If I am correct then our suffering is not in vain."

Explaining he could have visitors two Sundays a month, he told Coretta, "I hope you can find some way to come down. I know it will be a terrible inconvenience in your condition, but I want to see you and the children very badly." He asked her to notify Wyatt Tee Walker to come, too, because there were urgent things he wanted to tell him. As always, he asked for books, along with certain of his sermons, with instructions on where to locate them in his files. He asked for the dense volumes of *The Systematic Theology of Paul Tillich*, works on Jesus and Gandhi, a Bible, a dictionary, and a radio. He concluded with a message to his family: "Please ask them not to worry about me. I will adjust to whatever comes in terms of pain. Hope to see you Sunday."

One reporter asked Warden Balkcom if King could be assigned to ministerial duty but was rebuffed; Reidsville already had a chaplain. The *Amsterdam News* predicted King's four-month sentence would entail hard labor on a public road gang.

Hollowell received a call in the mid-afternoon from Daddy King's friend A. T. Walden, a prominent Black Atlanta lawyer of the previous generation, who was at Abram's office. Also working alongside Abram that afternoon was a young lawyer named Charles Wittenstein, a Brooklyn native who had come to Atlanta eight years earlier to support the cause of civil rights. Wittenstein made the same discovery that George Stewart had: because of a holiday, they were by one day still within the month window to appeal King's traffic sentence. If they submitted a bill of exceptions to appeal within the next few hours, King could be freed on bond while that appeals process went through.

To Hollowell, this was dramatic news. He jumped into his car to get over to Abram's office and go through the statutes with the other lawyers. Once satisfied that this idea was exactly what they should pursue, he grabbed one of Abram's typewriters and, without notes, wrote the first section of the motion they would file. Abram's secretary went to work on cleaning up Hollowell's rapidly written draft, and the attorneys agreed that it was ready to go less than an hour later.

The problem was that the business day was nearly over, and Hollowell would never make it to Decatur in time to file the motion with Mitchell. The month window was closing fast, so Hollowell resolved to call Mitchell on the phone and, however improbably, persuade him to accept the document late that night. Miraculously, the lawyer reached Mitchell and, ignoring the tense hearing earlier that day, implored the judge to let him just slide the papers under his door. Technically, with a little indulgence, they would have been delivered on that day. Then he asked if Mitchell would just insert the correct date in the record when he picked them up in the morning.

The judge hemmed and hawed but eventually said yes. Stewart had already talked to Judge Mitchell by this time. Would Mitchell have otherwise offered King's defense team this favor? And yet Hollowell must have believed there was some chance that the judge could be won over as well. Mitchell told him to appear before him the next day.

Hollowell now had reason for hope. He left Abram's office and began driving toward Decatur.

■ ■ ■

Seigenthaler drove Bobby to the airport for a flight after his meeting with the chastised "bomb throwers." Bobby's anger at them had apparently dissipated, and Seigenthaler could see he was genuinely galled at King's being imprisoned for a traffic citation. Bobby said, "I can't understand why . . . the American Bar Association doesn't say to this

Judge in Georgia . . . it's a basic tenet of American jurisprudence that you have to provide bond. This man is not an outlaw or criminal; he's an American."

Bobby, as usual, knew more than he was letting on, because he had almost certainly discussed the King situation with his brother several times before he dressed down Martin and Wofford—both before and after JFK's call to Governor Vandiver that morning. Ever since Wofford's call to Morris Abram inaugurated the Kennedy campaign's involvement in the King situation, Bobby and his brother had been working quite effectively to fix this thorny political problem through quiet back channels, and then Wofford, Martin, and Shriver had so clumsily transformed it once again into an unpredictable public relations issue through their unsanctioned intervention.

Still, Bobby believed it was a disgrace that no one had had the courage to contradict Judge Mitchell, who was making a mockery of legal procedure. While he had been only an indifferent law student, Bobby was fueled by a strangely Puritan moralism (so different from Jack's own inclinations) and remained fascinated by the law and its application. Talking more to himself than to his aide, he muttered, "I'd like to just express on behalf of one lawyer in this country just what I feel . . . I'm not going to call him; I just think that too many people would think I was trying to do something political about it." Bobby was wrestling with something. Without telling Seigenthaler about his conversation with the governor, he imagined out loud that if he just phoned the judge as a lawyer, simply offering advice about a legal question, maybe the political damage could be minimized. The clear-eyed strategist in him, however, understood the risk that this would entail.

Seigenthaler answered, "There's a great deal of downside exposure. People in the South are going to be mad about you calling up the judge."

"That's right . . . I don't think I'll do it. I'm not going to call him. But I'll tell you this. I resent it."

"Just think about it a minute as a lawyer," Seigenthaler said. "I just tell you, I wouldn't do it . . . I don't know a lawyer who's not involved in a case who would do something like that . . . who would call the judge himself." Bobby recognized that a man's life was at risk in that southern prison, and Seigenthaler could see how torn he remained. Still, it seemed from Seigenthaler's perspective that it was too great a hazard to the campaign.

"I think you're right," Bobby said as he set off with a stack of work to do on the flight. Bobby would be speaking in Philadelphia that evening, including to six hundred people in front of the Kennedy office on Chestnut Street near City Hall. Seigenthaler thought that had settled it.

But Bobby did try calling Judge Mitchell at some point in the day, but he couldn't reach him. Bobby tried another number he got from Governor Vandiver: that of George Stewart. This Georgian picked up.

Stewart told the campaign manager that his friend Mitchell was open to allowing King out on bail, but the three of them needed to talk in the morning—at 8:00 a.m.

■ ■ ■

Nixon's team was being peppered with questions about King's imprisonment. It was not just reporters who were asking; Republican headquarters in D.C. also demanded to know what to say. Nixon would write two years later that he told his press secretary, Herb Klein, "I think Dr. King is getting a bum rap. But despite my strong feelings in this respect, it would be completely improper for me or any other lawyer to call the judge."

Klein got the picture and went out to face the reporters. When the question came, he simply said two words, "No comment." It was as close to silence as he could get.

■ ■ ■

Five hundred people packed into Atlanta's Mount Zion Second Baptist Church for an emergency meeting led by King's friend the Reverend Ralph Abernathy. Daddy King showed his stout stuff, telling them, "If my child can sit at Reidsville and take all that—I can certainly keep my head up and keep praying—for he's sitting there tonight for every Negro in the world." Somewhat more ominously, he also said that he didn't think his son could "make four months." Bridging the generations, Lonnie King spoke alongside Daddy King, saying the sit-in arrests had finally united the Atlanta Black community behind the student movement.

Abernathy, used to being at King's side, said that instead of being in the pulpit, he wished he were "down on the road gang with my good friend." He told the crowd that King was "the Moses of the 20th century, the greatest religious leader of modern time," and announced he was planning a motorcade to drive to Reidsville so they could pray for him outside the prison.

■　■　■

When John F. Kennedy landed at LaGuardia long after midnight, at the end of a grueling day of campaigning in Michigan, he was confronted about his call to Coretta Scott King by a gaggle of reporters. He is said to have muttered to an aide something about a "traitor" in their campaign.

Then he regained his usual equanimity and took a few questions. Regarding the call, he simply said, "She is a friend of mine and I was concerned about the situation." The answer was soothing and amiably distant. Mrs. King and Kennedy had never met, however, and in the remaining years of his life they never would.

Reporters heard differing things. The *Constitution* reported Kennedy as saying, "I had nothing to do with his release." Did Kennedy think that Bobby's (unanswered) call to the judge had already achieved the desired outcome, in which case the statement would have been, in the narrowest sense, true? In any case, the odd phrasing went unnoticed. JFK waved and wished the reporters good night, and after making yet more campaign calls, he settled in for his few hours of rest.

DAY 9: THURSDAY, OCTOBER 27

Some time before two in the morning, Louis Martin was woken by his bedside phone. An energetic voice on the line snapped him to attention: "Well, I talked to that judge down there . . . We're going to spring him."

Martin wasn't dreaming. This was real, verging on the inconceivable. Bobby Kennedy went on, saying he gave this judge a stiff talking-to about freeing King: "I told him to get him out of there or I'll take care of him, and I gave him hell."

Momentarily speechless, Martin had difficulty absorbing this message, especially after the dispiriting conversation they had had just hours earlier. Bobby sounded like a different person, almost giddy with pride at what he had done. Martin replied, "We now make you an honorary brother." Bobby laughed.

Bobby, of course, had exaggerated. Perhaps he hoped that Martin would convey the story of his tough talk to Black voters, or maybe he just wanted Martin to be happy with him.

Despite Bobby's tale about talking to Judge Mitchell, it was in fact Stewart to whom he had spoken. The second and most important call—this time between Bobby and the judge for real—was scheduled for 8:00 a.m. The tone of that conversation would turn out to be much less adversarial than that of the fictitious one described by Bobby, but he was making things happen nonetheless.

■ ■ ■

King's health, after all he had endured over the past eight days, was starting to suffer. He was stricken with a vicious cold and a bone-weary feeling. Eight consecutive nights on dank, hard prison mattresses in three different cells, along with the raw fear of a nighttime trip to Reidsville, had left his body vulnerable, and he wasn't sure how much longer his spirit could hold out, either. The bangs and shouts of prison life woke him early, and he sat in his white uniform, praying and reading the books he had with him: *Victor and Victim: The Christian Doctrine of Redemption* and Dante's *Divine Comedy*. Cockroaches scurried along the walls.

To his surprise, prisoners frequently slipped notes into his cell. He'd received nearly twenty already. They relayed that prison officials had warned inmates not to speak to him. One note informed him that the prisoners were willing to stage a strike to protest his being held at Reidsville. He was moved by the offer but did not know what repercussions such a strike might entail, and he wrote back advising them not to act.

While many just wanted to express concern for him, or to say how much they respected him, others asked him to speak out about conditions at Reidsville. They told him that their letters were intercepted, and that the prison ignored their physical ailments. King tried to respond to each note, finding ways to get encouragement back to whomever he could, and promised that he would speak up once on the outside.

These messages lifted King's mood, but the guards at Reidsville were even crueler than he had expected. King was deeply affected by his time there and resolved that prison reform must become part of his work. Guards refused to call him "Reverend," which was humbling, but far from the worst thing he experienced or witnessed. He saw guards speaking to the prisoners as if they were animals. Their cruelty and callousness drove the inmates deeper into a state of bitterness, though he could not help but see something good in these prisoners as they respectfully nodded to him as he walked past.

After just thirty hours in solitary confinement, King was taken from an individual cell into a dormitory housing other newcomers, from which he would eventually be transferred to his work detail. Warden Balkcom had evidently made a decision quickly, even though he had told press the day before that it might take weeks. In the bunk below King was the young man accused of murder during a prison fight the week before. Whether this was a coincidence or an attempt to intimidate him, King resolved to keep as calm as he could.

■   ■   ■

"Kennedy Phoned to Express Concern, King's Wife Says," read the headline on the first page of *The Atlanta Constitution*, above a reprint of Anthony Lewis's *New York Times* story. Lewis reported that there had been no Kennedy campaign release about the incident, but he confirmed that Mrs. King had indeed received a call. Mayor Hartsfield claimed to have no knowledge of any of it, remarking only that the state government was in a "picklement over this case."

Coretta was quoted as saying,

Sen. Kennedy said he was very much concerned about both of us. He said this must be hard on me. He wanted me to know he was thinking about us and he would do all he could to help. I told him I appreciated it and hoped he would help. It certainly made me feel good that he called me personally and let me know how he felt. I had the feeling that if he was that much concerned, he would do what he could to see that Mr. King is let out of jail.

The *Constitution* asked if her husband would endorse Kennedy, but she replied he had been clear he would not endorse either candidate, and she knew of no change in that stance. When asked if Nixon had reached out to her, Coretta replied, "He's been very quiet." While she'd gotten calls from Chester Bowles, Mahalia Jackson, and Harry Belafonte, there had been nothing from Nixon. The *Times* noted that Republican headquarters was asked for "some kind of statement on the King case from Vice President Nixon or from Republican campaign officials here. An aide said the Vice President would have no comment."

Pressure for King's release was mounting in the pages of the country's major publications. One *Washington Post* editorial was titled "Chain-Gang Justice," decrying what was being done to King, which made Georgia look to the world as racist as South Africa. *The Christian Science Monitor* said that Mitchell had unintentionally "given an invaluable boost to the Southern Negro campaign for equal treatment. He did so by meting out patently unequal treatment to the Reverend Martin Luther King." They noted how Brooklyn's representative Emanuel Celler urged Eisenhower's Justice Department to file an amicus brief in Georgia on King's behalf. The NAACP asked Kennedy and Nixon "for the strongest condemnation on your part. We urge you to do so today."

The American Jewish Congress wired Vandiver urging him to pardon King, though he told reporters he had no such power as governor. The AFL-CIO's president, George Meany, sent a similar plea. Vandiver, for one, was experiencing another sort of fallout from the crisis, because four lieutenant colonels—an honorary title Georgia governors bestow to whomever they wish—resigned in protest over his alignment with Kennedy, who now gave the impression of supporting King. Vandiver could only wonder what would happen if word of his outreach to a sitting judge on King's behalf ever got out.

The Kennedy campaign's Georgia co-chair Griffin Bell assured the press once again that Kennedy was keeping his pledge to stay out of the King matter. He'd heard nothing about a call to Mrs. King. At every level of the Georgia Democratic Party, everyone was holding on.

■ ■ ■

At 8:00 a.m., the phone rang, as promised, in George Stewart's office. Judge Mitchell, not wanting to be overheard in the courthouse, took the call from Bobby there. Bobby was ringing from a pay phone on Long Island, where he was to give a speech to rally Democrats later that day. He sounded congenial, reiterating what he told Stewart the day before: "We would lose the state of Massachusetts" if King was left in prison, so it would be helpful if they let him out. The lawyer in Bobby brought up the constitutional requirements for bail in Georgia, but Mitchell was not interested in all that; he already had legal grounds for releasing King and had known what he would do since the previous day.

Mitchell said, "Bob, it's nice to talk to you. I don't have any objection about doing that." This was a purely political call. Bobby extended a future invitation to D.C. Now there was a story for white Georgia voters when news broke of King's release.

There was one problem, however: Judge Mitchell did not tell Bobby that he was about to announce to the press—likely as a way of justifying his sudden reversal—that the Kennedy campaign had called him on King's behalf.

Maybe this young man didn't understand they'd been playing pretty hard politics in Georgia for a while.

■ ■ ■

"He has to do this," Jackie Robinson pleaded. "He has to call Martin right now, today. I have the number of the jail."

Nixon's public relations and speechwriting aide William Safire had admired Robinson since he was a kid, watching his feats as a four-sport athlete at UCLA. Safire was sold on what his childhood hero, and crucial campaign surrogate, was telling him: the King matter could no longer wait. He brought him to see the campaign manager, Finch, in the midwestern hotel where the staff was staying. Nixon had stumped in Ohio on Wednesday and in Michigan on Thursday. Finch had also been getting pleas to help King from others around the country who saw him as one of the few ways to reach the candidate before he brought Robinson in to see Nixon.

Jackie Robinson had risked so much for Nixon: his newspaper column, his job, his standing in the civil rights movement. Already aggrieved that Nixon had not backed Lodge's pledge to appoint the first Black cabinet member—and had then compounded the insult by refusing to campaign in Harlem—he was now angry that Martin Luther King was languishing in jail while his candidate stayed silent. Robinson's wife, Rachel, had never thought highly of Nixon, and he feared she was being proved right. Knowing that other advisers were, in Robinson's words, "counseling him not to rock the racial boat," Robinson understood he was likely to fail. But what these other aides said ultimately did not matter; Nixon was his own adviser. It was his choice.

Only ten minutes later, Robinson walked out of the meeting with Nixon wearing a look of pained frustration; Safire thought he saw tears in his eyes. Robinson bitterly told Safire, "He thinks calling Martin would be 'grandstanding.'" Hitting the wall against Nixon's resolute caution, Robinson shook his head, muttering, to Safire's horror, "Nixon doesn't deserve to win."

Nixon would later claim it was all very simple: Attorney General Rogers could not get approval from the White House to make a presidential statement that the administration was looking into King's case. Nixon said he had asked the attorney general to see if King's federal civil rights had been violated, and to get the White House involved. But Rogers, for his part, maintained that he had advised Nixon to speak out. Another clue comes from a note in the Nixon Library's King file. It is not certain who on the campaign it is from but is signed by "R" and reads: "This is too hot for us to handle."

When Nixon wrote his post-campaign memoir, *Six Crises*, he placed the blame on the bureaucracy of the Eisenhower White House, likely hoping to win over Black voters in the future. In an interview with

Simeon Booker, Nixon continually referred to the White House, leading Booker to believe that he really meant Eisenhower. Perhaps Nixon had expected the president to make a statement about King, but when had the general stepped into the spotlight to speak out about civil rights? Finch would maintain that Nixon tried calling the White House, but "some hang-up occurred someplace." The "hang-up" was likely in the Nixon camp, perhaps in the candidate's own heart.

Robinson was tempted to quit the campaign and to speak out against Nixon. But just as he faced this crisis of doubt, he got a call from Branch Rickey, his former Brooklyn Dodgers general manager, who had supported Robinson throughout his trying baseball years. When the Republican Rickey heard that the Democrats were asking his star to abandon the GOP, he tracked Robinson down to persuade him to remain on the side of the Republicans. Rickey spoke to Rachel Robinson as well, learning that Bobby Kennedy had called her that morning to see if Robinson would make the switch. Despite her own wariness toward Nixon, she told her husband to keep going.

■　■　■

That same day, John Calhoun finally heard back from the Nixon campaign. A Republican staffer relayed a simple, chilling message from Nixon: "He said he would lose some black votes, but he'd gain white votes, so he was going to sit it out, and he wouldn't say anything."

Nixon would later say he never got any warning about how the King situation could affect his standing with Black voters, but Calhoun remembered being told, "The Vice President got your message . . . yes, he understands."

Nonetheless, Calhoun would keep asking for funds to make the case for Nixon to Black voters. Eventually, he secured three hundred dollars to print campaign literature in Atlanta, and he felt confident that he could reach the Black Republicans he knew best. But he would not have the kind of story that Louis Martin could tell his voters—not at all.

■ ■ ■

For the third morning in a row, Judge Mitchell convened his court. The crowd that had packed the courtroom two days earlier had evaporated. Maybe it was the bomb threat the day before; maybe expectations were low for this procedural hearing on Hollowell's motion to have King released on bond. A.D. was the only member of the King family able to attend, though he was joined by Abernathy. Yet soon after opening the morning session, Judge Mitchell delivered shocking news to the few who were present. With an earnest air, the judge announced that he had been more carefully reading the laws of the State of Georgia since Hollowell had filed his bill of exceptions the day before.

It was now his considered conclusion that for a misdemeanor King should be free while the verdict was being appealed.

The courtroom stirred with amazement. Mitchell went on: the question was no longer whether King should be held, but simply what amount the bond should be. Hollowell jumped in to propose, based on the testimonies to King's good character in this courtroom, that it not be more than a thousand dollars. Jack Smith countered with two thousand dollars, and Mitchell went with the larger figure without much deliberation. It was a parting shot directed at King, but Hollowell knew he had achieved a significant victory: they could bring King home for the time being. Hollowell had the bond money ready within an hour.

In the meantime, Mitchell assembled the press and proceeded to read a statement. Clearly, he wanted the nation, and his hometown, to know why he had so unexpectedly reversed his decision. "Ladies and gentlemen of the press, as you no doubt know, pressure has been put upon me in this case urging the release of the defendant and people of other views urging that I deny his release. The pressure favoring his release has even come from those close to the presidential candidate."

Having dropped that bombshell, Mitchell offered up the paradox that nothing—nothing—could have affected his lofty, unprejudiced legal judgment while giving the impression that something in fact had: "However, I would like to say that this pressure has not influenced me in any of my decisions in this matter . . . I have followed the law." He claimed to have done that in revoking King's probation, and now in concurring with Hollowell's reasoning in his bill of exceptions. "Therefore, I have no alternative except to grant bail during this appeal in this portion of the case pending before me now." After Mitchell had boxed himself into a legal corner, it turned out it was Hollowell who offered him an escape route.

Reporters immediately pressed Mitchell for more details on this contact with someone close to a presidential candidate, but he said he could not give more details while continuing to do so. He said he had not heard from the Nixon side; it was a Kennedy brother, not the candidate, and when asked then whether it was Bobby or Teddy, he said, "Well, I will say that I have never heard Ted's name mentioned."

Abernathy then said to reporters his soon-to-be-famous phrase: "Time for all of us to take off our Nixon buttons." As Hollowell raced to get the release papers in order, students and Black community leaders were already planning King's welcome-home rally. They wanted to make it as big as possible, and to hold it that night, if they could just get him home.

Hollowell now rushed to get Judge Mitchell's paperwork to the state corrections director, granting the state prison permission to release King. The DeKalb County sheriff confirmed that King did not have to be returned to his custody, but a corrections official said that in order to let King go, they needed documentation of King's bond payment to be presented at Reidsville. A journalist from CBS Atlanta's Channel 5, Ed Blair, asked Hollowell how he was going to get to Reidsville to retrieve his client. Hollowell responded that he would drive, of course. But Blair had a proposition: he would charter a plane for Hollowell if his cameras could record the first interview with a liberated Dr. King. That was an easy call for Hollowell: every minute mattered when a client was in Reidsville.

Blair was not the only person planning to fly to Reidsville to witness King's release. NBC's Channel 2 and a film company both got their own planes, and Reverend Abernathy, Wyatt Tee Walker, and

A.D. chartered one as well, in place of their earlier idea of a prayer caravan driving to Reidsville. The SCLC team wanted to bring King home to Atlanta as quickly as possible, unable to relax as long as he was in prison. So now, four small private planes raced toward the same destination.

■   ■   ■

At Kennedy headquarters, the press staffer Roger Tubby was telling John Seigenthaler, "Crazy judge down there says Bobby called him on the phone. And I'm getting calls; what should I say?"

Seigenthaler said, "Just flat deny it. I put him on a plane last night." He repeated the story of how Bobby had said he would not call the judge. "Yes, he was thinking about it. That probably got around and somebody picked that up maybe . . . Forget it, he didn't do it."

Martin was at the CRS office that morning when he heard from Tubby that the campaign was planning a press conference. Martin said, "What do they want to hold a press conference for?"

The press aide told him, "Well, they're trying to deny that report on the wire that Bobby called Mitchell."

"Well, he did," Martin said, thinking of the call he had received from Bobby in the middle of the night.

"No, they're going to have a press conference and deny it."

Martin ran out of his office and back down K Street as he had done the previous day. He needed to stop the press team from going on the record with something that not only was untrue but undercut Martin's goal of connecting with Black voters.

Arriving at 1001 Connecticut Avenue, Martin found Tubby and, catching his breath, said, "Listen, don't put out any denial yet, because the facts are, he's made the call." He pleaded, "For God's sake, don't call any press conference. Cancel this thing. Bobby did call him."

Tubby said no, he'd already denied it because Bobby had not done this. He had just spoken with Bobby's assistant John Seigenthaler, who was sure Bobby had not called. Martin said, "Listen, Bobby called me and said he called him. We'll be embarrassed."

The two partners must have missed each other in the CRS office because Wofford was not operating with an understanding of what Martin already knew. Wofford's phone rang and he heard the distinctive, halting delivery of the NBC journalist David Brinkley: "There's a crazy story coming over the wire that now a brother of the Senator has intervened, and called the Judge directly to get King released." He asked if "a brother of Kennedy had called the Judge in Georgia to get King off. Could this be true? And which brother?"

Wofford did not think that Ted, organizing the campaign in California, could have done such a thing. And after the flogging he'd received from Bobby the day before, he could not fathom that he might have done something. He concluded, "It just can't be true, David."

"Well, we're going on the air in about ten minutes. Should I disregard this story?"

"I think you can. It just can't be true." Brinkley said he would take his word for it and not mention it on the evening news.

■ ■ ■

Hollowell attempted to shake Warden Balkcom's hand, but seeing a cameraman next to him, the prison official said, "Hell, no, don't do that. You want me to lose my job?" Balkcom would not have survived so many different gubernatorial administrations without political savvy. He used to offer his Tattnall County home cooking to legislators he intended to win over. This charm, however, did not completely mask the toughness needed to rule over a citadel like Reidsville.

Once Hollowell smoothed over the awkward interaction, King was brought in and the paperwork was approved. Balkcom admitted, "I'm sure glad to see you fellas. We've about burned out three telephone transformers with all the calls we've been getting."

King changed back into his usual somber black pastor's suit. He almost left without his license, which was being held in the prison office, but remembered it. He put it back into his wallet; a driver's license had started the whole saga, after all. He walked through the prison gates, carrying his belongings in two brown paper bags. As of 3:46 p.m., he was a free man. Hollowell was moved by a chant rising from the segregated Black section of the prison, beginning with a prisoner whose cell faced the front: "Long live the King! Long live the King!"

Hundreds of hours of film documenting the rest of King's life survive, offering a sometimes haunting vision of just how he spoke, how others related to his physical presence. Almost nothing from those nine days in 1960 survives on film, and the brief minute of black-and-white footage, showing King emerging from Reidsville accompanied by Hollowell, Walker, and Abernathy, is a rare surviving relic. It is Hollowell who mostly fills the frame—tall, impressive, and clearly pleased at the turn of events. King's demeanor as he nears the camera is more reserved; as always, he is the eye at the center of the storm that formed about him. King, Hollowell, Walker, and Abernathy exchange smiles as they pass through the gated opening in the chain-link prison fence.

The minister steps forward to speak with Blair, and the other reporters crowd in. "Dr. King, you've heard the reports that Senator John Kennedy's family brought influence to bear to win your release from prison; would you comment on that?"

King says slowly and methodically, looking straight into the camera,

Well, I owe a great debt of gratitude to Senator Kennedy and his family for this. I don't know the details of it, but naturally I'm very happy to know of Senator Kennedy's concern and all that he did to make this possible. I might say that there are no political implications here, I'm sure the Senator did it because of his real concern and his humanitarian bent, and I will always say that I am deeply indebted to him for it.

To another reporter outside the prison, King would say, "I understand from very reliable sources that Senator Kennedy served as a great force in making the release possible . . . I think a great deal of Senator Kennedy." He did not know the full story, but King said, "The Kennedy group did make definite contacts and did a great deal to make my release possible." King said he had not heard from Nixon and knew of no efforts to help him from anyone on the Republican side.

While it has generally been thought that King never seriously considered an endorsement, he said, perhaps moved by his freedom, "I think I'll wait until a day or two before the election, then state who my personal preference happens to be." He nodded, bringing the short interview to a close, and the group moved on toward the airfield, eager to reach Atlanta and the long-delayed homecoming celebration.

■ ■ ■

Louis Martin managed to get the press conference called off, but Seigenthaler soon got Bobby on the phone: "Bob, you'd never believe the story that the AP has got out." Bobby was still in New York; his brother was hitting four boroughs from Eastern Parkway Arena to Sunnyside Gardens, and doing two Seventh Avenue rallies.

Bobby replied, "What's that?"

"That crazy judge says—he's going to be a real idiot—he says that you called him on the telephone complaining about this." Seigenthaler added, "He thinks you're a young whippersnapper sticking your nose into the judicial process of the State of Georgia. I told the press section of the National Committee that you didn't do any such thing as that and for them to issue a denial."

"What did you say?"

"I told Tubby to put out a denial."

There was a long pause. "John, you'd better get Tubby to put out another statement. I did call him." Seigenthaler was in shock. "I just got so pissed off and I did it." Getting warmed up, Bobby explained more: "I kept thinking that it was so outrageous. When I got off the airplane, I'd made up my mind that somebody had to talk to that judge."

"I can't believe it," Seigenthaler said.

"Yes, it just burned me all the way up here on the plane . . . The more I thought about the injustice of it, the more I thought what a son of a bitch that judge was. I made it clear to him that it was not a political call; that I am a lawyer, one who believes in the right of all defendants to make bond." He claimed to have no knowledge that the judge was going to divulge their conversation, but figured the judge saw some political gain in doing so.

All that off his chest, Bobby told the still stunned aide to gather the CRS team together and draft a statement, as innocuous as possible. So it was Seigenthaler who confirmed the story for Wofford, and Wofford was in as deep a state of disbelief as anyone else. The mavericks had just been outdone.

Seigenthaler told Wofford, exaggerating slightly, "He just woke up this morning and he was so damn mad that that cracker judge should put a decent American in jail for driving with an out-of-state driver's license, clearly on the grounds of color, and screwing up his brother's campaign to boot, that he just got the judge on the phone and said to him, 'Are you an American? Do you know what it means to be an American? You get King out of jail!'"

That manner would not have astonished anyone who knew of Bobby's reputation for abrasiveness. But there was more to Bobby than just this pugnacity; there was vulnerability and a concern for injustice as well. As O'Donnell noted, "Jack was the tough one. Not Bobby. Jack would cut you off at the knees. Bobby would say, 'Why are we doing that to this guy?'" Bobby was the family's most sensitive boy, sticking closest to his mother, struggling to make friends at new schools, physically clumsy in a family that prized athleticism. He was seen, not without cause, as needlessly obnoxious—a young man concealing his insecurities by way of a stern and unyielding manner. Jack's cheerfulness seemed immune to whatever the world threw at him, while Bobby's emotions remained apparent to all around him. Jack could charm, and Jack could forgive, but it was hard to find these qualities in his younger brother, who saw things in starkly moralistic terms and was prepared to do whatever was necessary. Yet as Arthur Schlesinger put it, "John Kennedy was a realist brilliantly disguised as a romantic, Robert a romantic stubbornly disguised as a realist."

Wofford, Martin, and Seigenthaler set about the business of damage control. The first order of business was to craft a statement denying that their boss had asked for a favor from a sitting judge, which would land them in deeper trouble.

Finally, they came up with a statement that read, "Robert F. Kennedy said tonight he telephoned Judge Mitchell to inquire as to whether the Rev. Martin Luther King had a constitutional right to bail. Mr. Kennedy said he did this after many inquiries were made at his office concerning this matter." They concluded, "That is the extent of the matter and any suggestion that interference was involved is untrue."

■ ■ ■

Sitting in a single-engine plane in a field near Reidsville with Hollowell, Abernathy, A.D., and Walker, King was at last ready to lift off. Just as the pilot started the engine, however, they heard a grinding sound, then paralyzing silence. They were momentarily frightened that someone had sabotaged the plane—a final attempt to kill King. But then the engine coughed and roared to life. The little plane jumped forward, sped along the short runway, and rose over the roads King had traveled in the back of a police car on Wednesday night. Reidsville shrank behind them into the countryside, swallowed by the dusk.

They landed at the Peachtree-DeKalb Airport in Chamblee, north of Atlanta, just past 5:50 p.m., with a few dozen family members and friends awaiting them, along with expectant photographers and reporters. The men emerged, waving, and King's family surrounded him, happy and grateful to be reunited. Yoki and Marty shyly stood alongside Coretta as she embraced and kissed her husband. Eight students, with signs reading, "Welcome home, Dr. King," surrounded the exuberant family. Marty jumped into his father's arms and King lifted him up—Marty's wish to see his father return on a little plane come true. Yoki, in a plaid school dress and with a bow in her hair, looked up at her dad. Reporters asked King if he was now voting for Kennedy, but King quietly said that as the leader of a nonpartisan organization he would not publicly disclose his choice. He thanked the prison warden for his treatment.

The family had chartered a long black limousine to take them home, and they climbed inside to head down the highway. As they approached the Fulton County line, they suddenly saw three hundred students assembled to greet King. They stood just feet from the border, but they would not step into the county that had jailed him without just cause. King told the driver to stop, and the little caravan following close behind slowed. The students were dressed in their finest sit-in suits and dresses. They had borrowed four buses from the colleges, and when those were full, some forty more cars drove groups of students to this impromptu rally to thank King for all he had endured. He had stood with them, and they wanted to communicate that they had not forgotten him during those nine days. As King stepped out and waved, the minister was lifted onto someone's shoulders so all could get a clear view of him. The students roared, "Welcome home, Dr. King."

At that moment, the young white *Journal* reporter Pat Watters witnessed something that changed his life. King looked younger and more vulnerable than Watters had imagined: "not softness, not naïveté, but somehow hurtable." Crowded along the edge of the road in the light of a full moon, the students seemed unbreakably unified. They linked arms and began to sing a song Watters had never heard before: "We Shall Overcome." The human chain swayed as the students sang in the fall moonlight.

Watters stepped out of his car and into the soft evening wind. The students stood exposed on a roadside so near DeKalb County, targets for anyone hiding in wait, and Watters was overwhelmed by how unafraid they appeared. He tried to catch the words of this unfamiliar song. He heard the line "We shall overcome some day." There was such hope, such assurance, in these words. As he stood on the shoulder of a Georgia highway, all that Watters had accepted growing up in the Jim Crow South was thrown into sharp relief.

Watters felt the need to stand with these students, who he was suddenly sure would prevail, and found himself weeping. That night marked the beginning of a transformation, and three years later he would leave journalism to devote himself to the work of the Southern Regional Council for racial equality. He would recall in his memoirs how "We Shall Overcome" could be heard at each significant moment of the civil rights movement over the next eight years.

King just had time to change clothes before heading to the church he had known his whole life. Hollowell quietly returned to his office. After a few hours, he made his way to Ebenezer and spoke briefly, though the gratitude he was shown was muted. As was so often the case in Hollowell's life, the attention was not on him; he had done his job. His tireless legal work to get King out would be forgotten in the rush to praise the Kennedys. For the attorney Howard Moore, who was mentored by Hollowell and knew how unflappable he was, the following days were one of the few times he ever saw Hollowell appear wounded. He was no self-promoter, but Hollowell would have liked to receive more thanks for what he had done.

Hollowell was, however, gratified to receive a late-night phone call from Thurgood Marshall, who drawled, "Well, Don, I see that everybody except the lawyers is responsible for getting King out of jail."

As for Lonnie, he had never seen a church this packed so late at night; the service would still be going strong at one in the morning. The students had worked for hours getting word out all over campus and along Sweet Auburn, assembling the crowd they believed King deserved.

The welcome-home service was titled a "thanksgiving prayer service." Eight hundred people responded with fervor when Daddy King said of Kennedy, "It took courage to call my daughter at a time like

this. He has the moral courage to stand up for what he knows is right."
Daddy King came out strong, holding nothing back. "He can be my
president, Catholic or whatever he is. I've got all my votes, and I've got
a suitcase, and I'm going to take them up there and dump them in his
lap."

The charged response made the sanctuary feel like a political rally.
To the young Reverend Moss, it was an electrifying moment, with
people around him going wild for Daddy King's endorsement. Daddy
King admitted to having been against Kennedy because "he is a Catholic and I couldn't go that way." Yet that one call to his daughter-in-law,
showing sympathy for what Black people faced, changed his view. When
King junior came to the lectern, the contrast between the elder King's
emotionality and his son's cooler, more cerebral style had never been
starker. He said only one thing regarding the election: "I never intend
to be a religious bigot. I never intend to reject a man running for president of the United States just because he is a Catholic." It was a statement that could certainly be interpreted as favoring Kennedy, though
it was only a statement against discrimination. But King, still suffering
from a viral fever that he had developed in prison, did not feel like
talking about politics for long; instead, he focused on the meaning of
suffering to their emerging cause.

King recounted the handcuffing around 3:30 a.m. and the long,
harrowing ride to Reidsville, and declared that he would endure it
again for the cause of equality. He said Black people must "master the
art of creative suffering . . . We must be prepared to suffer, sacrifice and
even die." It was a night of celebration, but also a night of reckoning.
"We must continue to have the courage to challenge the system of
segregation—an evil which no righteous person can accept whether it
is in schools, libraries, public parks, Christian churches, at lunch counters." Segregation is "an evil which must be removed from our society."

Then, for a moment, he let a smile pass over his face when he said
he must be "a dangerous man" if they had to chain and handcuff him.
King circled back to where it had all begun: the sit-in. He reminded
the crowd that after all the attention that had been paid to him over

the last few days, when he had gone down to Rich's more than a week earlier, he was a follower, not the leader. He praised the students for "creative and victorious moments last week. They created the atmosphere for all that is taking place in Atlanta today."

Lonnie was jubilant. Everyone was joyful that night, but he had been released from the guilt that had dogged him for the past nine days. Now here they all were together, singing, safe.

TIME TO DETONATE

Since he had started working for the Kennedy campaign, Louis Martin's rallying cry was "Let's get all the horses on the track!" All the CRS's horses were lined up—endorsements, ads in the Black media, support from local vote getters and organizations—but where was the opposition's final play for Black voters? Martin spent all day Friday fretting, and the next morning, too, wondering when his opponents would do what seemed obvious: utilize the years of work Nixon had put into building relationships with Black leaders like King.

While the Kennedys might feel relieved that the white-focused media had moved on from the passing attention given to the Georgia calls, Martin was still unsure whether they had taken full advantage of the incident to increase Black voter turnout. To the extent that they had covered the Kennedy's involvement, the press mostly focused on the mystery of what had happened between Bobby and the judge, and Martin did not want the impact of Jack Kennedy's earlier sympathetic call to Coretta to be lost on voters.

Martin was now confident they were going to win a higher percentage of the Black vote than Nixon, but wondered if the total number of those votes would be enough to win them the election; after all, both candidates were still seen as largely uninspiring by many in the Black community. In his mind, there was a dangerous difference between adequate and full turnout. Martin sensed that "it was going to be a tight contest so every darn vote counted. I don't care where we found it. We had to get it. We were anxious to make sure that we got the blacks to the polls because we knew that if they got there, they'd vote the right way." He compared the election to setting up a horse race: "If they don't run that day, that's it."

Following King's release, Martin and Wofford resumed their habitual brainstorming, even though they remained hamstrung by Bobby. Doing nothing seemed ridiculous with the election so close. They had to fully leverage their momentary political advantage and do so quickly, and invisibly. They considered how effective the National Conference on Constitutional Rights before Kennedy's Harlem speech had been just weeks earlier. Could they do something in that vein, but even more ambitious?

Martin had an idea: a hard-hitting pamphlet laying out the entire King crisis for Black readers, highlighting what Kennedy had said, and sandblasting Nixon for what he had not. The two of them believed Nixon had been a moral coward and that he should pay for it. As they kept batting ideas back and forth, they realized that Martin already had the distribution channels to get an explosive little pamphlet into the hands of Black voters.

It would be the consummate Louis Martin play—one his whole life had been building toward. A story from Martin's time campaigning for FDR in 1944 suggested he had what was needed to pull off a plan this risky. When Martin went to New York City to rally the growing urban Black vote, he saw a story in a Black newspaper that quoted the new vice presidential nominee Harry Truman as saying store owners should be able to serve whomever they pleased—or not. Knowing the story could blow up and cost Roosevelt critical Black votes, Martin drafted a made-up interview to present Truman as being against segregation. When he could not reach Truman's traveling camp to get approval, and with a few hours left before weekly Black newspapers' deadlines, the rookie DNC staffer had to decide whether to publish a statement in the

candidate's words without his permission—and this was a candidate
Martin had never met. Martin chose to send out the Truman denial,
consequences be damned. His informed gamble was that white folks
would never notice anything in the Black press. To white journalists,
it "might just as well have been written in Chinese for all they knew."

Could he do the same thing again, but on a bigger scale? Martin's
fearlessness came from having confronted racism in its most terrify-
ing forms. He could still see the Spanish-moss-covered tree branch on
which two Black men were lynched in his childhood hometown of
Savannah, Georgia; the branch had been cut down and displayed on
the steps of a church two blocks from his house. After that, anytime he
saw a group of white people talking together as a child, he wondered
in panic if they were gathered for a lynching. As he would say, "I was
twelve years old, and I was scared to death." He did not believe people understood the terror he'd lived under. His physician father might
have been an Afro-Cuban immigrant who believed he would be ex-
empted from racism by his financial status, but Martin's Black American mother knew better. When a new patient once came through the
office's front door, Dr. Martin's receptionist found him napping and
implored, "He's a white man." The doctor rose so quickly that even the
child Louis understood these words implied a racial power structure
that his father was forced to acknowledge.

Kennedy's call to Coretta was something almost beyond his wildest
imaginings—an act so human, so timely, and so compassionate, but
seemingly above the political fray . . . perfect (at least by the standards
of the era). Martin would not have to say outright that Nixon was a
racist; he felt confident that evoking outrage toward Nixon's lack of
compassion and empathy would resonate in the Black community because it resonated with him.

Wofford asked Martin how they could possibly pull the plan off,
given Bobby's directive. In answer, Martin dialed up Shriver in Illinois,
confident their boss would support them. Laying out the idea, Martin
explained the media habits of the people he wanted to reach, saying,
"They don't read the *New York Times* or the *Atlanta Constitution*."

Regarding the pamphlet, Shriver asked, "What do you want to put in it?"

Martin explained that they would simply highlight indignant statements that Black leaders like Daddy King had already made publicly.

"So you don't need to editorialize or make any new statement?" It was clear where Shriver's sharp mind was going.

In the end, Shriver made the decision to go ahead, against his brother-in-law's orders. "Okay. We've got to use these wonderful quotations of Mrs. King, Martin Luther King Jr., and his father. That's not propaganda, it's just reporting what has been said. Bobby couldn't object to that." Of course, Bobby might well object, but Shriver wasn't going to give him the chance: "Then you don't need to ask Bobby's permission. He might say no, but what you're planning is not within his ban. Let's do it. If it works, he'll like it. If we don't do it, and we don't get enough Negro votes, he and Jack wouldn't like that, and we would all be kicking ourselves for a long time."

With their boss taking responsibility, Wofford was thrilled. The quotations indicting Nixon were powerful. Martin told Shriver they would figure out a way to produce and distribute the campaign literature, while Shriver quickly found a way to finance the covert project without asking the campaign for funds, never explaining where the money came from. The marketing genius in Shriver realized, as he later put it, "we had a terrific propaganda coup." He knew his in-laws were political sharks, but he also saw them as fundamentally decent people capable of an empathetic gesture like calling Coretta, even if the political equation hadn't been fully figured out.

Martin and Wofford called Coretta, writing down what she remembered from her conversation with their candidate and how it made her feel. It took them six hours to get the piece ready to be printed. They attempted to further hide their tracks by saying that the pamphlet was published by a group of respected Black ministers even if they were not involved editorially. Marjorie Lawson contributed as well: she had been focused on winning the support of Black churches, which could serve as distribution sites. The team called their fictive organization the Freedom Crusade Committee, listing as its head their friend from Philadelphia the Reverend William Gray. They decided not to mention Bobby's call to the judge, given its questionable legality.

The pamphlet was titled *The Case of Martin Luther King*. When opened, it featured Coretta's quotations above Daddy King's, and then at the bottom of the page was King junior's statement that Kennedy "served as a great force in making my release possible." Their use of King's words made it sound like an endorsement: "I hold Senator Kennedy in very high esteem. I am convinced he will seek to exercise the power of his office to fully implement the civil rights plank of the party's platform." Alongside a statement by Abernathy was a quotation from the Reverend Gardner Taylor: "All Americans can rejoice that Dr. Martin Luther King and all the sit-in students are now out of jail." He hailed Kennedy for "moral leadership and direct personal concern" and indicted Nixon for being "so insensitive to a case which has world-wide implications."

When they added in bold a headline reading, "'No Comment' Nixon Versus a Candidate with a Heart, Senator Kennedy," they were clearly going beyond the editorial boundaries established by Shriver. They decided to run the headline anyway.

Then came one last decision—paper size and color. They went with a simple tri-fold format, on robin's-egg blue. When they were done, Shriver ordered fifty thousand pamphlets printed in Washington and, by midweek, five hundred thousand to be run off in Chicago. This number would grow quickly. Shriver and Wofford would later put it at around two million; Martin believed it was three million. No one remembers who gave it the name by which it has gone down in history and campaign lore, but the light blue paper it was printed on served as inspiration: it would be called the Blue Bomb.

The next morning, Wofford, Martin, and Shriver received a message they had been awaiting for weeks: Kennedy would indeed sign the recommendations coming out of their New York Conference on

Constitutional Rights. Kennedy instructed Wofford to go to Washington National Airport to meet him as he passed through town, saying for "Harris to bring out the damn paper." Campaign higher-ups had never been enthusiastic about this report, and would have preferred to let it be forgotten in the closing days of the campaign, but they were prevailed upon to have Kennedy sign it.

Taking his son Daniel with him, Wofford drove along the Potomac River in Alexandria, Virginia, on a beautiful fall day. When he arrived at the airport, he was happy to see Kennedy had his daughter, Caroline, with him. He handed the document to Kennedy, who read over the detailed proposals for civil rights action and then looked up at Wofford. He asked, "Don't you think we've shot our bolt in all this? Do we have to do it?" With an expression that was half hopeful, half sly, Kennedy said, "Tell me honestly whether you think I need to sign and release this today, in order to get elected Tuesday. Or do you mainly want me to do it to go on record?"

Wofford knew what Kennedy was really asking. The unexpected events of the last two weeks had given the CRS more than they could ever have hoped for, and they might have the Black votes they needed without another set of future promises. This policy document was not going to sway many voters, not now. Wofford paused, knowing he was expected to return with a signature. But unable to refuse Kennedy, he said, "No, you don't need to sign it."

Kennedy declared, "Then we can wait, and release it when I'm elected. You can consider me on record," he said, smiling, "with you." This was Kennedy charm up close. "Let's issue it right after the election." Having settled the matter, Kennedy said, "Let's go out to the plane."

Wofford strolled with Kennedy out onto the sunlit tarmac where his private plane was waiting. On parting, Kennedy made a surprising remark, one of the few he ever made about the events surrounding King's arrest and release. He casually said, "Did you see what Martin's father said? He was going to vote against me because I was a Catholic, but since I called his daughter-in-law, he will vote for me. That was a hell of a bigoted statement, wasn't it? Imagine Martin Luther King having a bigot for a father!" The candidate smiled, waved farewell, and added, "Well, we all have fathers, don't we?"

Wofford was left holding the unsigned papers.

■ ■ ■

Nixon knew it was time to roll out the old general, still the most potent weapon the GOP possessed. President Eisenhower's wife, Mamie, had taken Nixon aside, saying Ike's health meant his appearances would have to be limited, but she asked that he not tell the president that this was the reason he was being sidelined. Eisenhower was puzzled and angry about his small role in the campaign. Nonetheless, the White House announced on Monday, October 31, that President Eisenhower would campaign in New York on Wednesday and in Ohio and Pennsylvania on Friday.

Kennedy had been relieved that the beloved president had stayed out of the fray, but it was inevitable that with Eisenhower flashing his trademark smile, the polls would start to shift in Nixon's favor. On Monday, Kennedy was in Philadelphia, speaking to Temple University students leaning out of dorm room windows to see him. It was a drizzly, cloudy day, with Kennedy campaigning in a raincoat and hat, an item he disliked and rarely wore. It has been assumed that Kennedy never spoke about the King affair in any public way (with few references even in private), but he mentioned it that afternoon when campaigning in a Black neighborhood of Philadelphia. At a campaign stop at the Raymond Rosen Apartments, Robert Nix, a local Black political leader, introduced Kennedy and recounted that he had been crucial in getting Dr. King out of prison.

During Kennedy's turn to speak, he ruefully told his audience, "And with Martin Luther King in jail, Mr. Nixon's headquarters issued a statement 'No comment.' If that's what you want, you can have him." Kennedy closed with his well-honed theme of moving forward and left to applause.

That same day, Halloween, Bobby called political allies in Georgia to say he had not meant to interfere in the legal affairs of the state, that he had only tried to gather information about King's case. Not quite a disavowal, it could serve as a veiled apology if one was needed to soothe bruised white feelings. Yet Bobby did not want to undercut his brother the way Nixon had undermined Lodge's cabinet pledge. Bobby said later in the week that he and JFK got involved because "we were all anxious to make sure that justice prevailed, whether we lose the state of Georgia or win the state of Georgia." He added, "Sen. Kennedy felt very strong in connection with this matter." When pressed on the *Today* show, he said, "I think Sen. Kennedy did—and the rest of us did—what we thought was right under the circumstances. And we would do it again."

■ ■ ■

With King's doctor ordering bed rest due to the virus he began feeling at Reidsville, the SCLC canceled a press conference. He still planned to travel to Nigeria, however. While King recovered, his father delivered a sermon; the one he gave at the 10:45 a.m. service on Sunday morning, October 30, was titled "Self Denial."

King still faced hearings in January regarding his appeal, which, if he lost, could result in a four-month sentence. Despite Mitchell's reversal, the judge was not someone King could ever trust, especially because Mitchell's calculus might change after the election. But King would have to face that possibility another day.

For all his idealism, King was always clear-eyed about politics, but he refused to be cynical enough to imagine that it was all about expediency. He said later of John F. Kennedy, "There are those moments in history—that doesn't always happen, doesn't happen often—that what is morally right is politically expedient, politically sound. And I would like to feel—I really feel this—that he made the call because he was concerned. He had come to know me as a person then. He had come to know more about this problem. Harris and others had really been talking with him about it."

In the end, King respected Kennedy's actions because the candidate "didn't know it was politically sound. It was a risk because he was already grappling with the problem of losing the South on the religious issue." In shifting and at times bitter racial winds, there was no way for Kennedy to accurately judge the utility, or the foolhardiness, of his call to Coretta. For Kennedy, a man of infinite political calculation, it was a roll of the dice.

Above all, King felt genuinely hurt by Nixon, who had let him down in such a dangerous way; Nixon had behaved, when it mattered most, as if "he had never heard of me." King said he saw now with greater clarity the gulf between the two ambitious candidates. True, he had been drifting toward Kennedy—based on his decision to hire people like Wofford—but he saw now why these staffers had become so invested in their candidate.

The reputation Nixon had earned as an opportunist, which King had been willing to ignore, seemed to have been sadly confirmed. Of his misgivings regarding Nixon, King later said, "So this is why I really considered him a moral coward and one who was unwilling to take a courageous step and take a risk. And I am convinced that he lost the election because of that. Many Negroes were still on the fence, still undecided, and they were leaning toward Nixon." Daddy King, swayed by Nixon's betrayal, encouraged his son to go ahead and endorse Kennedy, as Morris Abram was also prodding him to do.

Once King was healthy enough, he traveled to Harry Belafonte's Fifty-Seventh Street office in New York, along with the advisers Stanley Levison and Clarence Jones. Belafonte had told King on the phone before the meeting, "You have to stay above this fray." While Belafonte had himself endorsed Kennedy, even appearing in an ad at Louis Martin's urging, the singer saw King's unique moral platform as something to protect. Levison suggested that King walk a delicate line between thankfulness and a fateful move into partisanship. Belafonte later heard that the Kennedys were not happy with King's lack of an endorsement but that they had not been terribly surprised by the decision, either. Bobby even later expressed rueful admiration for King's political savvy in not giving them all they wanted.

In a news conference on Tuesday, November 1, King confirmed that he would not endorse either candidate: "The role that is mine in the emerging social order of the South and America demands that I remain non-partisan. Thus, devoid of partisan political attachments, I am free to be critical of both parties when necessary." But, he added, "Sen. Kennedy exhibited moral courage of a high order."

King said he knew of Black leaders now switching to Kennedy. This included his friend Abernathy, who said that Kennedy's call to Coretta "was the kind act I was waiting for. It was not just Dr. King on trial—it was America on trial." In another essentially Democratic rally in Ebenezer—without King present—Abernathy preached, "Since Mr. Nixon has been silent through all this, I am going to return his silence when I go into the voting booth." In Mississippi, one NAACP leader who switched from Nixon because of Kennedy's intervention was Medgar Evers.

Dora McDonald, King's secretary, wrote back to one of his admirers that although King would not make an endorsement, "Dr. King intends to support Senator Kennedy—feeling that he has the best program for the hour."

King never got to cast that vote. A Montgomery probate judge ruled he could not get an absentee ballot because he had not paid a poll tax in the last two years. King sent a canceled check showing that he had tried to pay. With a pained grin, he noted that "the state of Alabama and I have had frequent disputes." Nor could he vote in Georgia, having not registered there during the tumultuous move back home.

■ ■ ■

Shriver called Martin and Wofford on Tuesday, telling them he wanted to print 250,000 more Blue Bomb pamphlets. That figure was soon upped to half a million. With that, they could flood Chicago churches over the weekend, as well as Wisconsin—in particular, Milwaukee, Racine, Kenosha, and Madison. This last-minute distribution, coming only days before the election, would be an emotional appeal with what they hoped would be maximum impact. Shriver later said that the Blue Bomb "was like a shot of lightning in the middle of the night. You can't imagine what effect that had . . . like a prairie fire."

The *Amsterdam News*'s estimation was that Kennedy's call would help him earn around 70 percent of Black New Yorkers' votes. Local Black GOP leaders were lamenting the lack of funding they had been given for organizing, always a bad sign for a campaign's prospects. One Black GOP leader admitted, "They have almost written us off." Yet some Black Republicans remained loyal, still frantically calling Morrow for help. In Atlanta, a group of Republican ministers issued another endorsement of Nixon, but Daddy King was not among them.

Most public polls still showed Kennedy narrowly ahead. Kennedy had been confident about the outcome after the debates, but now he was starting to wonder if he would lose. Yes, he had the crowds, the excitement, even some residual momentum from the debates, but Nixon had the general. Eisenhower packed Cleveland's Public Square on Friday with thirty-five thousand people, and the old campaigner's dander was clearly up—revealing, if not genuine enthusiasm for his VP, an active disdain for Kennedy. A week earlier, Kennedy had felt secure, but as Eisenhower headed out on the trail, he said of the president, "With every word he utters, I can feel the votes leaving me. It's like standing on a mound of sand with the tide running out. If the election were held tomorrow, I'd win easily. But six days from now, it's up for grabs."

When Lyndon Johnson heard about the call to Coretta while on his campaign plane, he said, "Goddammit, I didn't know those Kennedys were so smart." Johnson's home state could decide the election, and he thought this call could sway enough Black Texans to break their Republican ties. Regardless, Johnson told Kennedy, "We'll sweat it out—but you'll have the privilege of knowing that you did the right thing."

In the week leading up to the election, Louis Martin's every call, every telegram, was dedicated to advancing the Blue Bomb. He sent out four hundred personalized telegrams to every Black newspaper editor and community leader he knew, drawing on two and a half decades of relationships, urging each of them to write as much as possible about the election-defining story of how Kennedy was "moved to show his concern on this outrage against blacks and against Martin Luther King." Martin wrangled endorsements from some traditionally Republican papers like Norfolk, Virginia's *Journal and Guide* and the *Amsterdam News*. King, when asked what swung Black voters to the Democrats, stated, "The Democrats did a great deal of work in Negro areas, and especially in the Negro press. They did an excellent job of public relations."

Once he had sent out the telegrams, Martin moved to the phones. The editor called every Black Democratic leader with an organization he knew of, urging them to get messengers out on the street: "Pass the word through the ghettos and the bars," as well as beauty salons, barbershops, and pool halls. Raymond "Silver Fox" Jones, a Harlem operative, promised Martin, "I'll get the boys out in the streets." Unions helped get them out, too, from New York to Detroit. Multiplied hundreds of times, Martin's efforts created momentum, and CRS efforts over the last few months had primed Black voters to start liking Kennedy. Now, with Kennedy's call to Coretta, the CRS had the right closing strategy to solidify that trust.

Martin was proud of how well and how painstakingly they had baked the cake, but his actions showed how important he thought this final effort was, and he was now working fourteen hours a day to push the Blue Bomb "to be the dramatic thing" in cities like Detroit, Philadelphia, Chicago, New York, Cleveland, and Los Angeles.

He and Wofford were prepared to meet the demand, with hundreds of thousands of copies heading out on buses, trains, and planes. A CRS associate, Franklin Williams, described the Blue Bomb as "electricity."

■ ■ ■

Jackie Robinson was a hero because he was stubborn. His prodigious talent on the baseball field had left fans, coaches, and fellow players in perpetual awe, but what differentiated him from other supremely talented players was his inability to give up, to quit when it was the sensible thing to do. He endured verbal abuse and raw racism because he refused to surrender to anyone. Those same character traits also led him to refuse to abandon Nixon. Reversing course was not in his makeup. His friend Dr. Kenneth Clark, famous for his white and black doll study that was used as evidence in the *Brown v. Board* hearings, said that the moment had come to make the switch, given how the Democrat had aided King. Yet in these final, frantic days, Robinson fiercely held on to his sense of being truly independent, not a partisan—someone who was actively choosing Nixon. When pressed, he remembered his instinctive dislike of Kennedy, but above all, no matter how distraught he felt about Nixon's inaction, he believed that a man's promises mattered.

Despite the attractiveness of what Robinson called a "shrewd political move" by Kennedy, he decided to do all he could to propel Nixon to victory in the final inning. Nixon sent him a letter the Friday before the election, as though aware of Robinson's disappointment in him. He wrote of the King case that it would have been easy for those not in the administration to make "a 'grandstand play.'" Robinson forged on.

In the final issue of *Jet* before the election, the reporter Simeon Booker characterized Black Republicans as feeling "woefully weak in organization, resources and manpower at a time the Party stood a chance of making the best inroads into the Negro vote." *Jet* reported that the GOP felt Nixon was popular enough not to need a concentrated effort in the Black community, even though the reporter did not see as many Black people at Republican events as he did at Kennedy's rallies. To the National Urban League's Lester Granger in the *Amsterdam News*, what the Democrats seemed to have this year that the GOP lacked was "a most able corps of Negro troubleshooters, hatchet men, advisers and interpreters."

Still, the *Jet* article ended with a Black Republican expressing hope they could "make enough gains in our communities to push Nixon through . . . The improvement will be noticed in the final days of the campaign."

While Robinson was still stubbornly on the road, the other major Black Republican surrogate, Morrow, was at the White House, sidelined when he was needed most.

■ ■ ■

On Sunday in Atlanta, King sat for a long radio interview targeted at Black listeners, and the election hovered over the discussion. Nimbly evading the usual endorsement pressures, King hoped that Kennedy would adopt a "forthright position" on segregation, whereas he feared that a potential Republican administration would engage in "too much disagreement and double talk." Explaining that he had spoken with Kennedy twice, the minister admitted, "I was very impressed with his intelligence and his understanding of the problem and honesty in discussing it." This seemed to be another endorsement in all but name. King said, "I think more and more [Kennedy] has demonstrated a great deal of courage, and this has been impressive."

The *Constitution*'s moderate editor, Ralph McGill, wrote of King's jailers, "They alone provided him with the opportunity to exert and reveal his undenied courage. As the late Mahatma Gandhi demonstrated, neither jail nor physical assaults are an answer when the moral force is on the other side." A misdemeanor leading to a late-night transfer to the state prison "was so obviously a discrimination that the conscience of the nation was outraged against the South." He advised those who were upset about Bobby's call to "cast the first stone at those who made Georgia vulnerable to a charge of injustice. Without them, there would have been no call."

Editorials like McGill's were moving more than undecided Black voters; they were starting to elevate King's status and viability as a national leader. *Life* magazine wrote of how being a sit-in martyr gave King new prestige. *The Pittsburgh Courier* reported how the thought in Atlanta was, "These white folks have now made Dr. Martin King Jr. the biggest Negro in the United States." In wanting to crush him as a regional voice, his enemies had inadvertently helped create something Harris Wofford had only dared dream of: an American Gandhi.

As the day of decision neared, King was now seen as not only a man influencing a crucial voting bloc but a figure who might well have the capacity to rise above politics itself. Nixon and Kennedy were scrambling to ascend to the pinnacle of political success, and King was seeing, for the first time, what it might be like to rise in moral stature above men like them. Not just as a nimble activist leader, not just as a Black leader on par with Wilkins and Randolph, but as a new national force.

What hath Judge Mitchell wrought?

■   ■   ■

Kennedy was back in New York, speaking at Grand Concourse and Fordham Road to more than twenty thousand supporters. Kennedy said that Nixon "in the last seven days has called me an economic ignoramus, a Pied Piper, and all the rest. I just confine myself to calling him a Republican. But he says that is really getting low." On the surface, Kennedy's charm and wit seemed fully intact, the soul of confidence and bonhomie. By late in the day, however, Kennedy was so consumed by anguished second-guessing that he experienced, to the astonishment of campaign aides, a raging meltdown. His gut told him that they should be campaigning in California (he would be proved correct) instead of tracing well-worn and secure East Coast cities. Sensing they were making a devastating error, soaked from the rain, and two hours behind schedule as they worked their way across Long Island, he uncharacteristically said he would not go on to the Upper East and West Side crowds awaiting him. Instead, he told the driver to take him back to his hotel.

Nixon had reached a breaking point from the pressure weeks before. While sitting in the back seat of a car in Iowa following a poorly designed schedule with too few destinations, he savagely kicked the front seat, breaking the frame and knocking a long-suffering aide in the kidneys. Before Election Day, Nixon would punch a consultant in the ribs for not running an errand. Nagging physical ailments were dragging him down, but what was hurting more was an unwillingness to break his convention promise to visit all fifty states, given the time he lost in the hospital owing to his knee injury. His stubbornness compounded his exhaustion as he demonstrated a lack of strategic vision in the last, draining hours of the campaign.

■ ■ ■

As the Blue Bomb continued to roll out, Martin and Wofford's attention was focused on the final Sunday before the election. They had to figure out how the pamphlets would get into as many Black churches as possible. Their secret play was shaping up to possibly be one of the great covert political moves in American history. Late Saturday night, Wofford was lugging heavy boxes of Blue Bombs onto Greyhound buses bound for Virginia and the Carolinas. He could not help but feel inspired as he watched the buses pull away with the first hints of dawn.

Twenty thousand people were out at 3:00 a.m. at an unusual campaign stop in Waterbury, Connecticut. It was a rare middle-of-the-night chance to greet Kennedy, followed by an event with more than forty-five thousand people on the New Haven Green later in the morning. Kennedy was back on track, determined to outwork Nixon. They were almost home.

In Chicago, Shriver had been calling every Catholic activist and education contact he could think of to hand out his blue pamphlets, particularly on the South and West Sides of Chicago. In Washington, Martin was also on the line with Chicago contacts, drawing on his years reporting for the *Defender* and the time he had spent living in Hyde Park. More than a quarter of a million pamphlets would be distributed in Chicago that Sunday, primarily at Black churches.

Shriver wanted to see it all happen, to personally help hand out the pamphlets. This would make a splendid morning activity for his daughter, Maria, on her fifth birthday, as well as for her six-year-old brother, Robert. The three Shrivers stood outside Chicago's Ebenezer Missionary Baptist Church and talked to every worshipper they could. What Shriver experienced that Sunday morning was extraordinary. Parishioners grabbed the pamphlets as they entered, and Shriver, to his delight, saw them clutching them as they filed out. The worshippers looked energized by the contents. The same enthusiasm was building from St. Louis to Philadelphia to New Orleans. Few, if any, on those church steps realized they had just encountered the man in charge of Kennedy's Civil Rights Section.

■   ■   ■

Dr. King's Sunday sermon at Atlanta's Ebenezer was called, appropriately enough, "Eight Days Behind Bars." The words of the sermon have been lost, but were inspired by the lesson that morning from Revelation 2:1–10, which include:

> You have persevered and have endured hardships for my name, and have not grown weary. Do not be afraid of what you are about to suffer. I tell you, the devil will put some of you in prison to test you, and you will suffer persecution for ten days. Be faithful, even to the point of death, and I will give you life as your victor's crown.

Certain Bible verses were hardly abstract to King; they expressed a terrible reality he would face again, but not this day. After his release,

he wrote to L. Harold DeWolf, his Boston University theology professor, "I think I received a new understanding of the meaning of suffering and I came away more convinced than ever before that unearned
suffering is redemptive." Following the service, there was a homecoming dinner in the Fellowship Hall under the sanctuary.

By Sunday evening, Wofford was getting reports of entire Black
congregations, Baptist and AME, standing and vowing to vote for
Kennedy. When the Harlem operator Silver Fox Jones called Martin,
he told him of reports his men were bringing back from the Harlem bars that everything was going to go Kennedy's way. Martin loved
hearing it all. Their excitement was building.

While the election was anticipated to be close almost everywhere,
most eyes were on the South, with *The New York Times* calling it the most
influential election for the region since 1860. Could the Democrats
keep their party together with papered-over civil rights differences?
Would Nixon break the Democrats' long-standing control of the region? And, whoever won, how would the results affect the prospect of
advancing civil rights?

■   ■   ■

Nixon made his closing appeal to Americans in a televised event
from Chicago, after numbingly long days that included Wisconsin,
Michigan, and the day before, astonishingly, Alaska—a final flourish
of insane scheduling. During a telethon on the last day before the
election from Southfield, Michigan, Nixon took questions from callers. When asked about sit-ins, he said that it was wrong for stores to
segregate Black customers and that as president he would work to stop
such discrimination.

Meanwhile, in Boston, hundreds of thousands of fellow New En-
glanders packed the old winding streets to see Kennedy; it took his
car an hour and a half to get to the Boston Garden from his hotel and
from there to Faneuil Hall. In Kennedy's final televised statement, he

summed up his stirring but vague message, "This is the choice, then, in 1960. Shall we go forward?"

Three major polling companies predicted Kennedy would win, with one other predicting that Nixon would. One polling expert said, "It can go either way. This has been the most volatile campaign since we began taking samplings in 1936. I have never seen the lead change hands so many times." Gallup had Kennedy up by only one, a drop from the previous poll, suggesting Nixon's trajectory might overtake that of Kennedy by Election Day.

■ ■ ■

After nearly three months in D.C., spending almost all their waking hours side by side, Wofford and Martin parted. Martin said goodbye to drive west, home to Chicago. He passed through the hills of western Pennsylvania and the flatlands of Ohio and Indiana, traveling across a vast heartland preparing to elect a president. He was driving to Illinois to help with the final push, because his state was too close for anyone's comfort; even Mayor Daley lacked complete confidence in the outcome. When Martin got to Chicago after the long ride, he could have gone home to his family in Hyde Park, but no one ever second-guessed his work ethic. He headed straight to a precinct on the South Side he thought would be crucial the next day. His mission to maximize turnout was not over yet.

"IT WAS A SYMPHONY"

From the moment the sun rose on a brisk, bright day, Atlanta voters flocked to the polls. Fulton County was breaking records, exceeding one hundred thousand voters for the first time. A *Daily World* reporter thought the King case increased interest in the election. Because Nixon had made Georgia a battleground state, observers predicted the results would reveal an active two-party race there for the first time in their lives. This had been Nixon's fervent hope back on August 26, when vast crowds of Atlantans came out for him.

Kennedy voted at a quiet library at the base of Beacon Hill. On Election Day, a candidate needs to get out of the way of the staff, party workers, and voters who will determine the outcome. In the cool morning, there was hardly a cloud in the blue sky as Kennedy and Jackie flew to the Cape, home to Hyannis. Shriver arrived later in the day with Eunice, and the family awaited the results together. On the lawn, the brothers broke out a football in the afternoon before Jack took a nap. They were far from getting any real details, but indications were that north of sixty-nine million Americans were voting that day—a record-shattering turnout.

After less than five hours of sleep in the preceding seventy-two hours, Nixon would sleep for two more before rising again to vote in Whittier, California, his hometown. After he voted, an impulse to break free from the confines of the long campaign hit him. Nixon took off down the California coast in a convertible, ostensibly to show the landscape to a military aide who had never seen it. They stopped to see Nixon's mother, swung by his birthplace, Yorba Linda, and then continued south. Nixon expected to turn back around at San Diego, but when he learned his car mate had never been to Tijuana, the vice president decided to head out of the country, with a Secret Service officer and a policeman in tow. Election Day limbo has made candidates do odd things, but Nixon's Mexico jaunt remains one of the stranger such episodes.

After asking a border agent for recommendations for Mexican food, they set off to eat and drink margaritas. Back across the border later in the day, they looked at the ruins of the Mission San Juan Capistrano. Nixon relished the solitude of the empty chapel, sitting in the back pew. After getting a pineapple milkshake, the candidate was too exhausted to do any further driving, and he turned the wheel over to the Los Angeles Police Department officer for the rest of the trip back to Los Angeles and the long night ahead.

In D.C., Wofford wondered how to pass the time. Silver Fox Jones called him to say, "Well, just take it easy now. It's over. We've done our part. I want you to know that this thing that you and Louis and others were doing . . . it was a symphony, man, it was a symphony." No compliment meant more to Wofford than the approval of an old political ward battler. Wofford would say later that the Kennedy brothers "moved in action and responded in action," and so had they. Arthur Schlesinger said of the Kennedys, "They were not systematic calculators but brilliant improvisers."

Wofford had to trust he had done enough. He learned of a late afternoon showing of a favorite movie, *Viva Zapata*, with Marlon Brando. While working at his old law firm, whenever the film was showing nearby, he brought anyone he could in the office to make sure they saw it. He decided to sit in the darkness, allowing himself to be distracted by the story of a doomed radical speaking for the dispossessed.

In the film, a pair of idealistic young brothers help lead a revolution, are tempted by power, and then make a heroic stand before they are killed. The final shot is of a horse without a rider.

In Chicago, Louis Martin's nine-year-old daughter, Toni, was happy to have her dad home. Toni had two younger sisters and two older ones already out of the house. As the Martins settled before the television in their home on a grassy, tree-lined Hyde Park street of brick houses owned by Black professionals and University of Chicago professors, they were like millions of American families doing the same—experiencing the novelty of watching the tense election results in real time on a flickering black-and-white screen. Toni was aware that her father had been working on this election, but she could not quite decipher the meaning of each state report coming in, how it all added up. She tried to follow her parents' running commentary on each update. Tonight, Toni would get a civics lesson through their dissection of what each state meant for Kennedy, until she fell asleep as the returns crawled in past midnight.

All his life, Kennedy had demanded constant company, but Nixon had a strong desire to be left alone. This was especially true on an election night, when Nixon preferred to hide away, curling up in a chair to keep a running tally on a legal pad. After his Tijuana escape, he had holed up at the Ambassador Hotel (the site where, eight years later, Robert Kennedy would accept victory in the California primary). Aides would gingerly bring in numbers, offering few observations; Nixon knew every inch of the nation's intricate political landscape, exactly where he was succeeding and where he was showing vulnerabilities.

Early in the evening, Nixon dismissed TV anchors' talk of Kennedy's cruising to an assured victory. He knew his totals would go up as the night went on and the tide rolled west toward his home state. Illinois was looking good for JFK, but the downstate vote would even things up, and nothing would be decided until Chicago's votes were released. Nixon was pleased he was hanging on so well; he had a chance. The race was tight even in the state of Texas; Kennedy's move to include Johnson on the ticket should have clinched it, but hadn't so far.

Bobby, a continent away, was surrounded by wired-up phones and teletype machines delivering news. Kennedy would wander through, go to the television to see what was being reported, offering wry commentary as if he were a news anchor and not the candidate. Based on data being delivered to Bobby, the younger brother was apprehensive. "We're being clobbered," he said. Then the poll closings in the South brought good news; Georgia and the deep Democratic South were coming home. But Nixon was carrying Florida and was close in North Carolina—good signs for the vice president.

Kennedy's lead in the popular vote, if not in the crucial Electoral College count, was decreasing as the West started coming in. As the states fell, Kennedy stayed just ahead as he and Nixon each struggled toward 270 Electoral College votes, with many states too close to call. There have been closer elections in American history, but this was the last election that was essentially fought in every section of the country with excruciatingly slim margins throughout. Eighteen states came down to three percentage points or less.

Louis Martin's family knew he could be a worrier. By midnight in Chicago, he and the country saw that Ohio was among the midwestern states going to Nixon. As he always seemed to, Nixon was clawing his way back.

Nearing midnight in the West, with the math in states like New York and Illinois starting to let him down, Nixon felt compelled to say something, even if there was, at this point, no need to concede. He went to write his remarks on his trademark yellow pad of paper. But Finch stopped him, saying he should let all the votes be counted, because he was closing Kennedy's popular vote advantage: it was under a million and falling. Kennedy appeared to be only four electoral votes short of winning, but the vice president was close to his rival in enough states that it was possible that Illinois and Texas could give him the narrowest of victories. He went before the cameras around 3:00 a.m. in the East, his wife Pat's drawn face revealing the pain he would not allow himself to show, and said if present trends continued, he would not be president.

Yet it still was not over, as Nixon learned that his deficit in Illinois was shrinking. He went to sleep in hopes of waking up to a reversal of fortune, as Woodrow Wilson had done in going to bed assuming he had lost, then waking up president-elect with the morning's victory in California. With Illinois in doubt again, after 4:00 a.m., *The New York Times* replaced its "Kennedy Elected" headline with "Kennedy Is Apparent Victor."

In D.C., Wofford was long past his Brando movie and immersed in the numbers on television, which continued to shift deep into the night. He saw with horror that Illinois might well go for Nixon. They had lost Ohio, and Nixon was proving strong all throughout the Midwest; it was not beyond thinking that the vice president would somehow win, stealing Wisconsin. California was too close to call. Nixon had made many questionable strategic moves, but those within the Kennedy circle had always found it difficult to understand the vice president's appeal; worse, there was the fear that maybe the nation was not ready for Jack. It was easy for Democrats to see Nixon as trite and plodding, but perhaps in his striving, endurance, and guts the people saw themselves.

Bobby was constantly on the phone throughout the night with Mayor Daley, who reassured him that Chicago would overwhelm downstate GOP vote totals. At 4:00 a.m., Kennedy walked the short path back to his house to go to sleep, feeling somewhat confident that he had it; he could not conceive of Daley letting down his father, Joe Kennedy.

Wofford was stubborn, refusing to turn off the television until it looked, at dawn, that by the shakiest of margins they had somehow done it—elected a Roman Catholic candidate, elected the youngest man ever to the presidency, a man who gloried in being smart, alert, alive, not the liberal Wofford might have wanted, but a man capable of listening and of growth. Soon the nation would be waking up in anticipation of Kennedy's televised appearance in Hyannis.

Wofford sensed that Black voters seemed to have provided, in their surging turnout, the winning margin in state after state. He would

soon begin to wonder what those Black vote totals meant. The unexpected events of the last three weeks had led the nation to a racial
reckoning. One way or another, the country found itself between a
new president and a King.

■   ■   ■

Talking to reporters the next morning, an exhausted Bobby credited
the debates with being key to getting voters comfortable with electing
Kennedy, but added, "I think the Negro vote helped a lot." Asked if
his call to Judge Mitchell helped to make that happen, Bobby smiled
and said that it had. He shared his assessment that Nixon should have
focused on the Black vote in the North and forgone the temptation
of trying to win the white South. Nixon could have come out against
bigotry instead of thinking he could win the whole country by staying
silent. Then again, left unsaid was how Kennedy moved more deftly in
this respect, selecting Johnson to hold white southern voters while the
CRS pushed for Black Americans.

The Atlanta Journal wrote, "A good argument can be made for the
proposition that Judge Oscar Mitchell of DeKalb County Civil and
Criminal Court elected John F. Kennedy as the next president of the
United States." This startling assertion would soon gain traction, but
for Atlanta students its truth was already evident. The headline in the
Inquirer proclaimed, "Negroes Clinched Kennedy Win: Negro Surge
Gave [Democrats] Key States."

But not everyone in Atlanta felt the same way. Mayor Hartsfield
moaned to friends of feeling embarrassed that Atlanta's Black voters
had still given the majority of their votes—56 percent of them—to
Nixon. Even as party strategists, reporters, and academics were beginning to pore over the voting data, noting the significant, nationwide
shift in Black voting patterns, somehow, after everything the mayor
felt he had done for King, his pleas for them to vote Democratic had
fallen short. He took it very personally.

But those close to King did not; their middle-class Black community along Sweet Auburn had been voting Republican for a long time, after all. The numbers actually showed a move toward Kennedy that was, for those who had so feared for King's life, gratifying. For Georgia's Black voters, generations of persecution by Democrats were felt more keenly than a single gesture made by the idealistic Kennedy, no matter how appreciative they were. It was still hard to vote for a party headed by Vandivers and Mitchells, and there was no disregarding the Republican John Calhoun's superb organizing skills. Yet many votes had shifted after all the twists and turns of campaigning; that much was also clear. Change had come to Sweet Auburn.

Equally evident was another turn, one that promised to alter Georgia politics for decades: DeKalb County gave the Republicans a surprise victory, one that local politicos attributed to the King affair. Even in a national GOP landslide four years before, Eisenhower put up only 40 percent there; now the Republican candidate received more than 50 percent of votes. A Democratic county official said, "If Kennedy hadn't made that telephone call, he would have taken this county. It isn't our fault; Kennedy made it himself."

Nixon might not have won Georgia, but the *Constitution* proclaimed that he had garnered the highest percentage of votes for a GOP candidate since before the New Deal—nearly 38 percent.

White voters in DeKalb County and Black voters in Fulton County were, in retrospect, harbingers of a massive political realignment that would transform the South. For now, the totals were just a taste of what was to come. All that was needed to cement this tectonic shift was some future, epochal event—say, the signing of a civil rights bill by a Democratic president, with a Martin Luther King standing by to receive the pen. When in fact this happened, President Lyndon Johnson muttered, "We have lost the South for a generation," but he was too optimistic. It would be far longer than that.

"THEY JUST ALL TURNED"

Nixon slept until noon on Thursday following the election. He decided he needed to return to a Washington schedule, so his chauffeur, John Wardlaw, picked him up. Seeing the man he had known for eight years slink dejectedly into the back seat, Wardlaw, who was Black, confessed to him, "Mr. Vice President, I can't tell you how sick I am about the way my people voted in the election. You know I had been talking to all of my friends. They were all for you." He added something that Nixon would hear again, many times, but not as bluntly: "But when Mr. Robert Kennedy called the judge to get Dr. King out of jail—well, they just all turned to him."

William Safire, who witnessed Jackie Robinson's tears of frustration, told Finch, "Their Martin Luther King gambit paid off handsomely." Nixon agreed, later admitting, "I just didn't realize such a call could swing an election. The Democrats whipped up a fury in the Negro areas. I was painted a villain, and my entire record was erased within a few weeks."

His actions, or inaction, during those nine days left a wound that would never heal. Nixon was publicly restrained, but some indication of the emotion he felt after losing the Black vote can be found in a note dated a week after the election. Finch passed on to Nixon a proposal that he send a response to all those who had contacted him about King, given that "the guy is out now, but there might be a chance to do a little spade work." He added, "We show sincerity and so leave it up to JFK to show where he stands as soon as he gets into office." The campaign even drafted a letter Nixon could use, which included the lines "It was good of you to communicate with me in regard to the recent arrest of Rev. Martin Luther King, Jr., an incident about which I was deeply concerned. I know that my satisfaction in Dr. King's subsequent release was shared by millions."

In response to Finch's suggestion that he send out these conciliatory notes, Nixon scrawled his reply in large letters: "NO."

There is one letter to King written after 1960 in Nixon's files. During his 1962 gubernatorial campaign, Nixon declined an invitation from the Southern California–Nevada Council of Churches to speak alongside King. He sent King a note lacking the familiarity of their 1950s letters, but saying, "I look forward to future meetings and discussions when all of us can join together in a realistic appraisal of race relations problems." There is no record of any such meeting ever happening, or of further contact between them. It was as if, for Nixon, the Reidsville incident were cause not for apology but rather for a sundering, the rejection of a relationship that had begun with such promise.

In an April 1962 *Ebony* profile, Nixon would still appear to be haunted by the King crisis, alternating between contrition and self-justification. Nixon maintained, "I could have become President. I needed only five per cent more votes in the Negro areas. I could have gotten them if I had campaigned harder." He thought his record and relationships were strong enough, but "then the Rev. Martin Luther King Jr. case came up." Louis Martin's impact was known even if his name was not: "The Democrats used this incident as a symbol of my unconcern in an all-out drive in the big city Negro areas." Nixon claimed he worked to help free King, but thought he should not publicize "something which is a matter of confidential government business." As for what Bobby had done, Nixon wanted the attorney general to stop getting credit because "this was unethical. I agreed it was a bum rap (for King) but as a lawyer, I know if you call a judge in a case, you're guilty of contempt and this is a violation of canons of legal ethics. Bob Kennedy called the judge but this did not get him out of the jail—not so—it was public opinion."

Calling it a "fast moving campaign," Nixon presented himself as an idealistic political naïf: "There was some doubt . . . in the effectiveness of the Democratic use of the King case. At first our party people were not aware of the tremendous impact . . . We had no idea the Democrats were concentrating so much in the Negro areas on this 'No Comment' business." He warned of the direction in which Republicans were moving, in light of the right-winger Barry Goldwater's rise to power: "Our party would eventually become the first major all-white political party. And that isn't good."

Even in 1960, Republicans were quicker than Democrats to understand that the King crisis had effectively transformed the election. At a White House meeting with Nixon present, President Eisenhower, interpreting his vice president's loss as a repudiation of his administration, muttered to his staff that Lodge's cabinet pledge had "just killed us in the South." What also peeved the president was his belief that they had fruitlessly made a good faith effort on civil rights, yet fewer Black people voted for Republicans than in 1956. He declared that Black voters "just do not give a damn."

Nixon, for his part, grumbled to Eisenhower that the Black vote was "a bought vote, and it is not bought by civil rights," a sign of bitterness that would only grow in years to come. This was a view he had never, to anyone's knowledge, expressed before.

In December, a still sore president said to a group of business leaders visiting the White House that a "couple of phone calls" kept Republicans from winning. No reporter followed up to ask which calls he was referring to; it was clear just how important the Kennedy calls had become to Republicans smarting from this defeat. Yet despite the quick assessment that these phone calls had made all the difference, no one apparently reached out to Morrow to see what he thought of the decline in the GOP's share of the Black vote.

Morrow, for one, knew all too well what had happened to his dream:

> This act won the election. Kennedy's action electrified the entire Negro community and resulted in tens of thousands of Negro voters going over to the Democrats' banner. Many factors contributed to Mr. Kennedy's election—which was close—but one incontrovertible fact is evident. He carried the crucial, essential Negro vote. He had keen, intelligent Negro advisers, and he obviously listened to them.

This was a subtle tip of the hat to Louis Martin, as well as a pained observation that at least one candidate had listened.

Morrow hoped Republicans would learn two lessons. First, "the strategy of wooing the solid South and ignoring the available Negro vote was a costly blunder." Morrow thought he had seen in Nixon an ability to listen, an affinity with the disenfranchised. But having assumed such feelings were enough, Nixon lost this community's trust, and now he seemed well on his way to assisting the GOP in losing its way with African Americans entirely.

Second, Morrow assessed, "white people must stop believing they 'know the Negro.' For a long while to come in this country, it would be well to ask knowledgeable Negroes for an objective assessment of the Negro attitude and mood on a given subject." This ability to listen would prove difficult for both parties to master (if indeed either ever has). But insensitivity would be weighed by Black voters alongside outright hostility to their citizenship.

Morrow would never leave the party, but he never again held any position of political responsibility, at any level—national, state, or local.

Jackie Robinson lost his newspaper column in the *New York Post* as a result of his support for Nixon. He retained a column in the Black *Los Angeles Sentinel*, and there he wrote that he could only hope Kennedy would "curb the power of the southern segregationists in his camp," those who still "have their feet on the Negro's neck!" As angry as he was at Nixon, he continued to treat the vice president's racial insensitivities as a mistake and Kennedy's as a deep character flaw—particularly the new president's dealings with segregationist governors. He predicted that unless the new president worked to make equality real in America, he would not be able to advance democracy abroad.

■   ■   ■

The fact that King had been an inadvertent kingmaker dawned on Democrats slowly, perhaps because winners luxuriate in victory rather than confront the critical realities responsible for a win. Recognizing that Black voters had mattered would have created not only a sense of obligation but also a sense of embarrassment in a party so riven by the civil rights movement. Still, some saw something noble and important in what had just happened. "Senator Kennedy took a risk in his campaign," Eleanor Roosevelt said, "when he telephoned and promised to help the Rev. Martin Luther King." She believed, "It may well be that similar risks will have to be taken to save humanity from itself."

It was also true that some in the CRS insisted that one moment should not obscure the reality of what months of organizing had also achieved. Even Louis Martin was hesitant to say that one call had turned Black America. He was proud of the hard work the CRS had done— the cake they had made—and now everyone, it seemed, was interested only in the icing on the top.

Marjorie Lawson later said of the phone call to Coretta, "I thought it was a disservice to Negro voters to say that they were so childlike that one telephone call made to one woman would turn a whole voter group to, or against, a candidate." She thought that what really mattered was that "for the first time, a candidate had made a staff and funds available in recognition of Negro voters and had helped them organize and get out the vote." Believing that the entire story could be reduced to a single call was to ignore "organizational work that had been done."

What the call meant to the North Carolina A&T State University president and CRS ally Sam Proctor was "an existential affirmation before black people that this candidate cared about our well-being, showed respect for us." He said Black communities had been choosing presidents based on who would hurt them least, and Kennedy looked "light years ahead of anybody else, because other people hadn't made any such gestures." Franklin Williams, who ran a voter registration drive for the CRS at churches nationally, was convinced the call tipped the election to Kennedy, calling it "a major factor in influencing unconvinced millions of blacks to support this young man from Massachusetts . . . You couldn't have bought that kind of publicity." Understanding its power meant understanding its context: "These were desperate times and there were very few lights of hope for us." As Andrew Young put it nearly sixty years later, "No presidential candidate had ever expressed any concern for anybody Black in any situation."

What is indisputable is that the Democratic share of the Black vote rebounded from the previous presidential election by seven percentage points, to a commanding 68 percent. For an election decided by less than a percentage point overall, this shift was more than enough to put Kennedy in the White House. The Kennedy campaign reversed the rising tide of Black support for Republicans, which had increased from 21 percent in 1952 to 39 percent in 1956. Even Louis Martin thought Nixon would build upon this trend. But it was not to be.

Black American votes for the GOP had decreased by seven percentage points, to 32 percent. And despite Nixon's poor performance, never again would a Republican do as well as Nixon did with Black voters. The CRS's efforts changed the direction of a trend line, and the Republican Party never approached Nixon's 1960 margins again. As Joshua Farrington writes in *Black Republicans and the Transformation of the GOP*, "The 1960 election proved to be a decisive turning point in the GOP's relationship with black voters."

Though it can never be precisely known just how many voters were swayed by the Blue Bomb, or the Kennedy calls, or any specific actions taken by the CRS during the campaign (polling still being a primitive instrument), we can study some small pieces of data to try to gain a sense of what really happened in 1960. Kennedy's pollster Louis Harris happened to survey Black voters both before and after the call to Coretta in six states and found that Kennedy's existing lead increased in Illinois, Pennsylvania, and Maryland. In North Carolina, his support increased from 47 percent to 88 percent, while the margin of how far ahead Kennedy was in Texas and New York declined, but not dramatically.

Martin would say you had to get the horses on the track; Election Day is a race. Key urban wards across the country increased their support for Democrats by ten percentage points or more compared with 1956, in many cases voting at a rate of around 75 percent for Kennedy. The Democrats' 7 percent increase in Black support also does not fully explain just how pivotal the CRS's efforts proved to be. Martin's greatest concern was not the percentage, per se, but the total Black turnout, which could make or break winning margins in close states where Nixon was poised to do well with white voters.

Nationally, data showed that Black turnout was indeed higher than in previous presidential election cycles. There was also plenty of anecdotal evidence that in crucial areas the turnout was beyond even the CRS's dreams. All this, when energy for Kennedy before the convention had been lukewarm at best. Seen in this light, the turnout Martin was aiming for was a remarkable achievement. Without this increase in the number of Black voters, Nixon would have narrowly won the popular vote and could well have won in the Electoral College by a landslide. The political science professor David Niven found in his book *The Politics of Injustice* that Black voters made the difference for Kennedy in nine states, accounting for 142 electoral votes.

Of course, any number of slight shifts in voting patterns could have altered a race that close: the rise in unemployment in the weeks before the election; a Roman Catholic Democrat running against a Protestant (Kennedy lost some Protestant votes in the South, where he won anyway, and gained Catholic votes in places he needed them, such as New York). Still, a *New York Times* article announced, "Negro Vote

Held Vital to Kennedy," singling out the call to Coretta as the turning point. The reporter Anthony Lewis estimated that the 250,000 pamphlets given out in Chicago might have made the difference in a state that Kennedy won by a little over eight thousand votes. This piece was followed by a *New Republic* study of the Black vote that found that Kennedy would not have been president without these voters. The article discussed how there were more Black votes for Kennedy than his slim margin of victory in states like Illinois, Michigan, New Jersey, and South Carolina. The *Times* reported similar outcomes in Texas and North Carolina as well.

The idea that Kennedy owed his presidency to Black voters gained further traction when Theodore White published his groundbreaking book, *The Making of the President, 1960*. White had interviewed Wofford, and when the book became a runaway bestseller, many white Americans began to understand the importance of Kennedy's call to Coretta for the first time. White singled out the "hard work" of the CRS, "led by the able Sargent Shriver and Harris Wofford." (Louis Martin went unmentioned, as he would in many future books.)

White pointed to eleven states where Black voters gave Kennedy the margin of support he needed to win, and five in particular where, if the 1956 election margins by race had repeated without Democrats' improvement, Kennedy could not have won them. He also pointed out that the Kennedy campaign proved dominant in a number of important Black-majority wards in Chicago and Detroit. Though White's account of Kennedy's efforts to help King was not entirely accurate, the story was now out there, irrevocably part of a growing legend. Wofford, for his part, saw his conversations with reporters like White and Anthony Lewis as part of a larger effort to not only help people understand Kennedy's victory but also ensure that the civil rights struggle would not be conveniently forgotten by the new administration; the Black vote was now visible and invaluable.

To Wofford, Kennedy's call also revealed something about the man who made it—one who was imperfect, vulnerable to temptation and to stress, and not noticeably inclined to think about, or empathize with, the pain of Black Americans. While the pressures on Kennedy were nothing compared with King's suffering in his cell, Wofford still recognized that JFK had found himself in a deeply uncomfortable situation, achingly close to the presidency and whipsawed by the (morally incomparable) demands of two very different blocs of voters. Though he told the story hundreds of times, Wofford never lost the note of wonder in his voice as he described a candidate under unrelenting pressure—a candidate who certainly did not have to call a stranger in distress, one whose husband's notoriety among white voters could derail his hopes of becoming president. He reflected, "Most people in life and in politics, and certainly Jack Kennedy, have mixed motives. He wanted to win the election and he also liked to do the right thing. That's why the call to King is a test of what sort of a fellow he was."

Wofford saw the call as an example of the Kennedys being their best selves, just as their decision to allow King to be wiretapped years later was an example of them at their worst. Though it surely helped that Kennedy had men like Wofford, Martin, and Shriver around him, he passed a test of decency in 1960 that Nixon failed.

Bobby's actions during those nine days have long been mischaracterized, first by Bobby himself and then by historians in coming decades who took his word at face value. But in his 1964 oral history of the Kennedy presidency—which was published posthumously in 1988—he offered something closer to the truth. He refuted the story he had spun in the immediate aftermath of the election, in which he impulsively called Judge Mitchell out of moral outrage and in which the cowed judge backed down in the face of his anger. In the oral history, he hinted at the Vandiver back channel and described his easy, almost convivial, conversation with Judge Mitchell.

As to why Bobby himself intervened after telling the CRS not to, Wofford guessed there was a simple answer: "Once having started it . . . you want to finish the job." The Kennedys prioritized problem solving over virtuous gestures. This mentality was summed up by Wofford as

"We're in it, so we better win it." After JFK made an early morning call to Vandiver, prodded by Hartsfield's invented story of his interest in King's fate, Bobby had to quietly lay it all to rest. No one can say that the Kennedys weren't good at back-channeling.

One could imagine that the CRS did little to win King's freedom—except that the Kennedy brothers would never have involved themselves in such a risky affair, so close to the election, had Wofford not called Morris Abram that Saturday morning. And even after that call, the CRS kept pushing the campaign to do more, cultivating and directing public pressure to free King. It was the CRS, too, that orchestrated JFK's call to Coretta through Shriver—which made it incumbent upon the campaign to match words with actions. The Kennedys might have finished the job, but the CRS started it, and without the efforts of Martin, Wofford, and Shriver the Kennedy campaign might well have remained silent.

Martin and Wofford, not knowing better, continued to tell the story of Bobby's berating Judge Mitchell for decades. King himself, in his Kennedy Library oral history, showed he never knew the facts of Bobby's intervention. He simply accepted the story of the spontaneous call to the judge.

Though he was grateful to be out of jail, King sensed with growing unease that the story of his release was all too convenient for certain white politicians. He emphasized that "the Kennedy family did have some part, at least they expressed a concern and they did have some part in the release, but I must make it clear that many other forces worked to bring it about also." It was a difficult rhetorical line to walk, but even the day he emerged from Reidsville to face reporters, he knew that his story was bound up with the sit-ins, with the resilience of his Atlanta community, with the way his family and staff had worked against odds that white reporters did not understand. He knew that long-standing relationships between men like Daddy King and John Calhoun and imperfect white allies like Hartsfield prepared the ground on which he eventually walked free. And as he passed through the foreboding gates of Reidsville, he was standing next to the commanding

Hollowell—a Black lawyer who refused to be intimidated by white judges and prosecutors.

The Atlanta students, for their part, refused to give all the credit to the Kennedys. One *Inquirer* headline read, "King: Public Freed Him." The SCLC's Wyatt Tee Walker claimed, too, that broad public support for King was responsible for his release:

> If there was any critical pressure that brought the judge to this new position, certainly the hundreds of thousands of telegrams, letters and calls from all over the nation had its impact on the conscience of the court. Coupled with the brilliant handling of the team headed by Donald L. Hollowell, the judge really had no choice but to grant bail.

Walker wanted to wrestle the story back under control before it was completely wrenched from their hands.

Nonetheless, Wofford's heroic account of the Kennedys' actions was accepted by many, and its simplicity gave it great utility. As Governor Vandiver said in an interview years later, "Those of us who knew [the true story]—the only ones—we went underground, we didn't tell anyone either."

"Us" meant Vandiver, George Stewart, Bob Russell, Bobby Kennedy, and the new president, and "underground" often meant taking certain facts to the grave. Of those five individuals, only Vandiver reached old age, and his late-in-life account sheds unique light on the real story. Vandiver first began to talk in a 1967 Kennedy Library oral history, but comments on sensitive negotiations he'd conducted with Kennedy and his Georgia associates were only included in an addendum that remained sealed for many years. In interviews conducted long after his political career was over, Vandiver was more open, even displaying a touch of pride in his odd entanglement with King—quite a change from his earlier belief that the matter was political poison.

President Kennedy himself apparently told Theodore White aspects of the story on deep background. White went to Atlanta to ask Vandiver for more details, but he did not get the real story from the governor, because Vandiver still had political ambitions. And so the story remained unbroken for decades—except for a brief interlude in 1960, in the wake of a Christmas party livened with perhaps too many spirits. A *Journal* reporter picked up on how George Stewart had set up Bobby's call to Judge Mitchell, and subsequently published a story that quoted Stewart taking credit for something that had turned out to help his party. Stewart said, "Since King had to be released under the law anyhow we might as well get in a good lick for the national Democratic party and the state by showing the nation anyone can get justice down here." He added, "The Kennedys were interested in King and Nixon wasn't." After that, Stewart remained silent about his role and died a decade and a half later.

In later years, in certain Georgia circles, the effort to help Kennedy help King might be discussed quietly at parties or at funerals, but never around strangers. By the close of the decade, many of those involved had died, including King himself, and the official story held firm, gleaming like Georgia marble.

■   ■   ■

After the election, the exhausted president-elect retreated to his father's West Palm Beach mansion and relaxed with his adviser John Kenneth Galbraith, the six-foot-eight professor of economics at Harvard. The two men had a comfortable, frank rapport. Galbraith was the only person to have recorded Kennedy's own thoughts about the King affair in the immediate aftermath of the election.

After a day spent walking beside the ocean with Bobby and Ethel, they all gathered for dinner at the grand Louis XIV mahogany dining room banquet table and refought the election. Kennedy said of Nixon, "He sat out the jailing of Martin Luther King." Galbraith remembered the brothers saying that they had "acted individually; neither knew

what the other was doing." Historians long mistook this statement for the truth, and it has taken decades for the reality of what actually happened to emerge. Later testimony from Vandiver and Mitchell confirms what the Kennedy adviser Dick Goodwin and other family members also claimed: that the brothers were in constant communication in those days. They are sure that Bobby would not have made such a critical decision without Jack's approval.

Kennedy said one more thing to Galbraith about the unfolding of the King crisis. In his typically dry manner, he shrugged off any suggestion that he deserved praise: "The finest strategies are usually the result of accidents."

■   ■   ■

In Chicago, two days after the election, Louis Martin picked up his home phone, surprised to hear the familiar can-do tone of Shriver. Shriver was not interested in reminiscing; he ordered Martin to "get back to Washington . . . We've got to recruit a whole leadership here with this new government. We've won it. Now we've got to do something with it." Shriver called Wofford as well, saying, "If you thought you were going on vacation, enjoy it quickly—between now and Sunday. Monday morning we get to work. Jack has asked me to organize a talent search for the top jobs—the Cabinet, regulatory agencies, ambassadors, everything. We're going to comb the universities and professions, the civil rights movement, business, labor, foundations, and everywhere, to find the brightest and best people possible." They had three days to learn how an American government transition worked before showing up at the Mayflower Hotel in D.C.

Suddenly Louis Martin was exactly where he needed to be. His goal was to build Black political power, and he would do that by becoming the ultimate background adviser, finding qualified Black candidates to appoint to posts dealing with more than just Black affairs. No matter what position came up, Martin would have a stellar candidate to pitch—one who just happened to be Black. Shriver and Wofford were amazed at what he dubbed his "Who's Who of Negro experts of one kind or another." He quickly had a list of 750 strong prospects. Eight years on, he was still crossing people off that list whenever he was able to get them into pathbreaking roles. As he would put it, "There was an opportunity for the first time to try to slip—as the boys used to say—a few brothers in here."

His position for the next eight years would be deputy chairman of the Democratic National Committee, a job he found well suited to cultivating a generation of Black presidential appointees—among them, the first Black cabinet secretary and Supreme Court justice. That being said, if Martin felt (justifiably) snubbed by being assigned to the DNC instead of to the White House, he never said so in writing. Later, President Johnson would turn to Martin more and more regularly as an adviser and even as a confidant.

Martin justified his behind-the-scenes appointment by saying that he did not want racist opponents knowing of his access to power, nor did he want Black Americans to criticize him, as they had Morrow, as "some black sitting in the White House assuming that he had some power and was telling how they should run the country for blacks." Martin had a full pass to the West Wing, but Wofford still thought the Kennedy administration had missed an opportunity to hire a man of Martin's talents to be at the president's side on a daily basis.

Wofford would later write, "Louis and I continued through the next decades to be on call for Shriver." They continued to support Shriver's endeavors such as the Peace Corps that survive to this day as his legacy. The three close colleagues would weave in and out of each other's lives, a loose but affectionate partnership forged during the 1960 election. What happened during the race to save King's life would continue to play a powerful role in their lives.

■　■　■

While the new administration took shape, the old one packed up, its members choosing their soft landing places. Morrow expected, along with the rest of Eisenhower's departing staff, to be recommended for some lucrative post by the president. At the final Christmas party, however, Eisenhower took him aside with a pained expression and told him that no one he knew seemed to need his services. Morrow found himself, somewhat like Vice President Nixon, left adrift and unemployed by the Republicans' loss.

During his limbo, he published his White House diaries, which he titled *Black Man in the White House*. The book, even as it honored the president he served and a vice president he admired, stirred more than a few pots in Eisenhower's circle. It revealed Morrow's frustration at not having been listened to, his sense of being invisible, and his opinion on the mistakes Nixon had made at the end of his campaign. Morrow expressed disappointment that Nixon didn't seize the chance to win the Black vote.

It would take nearly three years before his Republican connections paid off with a high-level position at Bank of America. By then, Nixon, having lost the governor's race in California, had established himself as a New York lawyer literally across the street from Morrow's offices. Morrow never became part of Nixon's inner circle, though Nixon said of him, "His career would have been bright if I had won." Morrow served as a mentor to minority executives facing the same frustrations he encountered at CBS, the White House, and now the world of New York banking, telling them, you can "be in it but not of it."

To outsiders, Morrow seemed to have fulfilled the American dream, but he felt that he had fallen just short. He was denied access to the corridors of power that others of his stature passed through freely. In the end, he hoped there would be change, and if not that, he felt his existence at least offered "a certain nuisance value." Morrow's path as "the first" was marked by pain that he could not easily forget, but he developed a wry perspective on events—even titling his last autobiography *Forty Years a Guinea Pig*.

As for the defeated vice president, his time in Washington appeared to most observers to be at an end. Yet the man who equaled FDR for being on the most national ballots—five each—sensed his time there was not quite over. As night fell on the day of Kennedy's inauguration and galas got underway across the city, Nixon asked his driver to take him back to the Capitol before taking him to the airport for his flight to California. Alone, the former vice president looked out from a balcony atop the dome toward the Washington Monument and the Lincoln Memorial, shimmering white in the cold distance. He later wrote, "As I turned to go inside, I suddenly stopped short, struck by the thought that this was not the end—that someday I would be back here. I walked as fast as I could back to the car."

■ ■ ■

The Georgia Court of Appeals finally put to rest the case that sent King to Reidsville. The appeals court invalidated Judge Mitchell's twelve-month sentence and declared King's infraction a paid traffic violation. The Atlanta sit-ins, however, were not over. At the end of the monthlong truce, Mayor Hartsfield still had not secured an agreement to desegregate downtown stores. The students went back to the picket lines, with the KKK marching in opposition, but this time Daddy King was out there holding a sign with the students.

A deal was eventually reached with Mayor Hartsfield and white business owners in March, though desegregation would not happen until the fall of 1961, when Georgia schools were finally to be integrated after seven years of resistance to *Brown*. At the start of that school year, nine Black students would walk into formerly all-white high schools, and President Kennedy praised the fact that this occurred "with dignity and without incident." He asked other segregated school systems to "look closely at what Atlanta has done." Nor was racist violence able to deter the integration of the University of Georgia, the culmination of Donald Hollowell's work.

Days later, Black customers were seated in the Magnolia Room for the first time. Less than a year after students had displayed their willingness to risk their lives to integrate downtown Atlanta, that goal was calmly realized. As their struggle approached a kind of culmination, Lonnie King finally began to take stock of the stress he had been under for so long: he was diagnosed with an ulcer.

■   ■   ■

One especially important implication of the 1960 election was noted by A. S. "Doc" Young in the *Los Angeles Sentinel*: "Today, a Negro stands no chance for the presidency . . . because of cancerous racial prejudice. But certainly behind Kennedy's victory lies the suggestion that 25 or 50 years hence, particularly in view of the rising tide of color throughout the world, a Negro might occupy the White House, as head man." Bobby was ridiculed a few months after the new administration took office when he said much the same thing: "There's no question that in the next thirty or forty years a Negro can also achieve the same position that my brother has as President of the United States."

Having dedicated his life to creating equal opportunities for Black Americans in politics and other fields, Louis Martin would no doubt have been amazed to learn that the nation's first Black president would come from his Hyde Park neighborhood forty-eight years later and that he lived two blocks down Greenwood Avenue from where Martin watched Kennedy's victory with his family.

EPILOGUE: THE DUNGEON SHOOK

April 1968

Those nine days in late October were defined by the actions of men who were astonishingly young: King was only thirty-one, Wofford and Bobby were thirty-four, Shriver was forty-four, and JFK was forty-three. Louis Martin and Nixon were the oldest, aged forty-seven.

Nearly all of them would come together again one final time. This last meeting took place a long way from 1960, the year when three mavericks imagined that politics could be something different, something daring. Those intervening eight years seemed like a lifetime, but Martin Luther King would reunite them.

■　■　■

It was pouring in Atlanta that night. The city was bearing the brunt of the same storm system that had thundered down on Memphis's Mason Temple the night before, where Coretta King's husband promised they would reach the promised land—"though I may not get there with you." When the phone rang, Coretta was resting in bed after an afternoon of shopping with Yolanda for her Easter dress. It was Jesse Jackson; he reported that her husband had been shot. She wrote that she felt "not surprise, but shock—that the call I seemed subconsciously to have been waiting for all our lives had come." She was afraid to ask how serious it was. Minutes later, a call from Andrew Young confirmed the wrenching news: "Well, I tell you, it's pretty bad, and you need to come right away. He's not dead yet."

She was already thinking, this time Martin was gone. Within half an hour, Atlanta's mayor, Ivan Allen Jr., arrived at the house with his wife, offering to escort Coretta to the airport for a flight to Memphis. In a private waiting area at the Atlanta airport with King's secretary Dora McDonald, the mayor came to her and confirmed the devastating truth: King was gone. She turned around, to be back home with the children.

The Atlanta police chief, Herbert Jenkins, traveled through the drenching rain to inform Daddy King of his son's murder, while both men stood in the empty Ebenezer sanctuary. As it was for Coretta, this was news that shocked him in its timing, not its eventuality. He went home to tell Alberta. When he spoke to Coretta, he said, "I always thought I would go first."

For the next week, King's city would be the center of the nation. The Reverend Ralph Abernathy would evoke the book of Genesis: "Let us slay the dreamer, and see what shall become of his dream." As the news spread, thousands began to make plans to convene on a redbrick Baptist church in Sweet Auburn.

When the news reached him, Lonnie King was in Gaffney, South Carolina, helping the local school board implement integration. He canceled his evening meeting so he could return home.

Two days after Lonnie arrived in Atlanta, he found himself standing in a line of silent thousands, winding through the Spelman chapel to view the body of his friend, brought home the day after his death.

Lonnie had drifted away from direct action, leaving Atlanta for How-ard Law School, burned out from the student movement, and so he had seen little of King in the past six years. The last time they had actually talked was a few years before, when Lonnie was in Columbus, Ohio, de-livering a speech. Hearing King was coming to the area the next day, he stayed on and went up to King after his address, where they hugged and caught up on where life had taken the two of them. In the early months of 1968, whenever Lonnie was home visiting family, he took advantage of being able to hear King preach from the Ebenezer pulpit.

After meditating on the sight of King under a sheet of glass, ly-ing in a simple bronze and African mahogany casket, Lonnie went home. There he sat, distraught, when the phone rang. It was a voice he was surprised to hear, calm but firm. Coretta was on the line, asking him if he would be available to help organize the upcoming funeral at Ebenezer. A bit stunned, Lonnie asked what she meant.

The widow explained, "Wyatt Tee will be handling the pulpit ar-rangements, but I need someone at the church to handle all the logis-tics outside the church—who gets in, the lists of special guests . . ." She added there would be two funerals, one at Ebenezer, another in front of Morehouse, where Dr. Mays would offer the eulogy, and a long walk between the two, with 10,000 people expected to follow the casket (the actual crowd was later estimated to number 150,000).

Confused, given that he was not part of King's immediate staff, Lonnie replied, "Coretta, why are you asking me to do this? You have all these folks who worked for your husband."

She said simply, "Lonnie, would you do this for Martin?"

"Yes, ma'am." And so Lonnie reached out to old student organizing friends like Charles "Sit-Down" Black. Lonnie thought no one would be better at finding marshals for the march to the Morehouse campus quadrangle—a hunch confirmed when he learned Black was already working alongside Dr. Mays and other Atlanta University Center college leaders to train students to line the memorial route. The old networks were stirring back to life.

▪ ▪ ▪

Harris Wofford, by then president of SUNY Old Westbury, was speaking at a conference at Dartmouth College when the news arrived. Surrounded by strangers, Wofford sat down to take in his friend's fate on TV, recalling all the times King had eluded death. The screen showed Bobby Kennedy speaking at an open-air rally in Indianapolis. On a dark, rain-lashed night, the candidate for president stood on a flatbed truck under poor lighting, appearing shrunken in his flapping raincoat, his manner deliberately calm and straightforward. His mostly Black audience, gathered an hour before, had not yet heard that King was dead. Thus, Wofford heard the confirmation of King's death from a man of whom both he and King had long been wary.

Scrambling to leave New Hampshire to join the King circle, Wofford was haunted by the news clip that followed of words King had spoken in Memphis, looped over and over to fill hours of coverage: "And so I'm happy tonight; I'm not worried about anything; I'm not fearing any man. Mine eyes have seen the glory"—and here King reeled, suffering from a fever in the thundery heat of a city under a tornado watch, almost collapsing into the arms of Abernathy and Young, and concluding with the words—"of the coming of the Lord."

▪ ▪ ▪

On the night of the assassination, after hours of busy signals, Bobby finally got through to Coretta at nearly two in the morning and offered, along with his condolences, a couple of reassurances. He informed her that he had already ordered three new temporary phone lines to be installed at the King house on Sunset Avenue in the morning, and he wanted to make available to the family an airplane to fly her to Memphis the next day to bring home the body of her husband. Coretta thanked him for his help, saying later that year, "I felt that he was a friend." She continued, "I still had the feeling that my husband was at Reidsville and [Bobby] was concerned."

Bobby had said to Xernona Clayton, the King family friend who first answered his call, "My family has experience in this sort of thing."

Some SCLC staffers felt that accepting the offer of a plane was inappropriate given Bobby Kennedy's candidacy for president, but Coretta disagreed, later saying, "I don't really see anything wrong with it in this crisis period; one friend to another friend." In a later interview, she recalled the phone conversation she had had with Jack Kennedy eight years before. She felt that such reservations obscured an essential truth about the Kennedys: "Although they were political figures . . . they were human beings first, and their humanness reached out to the needs of other people."

This was not the first time the fateful 1960 call had found an echo in a later moment of crisis. When King was arrested while leading a march in downtown Birmingham in 1963, he was kept in isolation in the Birmingham jail without access to a lawyer or a phone to call his wife for nearly two days. Frightened, Coretta thought back to Kennedy's campaign call and phoned the White House for help. She received two calls from Bobby, then the attorney general, and one directly from Kennedy. The president said he was seeing to it that the Alabama authorities treated her husband fairly, and that she would soon be able to speak to King, which she did, fifteen minutes later.

In that phone conversation, after learning that the president had inquired if his wife was feeling well after giving birth to their daughter Bernice, King expressed appreciation for the president's assistance and was adamant that Coretta and his staff ensure that the press be informed that the call had taken place. With the Birmingham campaign slow to get off the ground, it was imperative to get the news out now that the Kennedy administration was at last paying attention. Within days, the nation would be unable to turn away from the images of the police dogs and fire hoses wielded by Sheriff Bull Connor and his men.

It seemed that what King had faced in Reidsville steeled him for solitary confinement in the Birmingham jail. King would write of those first nights, "You will never know the meaning of utter darkness until you have lain in such a dungeon, knowing that sunlight is streaming overhead and still seeing only darkness below." There he wrote the public letter that would become a defining document of the civil rights movement. Birmingham was a campaign that King chose and directed, using all that he had learned since Montgomery, proving against all odds that direct action could move a country to see his cause as nothing less than a response to a moral crisis. After two years of presidential diffidence—and at times indifference—the brutal news coming out of Birmingham convinced a young president that there was no going back. King's Birmingham campaign forced Kennedy out of his habitual caution and persuaded him, at last, to speak out in favor of civil rights legislation.

■   ■   ■

After being notified of King's death, President Johnson got on the line with his adviser Louis Martin and his aide Joseph Califano, asking them to gather as many Black leaders as they could at the White House the next morning. It would be the second time Martin spent the entire night at the White House—Kennedy's death being the first, when Martin helped a stunned Shriver prepare for the funeral of a man they had helped elect.

Reports of rioting following King's assassination came in from major cities, including neighborhoods only blocks away. When the White House meeting was convened, Martin was not present, having been held up at the gates by the Secret Service as they checked the trunk of his car. Finding golf clubs, they wondered if he might be part of the looting. So the vice-chair of the DNC, the man who had just placed Thurgood Marshall on the Supreme Court, waited while calls were made to put an end to the indignity.

Martin was pulled in many directions that week: working for a beleaguered president he still believed in; mourning a leader in King whom he deeply respected; and, as a father, having his daughter Anita's wedding reception at the Mayflower Hotel the night after the assassination. Despite everything, Louis Martin was intent on going to Atlanta no matter how much the president needed him.

■ ■ ■

While it looked as if all the world were going to descend on King's funeral, one man had reservations. Richard Nixon, favored to win the 1968 Republican nomination, convened his advisers and told them that while it was expected that candidates should pay their respects, he was having a momentary crisis of conscience. Nixon felt a pull to go, but, he said, "it's not credible. I mean, I don't—yes, he's a national leader, but I don't like taking advantage of going to a funeral and being there when Martin Luther King and I were not good friends."

Advisers argued that not attending would actually draw more attention to the reasons their friendship had ended than his joining the vast sea of dignitaries. Nixon called his stolid campaign manager, John Mitchell, who thought going would make him seem like "a prisoner of the moment," leaving unsaid the truth that holding on to southern delegates would be a lot easier if Nixon did not go. Much about their party had changed in the years since 1960. Jackie Robinson wrote in 1963 of fears that he and Morrow shared: "The danger of the Republican Party being taken over by the lily-whitest conservatives is more serious than many people realize." Goldwater supporters in Georgia would purge Black leaders like John Calhoun from the party leadership in 1964.

William Safire, however, offered a painful reminder of how Nixon's reluctance to act in 1960 had backfired. Still, Nixon argued that to attend would be "grandstanding." Safire reminded his boss that was exactly the word he had used when he had disappointed Jackie Robinson and Nixon did not want to make that same mistake again.

What if, Nixon wondered aloud, he flew down to Atlanta privately, without publicity, to pay a quick visit to Mrs. King, offer his condolences, and be done with it—leaving unsaid how similar to JFK's call to Coretta this gesture would be. His aide Dwight Chapin and his advance man Nick Ruwe were tasked with making it happen. Ruwe hired an Atlanta limousine driver and told him, "This can never be talked about."

The next afternoon, Ruwe drove Nixon and Chapin to the Kings' humble home in Vine City—a typical redbrick split-level, with the exception of the security bars over all the windows. Nixon was soon chatting with the four King children and then went to speak with Coretta in her bedroom. For three days, her bed had served as central planning for the Memphis march, the succession process at the SCLC, and the funeral. Mrs. King, propped up by pillows in bed and surrounded by telegrams and newspapers, was gracious as Nixon took her hand. After fifteen minutes, the candidate excused himself and said he was now going to visit Daddy King. He was there for half an hour and soon flying to Key Biscayne, feeling good about the effort. Late that evening, Nixon asked Chapin to come to his villa and said, "Dwight, how's our trip to Atlanta playing?"

Playing? Nixon had ordered it all to be private. Chapin went back to his room to figure out if the visit had leaked. One Atlanta reporter had picked up on the quick visit, but otherwise their plan had worked perfectly—silent as could be. When Chapin brought Nixon that news, the furious candidate exploded. "Damn it. I'm going to have to go back there and go to that funeral." Chapin made new flight and hotel reservations.

■   ■   ■

On Palm Sunday in Washington, two days before the funeral, Bobby's adviser Peter Edelman and his fiancée, Marian Wright, picked up the senator and his wife to head for the church of the Reverend Walter Fauntroy, a longtime friend of King's. As Edelman drove, they saw smoking hulks of buildings along street after street. More than twelve thousand National Guardsmen still patrolled D.C. neighborhoods. Parishioners on Ninth Street stepped over debris and broken glass. Eight

years after her Spelman sit-in days, Marian Wright was counsel to King's
Poor People's Campaign and an advocate for children in poverty. She
had just heard King speak at a Washington National Cathedral service
four days before his death, talking about his upcoming Poor People's
March. She would return to Atlanta for the sake of her "slain young
prophet."

When Ethel and Bobby arrived in Atlanta the next afternoon, they
first stopped by Sunset Avenue to visit with Coretta. Like his brother
when he made his fateful 1960 call, Bobby had never met her. The
limo pulled up to the King home in the late afternoon, and after greeting each of the King children, they were ushered back to Coretta's
bedroom.

There had been so many visitors to Coretta's bedside that it no
longer seemed odd to have Ethel and Bobby there. It was as if they had
known each other for years, and in a sense they had. Political violence
having racked both families, they understood realities few others had
experienced.

The night of his brother Jack's assassination, there had been a
haunting reminder of the events of late October 1960. A reporter from
Atlanta's WSB station asked Martin Luther King, "Many have said you
helped put President Kennedy in the White House. In light of what
has happened, do you regret that?"

King answered that night, "There are those who contend that
the Negro vote had a great deal to do with President Kennedy being elected, and that many Negroes were influenced to vote for the
President because of a call he made to my wife during an arrest here
in Georgia. Now, if this had anything to do with it, I certainly don't
regret it because I think President Kennedy made a most significant
contribution in civil rights."

After informing Coretta that their sister-in-law Jackie, despite usually avoiding public gatherings, would indeed be attending the service
and would stop by for a few minutes the next day, Bobby and Ethel
rose and offered a goodbye. Next came a meeting with King's devas-
tated advisers, one that Kennedy dreaded but knew was important

to face. The pain in the room at the Hyatt Regency was palpable, the assembled faces etched with confusion and suffering. Where were they to go next? What was even possible, with King gone, with cities going up in smoke?

Bobby simply said that he was running for president to make a difference, that they could not erase generations of injustice, but that they had to go forward, somehow, together. Much later, after the doors of Ebenezer were closed, the lines of mourners gone until dawn, John Lewis, who had joined Bobby's campaign, arranged for the Kennedys to have a private moment by the casket at three in the morning. They entered the darkened church, with a profusion of flowers and a few flickering candles by the body. Bobby and Ethel knelt, crossed themselves, and said prayers quietly. When they stepped back, Lewis had a moment to himself to say goodbye to a big brother, a teacher.

■ ■ ■

Before heading to Atlanta, Wofford decided that he wanted to join Mrs. King for the memorial march in Memphis itself, the day before the funeral. He asked his sixteen-year-old daughter, Susanne, to go with him. On this muted and mournful day, there was no repeat of the violence that had marred the march King led for Memphis garbage workers just a week before. Later, at the Memphis airport, the grieving family packed the plane flying home for the next day's nationally televised funeral. Wofford and his daughter joined them. In Atlanta, Wofford reflected on what a strange way it was to celebrate his own forty-second birthday.

Wofford never formally joined King's staff but had continued to work to further the aims of the movement after the 1960 election. He had hoped to lead the Department of Justice's Civil Rights Division, but Bobby decided that Wofford would always put King's interests above his brother's—a point Wofford didn't dispute. He was made special assistant to the president for civil rights instead. Though he arranged a few short, strained meetings between King and Kennedy, he felt the new administration would not dare push for civil rights, at least not in a substantive, legislative way.

From the second floor of the Executive Office Building, Wofford had looked out at the West Wing, where his requests for action had gone ignored for months. After a frustrating first year, he asked the president to let him work with Shriver on building the Peace Corps. Wofford recommended that Louis Martin take over his job, because they had already worked together to bring about quiet advances in civil rights through the executive branch. He thought Martin could provide the president with a perspective he needed to hear. Eventually, Wofford left for Ethiopia to manage the Peace Corps in Africa, though Kennedy did not take Wofford's advice about hiring Martin. It was on Ethiopian radio that Wofford listened to reports from Birmingham, feeling the ache of not being alongside King.

Wofford was back in America by 1965, when John Lewis and other marchers were being beaten in Selma on "Bloody Sunday." Clare's pleas could not keep Wofford from heading to Alabama, at last putting his body on the line alongside King. One afternoon, on the long march from Selma to Montgomery, Coretta noticed Wofford resting by the side of the road. Seeing him for the first time in years, she came over to chat and mentioned the 1960 call, saying of Kennedy, "They say that his call to me made the difference, that it elected him President. I like to think so. He was beginning to do so much, he and his brother."

■ ■ ■

As he had promised, just after sunrise and a sprinkling of April rain, Lonnie stood at the front door of the church, equipped with a long and growing list of special guests. Charles Black and other former student organizers, equipped with walkie-talkies just as they had been during their sit-in days, readied teams of students wearing gray armbands to restrain the crowds during the procession. Around ten o'clock, long lines of limousines began to appear, and student marshals, staffers, and police officers struggled to hold back the estimated thirty thousand people along the blocks surrounding the church so that special guests could enter. Lonnie's list was focused on the famous, starting with Harry Belafonte, who was to sit next to the King family. No one would be surprised to see him there, but Belafonte brought with him many other celebrities, including Jackie Robinson, Mahalia Jackson, Aretha Franklin, Charlton Heston, Marlon Brando, Stevie Wonder, and Berry Gordy.

But difficulties arose. "I let Nixon in. He was accompanied by Wilt Chamberlain, and you could tell Wilt! They weren't on the list to get in, but I let them in." Lonnie had to be careful, because he was being closely observed by hundreds, many frantic to enter. Louis Martin approached with Whitney Young, and Martin, as a powerful political official, was ushered in, while Young, a major civil rights leader as head of the National Urban League, was inexplicably not on the list. Luckily for Young, Lonnie remembered the former dean of the School of Social Work at Atlanta University and how he had supported the students. "Come round to the side," Lonnie said, bringing Young in through the basement. Lonnie's options were dwindling, "because by this time I couldn't let a lot of others in; I didn't want to piss off that many other people."

All of them, the famous and the obscure, overwhelmed the sanctuary and Ebenezer's basement Fellowship Hall. Outside, restless crowds jammed in for blocks around. People watched from rooftops and from on top of cars, or climbed up street poles and trees to get as close to the old church as possible. No one had anticipated such a turnout. Recent punditry to the effect that King was irrelevant, a man whose time had come and gone, now seemed absurd.

Wofford entered the already sweltering Ebenezer sanctuary with the King family. The smell of chrysanthemums and lilies suffused the room, and the choir shifted in the chancel, ready to sing the old hymns. He saw Abernathy ready to preside over the service, looking overwhelmed as more squeezed in. Wofford noted the presence of his friend Shriver, far from the row where Bobby sat. While they were family, Shriver's choice to remain in the Johnson administration, serving a president Bobby so thoroughly distrusted, had strained their bond. Although Eunice was busy campaigning for her brother, her husband was preparing to fly to Paris as Johnson's ambassador to France, hoping to help bring an end to the Vietnam War. Wofford regretted the tensions between these two men, both of whom he admired. The sense of estrangement extended to members of Bobby's staff, who would later push Shriver away when he attempted to help carry Bobby's casket off the plane from California following his assassination.

Louis Martin, meanwhile, sat thinking of King. He had once talked casually with him in the minister's small Sunset Avenue home during a three-hour visit to Atlanta in 1964 on political business. He was impressed by the minister's ability to focus completely on the person before him. When King was awarded the Nobel Peace Prize, Martin spontaneously booked a flight to see the presentation. Invited to a King family reception at their Oslo hotel, he broke into tears listening to Daddy King talk with pride about his son. Unlike his political bosses, who tended to see King as a problem to be handled, to Martin the young minister was "an apostle of love, love for all members of the human family." Martin worked with the administration to coordinate logistics for the March on Washington and helped arrange the meeting between President Kennedy and the organizers at the White House afterward.

Martin believed that the Reidsville incident was a "turning point in King's life." Yet it was a turning point for many, because before King, "for generations, blacks lived in mortal fear of jail." No one had seen a leader like him before—how he kept "standing up to them in a manner that had never been done." Martin thought this was why photographs of King in handcuffs were so affecting: "His ability to turn a jail term into a badge of honor thrilled blacks."

Even at this dark moment, Martin refused to submit to despair. True, as he said in a speech soon after, "Our time seems to be out of joint and we live in a worried world. We have troubles abroad and a crisis at our doorstep." However, he could also see the changes that King had helped to bring about, the way he had managed to shift, as he often said, that great mountain of racism. Martin said later that April, "I feel optimistic. I believe the facts indicate we are moving—however much we might be stumbling—toward a better day."

At the service, Wofford—thinking back over the thirteen exhilarating, fearful, and triumphant years he had known King—wondered, "How had it all come to this?" A tape of King's "Drum Major Instinct" sermon, in which he had eerily summed up how he wished his life of service to be remembered, finished playing over the loudspeakers. The casket was brought out through the throng and placed on a rickety wooden wagon, to be drawn by two mules during the four-mile procession. The silence of witnesses gathered ten-deep along the steamy sidewalks was broken only by the muffled clop-clop of the mules' hooves. Wofford and his daughter, Susanne, found their place near the front of the procession and followed in the midday sun. The rain had evaporated, ushering in a humid Georgia morning that would overwhelm many on the way to the Morehouse campus quadrangle.

As the celebrated guests emerged from the church, some left immediately, and others fell in line behind the family. Nixon had worked out a plan with his advance man to have a taxi ready so that he could slip out the back at the close of the service, but he had been seated up front. Then, with the other candidates for president within hearing, his supporter Wilt Chamberlain came and placed his hand on his shoulder. "Are you going to march with us?" Nixon looked shocked.

Though Nixon received occasional heckles, most of the dignitaries were simply absorbed into the thousands about to march behind King's casket. Standing next to Ethel, pregnant with their eleventh child, Bobby kept his head down, draped his suit jacket over his shoulder, and accepted a cold cola from a bystander. The crowd seemed to stir as he passed, excited by his presence. He was surprised by the reminiscences of King's friends, who described his sometimes ribald, joshing sense of humor. "I'm afraid I never saw that side of him," Bobby admitted.

The great procession, at long last, began to flow. In that Holy Week before Easter, Wofford felt it was right they were all advancing as one: "For Martin King marching was also a form of liturgy—a way of making words become flesh." He later recalled, "As we moved up a long slope towards Morehouse College, fifteen, twenty abreast, we could look back a mile or so upon a sea of people that stretched beyond the horizon, and memories went back to other marches in Montgomery, Albany, Birmingham, Washington, D.C., Selma, Chicago, rural Mississippi, and Memphis."

At a sharp turn, Nixon spied his taxicab waiting down a side street, and he began to move toward an escape. He turned to indicate to Chamberlain that he was going to head to the airport. Chamberlain asked, "Can I get a ride?"

The Republican candidate tried to detach himself from the march as inconspicuously as he could, though the crowd was perhaps tipped off by the presence of a seven-foot-tall basketball star with him. He and Chamberlain squeezed into a taxi and were gone. It had taken two trips, the result of many changes of mind, but he had done something that might finally put the disquieting shadow of this old relationship with King firmly behind him.

The vast crowd passed by the famous clock of Rich's department store before finally converging on the Morehouse quadrangle.

As King's casket was lowered into the ground at the South-View Cemetery, Abernathy's benediction could barely be heard over the rain, which had begun again. After five days of chaos in the public eye, at dusk that day the King family was finally allowed some privacy to grieve and retreat to Sunset Avenue. Cameras stopped clicking, reporters left to file stories, and out-of-towners dispersed, heading back to the airport or to hotels.

Bobby Kennedy gathered his family and staffers that night in his hotel suite after an exhausting day. As he entered the packed room, Wofford felt his faith in Bobby growing—Bobby, the man who had so offended him during their first meeting eleven years earlier and who had excoriated him in front of Louis Martin. All of that seemed unimportant now.

True, Bobby's Democratic primary campaign had been chaotic and halting. Kennedy might lose the upcoming Oregon primary to Eugene McCarthy and would still have to overcome Vice President Humphrey, who could swamp him at the upcoming Chicago convention. But this struggle was about more than just winning an election; if King had taught them anything, he had surely taught them that.

Bobby Kennedy walked up to Wofford, shirtsleeves rolled up, blue eyes hollowed out from exhaustion yet intent. "Could you put things aside and join the campaign in California?"

■ ■ ■

The term "October surprise" is often associated with Nixon's own machinations while seeking the presidency. In 1968, Nixon's lead over Humphrey had evaporated in the closing weeks of the campaign, and he once again faced the prospect of defeat. Nixon also suspected that President Johnson would announce peace talks in Paris to end the Vietnam War in the final days of October. So he set to work, seeking to secretly scuttle the talks and extend the war past Election Day. Johnson suspected Nixon was engaged in near treason, but did not say so publicly. The historian John Farrell recently discovered H. R. Haldeman's long-lost notes from a late-night call with Nixon in October 1968, during which the candidate ordered his staff to throw a "monkey wrench" into the talks. Little noticed at the time, those same penciled notes contain revelations about Nixon's true feelings toward the civil rights movement. The moderate Nixon of 1960 was, by 1968, nowhere to be found. In those notes, Nixon instructs Haldeman and his staff to convey to southern politicians that he would, if elected, retreat on civil rights; in fact, he would "lay off pro-Negro crap."

After making a bargain with Strom Thurmond, the South Carolina senator who epitomized segregation, Nixon locked arms with

him to help him to secure the nomination. Nixon brought together the moderate side of his party with the hard right and mastered the dark art of the racist dog whistle. He believed that words like "law," "order," "welfare," "busing," "giveaways," "quotas," "crime," and "violence" would resonate with his "silent majority." As his adviser John Ehrlichman reflected, "Nixon always couched his views in such a way that a citizen could avoid admitting to himself that he was attracted by a racist appeal." This time there would be no racial moderate like Lodge throwing out promises. Jackie Robinson, never reluctant to state his mind, said, "The GOP didn't give a damn about my vote or the votes—or welfare—of my people." He came to bitterly regret his campaigning and wrote, "The Richard Nixon I met back in 1960 bore no resemblance to the Richard Nixon as President."

In many ways, Nixon's views and policies created the political realities of today. The arrest of King is not only the fulcrum on which the 1960 election pivoted but the dividing line between a moderate Republican vice president and the president who reshaped a political order that divides us still. Nixon's intuitive genius for exploiting racial divisions, born in the final stretch of the 1960 election, maintains its hold over us.

By way of his "southern strategy," Nixon took America's explicit rhetoric of racism and smoothed down its rough edges in public so that the Republican Party, the party of Lincoln, the party that Frederick Douglass called "the deck, [when] all else is the sea," could turn the solid Democratic South red by 1972 and keep it that way for decades.

The 1960 campaign stayed in Nixon's mind, informing the choices he would later make over the course of a presidency haunted by the past. He never stopped believing that the Kennedys played dirtier than he had in 1960, and he resolved to never be outdone on that front again. Knowing that Lawrence O'Brien, a Kennedy strategist, was head of the DNC at the Watergate office complex ate away at him. Though he was ahead in the polls throughout his 1972 reelection bid, Nixon sank to a level of criminality that would ultimately destroy his presidency. At the worst moment of the impeachment proceedings, wondering if he

would go to prison for obstructing justice, Nixon remarked, "The best political writing in this century has been done from jail." One wonders if he thought, however uncharacteristically, of King.

Of all the October surprises over the years, the arrest of Martin Luther King was a singular occurrence. The distribution of the Blue Bomb remains an enviable campaign feat. There was certainly some amount of subterfuge involved—Kennedy's manipulation of Vandiver, and Stewart's coaxing of Mitchell—but the Kennedy campaign's response to the crisis, especially the actions of Wofford, Martin, and Shriver, was imbued by a true surprise for the standards of politics: an uncommon sense of decency. Years later, Wofford said that Shriver, more than anyone he had ever known (other than Barack Obama, who was assigned the old Senate seat where Wofford sat after he was elected to that body in 1991), should have been president. And he would smile when recalling Louis Martin, thinking of how much fun they had together.

The reality of King's travails throughout the 1960s, however, was altogether harsher. King was certain of one thing: that suffering need not be meaningless, that it could be redemptive. During one march in the midst of his Chicago campaign, he was struck in the head by a rock, causing him to stagger, but he kept walking. He said, "I have to do this—to expose myself—to bring this hate into the open." He said repeatedly over a decade that he had no instinct for martyrdom, that he wanted to live a full life, but that he knew something dark in American life was going to claim him. When a filmmaker asked King how a movie about him would end, King replied, "It ends with me getting killed."

When King was at the height of his powers, on the verge of that transformational year of 1963, when he triumphed in Birmingham and channeled that momentum into the March on Washington, his friend James Baldwin published a short but powerful letter to his teenage nephew, which he titled "My Dungeon Shook." Baldwin offered a

lacerating assessment of what had been done to Black Americans and where they found themselves. He told his nephew, "The details and symbols of your life have been deliberately constructed to make you believe what white people say about you. Please try to remember that what they believe, as well as what they do and cause you to endure, does not testify to your inferiority but to their inhumanity and fear." Baldwin reminded him that part of the tradition from "whence you come" consists of poets who sang the great spirituals: "One of them said, *The very time I thought I was lost, My dungeon shook and my chains fell off.*"

The lines quoted by Baldwin—the "dungeon shook"—are found in at least three "sorrow songs" (as W. E. B. Du Bois and Howard Thurman called them): "I Am Free" ("Remember the day, I remember it well"), "You Got a Right" ("We all got a right to the tree of life"), and "Free at Last," the spiritual invoked by King in the conclusion of his "I Have a Dream" speech. King knew that dungeons were often mentioned in the Bible (twenty-two times, in fact) and that they represent more than a simple jail cell: a dungeon is a dark place designed to crush the soul. King declared during his Chicago campaign that "jail cells are not dungeons of shame, they are havens of freedom and human dignity." To King, who evoked the image of a dungeon many times, it was not just a preacher's metaphor; it signified something bitterly real. It was a phrase he would use over and over in the eight years after Reidsville—each time real, each time shaken.

Though Andrew Young, a future mayor of Atlanta, was not yet on King's staff at the time of the Reidsville incident, he was one of the few people King ever talked with about those hours riding to the prison. Young recounted, "He shared very little; that was unusual because he talked constantly about other tragic things. He used to laugh and tell jokes about being stabbed in Harlem, and he used to talk about when people came to his house with guns." But his transfer to Reidsville? "It was the thing he talked about least, and I decided that was probably the time when he came close to a nervous breakdown. He thought he was going to his death; it was probably when he decided he would not live a long and comfortable life." Young traced King's "paralyzing fear of being alone in jail" back to Reidsville, writing, "Martin's sojourn at the Reidsville prison brought out the best in John Kennedy, but it left scars on Martin that never healed."

When Young heard of the South African activist Steve Biko's death in police custody seventeen years later, he thought of how King's ride to Reidsville could well have ended the same way. The prison was nothing less than "an old Christian idea of the dark night of the soul: the moment of ultimate despair and hopelessness, and you almost have to go through that to find faith." After Reidsville, Young thought King understood that his life "was going to be one challenge and confrontation after another, and in a way he sort of became comfortable with the idea of his own death after that. He would tell me, 'Oh yeah, you all don't know what it is to be at the door of death.'"

During their late-night conversations, Young realized that Reidsville "was crucial to his decision to push ahead regardless; I think he kind of made that decision that night."

■   ■   ■

Shriver had imagined that he would continue his political career in Illinois after helping the new administration during the transition, but the chance to found the Peace Corps became the greatest challenge of his life. He overcame his brother-in-law's skepticism and made the Corps into one of the most enduring accomplishments of Kennedy's short-lived administration. Johnson made full use of Shriver as well, conscripting him to take on the superhuman assignment of running his War on Poverty while continuing to lead the Peace Corps. Working sixteen-hour days for the next four years, Shriver created programs like Head Start, Job Corps, Legal Services, and VISTA.

Shriver's aspiration to hold elected office was always thwarted. Vice President Humphrey nearly picked Shriver as his running mate in 1968. By the time George McGovern selected Shriver to be the vice presidential nominee in his campaign against Nixon in 1972, the race had already been lost. Shriver ran for the presidency himself in 1976 but fared poorly, doomed by perceptions that the era of vigorous liberalism he personified was over. His biographer Scott Stossel writes that "a good case can be made that Shriver, through the programs he started and ran, and through the generation of public servants he inspired, may have positively affected more people around the world than any twentieth-century American who was not a President or other major elected official or Martin Luther King." Seeing Shriver only as the embodiment of Great Society liberalism is to miss his true impact. His influence remained creative and effective. With Eunice, he nurtured a small initiative serving a thousand special needs children into the worldwide Special Olympics.

Louis Martin was both a masterful insider and someone willing to be, in Bobby's words, a "bomb thrower." When King's Birmingham campaign was playing out, Martin told the president during a cabinet meeting, "We need dramatic action understood by Negroes as clearly as the picture from Birmingham of Negroes being attacked by police dogs." That was the day Martin believed Kennedy made up his mind to move on civil rights legislation. When a Department of Justice adviser proposed removing public accommodation protections from civil rights legislation during a meeting in Bobby's office in 1963, Martin told the staffers about an Italian restaurant up in Silver Spring turning away Black customers. Martin said, "If one of my daughters got turned down there, I'd shoot him. And I'm an old man, and if I feel like shooting someone or throwing a rock, what do you think about Negros who aren't trained?" To the shocked faces, Martin said, "I'm telling you, that public accommodation bill has got to go in there, or we're going to have one hell of a war in this country." The protections remained part of the final bill.

Martin left Washington after Nixon's victory in 1968 to return to editing in Chicago, feeling he had accomplished what he had set out to do. As the years passed, his wife, Gertrude, felt some frustration that Martin never asked for any credit. But Martin understood how to play the system—how to operate without notice while allowing others to win acclaim. So that the Black elected officials he mentored around the country would have the resources needed to advance their policies, Martin helped found the Joint Center for Political and Economic Studies. When President Carter was in political trouble, Vernon Jordan and Andrew Young advised him to bring Martin on board. As in the 1960 campaign, Martin considered himself "a pinch hitter," and he liked helping Carter. Ten years after he left the DNC, Martin finally had his office in the West Wing, and his White House log reveals that he was visited by Wofford there on several occasions.

Martin's and Shriver's correspondence continued for the rest of Martin's life. After reading an article that called Martin the "godfather of Black politics," Shriver wrote that he was the "godfather of many of the specific actions taken on behalf of better race relations in the U.S.A." After a stroke placed Martin in a wheelchair in the late 1980s, Shriver wrote, "Even though I am hoping your recovery continues to make great progress, I cannot help but say that it would be more fun for me if I had a chance to talk to you. To hear your voice would be a warm consolation." Martin came back to D.C. one more time to receive the DNC's Lawrence O'Brien Achievement Award at the Capitol. Shriver and Senator Wofford proudly joined Martin. Even though the old editor was physically frail, his wit and his smile seemed unchanged.

Martin was the first African American to become a close adviser of three sitting presidents. Frederick Douglass spoke only three times with Lincoln, and Morrow was often ignored by Eisenhower, but Martin managed to become an effective president whisperer. At a celebration of his and Gertrude's fiftieth wedding anniversary, Martin recounted being in a cab in Liberia when the driver mentioned a village built by Americans during World War II. Locals had been able to smell the good barbecue the American cooked. The cabbie said, "You Americans back home are in the same boat: you can smell it, but can't taste it." Martin said to the gathering, so overcome that he could barely get the words out, "The one thing that would give me the greatest joy in life would be to make certain that everyone has a taste."

When Martin died in 1997, Wofford and Shriver were on the honorary planning committee for the funeral and honorary pallbearers. Shriver spoke at both the ceremony at Howard University's Rankin Chapel and at the service in Los Angeles, to which his son Robert took him. Shriver said, "Kennedy would never have telephoned Coretta Scott King to express his concern about her husband's imprisonment if Louis had not produced the idea. That idea and Kennedy's action definitely changed the election results in Illinois. I was there, and know what I'm talking about." Vernon Jordan called Martin "the unsung, unheralded, and to some, unknown hero of our times."

Martin and Shriver both hailed Wofford's upset victory in the 1991 special election for a Senate seat representing Pennsylvania; Martin wrote in the *Defender* that his friend had "imagination and guts. He was the most liberal, practical idealist I had ever met. He knew how to get things done and he was straight on the race issue." Wofford ran a new kind of campaign by proclaiming that all Americans had a right to health care—an idea Bill Clinton borrowed the following year for his presidential campaign. Though President Clinton was not able to enact universal health care, Wofford is still seen as the candidate who made the idea politically credible, even if the backlash to Clinton's efforts cost Wofford reelection. One of Wofford's proudest moments as a senator was when he stood behind President Clinton in the Rose Garden for the signing of a bill he had introduced, with Representative John Lewis co-sponsoring it in the House of Representatives: the Martin Luther King Holiday and Service Act. With Martin Luther King III and Representative Lewis next to Wofford, the law turned MLK Day into a national day of service. After his Senate defeat, Wofford led the Corporation for National and Community Service (AmeriCorps) for the rest of Clinton's term.

Wofford would end up playing an unexpected role in a few more events in recent political history. When Barack Obama's presidential campaign was embroiled in controversy related to the Reverend Jeremiah Wright's sermons, Senator Obama needed to deliver the speech of his life in order to right the ship of his candidacy. He decided to speak candidly and forcefully about race in American life, just as Kennedy had addressed Houston evangelical ministers about his Roman Catholicism in 1960. Wofford introduced Obama in Philadelphia that day, saying he had waited a long time to meet someone he thought the country needed as badly as the Kennedys. Wofford quoted what King once told him about what he hoped to find in President Kennedy: intelligence, political skill, *and* moral passion. He told the 2008 audience that he believed King would agree that Obama possessed all three. President Obama would award Wofford the Presidential Citizens Medal in 2012.

Around this time, Lonnie King was working on a late-life PhD dissertation after a long career in business and government administration, and he decided to give Harris Wofford a call, unsure if he was alive. After leaving a message, Lonnie soon received a voice mail in return that said, "Is this the Lonnie King who almost got me fired?"

Lonnie called Wofford back, saying, "Yeah, I'm the one." Lonnie remained a member of Ebenezer Baptist Church, having returned to Atlanta from Washington and Baltimore to teach at Georgia State. He expressed wistfulness about having left civil rights activism, saying, "We put democracy on cruise control after the 1960s and the folks who were opposed to us . . . they put their efforts to block us into overdrive."

In 2017, Lonnie and Charles Black spoke to supporters of the DREAM Act in Atlanta about the effective use of nonviolence as these students undertook sit-ins at their universities. Lonnie would declare that he had one more battle in him when he ticked off statistics about unregistered young Black and Latino voters in Georgia. Even though he was in his eighties, he planned to partner with churches and colleges on a new Georgia Student Movement. He was determined to organize young people one more time, saying, with the broad smile that persuaded Julian Bond to help him start a movement, "That's my last hurrah."

His death in March 2019 assembled the surviving Atlanta Student Movement veterans once more at Ebenezer to celebrate the leader who first brought them together. Under his online obituary is a comment from Marilyn Pryce Hoytt, one of the two women who went with Lonnie and Dr. King to the Magnolia Room: "Well done, brave warrior."

The Sam Nunn Federal Center now stands on the site of Rich's department store, and it boasts a thirty-foot-tall mosaic in the lobby portraying Lonnie and Dr. King being arrested together.

■   ■   ■

Many historians and reporters crossed the threshold of Harris Wofford's West End home in Washington over the years, seeking a sense of what it was like to sit across from figures such as King and Kennedy—to have known them not as monuments but as young men facing difficult, sometimes overwhelming choices.

Wofford was one of the last living figures from that era, but he wore the responsibility lightly. True, he was a godfather of the national service movement in America, among other historic achievements, but he was also happy to talk about the beer with Louis Martin that likely changed the outcome of the 1960 election. He loved a good story, but like Lonnie he was more inclined toward the future than the past, eager to strategize as he once did with a minister from Montgomery. He remained relentlessly attuned to what was next. Wofford was proud to be part of another equal rights movement, when, five years after Clare's passing in 1996, the person he met and fell in love with was a man. After fifteen years together, he married Matthew Charlton, writing a *New York Times* op-ed about their union.

Wofford often walked through West Potomac Park, just off the National Mall, to where the new Martin Luther King Jr. Memorial stands. Wofford went there because he missed his friend. King's resolute face, emerging from the stone in which his figure is carved, stares across the Tidal Basin to where the Jefferson Memorial stands, a perfect symbol of the tortured history of race in America. The statue's determined look reminded Wofford of how King appeared when facing a hard decision.

It would be on Martin Luther King Day 2019 that Harris Wofford died at age ninety-two. His public memorial service was held at Howard University, where he went to law school, where he and Louis Martin brought Kennedy to speak, and where a service for Louis Martin was held.

King's words are paraphrased in carved relief on the wall of the memorial: "Out of the Mountain of Despair, a Stone of Hope." It was Louis Martin who said, "It wasn't just a job with me. I looked on it as a lever, to move the mountain of racism." Along with Shriver and Wofford, the team found an opening and pressed their point of maximum leverage.

When King faced down his fears of solitary confinement, when he was arrested more than twenty times, he was attempting to deliver Americans from the stony encasement of racism. The struggle to shatter that rock, to break free from it, takes courage and more:

> The very time I thought I was lost,
> My dungeon shook and my chains fell off.

Martin Luther King Jr. being greeted by his family as he disembarks the plane that brought him home from Reidsville to Atlanta

NOTES

ABBREVIATIONS

AC: *Atlanta Constitution*
ADW: *Atlanta Daily World*
AI: *Atlanta Inquirer*
AJ: *Atlanta Journal*
AJC: *Atlanta Journal-Constitution*
DHP: Donald Hollowell Papers
JFKL: John F. Kennedy Presidential Library
LMP: Louis Martin Papers, Library of Congress
Lonnie King, interview: Lonnie King interviews with the authors, 2017–2018
NYT: *New York Times*
PC: *Pittsburgh Courier*
RNL: Richard Nixon Presidential Library
Wofford, interview: Harris Wofford interviews with the authors, 2016–2017

EPIGRAPHS

vii   *"Martin told me"*: Young, *Easy Burden*, 175.
vii   *"And Dr. King can"*: Dorothy Cotton, interview in *King*, History Channel, 2008.

PROLOGUE

3   *Coretta Scott King eagerly waited*: King, *My Life with Martin Luther King Jr.*, 176–77.
3   *The dining room at Atlanta's Paschal's*: Frank Wells, "King Held on Old Count as Sit-Inners Leave Jail," *AC*, Oct. 24, 1960.
3   *The word from Mayor*: Ibid.; "Rich's Declines to Prosecute Pastor King on Sit-In Count," *AJ*, Oct. 24, 1960.

4 *She knew her visits*: Coretta said of her husband and his fear of prison, "He needed and depended upon the support of people he loved." King, *My Life with Martin Luther King Jr.*, 179.

5 *she were imprisoned with him*: Ibid., 176.

5 *plates of food*: Marilyn Pryce Hoytt, interview by Jeanne Law Bohannon, July 13, 2018, Atlanta Student Movement Project, Kennesaw State University (KSU).

5 *there was no sign of King*: King, *My Life with Martin Luther King Jr.*, 177.

5 *Student leaders ran out*: Gwendolyn Iles-Foster, interview by Junior and Senior Everest high school students, 2012, D. C. Everest Oral History Project.

6 *The sullen, stubborn attitude*: Abram, *Day Is Short*, 129.

6 *"We now await substantial"*: "Rich's Declines to Prosecute Pastor King on Sit-In Count."

6 *"You gotta wait, there's people"*: Lonnie King, interview.

6 *DeKalb was Klan country*: King, *My Life with Martin Luther King Jr.*, 177.

6 *brief newspaper stories*: "DeKalb Seeks to Jail Rev. King," *AC*, Oct. 21, 1960; "King Faces Year in Jail on Old Count," *AJ*, Oct. 21, 1960.

7 *the weight of responsibility for King's fate*: Lonnie King, interview.

7 *As King talked with his brother*: Otis Moss, interview by the authors, May 27, 2017.

7 *"M.L. will be all right"*: Branch, *Parting the Waters*, 357.

7 *"Why are you releasing us?"*: Dr. Herschelle Sullivan Challenor, interview by Jeanne Law Bohannon, Aug. 25, 2017, Atlanta Student Movement Project, KSU.

7 *under the terms of the agreement*: "Rich's Declines to Prosecute Pastor King on Sit-In Count."

7 *have Coretta call his lawyer*: Iles-Foster, interview by D. C. Everest students.

7 *One young woman, Carolyn*: Tatum, "Atlanta Student Movement Historical Trail to Be Unveiled with Interactive Markers."

7 *through the glass doors*: *AI*, Oct. 31, 1960.

8 *his son's enemies might strike*: King Sr., *Daddy King*, 157.

8 *"I think I should choose"*: Rieder, *Gospel of Freedom*, 5.

9 *Martin's role has largely been neglected*: Louis Martin, despite Wofford's interviews with the author, did not get a mention in Theodore White's *Making of the President, 1960*—considered the definitive work on the 1960 election. He received only two passing references in both Theodore Sorensen's *Kennedy* and Arthur M. Schlesinger's *Thousand Days*.

9 *"It wasn't just a job"*: Poinsett, *Walking with Presidents*, 11.

10 *"too-liberal-in-law"*: O'Reilly, *Nixon's Piano*, 195.

10 *"bureaucracy, routine, rules"*: Stossel, *Sarge*, xv.

"IN TROUBLE"

11 *"We're in trouble with Negroes"*: Wofford, *Of Kennedys and Kings*, 47.

12 *most of any Republican*: Rigueur, *Loneliness of the Black Republican*, 311. As a swing voting community, Black Americans were evenly split in party identification by the first half of the 1940s, although Roosevelt hovered around 70 percent of the Black vote in his final three elections. Black voters went for Roosevelt by 71 percent in 1936, 67 percent in 1940, and 68 percent in 1944.

13 *connection with King*: Harris Wofford, interview by Berl Bernhard, #1, Nov. 29, 1965, JFKL.

13 *"good people, the right people"*: Martin Luther King, interview by Berl Bernhard, March 9, 1964, JFKL.

14 *for King's 1958 book*: Carson et al., *Papers of Martin Luther King Jr.*, 4:29.

14 *"You're making a big mistake"*: Belafonte, *My Song*, 215.

14 *"The time you've spent"*: Raymond, *Stars for Freedom*, 88.

15 *"had never really had the personal"*: King, interview by Bernhard, JFKL.

15 *"I don't think that it was a matter"*: Guthman and Shulman, *Robert Kennedy in His Own Words*, 66. Kennedy's quotation to a Black dentist on the campaign trail was "Doctor, I don't know

five Negroes of your caliber well enough to call them by their first names. But I promise to do better." Bryant, *Bystander*, 24–25.

15 *"Something dramatic must be done"*: King, interview by Bernhard, JFKL.

15 *Wofford got to work*: Wofford, *Of Kennedys and Kings*, 12–13.

16 *A bleak, open-plan office*: Ibid., 61; Lebovich, "Pelli's Renewed Investment Building."

16 *a substantive, civil-rights-focused*: Bryant, *Bystander*, 153; Sargent Shriver, interview by Anthony K. Shriver, *Kennedy's Call to King: Six Perspectives*, fall 1988, Independent Study, Georgetown University, JFKL Oral History Program.

16 *"cold as fish"*: Shriver, interview by Anthony K. Shriver, JFKL.

16 *lacked the national stature needed*: Harris Wofford, interview by Anthony K. Shriver, *Kennedy's Call to King*.

16 *bring on someone new*: Wofford, interview.

16 *inviting Martin to a Black advisory*: Louis Martin notebook and memoir draft, LMP.

17 *"We should work for"*: Louis E. Martin, interview by Ronald Grele, March 14, 1966, JFKL.

17 *"get into the act"*: Ibid.

17 *One meeting would end up*: Louis Martin, interview by David McComb, May 14, 1969, University of Texas Oral History Project, LBJ Library Oral History Collection.

17 *"mighty late in the day"*: Poinsett, *Walking with Presidents*, 73.

18 *"You don't know anything!"*: Lemann, *Promised Land*, 113.

18 *"You're talking about what we"*: Poinsett, *Walking with Presidents*, 73.

18 *"Don't have any relations"*: Harris Wofford, interview by Larry Hackman, May 22, 1968, #2, JFKL.

18 *"offend our good Southern friends"*: Wofford, *Of Kennedys and Kings*, 61.

18 *"Uncle Tom's Cabin"*: Ibid. In his unpublished autobiography draft, Martin discusses his respect for Dawson and particularly how he built his Chicago political organization.

18 *"You know, this man"*: Martin, interview by Grele, #1, JFKL.

19 *"Wait a minute, I wish"*: Poinsett, *Walking with Presidents*, 73.

19 *Martin's ability to speak Bobby's*: Wofford, interview. Wofford concluded that Martin "was able to deal with an Irish Mafia, talking their language, sort of rough." Bobby himself later said, "Louis Martin was the best, had the best judgment. I talked to him a lot. Harris Wofford was consulted, but he didn't have nearly the judgment that Louie Martin did." Guthman and Shulman, *Robert Kennedy in His Own Words*, 72.

19 *"If you want it"*: Martin, interview by Grele, #1, JFKL.

19 *The campaign manager's immediate trust*: John Seigenthaler, interview by Larry Tye, shared with the authors; Guthman and Shulman, *Robert Kennedy in His Own Words*, 72.

19 *Martin would walk out*: Louis Martin handwritten memoir draft, LMP.

19 *Martin and Wofford's desks*: Louis Martin notebook and handwritten memoir draft, LMP; Wofford, interview.

19 *Many nights, the two of them*: Shriver, interview by Anthony K. Shriver, JFKL; Wofford, interview by Hackman, #2, JFKL.

19 *going to Mass with Shriver*: Martin notebook and handwritten memoir draft, LMP. Martin rented a room in a Southwest waterfront building where several other Kennedy staffers stayed.

20 *He admired Martin's ability*: Wofford, *Of Kennedys and Kings*, 60.

20 *now he was on the phone each day*: Martin notebook and handwritten memoir draft, LMP.

20 *respected Wofford's knowledge of young*: This and Martin's other observations on Wofford are also from his notebook and memoir draft.

21 *Toni says they were hardly rich*: Dr. Toni Martin, interview by the authors, May 16, 2017.

21 *he showed up at the University*: Poinsett, *Walking with Presidents*, 5.

22 *"quicksand of racial relations"*: Martin notebook, LMP.

22 *forum on human rights at Howard University*: Martin, interview by Grele, #1, JFKL. The CRS's Frank Reeves, a professor at Howard, used his connections to have the CRS announce a "workshop

on human rights" to be held on the campus in the middle of the campaign. As a nonpartisan institution, the college felt it would need to invite Nixon as well, but the vice president declined (as the CRS had anticipated). Located past the university's old gates, up the hill off D.C.'s Sixth Street, Rankin Chapel's sanctuary still possesses a kind of intimacy, and one senses its history as a place where students spoke for equality, where great theologians and future leaders prayed and sang.

22 *This was the first time that Martin*: Martin notebook, LMP.

22 *"I regret that the Republican"*: Papers of John F. Kennedy, Pre-presidential Papers, Senate Files, Speeches and the Press, Speech Files, 1953–1960, Howard University, Washington, D.C., Oct. 7, 1960, JFKSEN-0912–058, JFKL.

22 *Leaving the campus, they were*: Martin notebook, LMP.

23 *Voter turnout would be*: U.S. Elections Protect, "National General Election VEP Turnout Rates, 1789–Present," www.electproject.org/national-1789-present; Flanigan et al., *Political Behavior of the American Electorate*, 73.

24 *It had taken him years*: Morrow, *Black Man in the White House*, 295.

24 *arrange White House parking spots*: Ibid., 123–24.

25 *"One hundred years ago today"*: Ibid., 295.

25 *"in a rear car"*: Ibid., 296.

25 *it was Nixon who went*: Ibid., 239–41; Morrow, *Forty Years a Guinea Pig*, 185–87.

25 *a 1959 Jet survey*: Rigueur, *Loneliness of the Black Republican*, 36.

26 *Nixon's midnight deliberations*: Morrow, *Black Man in the White House*, 293.

26 *pews, to observe Jackie Robinson*: Martin notebook and memoir draft, LMP; Louis E. Martin, interview by Ronald Grele, #2, April 7, 1966, JFKL.

27 *"I intend to cover"*: "Jailed," *Baltimore Afro-American*, Oct. 15, 1960.

27 *With Robinson crisscrossing the country*: Robert Healy, "Nixon Woos New Jersey Negroes," *Boston Globe*, Oct. 9, 1960.

28 *Georgians cheering for him*: White, *Making of the President, 1960*, 268–72.

28 *"The South is the wave"*: Thurber, *Republicans and Race*, 120–21.

28 *King and Nixon had first met*: Morrow, *Forty Years a Guinea Pig*, 117–18.

29 *"You're Dr. King. I recognized"*: King, *My Life, My Love, My Legacy*, 76–77.

29 *"rich fellowship . . . and fruitful"*: Nixon to King, Aug. 30, 1957, King, Martin Luther, Correspondence, 1957–1962, Pre-presidential Papers Collection 320, box 22, RNL.

30 *"To my friend"*: Kotlowski, *Nixon's Civil Rights*, 160.

30 *"My only regret"*: Frank, *Ike and Dick*, 154.

30 *"terribly distressed to learn"*: Nixon to King, Sept. 22, 1958, King, Martin Luther, Correspondence, 1957–1962, Pre-presidential Papers Collection 320, box 22, RNL.

30 *"It is altogether possible"*: Carson, *Autobiography of Martin Luther King Jr.*, 149.

"YOU CAN'T LEAD FROM THE BACK"

32 *"It might even mean"*: Carson et al., *Papers of Martin Luther King Jr.*, 3:462.

32 *"I need your help"*: Belafonte, *My Song*, 149–50.

32 *"People will expect me"*: King, *My Life with Martin Luther King Jr.*, 138.

32 *"the zenith of my career"*: Garrow, *Bearing the Cross*, 660.

33 *"the general strain of being known"*: Lewis, *King*, 109.

33 *"a pretty unprepared symbol"*: Loudon Wainwright, "Martyr of the Sit-Ins," *Life*, Nov. 7, 1960.

33 *"I can't afford to make"*: King, *My Life with Martin Luther King Jr.*, 158.

34 *American version of Gandhi's Salt March*: Branch, *Parting the Waters*, 259.

34 *The New York Times wrote*: Claude Sitton, "Negro 'Stand-Ins' Staged in South," *NYT*, Oct. 4, 1960.

34 *When describing King in 1960*: "Dr. King Attacks Apathy on Rights," *NYT*, Sept. 7, 1960; "14 Negroes Jailed in Atlanta Sit-Ins," *NYT*, Oct. 20, 1960.

35 *"anyone, including King, who comes"*: Carson et al., Papers of Martin Luther King Jr., 5:21.

35 *"He's not coming to cause"*: Garrow, *Bearing the Cross*, 128.

35 *In December 1959, King junior*: Sullivan, *Freedom Writer*, 196.

36 *King voted Republican*: Farrington, *Black Republicans and the Transformation of the GOP*, 91.

36 *At an event held at Mount Zion*: "Many Ministers Endorse the Republican Candidates," *ADW*, Oct. 11, 1960.

36 *"hypocritical" on the subject*: "Dr. King Attacks Apathy on Rights."

37 *Wofford's turn to assert himself*: Martin notebook, LMP.

37 *"the icing on the cake"*: Louis Martin used this phrase on multiple occasions, such as Martin, interview by Grele, #2, April 7, 1966, JFKL; Louis Martin to Anthony K. Shriver, *Kennedy's Call to King*.

37 *"tremendously scared of losing white"*: Wofford to Anthony K. Shriver, *Kennedy's Call to King*.

37 *instead of explicitly evoking "civil rights"*: Wofford, *Of Kennedys and Kings*, 63.

37 *"Kennedy can't win"*: Farrington, *Black Republicans and the Transformation of the GOP*, 93.

38 *"It took courage to call this conference"*: Wofford, *Of Kennedys and Kings*, 64.

38 *"This is the next President!"*: Martin notebook, LMP.

38 *"Are we going to vote"*: U.S. Senate, *Speeches, Remarks, Press Conferences, and Statements of Senator John F. Kennedy, Presidential Campaign of 1960, August 1 Through November 7, 1960*, 580.

38 *"Careful, Jack!"*: Branch, *Parting the Waters*, 344.

38 *"hit like a bomb"*: Martin, interview by Grele, #2, JFKL; Martin notebook, LMP.

39 *"I will attempt to appoint"*: Edward C. Burks, "Negro in Cabinet Pledged by Lodge," *NYT*, Oct. 13, 1960.

39 *"Whoever recommended that Harlem speech"*: Edward C. Burks, "Pledge on Negro Diluted by Lodge," *NYT*, Oct. 14, 1960.

39 *"move decisively toward the integration"*: Draft in Speeches and Writings File, LMP.

39 *"Can I get you to go"*: Lonnie C. King Jr., "On Student Movements and the Civil Rights Movement," Feb. 18, 2012, University of Georgia School of Social Work.

40 *Lonnie believed that if the students*: Lonnie King, interview.

40 *with the family of Howard Zinn*: Zinn, *Southern Mystique*, 132–34. Along with the Atlanta University math professor Dr. Lonnie Cross, an unaffiliated group of students also sat in at Rich's Barbeque Grill on March 5 and after that joined the efforts of the Committee on Appeal for Human Rights.

40 *"If you bring your Black ass"*: Lonnie King, interview.

40 *That was fine with Lonnie*: Ibid.

41 *"Remember that both history and destiny"*: Carson et al., *Papers of Martin Luther King Jr.*, 5:370.

41 *"Let us not fear going"*: Ibid., 369.

41 *"You're not merely demanding a cup"*: Ibid., 415.

41 *"There's something almost holy"*: Lefever, *Undaunted by the Fight*, 42.

42 *In mid-May, Lonnie led*: Gene Britton and Bruce Galphin, "Negro Marchers Diverted to Church," *AC*, May 17, 1960.

42 *The students had invited Dr. King*: Branch, *Parting the Water*, 301–2.

42 *"They were concerned we were"*: Lonnie King, interview.

42 *"If you had been from Mars"*: Lonnie King, interview by Bob Short, Reflections on Georgia Politics Oral History Collection, ROGP 086, Richard B. Russell Library for Political Research and Studies, University of Georgia Libraries, Athens; Kuhn, "There's a Footnote to History!," 587. The historian Clifford Kuhn's article on the 1960 King incident remains an excellent overview, and his interview with Ernest Vandiver was particularly groundbreaking, but we note one disagreement. Kuhn was skeptical of Lonnie King's claims of planning to influence the election, given the impossibility of anticipating how DeKalb County would claim King and send him to Reidsville, prompting a reaction from Kennedy. But Lonnie King was clear that all these outcomes surprised him (Lonnie thought Nixon would be the one to respond). We believe that

testimonies from student movement colleagues such as Otis Moss, about sending telegrams to the candidates concerning how King had been arrested in Atlanta with them (as planned), affirm that Lonnie foresaw that their sit-in could bring the issue of civil rights to the attention of the presidential campaigns.

42 *"this issue of civil and human"*: Lonnie King, interview by Jeanne Law Bohannon, July 19, 2017, Atlanta Student Movement Project, KSU.

43 *"The human rights for which"*: Carson et al., *Papers of Martin Luther King Jr.*, 5:538. The students' work on the Atlanta Student Movement was distinct from that of the SNCC, but many of the same Atlanta students were also involved in this growing national initiative.

43 *a message from Nixon*: "Kennedy Aided Truce in Atlanta Freeing 22 Sit-In Demonstrators," *NYT*, Oct. 24, 1960.

43 *"great suffering" soon to come*: "King Warns of Great Suffering," *Chicago Daily Defender*, Oct. 17, 1960.

43 *"If he stayed on the sidelines"*: Lewis, *Walking with the Wind*, 120.

43 *Six students followed King*: Branch, *Parting the Waters*, 346.

44 *"M.L., you don't need to go!"*: Ibid., 348.

44 *"I've learned that Nixon"*: Wofford, interview.

44 *"Do you really feel you"*: Harris Wofford to Taylor Branch, interview notes, Wofford Folder 957, Taylor Branch Papers #5047, Southern Historical Collection, Wilson Library, University of North Carolina at Chapel Hill.

44 *"To hell with that, Nixon"*: Wofford, interview by Bernhard, #1, JFKL.

45 *"No. You can't possibly"*: Wofford, interview.

45 *"I'm in a real jam"*: Ibid.

45 *"I have to participate now"*: *Harris Wofford: Slightly Mad*, dir. Jacob Finkel, Corporation for Civic Documentaries, 2017, documentary.

46 *"call M.L. and just remind him"*: Lonnie King, interview.

46 *"Just tell him that I asked"*: Lonnie King, interview by Bob Short, University of Georgia Libraries.

46 *came not from King's own fears*: Lonnie King, interview.

46 *Her strengths complemented Lonnie's*: Ibid.

47 *"M.L., let me say something"*: King, "On Student Movements and the Civil Rights Movement."

47 *DeKalb police spotted this Black man*: DHP; Gladney, *How Am I to Be Heard?*, 301. Police pulled King over on Clifton Road between North Decatur Road and Haygood Drive.

48 *"You and I are going down"*: Lonnie King, interview.

48 *"This is your hometown"*: Lonnie C. King, interview by Emilye Crosby, Civil Rights History Project, Library of Congress.

48 *"M.L., you can't lead from"*: Lonnie King, interview.

48 *"L.C., what time do you want"*: Lonnie King, interview by Bob Short, University of Georgia Libraries.

48 *"Ten o'clock on the bridge"*: Lonnie King, interview.

48 *readers of the* Atlanta Daily World: Taschereau Arnold, "Nixon and Lodge Endorsed by Bapt. Ministers Union," *ADW*, Oct. 19, 1960.

49 *telegram both Kennedy and Nixon*: Lonnie King, interview.

DAY 1: WEDNESDAY, OCTOBER 19

51 *Gallup's most recent poll*: Gallup, *Gallup Poll*, 1687.

51 *After working a night shift*: Lonnie King, interview.

52 *"the most rewarding experience"*: Lonnie King, "Cell Block No. 1–East-2," *AI*, Oct. 24, 1960.

52 *"We're not going to a funeral"*: "Sit-Ins Begin Here October 19," *AI*, Oct. 24, 1960.

52 *Martin Luther King was right where*: Descriptions of the October 19 sit-in are drawn from the King trial transcript in the DHP; *AJ*, Oct. 19, 1960; *AC*, Oct. 20, 1960; *ADW*, Oct. 20, 1960;

AI, Oct. 24, 1960, and interviews with Lonnie King. Specific quotations and additional sources listed. The King trial transcript in DHP allows for the first time a reconstruction of dialogue between King and the Rich's staff leading up to his arrest.

52 *They looked impressive*: With sisterly affection, Herschelle Sullivan later chuckled at how "the two muckety mucks, the two Kings, were at Rich's." She did not begrudge the two leaders the marquee sit-in target, because King was their inspiration and Lonnie was, as she said, "without doubt the singular leader of the Atlanta student movement." Herschelle Challenor, interview by Vicki Crawford, June 14, 2017, King Collection Oral History, Morehouse College.

52 *The Crystal Bridge had been built*: Clemmons, *Rich's*, 92–93.

53 *"a sit-in exercise as coordinated"*: "Negroes Sit-In at 8 Stores," *AJ*, Oct. 19, 1960.

53 *Picking up a ham and cheese*: Ibid.

53 *"We don't serve colored"*: Otis Blackshear, interview by Mike Mandel, Aug. 16, 1999, as quoted at the Sam Nunn Federal Center exhibit on the former site of Rich's department store.

53 *"a tree falling in the forest"*: Challenor, interview by Crawford.

53 *"Because the students asked me"*: "Negroes Sit-In at 8 Stores."

53 *"I am not the leader"*: Bruce Galphin and Keeler McCartney, "King, 51 Others Arrested Here in New Sit-In Push," *AC*, Oct. 20, 1960.

53 *"The decision as to when"*: "Negroes Sit-In at 8 Stores."

53 *"Until we get arrested or served"*: Ibid.

53 *Long's father was*: Jones, "Activist Gene."

53 *As everything shut down*: Lonnie King, interview.

54 *Four national chain stores*: "Negroes Sit-In at 8 Stores."

54 *A middle-aged man kicked*: "Sit-Ins Begin Here October 19."

54 *"The fountain is closed"*: "Negroes Sit-In at 8 Stores."

54 *the NAACP chose Hollowell*: Daniels, *Saving the Soul of Georgia*, 95.

54 *he or she sent word*: Charles Person, interview by the authors, May 12, 2017.

55 *Stone Mountain Ku Klux Klan*: "Formations' Observed: Tension, Action, Humor, Seen," *AJ*, Oct. 20, 1960.

55 *"a beautiful black mess"*: "Sit-Ins Begin Here October 19."

55 *waved his KKK card*: Galphin and McCartney, "King, 51 Others Arrested Here in New Sit-In Push."

55 *"astonishment, uneasiness, or dislike"*: "Formations' Observed: Tension, Action, Humor, Seen."

55 *"More power to you"*: "Sit-Ins Begin Here October 19."

55 *to take a nurse's exam*: Galphin and McCartney, "King, 51 Others Arrested Here in New Sit-In Push."

55 *Back at Rich's, Benjamin Brown*: "Sit-Ins Begin Here October 19."

55 *Lonnie had observed the Magnolia*: Lonnie King, Oral History interview, King Collection, Morehouse College.

55 *The glow of the crackling fireplace*: Clemmons, *Rich's*, 78–79.

55 *"Which of these organizations"*: This and the exchange that follows come from "Negroes Sit-In at 8 Stores."

56 *"1–2–3–4 don't shop"*: Ibid.

56 *"Now I'm handling this"*: Ibid.

56 *two elegant roommates embodied*: Blondean Orbert, interview by Jeff Clemmons, shared with the authors.

57 *"If you're going to participate"*: Lefever, *Undaunted by the Fight*, 66.

57 *"It was time for Jim Crow"*: Weaver, "Auburn University Student Recalls Being One of MLK Jr.'s Foot Soldiers."

57 *"sit at a little old nasty counter"*: Lefever, *Undaunted by the Fight*, 66.

57 *had a Rich's card*: Orbert, interview by Clemmons.

57 *Pryce could observe ladies*: Hoytt, interview by Bohannon, Atlanta Student Movement Project, KSU.

57 *Rich started to cry*: Raines, *My Soul Is Rested*, 90.

57 *work with the older Black leaders*: Sally Rich, interview by the authors, June 28, 2017.

57 *"We are sorry"*: This and the exchange that follows come from the King trial transcript, DHP.

59 *"Dear God, please don't let"*: Constance Curry unpublished memoir chapter, "Circle of Trust," provided to the authors.

59 *"could have done her in"*: Lonnie King, interview.

59 *"We want to sit down"*: "Negroes Sit-In at 8 Stores."

59 *"A house divided cannot stand"*: "14 Negroes Jailed in Atlanta Sit-Ins."

59 *Lonnie felt that Little could barely contain*: Lonnie King, interview.

60 *Other sit-in groups*: Richard Ramsay, "Atlanta Report," Oct. 19, 1960, *Southern Regional Council Papers*, series 4, reel 142.

60 *"The tin body of the wagon"*: Ibid.

60 *"I can't go to jail"*: Ibid.

61 *Judge James Webb was not*: Galphin and McCartney, "King, 51 Others Arrested Here in New Sit-In Push."

61 *Hollowell had been a buffalo soldier*: Daniels, *Saving the Soul of Georgia*, 16. Hollowell's background comes from ibid., as well as Hollowell and Lehfeldt, *Sacred Call*.

61 *"I was treated with less dignity"*: Daniels, *Saving the Soul of Georgia*, 19.

61 *He arrived in Atlanta*: Ibid., 30–31.

61 *He endured judges who turned*: Ibid., 6.

61 *getting a Black man, Willie Nash*: Ibid., 35–43; Hollowell and Lehfeldt, *Sacred Call*, 100–103.

62 *foremost civil rights lawyer*: Daniels, *Saving the Soul of Georgia*, 8, 94.

62 *"King is our leader"*: Ibid., 87.

62 *a chart on yellow notepad*: DHP.

62 *"What kind of trouble"*: Women of the Atlanta Student Movement, 2017 Women's History Month Finale Panel, March 31, 2017, KSU, soar.kennesaw.edu/bitstream/handle/11360/2407/WHM2017-transcription.pdf.

62 *"'Not guilty,' you damn fool"*: Raines, *My Soul Is Rested*, 86.

62 *getting them out of jail*: Daniels, *Saving the Soul of Georgia*, 87, 94.

63 *Lonnie's high school classmate*: Jordan, interview by the authors, June 23, 2017.

63 *"Man, have you lost your mind?"*: Lonnie King, interview.

63 *Hollowell had not known Dr. King long*: Hollowell and Lehfeldt, *Sacred Call*, 132–33.

63 *Judge Webb ruled that he must begin*: "Sit-Ins Begin Here October 19."

63 *Hollowell had gathered enough information*: Galphin and McCartney, "King, 51 Others Arrested Here in New Sit-In Push."

64 *some of Hollowell's clients did not*: Orbert, interview by Clemmons.

64 *King drafted in a blue-lined notebook*: Carson et al., *Papers of Martin Luther King Jr.*, 5:522. The lender's name is not recorded, but in another person's handwriting is the title "Great Issues," a Morris Brown College class that fall.

64 *"I will stay in jail"*: "Martin Luther King in Jail Over Sit-Ins," *York Dispatch*, Oct. 20, 1960.

65 *"a moral issue that needs"*: Galphin and McCartney, "King, 51 Others Arrested Here in New Sit-In Push."

65 *"This was a planned demonstration"*: Ibid.

65 *"We prefer jail to life"*: John Britton and Paul Delaney, "36 Bound Over to Criminal Court Following Downtown 'Counter' Demonstrations," *ADW*, Oct. 20, 1960.

65 *"If there is anywhere in the world"*: Galphin and McCartney, "King, 51 Others Arrested Here in New Sit-In Push."

65 *"If you persist in such vile"*: Ibid.

66 *"There was no question"*: Ramsay, "Atlanta Report," Oct. 19, 1960.

66 *Fifty-two protesters had appeared*: Galphin and McCartney, "King, 51 Others Arrested Here in New Sit-In Push"; Margaret Shannon, "25 Negroes, White Lectured, Jailed," *AJ*, Oct. 21, 1960.

66 *Lonnie was proud of the number*: "Jail, No Bail Group in Jail, Cheerful, Confident," *AI*, Oct. 24, 1960.

66 *dirt crusted so deep*: Person, interview by the authors.

67 *"You got a chance to bail out"*: Ibid.

67 *"smallest, dirtiest, dankest jail"*: Orbert, interview by Clemmons.

67 *Lonnie could not believe*: Lonnie King, interview.

68 *"They're too young"*: Raleigh Bryans, "Negroes Count on Atlanta as Moderate, Dr. King Says," *AJ*, Oct. 20, 1960.

68 *from an unlikely source*: "Did a Phone Call Elect Kennedy President?," *Negro Digest*, Nov. 1961.

68 *he was struck by the testy rivalry*: Martin memoir draft, LMP.

68 *New England private schools and summers*: Marjorie McKenzie Lawson, interview by Ronald J. Grele, Oct. 25, 1965, JFKL; Belford V. Lawson, interview by Ronald J. Grele, Jan. 11, 1966, JFKL.

68 *"look silly"*: Wofford, interview by Anthony K. Shriver, JFKL.

68 *arrange a meeting with King*: Marjorie Lawson, interview by Grele, #2, JFKL; Wofford, interview by Bernhard, #1, JFKL.

68 *she felt doubly marginalized*: Marjorie Lawson, interview by Grele, #2, JFKL.

69 *"the heart organizing and directing"*: Wofford, interview by Hackman, #2, JFKL.

69 *"more and more the strong man"*: Frank Reeves, interview by John F. Stewart, March 29, 1967, JFKL.

69 *The circumstances under which Reeves*: "Did a Phone Call Elect Kennedy President?"

69 *Abernathy, who had been arrested*: "Attempt Made on Life of SCLC Exec," *Tri-State Defender* (Memphis), Oct. 28, 1960; "Police, Gunmen Harass Vote Denial Witness, FBI Told," *Baltimore Afro-American*, Oct. 22, 1960; "Police Arrest 'Rights' Leader," *Los Angeles Sentinel*, Oct. 20, 1960.

69 *secure an endorsement from King*: "Did a Phone Call Elect Kennedy President?"; Reeves, interview by Stewart, JFKL.

69 *Reeves phoned Wofford to tell him*: Martin, interview by Grele, #1, JFKL.

70 *"How many votes will this"*: Martin notebook, LMP.

70 *"You don't know that sonofabitch"*: Ibid.

70 *"Instead of answering directly"*: Martin, interview by Grele, #1, JFKL.

70 *"Now you see why he's a leader"*: Martin notebook, LMP.

70 *On the first day of King's*: Reeves, interview by Stewart, JFKL; Martin, interview by Grele, #2, JFKL.

70 *Reeves phoned the SCLC's Wyatt*: "Did a Phone Call Elect Kennedy President?"; Reeves, interview by Stewart, JFKL.

71 *"What, if anything, could"*: Reeves, interview by Stewart, JFKL.

71 *Speaking to Wofford that evening*: Ibid.

72 *"the only lawyer who would help"*: Harris Wofford, interview by Carol Quirke, Dec. 19, 2011, SUNY Old Westbury Oral History.

72 *"I've had this nightmare"*: Wofford, interview.

72 *Coretta had a great-uncle*: King, *My Life with Martin Luther King Jr.*, 23.

72 *"they will do anything"*: Wofford, *Of Kennedys and Kings*, 12.

72 *"Corrie, I told you"*: Wofford, interview.

72 *"And the Lord came by"*: Harris Wofford, interview by Voices of the Civil Rights Movement, "Participating with Dr. King," Dec. 4, 2015.

72 *liver and onions, creamed potatoes*: "Jailed Sit-downers Denied Text Books," *Baltimore Afro-American*, Oct. 29, 1960.

73 *"fasting today in a spiritual act"*: Ibid.

73 *"It's the first food"*: Bryans, "Negroes Count on Atlanta as Moderate, Dr. King Says."

73 *On the women's side of jail*: Hoytt, interview by Bohannon, Atlanta Student Movement Project, KSU; Challenor, interview by Bohannon, Atlanta Student Movement Project, KSU.

73   *women were served fresh milk*: Challenor, interview by Crawford, King Collection, Morehouse College.

73   *interview with Atlanta's NBC affiliate*: WSB-TV newsfilm clip of Dr. Martin Luther King Jr., Oct. 19, 1960, Walter J. Brown Media Archives and Peabody Awards Collection, University of Georgia (UGA) Libraries, Athens, as presented in the Digital Library of Georgia.

73   *"Maybe it takes some degree"*: Bryans, "Negroes Count on Atlanta as Moderate, Dr. King Says."

73   *"As Negroes, we must bear"*: "Jailed Sit-Downers Denied Text Books."

73   *"I did not initiate the thing"*: Bryans, "Negroes Count on Atlanta as Moderate, Dr. King Says."

73   *"war on sleep"*: Young, *Easy Burden*, 176.

74   *how "convivial" King was*: Lonnie King, interview.

74   *"It is a means of showing"*: AI, Oct. 24, 1960.

74   *There were rumors in the Black community*: "Mayor Seeks Sit-In Truce but Picketing Continues," *AJ*, Oct. 21, 1960.

74   *Some two hundred college students*: Douglas Kiker, "Protest Drive Losing Steam?," *AJ*, Oct. 20, 1960.

74   *Judge Oscar Mitchell sent word*: "Rich's Declines to Prosecute Pastor King on Sit-In Count." The *Journal* records King as saying he found out about the suspended sentence on Wednesday evening after his arrest. King later stated in his JFK interview that he did not understand the looming problem of probation until he was kept from leaving jail on Sunday. We defer to the contemporaneous account, but based on Lonnie King's description to us of how King seemed unfazed in their time in Fulton jail, making no mention of the threat of prison until he was held back on Sunday, King might not have felt DeKalb County had the power to arrest him in Fulton County, and thus saw Wednesday's news as more of an irritant.

DAY 2: THURSDAY, OCTOBER 20

75   *Hundreds of students assembled*: Estimates were as high as two thousand students. Bruce Galphin and Keeler McCartney, "26 More Arrested in Sit-Ins; Many Counters Closed Here," *AC*, Oct. 21, 1960.

75   *A.D. and twenty-four students*: Ibid.; Shannon, "25 Negroes, White Lectured, Jailed."

76   *As A.D. and the rest of the students*: Shannon, "25 Negroes, White Lectured, Jailed."

76   *"had no intentions of creating"*: Shannon, "25 Negroes, White Lectured, Jailed."

76   *despite being busy representing*: Charles Moore, "2 Negroes Refused Entry to University," *AC*, Oct. 22, 1960.

76   *Twenty-five more Black protesters*: Shannon, "25 Negroes, White Lectured, Jailed."

76   *"modern slave quarters"*: Fleming, *Soon We Will Not Cry*, 66.

77   *More than half of the students*: Shannon, "25 Negroes, White Lectured, Jailed," and jailed list in *AC*, Oct. 20, 1960.

77   *Sullivan and other leaders set up*: Challenor, interview by Crawford, King Collection, Morehouse College.

77   *Norma June Wilson listened*: Atlanta Prison Farm rape story told in June Wilson Davis, interview by Jeanne Law Bohannon, May 19, 2017, Atlanta Student Movement, KSU, Stories from the Trenches: Women on the Move(ments), 1940s–2018, 2018 Women's History Month Finale Panel, March 28, 2018, Atlanta Student Movement, KSU. For farm details, see also Lefever, *Undaunted by the Fight*, 70. The civil rights movement from 1955 to 1968 forms a kind of modern American *Iliad*, a story based on true events but told and retold to mythic effect, a tale we tell ourselves to know ourselves by. It has become, with King its central hero, our most resonant civic story. Therefore, it takes an unusual new insight to reorder the way we have decided the civil rights saga unfolded. One such moment in understanding women as drivers of the movement and what they courageously endured in that role was provided by Danielle McGuire's book *At the Dark End of the Street: Black Women, Rape, and Resistance*. The movement looks very

different when these women's experiences are recovered and told with the horrors they faced in jail cells while daring to protest.

77 *Their prayers were not so much*: "Jail, No Bail Group in Jail, Cheerful, Confident."

77 *To pass the time*: Lefever, *Undaunted by the Fight*, 68; Hoytt, interview by Bohannon, Atlanta Student Movement Project, KSU.

77 *A few had textbooks*: "Jailed Sit-Downers Denied Text Books."

78 *"19 girls skipping"*: Lefever, *Undaunted by the Fight*, 68.

78 *Spelman students in particular*: Lonnie King interview; Lefever, *Undaunted by the Fight*, 63. In this sit-in arrest, at least twenty-one students were from Spelman, the rest divided among the other AUC schools.

78 *"You can always tell a Spelman girl"*: Zinn, *Southern Mystique*, 115.

79 *"Hello girls"*: Carson et al., *Papers of Martin Luther King Jr.*, 5:528.

79 *"Get out, King"*: Carson, *Autobiography of Martin Luther King Jr.*, 73–74.

79 *"dark and dingy street"*: Ibid., 74.

80 *"Fellows, before I can assist"*: Ibid., 75.

80 *Bernard Lee, slept in the bunk*: Branch, *Parting the Waters*, 352. This imprisonment changed many lives, perhaps none more than that of Bernard Lee, who became King's body man. Lee, almost invisible in King biographies (like A.D., he died young, leaving no memoir behind), followed King all the way to Memphis. Calling Lee a body man was literal: his speech patterns, mannerisms, and clothes made him an almost indistinguishable decoy for King.

80 *Lonnie's perspective was different*: Lonnie King, interview.

80 *"I was born looking up"*: Lonnie C. King, interview by Crosby, Library of Congress.

80 *he was assigned to clean*: Lonnie King, oral history interview by Ashley Burke, Georgia State University.

80 *He sensed a revolution coming*: Lonnie King, interview by Voices Across the Color Line Oral History Project, Atlanta History Center.

80 *Lonnie appreciated the fact*: Lonnie King, interview.

81 *"I am conscious of two Martin"*: Frady, *Martin Luther King Jr.*, 65.

81 *"an intensely guilt-ridden man"*: Fairclough, *Martin Luther King Jr.*, 49.

81 *felt like a movement retreat*: Ibid., 74.

81 *Lonnie saw a lighthearted King*: Lonnie King, interview.

82 *"modernistic substitute for the dungeons"*: "Jail, No Bail Group in Jail, Cheerful, Confident."

82 *"Have you seen this?"*: This and the exchange that follows come from "Julian Bond Discusses History of the Student Nonviolent Coordinating Committee," Feb. 2, 2010, University of Virginia School of Law.

82 *"You take this side of the café"*: Williamson, "Julian Bond." Lonnie's fear that sit-ins would peter out without more students joining was well-grounded, because this had been the fate of some NAACP student sit-ins in Oklahoma and Kansas two years before. Julian Bond's scholarly father had sat in a Pennsylvania theater in 1947 to protest discriminatory seating.

82 *not about waiting for NAACP lawyers*: Fort, "Atlanta Sit-In Movement, 1960–1961."

82 *Bond's experience of jail revived*: Alexander, "New Footage: Julian Bond's Final Atlanta Interview."

83 *"Good for you"*: Julian Bond, interview by Bob Short, Feb. 27, 2012, Georgia Politics Oral History Collection, Russell Library, University of Georgia.

83 *"freedom high"*: Andrew Young, interview by the authors, Aug. 29, 2017.

83 *Bond was reassured to find*: "Jail, No Bail Group in Jail, Cheerful, Confident."

83 *"extremely happy when I heard"*: Ibid.

83 *Lonnie cherished his hushed, late-night*: Lonnie King, interview.

84 *"There is something inherently depressing"*: Carson, *Autobiography of Martin Luther King Jr.*, 157–58. King wrote in a press release during this Atlanta imprisonment, "Sixteen hours is a long time to spend within a few square feet with nothing creative to do." Carson et al., *Papers of Martin Luther King Jr.*, 5:527.

84 *visits from his family*: King, *My Life with Martin Luther King Jr.*, 179.

84 *"It could be that your example"*: Wilkins to King, Oct. 21, 1960, NAACP Papers, Manuscript Division, Library of Congress.

84 *"highly organized, well-trained group"*: "Bible-Carrying Negroes Picket Atlanta Stores," *Lubbock Avalanche-Journal*, Oct. 20, 1960.

84 *Many, like the readers of* The Kansas City Times: "Jail Choice Made by Minister and 35," *Kansas City Times*, Oct. 20, 1960.

84 *it made only page thirty-nine*: "14 Negroes Jailed in Atlanta Sit-Ins." *NYT*, Oct. 20, 1960.

85 *"There are less provocative ways"*: "There Are Better Ways," *AJ*, Oct. 20, 1960.

85 *"can only breed resentment"*: "We Urge an End to Atlanta Sit-Ins," *AC*, Oct. 20, 1960.

85 *"a further strengthening of the position"*: Kiker, "Protest Drive Losing Steam?"

85 *"Our decision to stay in jail"*: "Jail, No Bail Group in Jail, Cheerful, Confident."

85 *"It is difficult to prophesize"*: King to "friend," Oct. 20, 1960, NAACP Papers.

86 *"performance and not campaign promises"*: Richard Nixon, Remarks of Vice President Nixon, Television Program, Channel 4, New York, online by Gerhard Peters and John T. Woolley, American Presidency Project, www.presidency.ucsb.edu/node/274056.

86 *"Mr. Civil Rights"*: Farrington, *Black Republicans and the Transformation of the GOP*, 59; Booker, *Shocking the Conscience*, 164.

86 *"Segregation, discrimination and prejudice"*: Farrell, *Richard Nixon*, 252.

86 *"most of us here will live"*: Farrington, *Black Republicans and the Transformation of the GOP*, 60.

86 *"one of the saddest days"*: Nichols, *Matter of Justice*, 161.

87 *"I am convinced that the future"*: Carl Rowan, "Who Will Get the Negro Vote?," *Ebony*, Nov. 1960.

87 *"Our God-given rights"*: "Intensification of Sit-In Campaign Is Seen in Atlanta," *Rome News-Tribune*, Oct. 21, 1960.

87 *Vandiver announced state troops*: "Atlanta Calls 'Sit-In' Truce," *Christian Science Monitor*, Oct. 24, 1960.

DAY 3: FRIDAY, OCTOBER 21

89 *Student protesters were back at Rich's*: "Mayor Seeks Sit-In Truce but Picketing Continues"; Bruce Galphin and Keeler McCartney, "Negro Picketing Continues but Sit-Ins Decline Sharply," *AC*, Oct. 22, 1960. Two students were arrested on Friday and sent to Fulton County Jail (John Britton, "Mayor Suggests 'Truce' in Demonstrations Here," *ADW*, Oct. 22, 1960; John Britton, "Mayor Hartsfield Orders Release from Jail of 22 Students Arrested Here," *ADW*, Oct. 23, 1960). The total for the week was seventy-nine arrests of seventy-three movement protesters, because six individuals who were released on Wednesday were arrested again on Thursday. Sixty-three total went to jail. Fifty-two including King had been arrested Wednesday, with thirty-six going to jail and sixteen having charges dismissed. Twenty-five Black protesters were arrested Thursday (not including an additional white counterprotester). The twenty-two students at the prison farm were let out Saturday. Thirty-nine of the forty-one held under state anti-trespassing charges had resisted taking bail by Sunday, with only exceptions like the Reverend Otis Blackshear doing so on Saturday to explain to his congregation on Sunday morning why he was arrested ("Negroes Agree to Halt Sit-ins for 30 Days Here," *AJC*, Oct. 23, 1960). Thirty-eight got out late Sunday while King was held, as is made clear in "Rich's Declines to Prosecute Pastor King on Sit-In Count." The *Constitution*'s "King Held on Old Count as Sit-Inners Leave Jail" missed the two students arrested on Friday in its count of sixty-one instead of sixty-three demonstrators who went to jail, and mistakenly said the students in Fulton County Jail were released Saturday, when that happened Sunday, as the *Daily World* and *Journal* reported. The AP's story, "Revive Traffic Charge to Jail Negro Leader" (*New York Daily News*, Oct. 26, 1960), had the correct total number of arrests of seventy-nine.

89 *a business owner replied, "Indefinitely"*: "Mayor Seeks Sit-In Truce but Picketing Continues."

90 *Students also kept up a twenty-four-hour*: John Britton and Paul Delaney, "Given Ten Days Each in 'Demonstrations,'" *ADW*, Oct. 21, 1960.

90 *"Flying squads of Negroes"*: "Negroes Sit In for Second Day in Atlanta," *Chicago Daily Tribune*, Oct. 21, 1960.

90 *Both SNCC and SCLC sent*: Otis Moss, interview by the authors, May 27, 2017.

90 *"I know I speak for"*: "23 More Are Seized in Sit-Ins in Atlanta," *New York Herald Tribune*, Oct. 21, 1960.

90 *"You can't get anywhere"*: "Negro Pastor Hits Sit-Ins, Kneel-Ins," *AC*, Oct. 24, 1960.

90 *"run smack dab over you"*: Fairclough, *To Redeem the Soul of America*, 67.

90 *He demanded, on day three*: Galphin and McCartney, "Negro Picketing Continues but Sit-Ins Decline Sharply."

91 *Mayor Hartsfield had seen enough*: William B. Hartsfield, interview by Charles T. Morrissey, Jan. 6, 1966, JFKL.

91 *"provide now the moral leadership"*: Britton, "Mayor Suggests 'Truce' in Demonstrations Here."

91 *Dick Rich was having a small*: Abram, *Day Is Short*, 127.

91 *"an unofficial mediator"*: "Mayor Seeks Sit-In Truce but Picketing Continues."

92 *What the mayor overlooked*: Ibid.

92 *"One day your parents"*: Otis Moss, interview by City of Atlanta, Atlanta Student Movement collection.

92 *Moss sent telegrams to both*: Moss, interview by the authors.

92 *"The actions of these unlawful"*: Associated Press, "Nixon Backer Blames Sit-Ins on Kennedy," *AC*, Oct. 22, 1960.

93 *Moss felt the weight of responsibility*: Moss, interview by the authors.

93 *Before joining the* Courier: Griffin, *Courier of Crisis,* Messenger of Hope.

93 *"ten years if necessary"*: This and the following exchange between Anderson and King come from Trezzvant W. Anderson, "In Jail with 40 Students 'I Had to Practice What I Preached'—Dr. Martin L. King Jr.," *PC*, Oct. 29, 1960.

94 *"at the last minute to go"*: King's description of their call as "last minute" is interesting. He is certainly talking about Herschelle Sullivan's and then Lonnie King's calls, but making them sound more like invitations rather than a follow-up to a long effort at convincing King. King's conversations with Wofford, hoping to evade the sit-in, certainly back up Lonnie's recounting that he had been pressing King to participate with them for some time (as other people's recollections also attest: John Lewis and in Branch's *Parting the Waters*, Glenn Smiley and Bernard Lee's memories of conversations with King during the SNCC conference). So while King was truthful that these calls came at the last minute before the sit-in, stating it as he did allowed him to conceal his own doubts about participating. It was only years later that Lonnie learned of King's conversations with the Kennedy campaign seeking to justify missing the sit-in, but his admiration for his friend was undiminished.

94 *"Oh, God, don't let him die"*: Matthews, *Kennedy & Nixon*, 18.

95 *"I didn't care for either man"*: Lewis, *Walking with the Wind*, 118.

DAY 4: SATURDAY, OCTOBER 22

97 *Harris Wofford watched his children*: Wofford, interview; Wofford, *Of Kennedys and Kings*, 13–14.

97 *"What the hell?"*: Wofford, interview.

99 *"If old Joe has his way"*: Wofford, *Of Kennedys and Kings*, 29.

99 *"Right now, I've got my eyes"*: Zengerle, "Man Who Was Everywhere."

99 *"I understand my boy"*: This and the exchange that follows come from an interview with Wofford.

100   *"You know I'm way behind"*: Wofford, interview by Blackside Inc. for "Eyes on the Prize," Oct.
        31, 1985, Henry Hampton Collection, Washington University Libraries.
100   *"Morris, Martin Luther King, Jr., is"*: Abram, *Day Is Short*, 126.
100   *"I'm supposed to be a civil-rights"*: Stein and Plimpton, *American Journey*, 90.
100   *"Can't you do anything?"*: Wofford, interview.
100   *"Atlanta's supposed to be the enlightened"*: Wofford, *Of Kennedys and Kings*, 14.
101   *"This is a scandal"*: Stein and Plimpton, *American Journey*, 90.
101   *"How in the hell do you"*: Abram, *Day Is Short*, 126.
101   *He stressed to Abram that Kennedy*: Wofford, *Of Kennedys and Kings*, 14. Wofford's and Abram's
        memories diverge on a key point, which is that Abram later remembered Wofford urging him
        to help get King out and then give the credit to Kennedy. The problem with this memory is that
        it is in conflict with Wofford's initial worry that making *any* linkage of the campaign to King's
        case without authorization would cause him great problems. This concern would not stop the
        CRS from later acting without concern for the consequences, but Wofford has been consistent
        through the years that he was hardly thinking so boldly on Saturday, that early in the crisis.
        Wofford's JFKL oral history interview predates Abram's book by a decade and a half. But the
        possibility cannot be dismissed that Wofford's motives from the start were more political than
        he ever felt comfortable acknowledging. Wofford maintained to us that this call was solely about
        helping his friend, that Abram misremembered his words in his later account. Wofford and
        Abram also disagree on whether Abram was already heading to this meeting, which Wofford
        remembered, or if Wofford's encouragement spurred him to it.
            Hartsfield's JFKL oral history account, however, contradicts both Wofford and Abram, say-
        ing that he and Abram cooked up the whole plan in advance, in person, and then sought to
        convince a reluctant Wofford. Hartsfield also said Bobby and Seigenthaler were in the room
        with Wofford during his call, which was certainly not true, further diminishing the credibility
        of Hartsfield's account. Given the incompatibility of Hartsfield's story with four men's memo-
        ries, and his implausible timeline (he presents Kennedy's call to Coretta, which happened four
        days later, as occurring right after his announcement), such assertions strike us as a legacy play
        at the end of a long career.
101   *"Yeah, come down at once"*: Wofford, *Of Kennedys and Kings*, 14.
101   *Raised in Fitzgerald, Georgia*: Abram, *Day Is Short*, 18–38.
101   *"We will not accept race mixing"*: "Hartsfield, Negro Leaders Huddle on Sit-in Truce," *AJ*, Oct.
        22, 1960.
102   *"to say what they really think"*: Ibid.
102   *"If you will give me a thirty day"*: Hartsfield, interview by Morrissey, JFKL.
102   *"distinct and marvelous southern prototype"*: Abram, *Day Is Short*, 94.
102   *When an Atlanta synagogue*: Martin, *William Berry Hartsfield*, 132–33.
102   *At seventy, Mayor Hartsfield*: Ibid., 130–31, 144–45.
102   *"an unusually effective leader"*: King Sr., *Daddy King*, 164. The Kings might not have viewed
        Hartsfield so positively if they had known how deeply the mayor feared an Atlanta run by a
        majority-Black population; Black voter registration in Atlanta was moving past whites for the
        first time heading into this election. Hartsfield often pondered how they could annex more of
        DeKalb County to head off such a future.
103   *"I believe William Hartsfield"*: Ibid., 116.
103   *When Daddy King called Hartsfield*: Ibid., 119.
103   *Flipping through them, he saw*: Hartsfield, interview by Morrissey, JFKL.
103   *hoopin and a hollerin"*: Ibid.
103   *"I will turn Martin Luther King"*: Ibid.
104   *John Calhoun heard the mayor's announcement*: Raines, *My Soul Is Rested*, 94–95; John Calhoun, in-
        terview by John Britton, May 23, 1968, Ralph Bunch Oral History Collection, Howard University.
104   *Vernon Jordan never forgot*: Jordan, *Vernon Can Read*, 49.

104 *Lonnie regularly had breakfast*: Lonnie King, interview.

104 *"A report!"*: This and the exchange that follows come from Abram, *Day Is Short*, 127.

105 *"the race was very close"*: Hartsfield, interview by Morrissey, JFKL.

105 *Calhoun had tried to reach*: Calhoun, interview by Britton, Howard University.

105 *Washington was a determined*: Morrow, *Black Man in the White House*, 33, 295–96.

105 *"Val, this is going to have"*: Raines, *My Soul Is Rested*, 95.

105 *Calhoun had previously offered*: Farrington, *Black Republicans and the Transformation of the GOP*, 105–7. A year before, the Republican Claude Barnett, head of the Associated Negro Press, offered to Nixon's press secretary, Herb Klein, that he could get Nixon stories targeted to Black newspaper readers all over the country, but was never taken up on the offer. The Nixon campaign was not printing Black-community-targeted pamphlets and did not bother to take money that a donor offered for a telecast aimed at Black voters.

105 *"John, I don't know whether"*: Raines, *My Soul Is Rested*, 94–95.

106 *"peace and quiet" offer*: "Negroes Agree to Halt Sit-ins for 30 Days Here."

106 *"At the end of that time"*: Ibid.

106 *Troutman had been spending a pleasant*: Wofford, interview; Abram, *Day Is Short*, 52–53, 58, 124, 128.

107 *"suspected the dark hand"*: Wofford, interview by Bernhard, #1, JFKL.

107 *"Who is this representative"*: This and the exchange that follows come from Abram, *Day Is Short*, 128.

108 *"I know this might lose"*: Wofford, interview.

108 *"Sit down and hold on"*: Wofford, *Of Kennedys and Kings*, 14.

108 *"He said what, Morris?"*: Wofford, interview by Bernhard, #1, JFKL.

108 *"But Kennedy knows nothing"*: Wofford, *Of Kennedys and Kings*, 14.

108 *"I hadn't checked with the campaign"*: Wofford, interview.

108 *"The Mayor knows that"*: Wofford, *Of Kennedys and Kings*, 14.

108 *"Well, you know, the Senator"*: Stein and Plimpton, *American Journey*, 91.

109 *"Hartsfield said what?"*: Wofford, *Of Kennedys and Kings*, 15.

109 *"If Senator Kennedy is asked"*: Abram, *Day Is Short*, 129.

109 *"As a result of having many calls"*: Wofford, *Of Kennedys and Kings*, 15. Even Hartsfield was now on message—with a lifetime of sensitivities to the southern handling of race to draw upon—backing up Kennedy's careful explanation. The mayor said to reporters, this time closer to reality, "It was thoroughly impressed upon me that the senator had no desire to interfere in what is a local matter, but that he merely wanted to express an interest, hoping the matter would be settled and realizing that Atlanta has a fine reputation for settling such matters." Characteristically, he was able to shoehorn praise for his city in at the close. "Did Kennedy Man Ask King Release?," *AJC*, Oct. 23, 1960.

110 *worked toward this outcome until eight*: Abram, *Day Is Short*, 127.

110 *unless all charges were dropped*: Ibid.

110 *Abram's daughter had gone without lunch*: Ibid.

111 *"Atlanta is getting a horrible image"*: This and the exchange that follows also come from ibid.

111 *"in terror that his company"*: Ibid.

111 *"he just wanted to sell shoes"*: Ibid., 128.

111 *"make martyrs out of them"*: "Rich's Declines to Prosecute Pastor King on Sit-In Count."

DAY 5: SUNDAY, OCTOBER 23

113 *"a pleasant, rotund little man"*: Abram, *Day Is Short*, 129–30.

113 *"Did Kennedy Man Ask King Release?"*: *AJC*, Oct. 23, 1960.

114 *"A lot of people I know"*: Layhmond Robinson, "Baltimore Study Uncovers Apathy," *NYT*, Oct. 23, 1960.

114   *"When the great spiritual leader"*: Martin G. Berck, "Rockefeller Opens 2-Week Drive in City,"
       New York Herald Tribune, Oct. 24, 1960.

114   *"Harris, you're just fucking everything up"*: Wofford, interview.

114   *Sunday's* Journal-Constitution *reported*: "Did Kennedy Man Ask King Release?" Vandiver as-
       sured reporters on Monday that Kennedy had "no authority to interfere, not any desire or
       intention." It had been only an inquiry that was made, and not a Kennedy staffer attempting to
       interfere in a Georgia situation. Vandiver did not record having a conversation with Kennedy
       at this point in the week in his oral histories, but *The Atlanta Constitution* on October 25,
       1960 (as well as AP coverage in other papers), quotes him as saying that he spoke to Kennedy
       on Saturday night and was reassured that their campaign would not mediate the King matter
       ("Vandiver Talked to JFK About King," *The Knoxville News-Sentinel*, Oct. 25, 1960).

114   *Vandiver later said that no such call*: Ernest Vandiver, interview by Clifford Kuhn, Jan. 25, 1994,
       P1994–02, series A, Georgia Governors, Georgia Government Documentation Project, Special
       Collections and Archives, Georgia State University Library (GSU), Atlanta.

115   *Almost no one seemed to notice*: Abram, *Day Is Short*, 130.

115   *Daddy King understood the depravity*: King Sr., *Daddy King*, 10, 20–28, 37–40, 67–69.

115   *"We must awaken the conscience"*: Charles Price, "Citizens Contribute $2000 to Sit-Ins," *Cleve-
       land Call and Post*, Oct. 29, 1960.

116   *"DeKalb Seeks to Jail Rev. King"*: AC, Oct. 21, 1960.

116   *"King Faces Year in Jail on Old Count"*: AJ, Oct. 21, 1960. DeKalb even provided to *The Atlanta
       Journal* the original terms of King's probation.

116   *"Stop spending your money"*: "Rich's Not to Press Sit-In Prosecution," *Women's Wear Daily*, Oct.
       25, 1960.

117   *"he grew in stature"*: King, *My Life with Martin Luther King Jr.*, 52–53.

117   *"Why did Daddy go to jail?"*: This and the conversation that follows come from ibid., 175.

118   *"He is one of my friends"*: Gladney, *How Am I to Be Heard?*, 300–301. Smith wrote, "He was re-
       ally arrested because the cop saw my white face, followed the car out to Emory where I was staying
       (taking my usual X-ray treatments) and arrested him for that, using the license as an excuse . . .
       but the real reason was me."

119   *"I've worked everything out"*: King, interview by Bernhard, JFKL.

119   *"But I would have to fine you"*: DHP.

119   *"I don't have time, I'm going"*: King Sr., *Daddy King*, 157.

119   *"be put to work and labor"*: "Rich's Declines to Prosecute Pastor King on Sit-In Count."

119   *The look of surprise*: Lonnie King, interview. As King said in his JFKL oral history interview, "It
       was such a minor case I didn't pay much attention to it, and never knew that the lawyer had
       really pleaded guilty." King, interview by Bernhard, JFKL. King said in sworn testimony in his
       subsequent DeKalb hearing that he never understood that he was on probation (DHP). Morris
       Abram speculated in *The Day Is Short* that believing DeKalb would seize him was why King did
       not want to leave Fulton County Jail, but King's testimony contradicts that (130).

120   *His visitors were cut off*: Trezzvant W. Anderson, "Martin Luther King Reveals: Prisoners Wanted
       to Strike over Him," *PC*, Nov. 5, 1960.

120   *"worried about what they might do"*: Ibid.

DAY 6: MONDAY, OCTOBER 24

121   *The deputy sheriff of DeKalb County*: "Rich's Declines to Prosecute Pastor King on Sit-In Count."

121   *Hollowell, along with the attorney Horace*: Hollowell and Lehfeldt, *Sacred Call*, 133.

121   *"a community trying honestly"*: "Rich's Declines to Prosecute Pastor King on Sit-In Count."

122   *Mayor Hartsfield appeared on WSB*: WSB-TV newsfilm clip of Mayor William B. Hartsfield,
       Oct. 24, 1960, Walter J. Brown Media Archives and Peabody Awards Collection, UGA Librar-
       ies, as presented in the Digital Library of Georgia.

123 *All day Monday, an increasingly frustrated*: Morrow to Finch, Oct. 24, 1960, E. Frederic Morrow Papers, 1925–1996, Amistad Research Center, Tulane University. This letter has long been missing from accounts of these crucial days, residing in a small portion of Morrow's papers that are at Tulane University, but the letter is the strongest evidence of how the costs to the Republicans related to the King situation were clearly explained to the top of the campaign. Finch also received memos from the RNC official A. B. Hermann pleading for them to run more Black newspaper ads, the same suggestion Martin persuaded Shriver to follow despite its considerable price tag. After being turned down, and then ignored after asking for just one Black-voter-focused pamphlet, Hermann eerily wrote, "This has been a very badly neglected area. I do not know why. I am fearful of it coming home to haunt us." Farrington, *Black Republicans and the Transformation of the GOP*, 106.

123 *Morrow's involvement with national Republican*: Morrow, *Forty Years a Guinea Pig*, 73–85.

124 *Eisenhower's team told Morrow*: Ibid., 86–93; Morrow, *Black Man in the White House*, 11–13.

124 *Once Morrow moved*: Morrow, *Black Man in the White House*, 17–18; Morrow, *Forty Years a Guinea Pig*, 98–100. Eventually, a religious young woman, in tears, took the assignment of being Morrow's secretary.

124 *"The White House is a little"*: Morrow, *Black Man in the White House*, 275.

124 *"We are proud of you"*: Eisenhower to Morrow, Jan. 10, 1955, E. Frederic Morrow Papers, 1861–1996, Vivian G. Harsh Research Collection, Chicago Public Library. Context of the meeting where Morrow used the phrase is in his *Forty Years a Guinea Pig*, 91, though Morrow slightly misquotes the Eisenhower letter.

125 *Outside work, he was apprehensive*: Morrow, *Black Man in the White House*, 43.

125 *"heartsick . . . the greatest cross"*: Ibid., 299.

125 *"it can keep him from"*: Carson et al., *Papers of Martin Luther King Jr.*, 7:502.

126 *"you people" needed "patience"*: Morrow, *Forty Years a Guinea Pig*, 163–64.

126 *"I could feel life draining"*: Ibid.

126 *Jackie Robinson, also in attendance*: Farrington, *Black Republicans and the Transformation of the GOP*, 76.

126 *"wondered if further constructive"*: Booker, *Shocking the Conscience*, 148.

126 *"crusader," but it certainly made*: Carson, *Autobiography of Martin Luther King Jr.*, 110.

126 *"Some kind of gesture"*: Morrow, *Black Man in the White House*, 93.

126 *"In most of the states where"*: Memorandum to Republican Party Leadership from E. Frederic Morrow, Nov. 6, 1958, Morrow Papers, Chicago Public Library.

126 *In a 1958 survey*: Perlstein, *Nixonland*, 125.

126 *"I say emphatically and categorically"*: Memo to Republican Party Leadership from Morrow, Nov. 6, 1958.

127 *"Dr. Martin Luther King, leader"*: This and all quotations from Morrow's letter can be found in Morrow to Finch, Oct. 24, 1960.

128 *"It was Democrats who arrested"*: Farrington, *Black Republicans and the Transformation of the GOP*, 109.

128 *The Nixon campaign was receiving*: King, Martin Luther, Telegrams, 1960, Pre-presidential Papers (PPS) Collection 320, box 22, RNL. In the Nixon Library, there is a long file of all the telegrams Nixon received pleading with him to do something to help King, from private citizens and NAACP chapters across the country.

128 *"Tell them that I would like"*: Kotlowski, *Nixon's Civil Rights*, 161.

129 *"Let me be consistent"*: This and the scene that follows come from Lonnie King, interview.

129 *Within two weeks, Lonnie*: "Lonnie King Could Lose Postal Job," *AJ*, Nov. 4, 1960.

129 *"Congratulations are pouring in"*: Louis Martin box, JFKL. John Seigenthaler also described Louis Martin as "elated" about the phone call to Coretta in his JFKL interview (#2).

There is a separate draft in this JFKL folder, written to be a statement released by Senator Kennedy, which sounds more like Wofford's writing, given its mentions of Gandhi: "Good news and bad news come together. The agreement reached this weekend in Atlanta under the leadership of Mayor Hartsfield was heartening to all Americans. It was an example of the kind of local and moral leadership this problem requires—the kind of leadership which brings people to reason together in good faith and with good will—the kind of leadership which has not been given by the Republican Administration in these last years of racial crises. The news that Dr. Martin Luther King has been sentenced to four months of hard labor for a minor traffic violation—driving with an out-of-state license—must shock the sense of fairness of all Americans. Mahatma Gandhi's technique of non-violent action which Dr. King has been using in his fight against racial discrimination always involves some rise of tensions and temper. But the technique stirs consciences—and it won freedom for India. I am sure that the American conscience will be stirred by this latest development and I hope that this will soon result in Dr. King's freedom."

Unlike the more conventionally professional press releases Martin would draft, this statement draws out the idea of "tension" rising out of the sit-in crisis—a concept King and Gandhi often invoked. Written in a loftier, more legal, and less political tone, it says, "Whenever there is unrest and tension, whether in racial or labor relations or in other problem areas, whether in any part of this country or the world, the President of the United States should be personally concerned." This draft makes the case that Kennedy showed moral leadership in the Atlanta situation, a quality Eisenhower was not displaying, from *Brown* to the present sit-in.

130   *"It doesn't matter if they"*: "Rich's Declines to Prosecute Pastor King on Sit-In Count."

DAY 7: TUESDAY, OCTOBER 25

131   *he was placed in handcuffs*: Margaret Shannon and Fred Powledge, "King Fights Term of Driving Charge," *AJ*, Oct. 25, 1960.

131   *"Protect him from what"*: Otis Moss, interview.

131   *front page of* The New York Times: *NYT*, Oct. 26, 1960.

131   *"walked arrogantly out with his prisoner"*: King, *My Life with Martin Luther King Jr.*, 177.

131   *"a well-known stronghold of the Klan"*: Ibid., 177–78.

132   *Students had wanted to protest*: "Rev. Martin Luther King Sent to a Georgia Chain Gang!," *New York Amsterdam News*, Oct. 29, 1960.

132   *courtroom, overflowing with 250 people*: Shannon and Powledge, "King Fights Term of Driving Charge."

132   *lanky form of Roy Wilkins*: Wilkins, Atlanta press conference, Oct. 26, 1960, NAACP Papers.

132   *flashbulbs popped all around him*: Jack Strong, "King Gets 4 Months in DeKalb Court," *AC*, Oct. 26, 1960.

132   *Hollowell and his team*: Vernon Jordan, interview.

132   *Judge Oscar Mitchell emerged*: Otis Moss, interview by Jeanne Law Bohannon, Aug. 25, 2017, Atlanta Student Movement Project, KSU; Charles Black, interview, May 18, 2017.

133   *Mitchell was from nearby Panthersville*: DeKalb New Era, Feb. 1, 1962; *AJC*, July 8, 2002.

133   *"a shrewd, bitter-end segregationist"*: Abram, *Day Is Short*, 130.

133   *As a World War II pilot*: Michelle E. Shaw, "Judge Jack B. Smith, 88: Known as a Kind and Professional Judge," *AJC*, Nov. 28, 2012, www.ajc.com/news/local-obituaries/judge-jack-smith-known-kind-and-professional-judge/CwVO2wjT3124aHWQdory5O/; "A Brief Biography of Judge Jack B. Smith," Judge Jack B. Smith, in Remembrance of, jackbsmith.blogspot.com/.

133   *"The State is ready"*: This and all quotations from the King hearing unless otherwise noted can be found in the King trial transcripts in DHP. In Donald Hollowell's files, only recently fully cataloged, there exist copies of typed transcripts (and quite tattered and worn) of the hearing itself. One includes all the courtroom exchanges and has handwritten Hollowell notes on what should be omitted for an abbreviated version. Discovering this has made it possible, along with newspaper and eyewitness accounts, to at last provide a fuller portrait of what occurred

that morning as well as during the Rich's sit-in. Historians have been seeking the official transcript for decades, and we were lucky to have finally located it at the Auburn Avenue Research Library on African American Culture and History, Atlanta-Fulton Public Library System. The "missing" transcript was in Hollowell's legal papers that were recently opened to the public. We thank the staff at Auburn Avenue for their help and professional dedication.

134 *With his imposing posture*: Daniels, *Saving the Soul of Georgia*, 39.

134 *Andrew Young compared him*: Ibid., 79.

138 *Charles Clayton told the press*: "Rich's Declines to Prosecute Pastor King on Sit-In Count."

141 *I'm going to indulge in a few*: Strong, "King Gets 4 Months in DeKalb Court."

141 *King sat composed as he absorbed*: Wainwright, "Martyr of the Sit-Ins."

141 *He thought Hollowell had argued*: King, interview by Bernhard, JFKL.

142 *Coretta was overwhelmed*: King, *My Life with Martin Luther King Jr.*, 178. Coretta remembered, "I felt so alone and helpless."

142 *the Reverend Samuel W. Williams*: Strong, "King Gets 4 Months in DeKalb Court"; John Britton, "Motion to Revoke Conviction of King Rejected Following Early Morning Transfer to Reidsville," *ADW*, Oct. 27, 1960.

142 *"Judge, you're killing me"*: "Judge Upset by Father's Plea," *Cleveland Call and Post*, Nov. 5, 1960.

142 *"Corrie, dear, you have to be"*: This and the conversation that follows come from King, *My Life with Martin Luther King Jr.*, 178.

143 *"As bad as this may seem"*: "Rev. Martin Luther King Sent to a Georgia Chain Gang!"

143 *"I made a boo-boo there"*: Wilkins, Atlanta press conference, Oct. 26, 1960.

143 *"a great many white people"*: Ibid.

143 *Hollowell was already working*: King, *My Life with Martin Luther King Jr.*, 178.

144 *Top Republican department officials*: White, *Making of the President, 1960*, 315.

144 *a friend of the court*: Anthony Lewis, "Protest over Dr. King's Arrest Was Drafted for President's Use," *NYT*, Dec. 15, 1960.

144 *Rogers, was on the campaign trail*: White, *Making of the President, 1960*, 315.

144 *"USE EVERY METHOD TO SEEK"*: Dr. Sedrick J. Rawlins to Vice President Nixon, Oct. 25, 1960, King, Martin Luther, Telegrams, 1960, Pre-presidential Papers Collection 320, box 22, RNL.

145 *"thus paving the way"*: Nixon, *Six Crises*, 362.

145 *"It seems to me fundamentally"*: Lewis, "Protest over Dr. King's Arrest Was Drafted for President's Use."

145 *The date on the existing memo*: If administration figures above Walsh had wanted the statement to be read by the president to reporters, such a text could have been written quickly; two sentences do not get delayed for nearly a week because the statement was not completed. Theodore White in *The Making of the President, 1960* wrote that the memo was sent for approval to the White House and to Nixon's campaign in Ohio. Taylor Branch in *Parting the Waters* casts doubt on this, noting the date on the memo.

145 *He and Louis Martin agreed*: Wofford, *Of Kennedys and Kings*, 16; Wofford, interview.

145 *Martin had another worry*: Martin memoir draft, LMP; Martin interview by Grele, #2, JFKL.

146 *Wofford believed that the Georgia co-chair*: Wofford, *Of Kennedys and Kings*, 16.

146 *"Don't issue it"*: Stein and Plimpton, *American Journey*, 91. Vandiver was adamant in his GSU oral history with Clifford Kuhn that he made no such deal with the Kennedy campaign this early in the crisis, particularly one demanding silence for secretly helping the jailed minister.

146 *"After all, we're interested in"*: Stein and Plimpton, *American Journey*, 91.

146 *On a hot August morning*: Wofford, *Of Kennedys and Kings*, 58–59.

147 *his own Irish family had endured*: Wofford, interview.

147 *"not a particular issue"*: Guthman and Shulman, *Robert Kennedy in His Own Words*, 66.

147 *"They are going to kill him"*: Wofford, *Of Kennedys and Kings*, 11.

148 *"Every hour that Martin spent"*: Belafonte, *My Song*, 217.

148 *"doing everything possible"*: Wofford, *Of Kennedys and Kings*, 17.

148 *"Can civil rights in some form"*: Louis E. Martin, "Dope and Data," *Chicago Defender*, April 28, 1956.

149 *"What do we do now?"*: Wofford, interview.

149 *"Who cares about public statements?"*: Stossel, *Sarge*, 163.

149 *"If these beautiful and passionate"*: Stein and Plimpton, *American Journey*, 92.

149 *"That's it, that's it!"*: Wofford, *Of Kennedys and Kings*, 17.

149 *"That would really make 'em"*: Wofford, interview.

149 *"That's the most beautiful thought"*: Stein and Plimpton, *American Journey*, 92.

149 *Wofford was still worried about*: Wofford, *Of Kennedys and Kings*, 17.

150 *"Mrs. King really needs"*: This and the other contents of the phone call come from Stein and Plimpton, *American Journey*, 92.

DAY 8: WEDNESDAY, OCTOBER 26

151 *It was around 3:30 a.m.*: Anderson, "Martin Luther King Reveals." In King's contemporaneous account, he estimated the time at 3:30. King later said in his JFK Library interview 3:00 a.m. and Coretta King wrote 4:30 in *My Life with Martin Luther King Jr.*

151 *"King! King! Wake up!"*: King, *My Life with Martin Luther King Jr.*, 179.

151 *He thought he was still dreaming*: Anderson, "Martin Luther King Reveals."

151 *"King, get up, put on your clothes"*: Coretta Scott King, interview in *American Idealist: The Story of Sargent Shriver*, PBS documentary.

151 *"Did ya' hear me, King?"*: Anderson, "Martin Luther King Reveals."

151 *the widow of James Brazier*: Hollowell and Lehfeldt, *Sacred Call*, 119.

152 *German shepherd in the back seat*: Andrew Young, interview by the authors. Young recounted to us that King told him about the police dog on this ride.

152 *never see anyone he loved again*: Ibid.

152 *"That kind of mental anguish"*: Young, *Easy Burden*, 175.

152 *"hell on earth"*: Daniels, *Saving the Soul of Georgia*, 116. King told Young that the torture of this ride made it the worst night of his life.

153 *King's first clue as to where*: Anderson, "Martin Luther King Reveals."

153 *some four hours into the journey*: Margaret Shannon and Gordon Roberts, "King at Reidsville as Hearing Held," *AJ*, Oct. 26, 1960.

153 *"exhausted and humiliated"*: King, *My Life with Martin Luther King Jr.*, 179.

153 *he was put through fingerprinting*: "Rev. Martin Luther King Sent to a Georgia Chain Gang!"; Jack Strong, "DeKalb Refuses to Release King," *AC*, Oct. 27, 1960.

153 *R. P. Balkcom, the forty-five-year-old*: Strong, "DeKalb Refuses to Release King"; Shannon and Roberts, "King at Reidsville as Hearing Held"; Francis X. Clines, "The 1992 Campaign: Off the Trail—Visits with Americans; Showing the Good Ol' Boys How to Play Their Own Game," *NYT*, Sept. 25, 1992; Georgia Senate, SR 108-R. P. Balkcom Jr. Memorial Highway-designate, www.legis.ga.gov/Legislation/Archives/19992000/leg/fulltext/sr108.htm.

153 *whispers went between cells*: Bass, *Taming the Storm*, 168.

153 *Governor Ernest Vandiver had achieved*: Vandiver's ambition discussed in Henderson, *Ernest Vandiver*, 34–35, 59.

154 *in March, at age forty-one*: Ibid., 110.

154 *Nineteen sixty had been the most difficult*: Vandiver, interview by Kuhn, GSU.

154 *keep stalling, as his predecessors had*: Henderson, *Ernest Vandiver*, 81–82, 87, 104–6, 114.

154 *Vandiver wanted to tinker*: Ibid., 102.

154 *"Wherever M. L. King, Jr., has been"*: Kuhn, "There's a Footnote to History!," 590.

154 *"Until now, we have had"*: Henderson, *Ernest Vandiver*, 124.

155 *The state patrol would ordinarily not*: Vandiver, interview by Charles Pyle, March 20 and July 28,

1986, Georgia Government Documentation Project, Special Collections and Archives, Georgia State University Library (GSU), Atlanta.

155 *John F. Kennedy was on the line*: In a *Journal* article on December 23, 1960, the first hints of such a behind-the-scenes exchange are alluded to, describing contacts as happening a day before King's release. Therefore, we believe it to have been on the twenty-sixth. Based on his conversations with Vandiver, Jack Bass in *Taming the Storm* agrees with that chronology.

155 *"Martin Luther King is in jail"*: Vandiver, interview by Pyle, GSU.

155 *It was at the Democratic National Convention*: Henderson, *Ernest Vandiver*, 121; S. Ernest Vandiver, interview by John F. Stewart, May 22, 1967, JFKL.

155 *"It's important to me"*: Vandiver, interview by Kuhn, GSU.

155 *"Well, he was driving a car"*: Vandiver, interview by Pyle, GSU.

155 *"Senator, I don't know"*: Vandiver, interview by Kuhn, GSU.

155 *"Yeah I know that"*: Vandiver, interview by Pyle, GSU.

155 *"I'll do what I can undercover"*: Vandiver, interview by Kuhn, GSU.

156 *it was Bob Russell's judgment*: Henderson, *Ernest Vandiver*, 37; Vandiver, interview by Pyle, GSU; Vandiver, interview by Stewart, JFKL.

156 *"No, not one"*: Vandiver, interview by Pyle, GSU.

157 *"Our friendship goes way beyond that"*: Vandiver, interview by Kuhn, GSU.

157 *"I don't know"*: Ibid.

158 *A. D. King was up early that morning*: King Sr., *Daddy King*, 157.

158 *worried about how he would withstand*: King, *My Life with Martin Luther King Jr.*, 179.

158 *"Dad, what's going to happen"*: King Sr., *Daddy King*, 157.

158 *Daddy King knew Reidsville was home*: Ibid.

158 *Daddy King had received calls*: Ibid., 153, 157.

158 *eight Black men on an Anguilla*: Newton, *Unsolved Civil Rights Murder Cases, 1934–1970*, 161. An all-white jury cleared the guards. The NAACP found they were ordered, without shoes, into a ditch filled with snakes.

159 *predawn stabbing at Reidsville*: "2 Convicts Indicted in Cell Deaths," *AC*, Oct. 21, 1960.

159 *"Inmates of Georgia State Prison"*: John Pennington, "Pleas for Penal System Probe Smuggled out of Reidsville," *AJ*, Oct. 27, 1960.

159 *"The conditions at Reidsville"*: Looney, "Segregation Order at Reidsville Prison."

159 *"It was on the outskirts"*: James Baldwin, "Nobody Knows My Name" (1959), in *Collected Essays*.

160 *"get King out this morning"*: This and the conversation that follows come from Daniels, *Saving the Soul of Georgia*, 116. In the news clip recorded that day, Hollowell says that he called the sheriff when this conversation occurred.

160 *Hollowell, however, was able to get*: Hollowell and Lehfeldt, *Sacred Call*, 134; Daniels, *Saving the Soul of Georgia*, 117.

160 *"astonishing swiftness"*: Britton, "Motion to Revoke Conviction of King Rejected Following Early Morning Transfer to Reidsville."

160 *Nathaniel Johnson*: Vernon Jordan, interview by the authors.

161 *"They all think this thing"*: "Flooded by Protests on King, Mayor Says," *AC*, Oct. 26, 1960.

161 *"We wish the world to know"*: "Trial Not City's, Mayor Emphasizes," *AJ*, Oct. 26, 1960.

161 *Organizations from all over*: "King's Imprisonment Stirs U.S.-Wide Wave of Criticism," *AC*, Oct. 27, 1960.

161 *"I think the maximum sentence"*: "Trial Not City's, Mayor Emphasizes."

161 *The Constitution suggested leniency*: "Leniency for King Is Wise Course," *AC*, Oct. 26, 1960.

161 *"because he is presently serving"*: Strong, "DeKalb Refuses to Release King."

162 *"I tried my best"*: Wofford, interview.

162 *Unexpectedly calm, Abram told him*: Ibid.

162 *"Sarge, I have been thinking"*: Strober and Strober, *"Let Us Begin Anew,"* 35.

163 *"Look, nobody wants to hear"*: Wofford, interview by Blackside Inc. for "Eyes on the Prize," Washington University Libraries.

163 *"The trouble with your beautiful"*: Wofford, *Of Kennedys and Kings*, 18.

163 *"If Jack would just call"*: Stossel, *Sarge*, 164.

163 *"All he's got to do"*: Branch, *Parting the Waters*, 361.

163 *"It's not too late"*: Wofford, *Of Kennedys and Kings*, 18.

163 *"Shriverize" was a verb*: Wofford, interview.

163 *"No, no. Where is she?"*: Branch, *Parting the Waters*, 362.

163 *apartment overlooking Chicago's Lincoln Park and Lake Shore Drive*: Shriver lived at 2430 N. Lakeview Ave. in Chicago. Liston, *Sargent Shriver*, 63.

164 *During the Battle of Guadalcanal*: Stossel, *Sarge*, 68–73.

164 *"Sargent Shriver, I think I'd like to marry you"*: Ibid., 113.

164 *"treat the disease of racism"*: Liston, *Sargent Shriver*, 85–88.

164 *"the house Communist"*: Stossel, *Sarge*, 141.

165 *both sides of the Civil War*: Ibid., 3–10.

165 *"You said you're supporting"*: Wofford, interview.

165 *"I'm coming up for the football game"*: Ibid.

165 *racing toward O'Hare, Shriver made*: Various previous versions of this incident, and a recent CNN reenactment in a documentary about the 1960 election (featuring only white campaign aides, with Louis Martin once again omitted), fictiously depicts Shriver frantically driving through a rainy evening to get to Kennedy.

165 *On Mannheim and Higgins Roads*: Shriver places his conversation with JFK as happening at the inn in his authorized biography and oral history in Strober and Strober's *"Let Us Begin Anew."* However, Branch, in *Parting the Waters*, has the conversation happening at the airport. The oral history done by Anthony Shriver with his father, held at the JFKL, has Shriver uncertain as to the location, but we believe it was at the O'Hare Inn—also based on Wofford's certainty on this point from conversations with Shriver afterward.

166 *rallies in 237 cities*: O'Donnell and Powers, *"Johnny, We Hardly Knew Ye,"* 203.

167 *Des Plaines, Libertyville, Barrington*: "Here's Route Kennedy Will Follow Today," *Chicago Daily Tribune*, Oct. 25, 1960.

167 *"intense physical pain"*: Schlesinger, *Thousand Days*, 95.

168 *"and that word was very often"*: Salinger, *With Kennedy*, 64.

168 *"The plane leaves at about ten"*: Strober and Strober, *"Let Us Begin Anew,"* 35.

168 *"Jack, I have an idea"*: Ibid.

168 *"I know you can't issue"*: Wofford, interview by Bernhard, #1, JFKL.

168 *"Jack, you just need"*: Stossel, *Sarge*, 164. The recent book *Kennedy and King* by Steven Levingston does not make clear that Wofford's call to Shriver about the possibility of the candidate's phoning Coretta took place the following morning—after Wofford and Martin forged the idea the night before. *Kennedy and King* also relies on a dubious account from Kenny O'Donnell (via his daughter Helen O'Donnell's *Irish Brotherhood*, published thirty-eight years after Kenny O'Donnell's death and appearing to lack a level of sourcing needed to back up its details in describing incidents) of O'Donnell's being part of Shriver's conversation with JFK in the hotel. That O'Donnell was present, much less approving, is simply not credible. Shriver was consistent throughout his life that he waited until O'Donnell walked out of the room before daring to present the idea. Shriver's caution is the more logical account, because O'Donnell, hardly an ally of the CRS staffers, would have very likely vetoed the idea.

168 *"Negroes don't expect everything"*: Stossel, *Sarge*, 164.

169 *"That's a good idea"*: Strober and Strober, *"Let Us Begin Anew,"* 36.

169 *"Dial it for me"*: Stossel, *Sarge*, 165.

169 *King needed a white lawyer*: King Sr., *Daddy King*, 157–58.

169 *"May I speak"*: King, *My Life with Martin Luther King Jr.*, 180.

169 *"Mrs. King, this is Sargent"*: Strober and Strober, *"Let Us Begin Anew,"* 36.

169 *"Just a minute, Mrs. King"*: King, *My Life with Martin Luther King Jr.*, 180.

169 *"Thanks, Jack," said Shriver*: Strober and Strober, *"Let Us Begin Anew,"* 36.

170 *get Bobby on the line*: Ibid.

170 *"going to blow up the courthouse"*: Shannon and Roberts, "King at Reidsville as Hearing Held."

170 *"We all like our Master"*: DHP.

170 *Lonnie King had not been present*: Lonnie King, interview.

171 *"We're waiting on a fellow"*: "Student Leader's Wife Terrorized," *AI*, Aug. 29, 1960.

171 *"this was an idea"*: Lonnie King, interview by Bob Short, University of Georgia Libraries.

171 *Dr. Mays, King's brother, A.D., and Wyatt*: DHP.

171 *"I don't think the Solicitor"*: This and all other quotations from the Wednesday court hearing before Judge Mitchell can be found in DHP.

172 *"This is a dark day"*: Britton, "Motion to Revoke Conviction of King Rejected Following Early Morning Transfer to Reidsville."

173 *"It's happened, man"*: Wofford, JFKL.

173 *"Kennedy's done it, he's touched"*: Wofford, *Of Kennedys and Kings*, 19.

173 *"I'll vote for him"*: Stein and Plimpton, *American Journey*, 93.

173 *"That's great, a Martin Luther King"*: Abram, *Day Is Short*, 131.

173 *The next call to reach Wofford*: Wofford, *Of Kennedys and Kings*, 19.

174 *"Kennedy made a series"*: "Rev. Martin Luther King Sent to a Georgia Chain Gang!" Martin could not have known how he might be blowing up the sensitive Kennedy/Vandiver covert maneuvers to free King. However, he always believed white people did not know what was going on in Black media, making any move on his part effectively hidden.

175 *"I can't get to him"*: Calhoun, interview by Britton, Howard University.

175 *traveling across the Midwest*: Morrow, *Black Man in the White House*, 296. Morrow said this conversation happened in Illinois, but also maintained it happened twenty-four hours before King was released, which would put Nixon in Ohio. Nixon was in Illinois the day after King was released, at which time the conversation would have made no sense to happen. We think it more likely he remembered the timing correctly, but not the exact midwestern state. Nixon got to the Midwest on the twenty-fifth, the day Mitchell revoked King's probation.

176 *"IT CALLS FOR THE STRONGEST"*: Mitchell to Nixon, Oct. 26, 1960, King, Martin Luther, Telegrams, 1960, Pre-presidential Papers Collection 320, box 22, RNL.

176 *"AN EXPRESSION FROM YOUR OFFICE"*: Leonard H. Carter to Nixon, Oct. 26, 1960, King, Martin Luther, Telegrams, 1960, Pre-presidential Papers Collection 320, box 22, RNL.

176 *"You must laugh heartily"*: Morrow Papers, Chicago Public Library.

176 *Nixon would be avoiding Harlem*: Farrington, *Black Republicans and the Transformation of the GOP*, 104.

176 *During Eisenhower's presidential campaign*: Morrow, *Black Man in the White House*, 296.

176 *"bad strategy"*: Ibid.

176 *Still, with one forceful remark*: E. Frederic Morrow, interview by Ed Erwin, April 15, 1968, Columbia Center for Oral History Archives, Rare Book and Manuscript Library.

177 *Simeon Booker of* Jet *asked to be moved*: Farrington, *Black Republicans and the Transformation of the GOP*, 106–7.

177 *"think about it"*: Morrow, *Black Man in the White House*, 296.

177 *"look like he was pandering"*: Matthews, *Kennedy & Nixon*, 172.

177 *Morrow thought back to Nixon's*: Morrow wrote, "One of the unsolved mysteries of the 1960 campaign is what happened to that Nixon." Morrow, *Black Man in the White House*, 293.

177 *Morrow headed back to the White House*: Morrow, interview by Erwin.

177 *"Kennedy goes the way"*: Stanley S. Scott, "Robinson in Memphis Indicates Negro Will Get Cabinet Post If Nixon Wins," *ADW*, Nov. 1, 1960; Allan Heim, "Robinson Goes to Bat for New Coffee Brand," *The Cincinnati Enquirer*, Oct. 28, 1960.

177 *"Did you know about that call?"*: Seigenthaler, interview by Tye.

177 *Bobby had been campaigning in Pittsburgh*: "Nixon 'Panic' Seen by Robert Kennedy," *NYT*, Oct. 26, 1960.

177 *he thought Martin would have informed Bobby*: Seigenthaler, interview by Tye.

178 *"landed on me like a ton"*: Shriver, interview by Anthony K. Shriver, JFKL.

178 *"You've gotten Senator Kennedy"*: Poinsett, *Walking with Presidents*, 82.

178 *"was going to get defeated"*: Shriver, interview by Anthony K. Shriver, JFKL.

178 *"Bob wants to see you bomb throwers"*: Wofford, *Of Kennedys and Kings*, 19.

178 *Wofford suggested that Martin go over*: Martin notebook, LMP; Martin, interview by Grele, #2, JFKL.

178 *Bobby simply liked him better*: Wofford, interview.

178 *how to handle the conversation*: Martin notebook and memoir draft, LMP; Louis Martin, "Up Front: New Senator, a Friend of King," *Chicago Defender*, May 18, 1991, clipping in LMP.

179 *"You know, Jackie Robinson is trying"*: Thompson, *Kennedy Presidency*, 87.

179 *going to blast the Democrats*: Draft in Speeches and Writings File, LMP.

179 *"they're going to blame the jailing"*: Thompson, *Kennedy Presidency*, 87.

179 *"What the hell do you mean"*: Louis Martin, interview by Robert Wright, March 25, 1970, Civil Rights Documentation Project, Bunch Collection, Howard University.

179 *"Wait a minute, don't talk about that"*: Thompson, *Kennedy Presidency*, 87.

179 *a moral framework Bobby would understand*: Louis Martin, interview by Ed Edwin, #3, May 2, 1985, Columbia University Oral History Collection.

180 *"Do you know that three Southern"*: Wofford, *Of Kennedys and Kings*, 19.

180 *"We said we wouldn't support King"*: Wofford, interview.

180 *"You bomb throwers probably lost"*: Stein and Plimpton, *American Journey*, 93. Seigenthaler wondered years later if Bobby and Jack discussed reaching out to the Kings the night before JFK's call to Coretta. Yet Shriver felt he saw in his brother-in-law's face the processing of a quite new idea, arguing against the Kennedys' having already considered an outreach to her.

180 *With their morale at its lowest point*: Wofford, *Of Kennedys and Kings*, 20.

181 *"You can't do this"*: Vandiver, interview by Kuhn, GSU.

181 *Once the two were together*: Charles Pou, "King Call Arranger Was George Stewart," *AJ*, Dec. 23, 1960. Stewart remembered saying on a call to Bobby, "If he is released, it might cost Georgia," with Bobby replying, "If he isn't released, it might cost us Massachusetts."

181 *Stewart told Mitchell a federal judgeship*: Bass, *Taming the Storm*, 169–71.

181 *Vandiver's fingerprints had to be effaced*: Jack Bass, interview, Feb. 2, 2018.

182 *"would affect my political future"*: Vandiver, interview by Kuhn, GSU. This was likely the second time they spoke that day, given that Jack asked the governor to report to Bobby if he could get King out.

182 *personally been to the governor's mansion*: Ibid.

182 *There were no special privileges*: Anderson, "Martin Luther King Reveals."

182 *"Hello darling"*: This and the other quotations from the letter can be found in Carson et al., *Papers of Martin Luther King Jr.*, 5:531–32.

183 *One reporter asked Warden Balkcom*: "Rev. Martin Luther King Sent to a Georgia Chain Gang!"

183 *Hollowell received a call*: Hollowell and Lehfeldt, *Sacred Call*, 135.

184 *"I can't understand why"*: John Seigenthaler, interview by Jean Stein, *American Journey* interview transcript, Jean Stein Personal Papers, JFKL.

185 *"Just think about it a minute"*: Seigenthaler, interview by Tye.

186 *"I think you're right"*: Ibid. Either Bobby's thinking shifted on the plane, or at every stage he believed that the less people knew, the better; the call had to be made for his brother's benefit.

186 *"Bobby would be speaking in Philadelphia"*: *Republican and Herald* (Pottsville, Pennsylvania), Oct. 27, 1960. *The Philadelphia Inquirer*, Oct. 27, 1960. Kennedy's Philadelphia office was located at 1431 Chestnut Street. Seigenthalar's recollection was of putting Bobby on a plane to New York (John Seigenthaler, interview by Ronald J. Grele, #2, Feb. 21, 1966, JFKL), but Philadelphia

was where Bobby spoke that evening. He was in Long Island, New York, the next day, which is where Bobby remembered calling Judge Mitchell from in his JFKL oral history.

186   *"I think Dr. King is getting"*: Nixon, *Six Crises*, 362.
186   *"If my child can sit"*: This and other quotations from the Mount Zion event come from Paul Delaney, "Mass Meet Supports Dr. King," *ADW*, Oct. 27, 1960.
187   *"traitor" in their campaign*: Wofford, *Of Kennedys and Kings*, 20.
187   *"I had nothing to do"*: Charles Moore and Gene Britton, "King Freed on $2,000 Bond, Flies Home from Reidsville," *AC*, Oct. 28, 1960.

DAY 9: THURSDAY, OCTOBER 27

189   *"Well, I talked to that judge"*: Martin, interview by Grele, #2, JFKL. There is a problem with what Bobby said to Martin that night, and with the timeline all historians have previously used. The investigative journalist Jack Bass was one of the few to ever get Judge Mitchell's side of the story, talking to him in the late 1980s about the King case back channels, information he included in *Taming the Storm*. The reporter became interested in the incident while working on an unrelated book and looked up the retired judge. Because his friend Vandiver had endorsed the writer's credentials, Mitchell opened up and explained that, actually, it was Stewart that Bobby got on the phone that evening. Then Bobby was to speak with him the next morning, fulfilling the judge's stipulation that a call from the Kennedy campaign was essential for Vandiver's political cover—and his own satisfaction. If we combine Mitchell's account to Bass with what Louis Martin consistently repeated throughout his life, of Bobby waking him up in the middle of that night (after the day's earlier tongue-lashing), this is something all previous histories have missed: Bobby had not actually spoken to the judge when he called Martin that night, only Stewart. The second, and most important, call was scheduled for 8:00 a.m. The tone and words of that actual conversation would be far from belligerent.
189   *"I told him to get"*: Draft in Speech file, LMP.
189   *"We now make you an honorary"*: Martin, interview by Grele, #2, JFKL; Martin memoir draft, LMP. Martin would call Bobby "honorary brother" for the rest of Kennedy's life, whether in memos, greetings in hallways, or a private code that let Martin always get into Bobby's office no matter what the attorney general was dealing with ("Tell him his honorary Brother needs his help"); this nod between them cemented a tie. Wofford, *Of Kennedys and Kings*, 22.
190   *King's health, after all he*: "Rev. King to Debate Sit-Ins with Ga. Newsman," *Jet*, Nov. 10, 1960.
190   *To his surprise, prisoners frequently*: Anderson, "Martin Luther King Reveals."
190   *King was deeply affected by his time*: John Pennington, "Prison Conditions 'Move' Dr. King," *AJ*, Oct. 28, 1960; Edward Peeks, "A Great Experience Says Dr. King of Sojourn in Prison," *Baltimore Afro-American*, Nov. 5, 1960.
191   *"Kennedy Phoned to Express Concern"*: Anthony Lewis, "Kennedy Phoned to Express Concern, King's Wife Says," *AC*, Oct. 27, 1960.
192   *"some kind of statement"*: "Kennedy Calls Mrs. King," *NYT*, Oct. 27, 1960.
192   *"Chain-Gang Justice"*: "Chain-Gang Justice," *Washington Post*, Oct. 27, 1960.
192   *"given an invaluable boost"*: "The Jailing of Dr. King," *Christian Science Monitor*, Oct. 27, 1960.
192   *"for the strongest condemnation"*: King files, PPS, RNL.
192   *The American Jewish Congress wired*: Douglas Kiker, "Jewish Body Asks Pardon for Dr. King," *AJ*, Oct. 27, 1960.
192   *Vandiver, for one, was experiencing*: "4 'Colonels' in Vandiver Staff Quit," *AC*, Oct. 28, 1960.
192   *Griffin Bell assured the press*: Ibid.
193   *At 8:00 a.m., the phone rang*: Bass, *Taming the Storm*, 169–71. Bobby said in his JFKL oral history only that he called the judge; it is likely he actually did not reach the judge the night before, and so then used another number from the governor to get the next best thing: Judge Mitchell's friend Stewart. According to Mitchell in Bass's interview, Bobby did not reach him at

the courthouse, so he phoned Stewart. We find Mitchell's account credible given how specific it was. Bobby hinted at a vagueness behind the myth when he acknowledged, "Whatever I said, he got him out." It was one day in Bobby's busy and consequential life, whereas these days were the most nationally relevant of Mitchell's life, so the details of the 8:00 a.m. call the next day with a prominent Kennedy would likely be something he would have clarity on.

In Bobby's JFKL oral history interview, he said he called the judge from the pay phone, remembering not a lot of small talk, asking mostly, "Will he get out on bail?" Soon after they rang off, the political transaction complete. Bobby would present a more aggressive picture of the call to others, but there was, as he admitted in his later oral history, little bluster and more politeness in the actual call.

193   *"We would lose the state"*: Pou, "King Call Arranger Was George Stewart"; "Governor Due Here This Noon," *Suffolk County News*, Oct. 27, 1960, marks Bobby's speech at the Huntington Town Hall as being that Thursday, and Bobby's oral history recollection was that he placed the call from Long Island.

193   *"Bob, it's nice to talk"*: Guthman and Shulman, *Robert Kennedy in His Own Words*, 70. Mitchell told Bass he never used this favor with the attorney general in terms of getting a federal judge-ship for himself, but he was successful in getting the DOJ not to deploy federal voting registrars into Georgia during the 1962 governor's race. Another likely apocryphal quotation from the call passed on to Wofford was Bobby saying, "If you're a good Democrat, you'll get him out of jail before sunset!" (from the *Slightly Mad* documentary). Seigenthaler reported Bobby telling him that he told the judge, "Are you an American? Do you know what it means to be an American? You get King out of jail!" Seigenthaler, in thinking why Bobby called the judge despite his counsel, believes it was a question of fairness that tilted Bobby toward phoning Mitchell. A great Bobby admirer, Seigenthaler concluded, "Bob Kennedy's the most moral man I ever met. This was an action that really upset him." Even if "it might cost him some votes . . . he thought the position of the judge was disgraceful" (Seigenthaler, interview by Grele, #2, JFKL).

193   *"He has to do this"*: William Safire, "View from the Grandstand," *NYT*, April 13, 1987.

193   *He brought him to see the campaign manager*: Safire, *Before the Fall*, 59–60. Harry Belafonte called Wofford, Frank Sinatra, and Sammy Davis on what he thought to be the Kennedy side urging action for King. Belafonte called Jackie Robinson to ask for Nixon's help but heard nothing back from the Nixon campaign. Belafonte, *My Song*, 218.

194   *Robinson's wife, Rachel, had never thought*: Rampersad, *Jackie Robinson*, 351.

194   *"counseling him not to rock"*: Robinson, *I Never Had It Made*, 139.

194   *Safire thought he saw tears*: Safire, *Before the Fall*, 59.

194   *"He thinks calling Martin"*: Safire, "View from the Grandstand."

194   *Nixon would later claim*: Farrell, *Richard Nixon*, 288.

194   *But Rogers, for his part, maintained*: William P. Rogers, interview by John T. Mason Jr., June 28, 1968, Eisenhower Administration Project, Butler Library Oral History Collection, Columbia University; Branch, *Parting the Waters*, 375.

194   *"This is too hot for us"*: Kotlowski, *Nixon's Civil Rights*, 161.

195   *In an interview with Simeon Booker*: Simeon Booker, "Richard Nixon Tells: What Republicans Must Do to Regain the Negro Vote," *Ebony*, April 1962.

195   *"some hang-up occurred someplace"*: Frank, *Ike and Dick*, 214.

195   *he got a call from Branch Rickey*: Long, *First Class Citizenship*, 191; Rampersad, *Jackie Robinson*, 351.

195   *"He said he would lose"*: Calhoun, interview by Britton, Howard University.

196   *"Ladies and gentlemen of the press"*: This and the following statements by Mitchell can be found in "King Released Under Bond," *AJ*, Oct. 27, 1960.

197   *"Time for all of us"*: "Abernathy in Georgia: 'Time for All of Us to Take Off Our Nixon Buttons,'" *Cleveland Call and Post*, Nov. 5, 1960.

197   *Hollowell now rushed to get*: Hollowell and Lehfeldt, *Sacred Call*, 135–36.

198 *"Crazy judge down there"*: Seigenthaler, interview by Tye, shared with the authors.

198 *"What do they want to hold"*: Draft in Speech file, LMP. Wofford's *Of Kennedys and Kings* puts Bobby's "honorary brother" call to Martin happening later that night, but we believe it was the night before given that Martin on multiple occasions told his detailed story of stopping a press conference based on what Bobby had told him in their late-night phone call. Given that it was on Thursday, October 27, that word of Bobby's call to Judge Mitchell was getting out, the phone call from Bobby had to come hours before that, in the middle of the night.

198 *"Well, they're trying to deny"*: Draft in Speech file, LMP.

198 *"Listen, don't put out any denial"*: Martin, interview by Grele, #2, JFKL.

198 *"For God's sake, don't call"*: Draft in Speech file, LMP.

199 *"There's a crazy story"*: Stein and Plimpton, *American Journey*, 93.

199 *"a brother of Kennedy had called"*: Wofford, interview by Bernhard, #1, JFKL.

199 *"It just can't be true"*: Stein and Plimpton, *American Journey*, 93.

199 *"I think you can"*: Wofford, interview by Bernhard, #1, JFKL.

199 *"Hell, no, don't do that"*: Hollowell and Lehfeldt, *Sacred Call*, 136.

199 *Balkcom would not have survived*: Clines, "1992 Campaign."

199 *"I'm sure glad to see you"*: Hollowell and Lehfeldt, *Sacred Call*, 136.

200 *Hollowell was moved by a chant*: Anderson, "Martin Luther King Reveals."

200 *"Long live the King!"*: Margaret Shannon and Douglas Kiker, "Out on Bond, King to Name Choice," *AJ*, Oct. 28, 1960.

200 *"Dr. King, you've heard the reports"*: WSB-TV newsfilm clip of Dr. Martin Luther King Jr., Oct. 27, 1960, UGA Libraries, as presented in the Digital Library of Georgia.

201 *"I understand from very reliable sources"*: Carson et al., *Papers of Martin Luther King Jr.*, 5:536.

201 *"I think I'll wait"*: Shannon and Kiker, "Out on Bond, King to Name Choice."

201 *"Bob, you'd never believe"*: Seigenthaler, interview by Grele, #2, JFKL. Historians have followed Seigenthaler's timeline of putting Bobby's call to Georgia, its fallout, and the writing of a press release all on the same day, but all that is improbable based on the judge's revealing the call the following day and Martin's rushing to stop their response the morning after Bobby called him in the night. Wofford's JFKL interview and memoir correctly put the scramble to clean up the Bobby story on the twenty-seventh. Given that Seigenthaler remembers getting Louis Martin to help draft the statement (Tye interview), it would have been impossible for this to have occurred the afternoon before Bobby's late-night call to Martin, when Martin always said he first learned about Bobby's outreach to the judge.

201 *his brother was hitting four boroughs*: "Kennedy to Stump in Four Boroughs," *NYT*, Oct. 26, 1960.

201 *"That crazy judge says"*: Seigenthaler, interview by Grele, #2, JFKL.

201 *"He thinks you're a young"*: Stein and Plimpton, *American Journey*, 94.

201 *"What did you say?"*: Seigenthaler, interview by Grele, #2, JFKL.

201 *"I just got so pissed off"*: Seigenthaler, interview by Tye.

201 *"I kept thinking that it"*: Stein and Plimpton, *American Journey*, 94.

202 *"I can't believe it"*: Seigenthaler, interview by Grele, #2, JFKL.

202 *"He just woke up this morning"*: Wofford, interview by Bernhard, #1, JFKL.

202 *"Jack was the tough one"*: Thomas, *Robert Kennedy*, 91.

203 *"John Kennedy was a realist"*: Schlesinger, *Robert Kennedy and His Times*, xiii.

203 *craft a statement denying*: Seigenthaler, interview by Grele, #2, JFKL. Seigenthaler's account makes it sound as if he learned Bobby made the call the same day as he saw him to the plane, but we believe it happened the following day. In another previously overlooked clue that the Mitchell call actually happened in the morning, Wofford recalled saying to Seigenthaler, "John, he called the judge this morning? How could he have done that?"

203 *"Robert F. Kennedy said tonight"*: Moore and Britton, "King Freed on $2,000 Bond."

203 *Sitting in a single-engine plane*: Peeks, "Great Experience Says Dr. King of Sojourn in Prison."

203   *Just as the pilot started*: Lewis, *King*, 128.

203   *They landed at the Peachtree-DeKalb*: Moore and Britton, "King Freed on $2,000 Bond"; Anderson, "Martin Luther King Reveals."

203   *"Welcome home, Dr. King"*: Anderson, "Martin Luther King Reveals"; "King, Negro Leader, Freed in Georgia on $2,000 Bond," *Baltimore Sun*, Oct. 28, 1960.

204   *The family had chartered a long*: Shannon and Kiker, "Out on Bond, King to Name Choice."

204   *"not softness, not naïveté"*: This and Watters's other reflections come from Watters, *Down to Now*, 53–62. Watters, a native of South Carolina and Georgia, was filling in on the civil rights beat. He had never seen King before this moment, when he noted King's vulnerability.

205   *King just had time to change*: Shannon and Kiker, "Out on Bond, King to Name Choice."

205   *Hollowell quietly returned*: Hollowell and Lehfeldt, *Sacred Call*, 137.

205   *few times he ever saw Hollowell*: Daniels, *Saving the Soul of Georgia*, 119–20.

205   *"Well, Don, I see that everybody"*: Hollowell and Lehfeldt, *Sacred Call*, 137.

205   *he had never seen a church this packed*: Lonnie King, interview.

205   *"It took courage to call"*: Moore and Britton, "King Freed on $2,000 Bond."

206   *"He can be my president"*: Shannon and Kiker, "Out on Bond, King to Name Choice."

206   *To the young Reverend Moss*: Moss interview, May 27, 2017.

206   *"he is a Catholic"*: Shannon and Kiker, "Out on Bond, King to Name Choice."

206   *"master the art of creative suffering"*: Moore and Britton, "King Freed on $2,000 Bond."

206   *"a dangerous man"*: Peeks, "Great Experience Says Dr. King of Sojourn in Prison."

207   *"creative and victorious moments"*: Moore and Britton, "King Freed on $2,000 Bond."

TIME TO DETONATE

209   *"Let's get all the horses"*: Wofford, *Of Kennedys and Kings*, 60.

209   *endorsements, ads in the Black media*: Martin, interview by Grele, #2, JFKL; Wofford, interview by Hackman, #2, JFKL. In *Jet*, Martin deliberately used font and color to make his Kennedy campaign ad buy indistinguishable from the usual *Jet* editorial content, save the inclusion of a minutely printed word in parentheses: "Advertisement." Per usual, Martin's ad linked JFK to FDR, the leader who inspired Martin to be a Democrat.

210   *"it was going to be a tight"*: Martin, interview by Anthony K. Shriver, JFKL.

210   *Martin had an idea*: Martin notebook, LMP; Martin, interview by Grele, #2, JFKL.

210   *A story from Martin's time campaigning*: Martin memoir draft, LMP.

211   *"might just as well have been"*: Martin memoir draft, LMP. Martin would never stop focusing on how racism manifested itself through the power of words. He became a journalist understanding that how one shaped a story shaped people's thoughts. From his first publication in high school on, he felt his work reflected "the horror and tragedy of racial discrimination and segregation."

211   *He could still see*: Poinsett, *Walking with Presidents*, 3.

211   *"I was twelve years old"*: Louis Martin, interview by Ed Edwin, # 10, Sept. 18, 1986, Columbia University Oral History Collection.

211   *"He's a white man"*: Martin memoir draft, LMP.

211   *because it resonated with him*: Martin notebook, LMP.

211   *"They don't read the* New York Times*"*: Stern, *Calculating Visions*, 37.

212   *"What do you want to put"*: Wofford, *Of Kennedys and Kings*, 22–23.

212   *"Okay. We've got to use"*: Stern, *Calculating Visions*, 37.

212   *"Then you don't need to ask"*: Wofford, *Of Kennedys and Kings*, 22–23.

212   *"we had a terrific propaganda coup"*: Shriver, interview by Anthony K. Shriver, JFKL. Given the reproductions done at local printers throughout the country, the numbers that were printed will never be precisely known.

212   *Martin and Wofford called Coretta*: Martin, interview by Grele, #2, JFKL.

214 *"Harris to bring out the damn paper"*: Wofford, interview.

214 *"Don't you think we've shot"*: Wofford, interview by Hackman, #3, JFKL.

214 *"Tell me honestly whether you think"*: Wofford, *Of Kennedys and Kings*, 28.

214 *"No, you don't need to"*: Wofford, interview.

214 *"Then we can wait"*: Wofford, *Of Kennedys and Kings*, 28.

214 *"Let's issue it right after"*: Wofford, interview by Hackman, #3, JFKL.

214 *"Let's go out to the plane"*: Wofford, interview.

214 *"Did you see what Martin's father"*: Wofford, *Of Kennedys and Kings*, 28.

215 *White House announced on Monday*: Felix Belair, "Eisenhower Adds 2 Crucial States to Campaign Trip," *NYT*, Nov. 1, 1960.

215 *"And with Martin Luther King in jail"*: Papers of John F. Kennedy, Pre-presidential Papers, Senate Files, Series 12, Speeches and the Press, box 914, Folder: "Rosen Apartments, Philadelphia, Pennsylvania, 31 October 1960," JFKL. Joseph Daughen, "Half-Million Cheer Kennedy Here," *Philadelphia Daily News*, Oct. 31, 1960; Philip Potter, "Kennedy," *Baltimore Sun*, Nov. 1, 1960.

216 *Bobby called political allies in Georgia*: Bruce Galphin, "His Call Misinterpreted, Robert Kennedy Says," *AC*, Nov. 1, 1960. Griffin Bell echoed Bobby's comment, saying the call had happened only because the campaign manager had been swamped with messages asking for information about King's fate. The *Constitution* called this "wise and welcome to those of us who support his brother." While they thought Mitchell's sentence was wrong, Bobby's call "went too far. We have indication from him now that he knows it, and this is a reassuring sign that common sense prevails in the Kennedy camp." "Robert Kennedy Reassures Us," *AC*, Nov. 1, 1960.

216 *"we were all anxious"*: "Bobby Kennedy Defends King Call," *AJ*, Nov. 3, 1960.

216 *"I think Sen. Kennedy did"*: Ruth Jenkins, "Intervention helped Kennedy Says King," *Baltimore Afro-American*, Nov. 12, 1960.

216 *With King's doctor ordering bed rest*: "No Plans on King, Fulton Discloses," *ADW*, Oct. 29, 1960; "NAACP Rally Draws 1,000," *Chicago Daily Defender*, Nov. 1, 1960. King was scheduled after the election to debate Georgia's Democratic chairman, James Gray, on a national NBC telecast concerning sit-ins, but Gray unexpectedly pulled out. King called his refusal a "tragic attempt of many leaders in the white South to live in monologue rather than dialogue." When told of King's response, Gray in turn replied, "He is a lawbreaker, and I don't think I should have any public association with him. I cannot, in conscience, engage in an exchange of views with a man who so obviously has such a studied contempt for the body of law which is both an Anglo-Saxon, as well as an American heritage." Gray added that Kennedy's calls had "made some folks mad, and it's going to cost some votes."

216 *October 30, was titled "Self Denial"*: "'Self Denial' to Be Dr. King Sr.'s Topic Sunday," *ADW*, Oct. 29, 1960.

216 *King still faced hearings in January*: DHP.

216 *"There are those moments in history"*: King, interview by Bernhard, JFKL.

217 *"didn't know it was politically"*: Ibid.

217 *"he had never heard of me"*: Ibid.

217 *"So this is why I really"*: Ibid.

217 *"You have to stay above"*: Belafonte, *My Song*, 219.

217 *even appearing in an ad*: Martin notebook, LMP.

218 *"The role that is mine"*: John Britton, "King Not Backing Either Candidate," *ADW*, Nov. 2, 1960.

218 *"was the kind act"*: Ibid.

218 *"Since Mr. Nixon has been silent"*: Ibid.

218 *"Dr. King intends to support"*: Carson et al., *Papers of Martin Luther King Jr.*, 5:537.

218 *"the state of Alabama and I"*: "Intervention Helped Kennedy Says King."

219 *"was like a shot of lightning"*: Shriver, interview by Anthony K. Shriver, JFKL. "Something very extraordinary happened and everybody became enthusiastic suddenly—overnight so to speak," Shriver remembered.

219 *The* Amsterdam News*'s estimation*: "Kennedy's Call to Mrs. King Won Votes," *Amsterdam News*, Nov. 1, 1960.

219 *calling Morrow for help*: Morrow, *Black Man in the White House*, 295.

219 *In Atlanta, a group of Republican ministers*: Farrington, *Black Republicans and the Transformation of the GOP*, 113.

219 *Cleveland's Public Square on Friday*: Laurence Burd, "Blasts Fiscal Shell Games as Ruinous," *Chicago Daily Tribune*, Nov. 5, 1960.

219 *"With every word he utters"*: Oliphant and Wilkie, *Road to Camelot*, 332.

219 *"Goddammit, I didn't know"*: Harris Wofford, interview by Bill Moyers, event for Corporation for Civic Documentaries at the New York Public Library, Jan. 13, 2016.

220 *"We'll sweat it out"*: Wofford, *Of Kennedys and Kings*, 21.

220 *In the week leading up to the election*: Martin, interview by Grele, #2, JFKL.

220 *"moved to show his concern"*: Martin, interview by Anthony K. Shriver, JFKL.

220 *papers like Norfolk, Virginia's* Journal and Guide: Martin, interview by Grele, #2, JFKL.

220 *"The Democrats did a great deal"*: Lillian S. Calhoun, "Says Dixie Bloc Can't Unseat Kennedy King Urges U.S. to Take Rights Stand," *Chicago Daily Defender*, Nov. 22, 1960. Interestingly, this article was written by Louis Martin's sister-in-law, the journalist Lillian S. Calhoun.

220 *"Pass the word through"*: Martin, interview by Grele, #2, JFKL.

220 *"Unions helped get them out, too"*: Edwin A. Lahey, "$5 in Phone Calls Key to Election?" *Fort Worth Star-Telegram*, Nov. 10, 1960.

220 *"to be the dramatic thing"*: Martin, interview by Grele, #2, JFKL.

220 *Detroit, Philadelphia, Chicago, New York*: Martin, interview by Anthony K. Shriver, JFKL.

221 *"electricity"*: Franklin Williams, interview by Anthony K. Shriver, *Kennedy's Call to King*.

221 *His friend Dr. Kenneth Clark*: Rampersad, *Jackie Robinson*, 351.

221 *"shrewd political move"*: Jackie Robinson, untitled, *Los Angeles Sentinel*, Nov. 24, 1960.

221 *a 'grandstand play'"*: Long, *First Class Citizenship*, 115. Jim Bassett, who did public relations for Nixon's campaign, remembers Nixon was asked to visit the Quinn Chapel AME Church, Chicago's oldest Black church. Nixon would not accept the invitation. Bassett recounted that Nixon was "in mortal fear of some kind of demonstration," keeping him away from visits into Black neighborhoods. There also was an offer for Nixon to have a meeting with top Chicago Black religious and business leaders. Nixon's aide H. R. Haldeman called Bassett two days before the event and said, "The boss says he ain't going to do that n——r thing in Chicago." Bassett complained that he "busted his ass to arrange this." All Haldeman would say was, "The boss says he ain't going to do that n——r thing" (Farrington, *Black Republicans and the Transformation of the GOP*, 104).

221 *"woefully weak in organization"*: Simeon Booker, "How Nixon Campaigns for the Negro Vote: Vice President, GOP Banking on Party's Rights Record," *Jet*, Nov. 3, 1960.

222 *"a most able corps"*: Lester Granger, "Manhattan and Beyond," *Amsterdam News*, Dec. 3, 1960.

222 *"make enough gains in our communities"*: Booker, "How Nixon Campaigns for the Negro Vote."

222 *"forthright position"*: "Negro Leader King All but Endorses Kennedy in Race," *Boston Globe*, Nov. 7, 1960.

222 *"I think more and more"*: Carson et al., *Papers of Martin Luther King Jr.*, 5:551.

222 *"They alone provided him"*: Ralph McGill, "An Essay on Dr. M. L. King," *AC*, Nov. 5, 1960.

223 Life *magazine wrote of how*: Wainwright, "Martyr of the Sit-Ins."

223 *"These white folks have now made"*: Anderson, "Martin Luther King Reveals."

223 *"in the last seven days"*: Remarks of Senator John F. Kennedy, Concourse Plaza Hotel, Bronx, New York, Nov. 5, 1960, JFKL.

224 *Instead, he told the driver*: Matthews, *Jack Kennedy*, 313–14.

224 *Nixon had reached a breaking point*: Frank, *Ike and Dick*, 213.

224 *Late Saturday night, Wofford was lugging*: Wofford, interview.

224 *Twenty thousand people were out*: Harrison E. Salisbury, "Senator Cheered," *NYT*, Nov. 7, 1960.

224 *In Chicago, Shriver had been*: Stossel, *Sarge*, 168.

225 *More than a quarter of a million*: Wofford, *Of Kennedys and Kings*, 24.

225 *Shriver wanted to see it all*: Shriver, interview by Anthony K. Shriver, JFKL. The South Side church was famous for its music and thought of as the birthplace of modern gospel with the infusion of spiritual songs with blues rhythm. The man mostly responsible for this development, Thomas Dorsey, had written "Precious Lord, Take My Hand," a song King would call for during his last moments in Memphis.

225 *"Eight Days Behind Bars"*: "'Eight Days Behind Bars' to Be Dr. King's Topic at Ebenezer Sunday," *ADW*, Nov. 5, 1960.

226 *"I think I received a new"*: Garrow, *Bearing the Cross*, 149.

226 *Wofford was getting reports*: Wofford, *Of Kennedys and Kings*, 24–25.

226 *bringing back from the Harlem bars*: Martin, interview by Grele, #2, JFKL; Wofford, *Of Kennedys and Kings*, 25; Poinsett, *Walking with Presidents*, 24–25.

226 *most influential election for the region*: Arthur Krock, "The South's Vote," *NYT*, Nov. 6, 1960.

226 *When asked about sit-ins*: Richard Nixon, Remarks of Vice President Richard M. Nixon, National Telethon, ABC Network, Southfield, Mich., online by Gerhard Peters and John T. Woolley, American Presidency Project, www.presidency.ucsb.edu/node/273809.

226 *Meanwhile, in Boston, hundreds of thousands*: Homer Bigart, "Kennedy Closes Drive in Boston," *NYT*, Nov. 8, 1960.

227 *"It can go either way"*: Charles Grutzner, "3 of 4 Election Polls Give Kennedy the Edge in Close Vote," *NYT*, Nov. 8, 1960.

227 *to drive west, home to Chicago*: Louis E. Martin, interview by Ronald Grele, #3, May 11, 1966, JFKL; Louis Martin, interview by McComb, LBJ Presidential Library. The day before the election, the *Defender* spoke directly to Black voters (in an editorial that might have been written by the former editor Martin): "We have a date with history. In looking at Nixon and the last eight years, we want a change, a new landscape, a new vista of hope and opportunity." Calling Nixon a man backed by the Grand Dragon of the KKK, they wanted Kennedy, "the man who saved Rev. Martin Luther King from the jaws of the monster of race prejudice in Georgia, the man who will transform America into a real democracy. To vote for him to-morrow is to meet our date with history. We must not fail" ("To-Morrow—Day of Decision," *Chicago Daily Defender*, Nov. 7, 1960). On the other hand, back in Georgia, the *Rome News-Tribune* was making their endorsement of Nixon a reminder of a white reaction that could cost the Democrats the election. They chided Kennedy's "cynical and determined bid for a majority vote by the intrusion of himself and associates in Georgia's affairs—the Martin Luther King case" ("We Support Vice President Nixon," *Rome News-Tribune*, Nov. 6, 1960). The *Los Angeles Times* warned with Georgia, "There has been resentment among white voters of Kennedy's sympathy phone call to Mrs. Martin Luther King Jr." ("AP Poll Puts Kennedy in Electoral Vote Lead," *Los Angeles Times*, Nov. 7, 1960). In Atlanta, the *Inquirer* had cited *The Wall Street Journal* on the late movement toward Democrats among northern Black voters, supposing Kennedy would do more for their pocketbooks ("Possible North-South Split in Negro Vote," *AI*, Oct. 31, 1960). Closer to home, however, they predicted that Nixon would win Atlanta Black voters two to one ("Negros Favor Kennedy in 7, Lean to Nixon in 2," *AI*, Nov. 7, 1960). That day, the man who so unexpectedly had influenced this race was not at a campaign rally or standing by a candidate. Instead, Martin Luther King was spending that Monday speaking to more than a thousand beauticians at a hairstylist conference in Atlanta at the Auburn Avenue Casino ("Keynote Speaker at Opening Session of Bronner's Beauty Clinic, Monday, 9 A.M.," *ADW*, Nov. 5, 1960). King's instinct was to be with working people, not politicians.

227 *When Martin got to Chicago*: Martin notebook, LMP; Martin, interview by McComb, #1, LBJ Presidential Library; Martin, interview by Grele, #2, JFKL. Somehow Shriver tracked Martin down by telephone to the South Side ward he was helping with, asking if he could meet him at the Merchandise Mart as soon as possible. Shriver had one last assignment, and it was not about the Black vote. He explained Republicans were making a play for Jewish voters by spreading

rumors of Joe Kennedy being an anti-Semite. Shriver wanted to counter this with a broadcast that night, but the problem was he had no airtime, script, or broadcaster. Other than that, the plan sounded good; Martin was happy to help. In a few hours, Martin performed his usual political magic to get on air with a persuasive message and a respected host, Philip Klutznick.

"IT WAS A SYMPHONY"

229 *From the moment the sun rose*: Marion E. Jackson, "Atlanta Turnout for Vote Is Big," *ADW*, Nov. 9, 1960.

229 *Kennedy voted at a quiet library*: White, *Making of the President, 1960*, 3–7.

230 *Nixon took off down the California coast*: Frank, *Ike and Dick*, 216–17; Nixon, *Six Crises*, 377–78.

230 *"Well, just take it easy"*: Wofford, interview by Hackman, #2, JFKL.

230 *"moved in action and responded"*: Ibid.

230 *"They were not systematic calculators"*: Schlesinger, *Robert Kennedy and His Times*, 193.

230 Viva Zapata, *with Marlon Brando*: Wofford, interview.

231 *Martin's nine-year-old daughter*: Dr. Toni Martin interview by the authors, May 16, 2017. The Martins lived at the time at 5301 S. Greenwood Avenue at East Fifty-Third Street.

232 *Bobby, a continent away*: White, *Making of the President, 1960*, 15–25; O'Donnell, *Playing with Fire*, 139.

232 *"We're being clobbered"*: White, *Making of the President, 1960*, 16.

232 *Then the poll closings*: Donaldson, *First Modern Campaign*, 144–47.

232 *he could be a worrier*: Trudy Martin Hatter, interview by the authors, May 16, 2017.

232 *Nearing midnight in the West*: Nixon, *Six Crises*, 385–86.

233 *"Kennedy Elected"*: This headline can be found in Kallina, *Kennedy v. Nixon*, 179.

233 *At 4:00 a.m., Kennedy walked the short*: White, *Making of the President, 1960*, 24–25, 345. Ironically, Kennedy was told he won California the next morning, but a week later, with heavily Republican absentee ballots coming in, in fact Nixon won it.

234 *"I think the Negro vote"*: Philip Potter, "Robert Kennedy Says Debates Won Election," *Baltimore Sun*, Nov. 10, 1960.

234 *Nixon should have focused*: Thomas B. Ross, "Kennedy Urges 'Supreme Effort,'" *Chicago Sun Times*, Nov. 10, 1960.

234 *"A good argument can be made"*: Harold Davis, "Did Judge in King Case Supply Kennedy His Edge?," *AJ*, Nov. 10, 1960.

234 *The headline in the* Inquirer: "Negroes Clinched Kennedy Win," *AI*, Nov. 14, 1960.

234 *Mayor Hartsfield moaned to friends*: Raleigh Bryans, "Mayor Pained by Negro Vote," *AJ*, Nov. 9, 1960; Ed Hughes, "Fulton Negro Vote for GOP Is Surprise," *AJ*, Nov. 10, 1960. Another subsequent estimate put it at 58 percent (Farrington, *Black Republicans and the Transformation of the GOP*, 113).

235 *"If Kennedy hadn't made"*: "DeKalb Goes GOP," *AJ*, Nov. 9, 1960.

235 *the* Constitution *proclaimed that he had garnered*: "Nixon's 38 Pct. a Record in Georgia," *AC*, Nov. 11, 1960.

235 *a massive political realignment*: Johnson won a stunning 94 percent of the Black vote nationally. Rigueur, *Loneliness of the Black Republican*, 311.

"THEY JUST ALL TURNED"

237 *"Mr. Vice President, I can't tell you"*: Nixon, *Six Crises*, 403.

237 *"Their Martin Luther King gambit"*: Farrell, *Richard Nixon*, 289.

237 *"I just didn't realize"*: Ibid., 288.

238 *"the guy is out now"*: "GG" to Finch, Nov. 15, 1960, King files, PPS, RNL.

238 *"I look forward to future meetings"*: Nixon to King, June 16, 1962, King files, PPS, RNL.

238 *"I could have become President"*: Booker, "Richard Nixon Tells."

239 *"just killed us in the South"*: Frank, *Ike and Dick*, 220.

239 *"a bought vote"*: Thurber, *Republicans and Race*, 133. The Kentucky senator and RNC chair, Thruston Morton, was quite open about why he thought his candidate lost. "We lost the Negro vote by a larger percentage than we have been," he stated, mentioning Illinois, Michigan, and Pennsylvania. Davis, "Did Judge in King Case Supply Kennedy His Edge?"

239 *"couple of phone calls"*: Lewis, "Protest over Dr. King's Arrest Was Drafted for President's Use."

240 *"This act won the election"*: Morrow, *Black Man in the White House*, 296–97.

240 *"the strategy of wooing"*: Ibid.

241 *"curb the power of the southern"*: *Los Angeles Sentinel*, Nov. 24, 1960.

241 *"Senator Kennedy took a risk"*: Eleanor Roosevelt, My Day, Nov. 14, 1960.

241 *"I thought it was a disservice"*: Marjorie Lawson, interview by Grele, #2, JFKL. This belief was echoed in Black Republican papers such as *The Philadelphia Tribune*, which wrote, "Negroes are satisfied with the froth, rather than the substance of politics . . . It is this kind of nonsense which blocks the progress of Negroes in politics; which prevents them from having any real power in government" (Nov. 8, 1960). A letter said, "Is THAT 'angelic' act supposed to suffice for 20 million Negroes?" (Nov. 22, 1960).

242 *"an existential affirmation"*: Sam Proctor, interview by Anthony K. Shriver, *Kennedy's Call to King*.

242 *"a major factor in influencing"*: Williams, interview by Anthony K. Shriver, JFKL.

242 *"No presidential candidate had ever"*: Young, interview by the authors.

242 *seven percentage points*: Rigueur, *Loneliness of the Black Republican*, 39, 311; Brauer, *John F. Kennedy and the Second Reconstruction*, 58–59. See also Bryant, *Bystander*, 187–88.

242 *to a commanding 68 percent*: Rigueur, *Loneliness of the Black Republican*, 311. Charts of the Black vote through election cycles put the number at 68 percent (though Gallup listed it at 70 percent). IBM and Gallup numbers from White, *Making of the President, 1960*. Without the Black vote increases, it is estimated that Nixon would have narrowly won the popular vote and would have had a landslide win in electoral votes.

242 *"The 1960 election proved"*: Farrington, *Black Republicans and the Transformation of the GOP*, 7.

243 *Kennedy's pollster Louis Harris*: Surveys of the Presidential Election in Various States, Robert F. Kennedy Pre-administration Political Files, 1960 Campaign and Transition, General Subject File, 1959–1960, boxes 43–45, JFKL; Sullivan, *Symbol of Virtue or a Strategy for Votes?*, 54–56.

243 *Kennedy's existing lead*: Kennedy surged in Martin's home state of Illinois, from 76 percent up to 82 percent, in Pennsylvania from 66 percent to 74 percent, in Maryland from 64 percent to 66 percent, and in North Carolina from being behind Nixon, 53 percent to 47 percent, to a lead of 88 percent to 12 percent. However, this increase was not found in every state: Kennedy's already high support in Texas, 83 percent, polled at 71 percent after the call, and New York fell to 63 percent from 66 percent. Connecticut was polled only after the call and found Kennedy at 68 percent.

243 *Martin would say you had to*: Martin, interview by Anthony K. Shriver, JFKL.

243 *Key urban wards across the country*: Scammon, "How the Negroes Voted"; Layhmond Robinson, "Negro Vote Gave Kennedy Big Push," *NYT*, Nov. 11, 1960; Lewis, "Protest over Dr. King's Arrest Was Drafted for President's Use"; White, *Making of the President, 1960*, 354; Sullivan, *Symbol of Virtue or a Strategy for Votes?*, 61–64. Kennedy's reversing the Republicans' 1956 progress could be seen in five South Side Chicago wards, where Kennedy went from Stevenson's 63 up to 78 percent; a Philadelphia ward where Democrats went from 74 to 84 percent; Ward 5 in Pittsburgh going from 68 to 78 percent; three largely Black New York City districts going from 64 to 75 percent; two Black Baltimore wards increasing from 48 to 74 percent; an important Memphis ward going from 36 to 68 percent; three Nashville Black wards flipping to the Democrats, with similar movement in areas within South Carolina, Texas, and Georgia;

predominantly Black Charles City County, Virginia, shooting from 19 to 65 percent, and the eight Black precincts of King's Atlanta improving from 15 to 42 percent. *The Chicago Daily Defender*, Dec. 1, 1960, recorded Black wards in its city went from 66 percent Stevenson to 80 percent Kennedy. It also reported Virginia and South Carolina Black voters went from a majority supporting Eisenhower to 60 percent for Kennedy.

After the election, *The New Republic* (Scammon, "How the Negroes Voted.") reported Illinois was won by fewer than 10,000 votes, with more than 350,000 Black people voting for Kennedy; Michigan decided by just over 65,000 with at least 225,000 Black votes for Kennedy; New Jersey taken by fewer than 30,000 with more than 125,000 Black votes for Kennedy; and South Carolina with a difference of under 10,000 with 60,000 Black residents registered to vote. Theodore White pointed to Delaware, Illinois, Maryland, Michigan, Missouri, New Jersey, North Carolina, Pennsylvania, Texas, and South Carolina as potentially due to Black vote margins.

243 *Martin's greatest concern*: Martin, interview by Anthony K. Shriver, JFKL.

243 *Nationally, data showed that Black turnout was indeed higher*: Flanigan et al., *Political Behavior of the American Electorate*, 76.

243 *anecdotal evidence*: White, *Making of the President, 1960*, 354.

243 *Black voters made the difference*: Niven, *Politics of Injustice*, 166–68.

243 *"Negro Vote Held Vital to Kennedy"*: Anthony Lewis, "Negro Vote Held Vital to Kennedy," *NYT*, Nov. 27, 1960. Kennedy took Texas by more than forty-five thousand while winning the majority of the hundred thousand Black voters; roughly seventy thousand North Carolina Black people voted for Kennedy when he won by below fifty-eight thousand; and South Carolina had a margin of fewer than ten thousand with more than forty thousand people supporting Kennedy.

244 *a New Republic study of the Black vote*: Scammon, "How the Negroes Voted."

244 *"hard work" of the CRS*: White, *Making of the President, 1960*, 354. A White article four years before ("The Negro Voter. Can He Elect a President?," *Collier's*, Aug. 17, 1956) on the rising Black vote in northern urban centers was a prescient indicator of what was to come.

244 *White pointed to eleven states*: White, *Making of the President, 1960*, 354.

245 *"Most people in life and in politics"*: Wofford, interview by Anthony K. Shriver, JFKL. Wofford told us, "Robert and John both, their changes came about because facts change; they were very realistic, they wanted very much to know what the real story was."

      Once they did, "the fact that Jack had made the call about which no one had checked—Bob had every reason to be angry with Louis and me and Sarge. We were under Robert Kennedy, and it was a big thing, the call to Mrs. King, and we hadn't mentioned it to Robert Kennedy or his team, so he first was just angry with us that we had done that on our own. [Bobby] was being his best self figuring out what to do. The call already made, he had to deal with that fact, and the best way to solve it, was, you know, to end King's arrest."

245 *the Kennedys being their best selves*: Wofford, interview.

245 *his 1964 oral history*: Guthman and Shulman, *Robert Kennedy in His Own Words*, 70–71.

245 *"Once having started it"*: Wofford, interview.

246 *King himself, in his Kennedy Library*: King, interview by Bernhard, JFKL.

246 *"the Kennedy family did have some part"*: Grier, "Martin Luther King Jr. and John F. Kennedy." This gentle insistence from King is evident in a recently discovered tape, long forgotten in a Tennessee attic for half a century, now held by the National Civil Rights Museum. Taped for a book that was never written, King recounts what each Kennedy brother did, but references, almost in a resigned way, all those close to him in Atlanta who worked to free him as well and whose efforts had been mostly overlooked.

247 *One* Inquirer *headline read*: "King: Public Freed Him," *AI*, Nov. 7, 1960.

247 *"If there was any critical pressure"*: Ibid.

247 *"Those of us who knew"*: Vandiver, interview by Pyle, GSU. Vandiver said, "Jack Kennedy thought that made the difference, he really did, he told me that."

247   *Vandiver first began to talk*: Vandiver, interview by Stewart, May 22, 1967, JFKL. This put historians such as Jack Bass and Clifford Kuhn on the hunt, both of whom did critical work before Vandiver's death, of pinning down otherwise obscured details of what happened.

248   *President Kennedy himself apparently told*: Vandiver, interview by Pyle, GSU.

248   *in the wake of a Christmas party*: Ibid.

248   *"Since King had to be released"*: Pou, "King Call Arranger Was George Stewart."

248   *in certain Georgia circles*: Vandiver, interview by Kuhn, GSU. Stewart was quoted about the back channel in the one *Atlanta Journal* interview (Pou, "King Call Arranger Was George Stewart") and then went quiet. Bob Russell died of cancer at age forty in 1965, with President Johnson attending the funeral.

248   *many of those involved had died*: Henderson, *Ernest Vandiver*, 201; *AJC*, Jan. 18, 1998. Stewart died in 1977.

248   *"He sat out the jailing"*: Galbraith, *Ambassador's Journal*, 6.

249   *Kennedy adviser Dick Goodwin*: Dick Goodwin, interview by authors, Jan. 23, 2017. It remains improbable that the Kennedy brothers "acted individually." Vandiver said they worked in chorus, Seigenthaler was not in a position to know, and the CRS was too busy, too committed to its own dangerous course, to ask. In an interview with us before his death, the assistant Kennedy speechwriter Richard Goodwin, the last living person who rode the Kennedy campaign plane, told us in response to this notion, "Let me assure you, Bobby never did anything, never made a move, without Jack approving it." The calls back and forth between them were constant.

249   *"The finest strategies are usually"*: Galbraith, *Ambassador's Journal*, 6.

249   *"get back to Washington"*: Louis Martin, interview by McComb, #1, LBJ Presidential Library.

249   *"If you thought you were going"*: Wofford, *Of Kennedys and Kings*, 68. With Martin and Wofford working as feverishly as before on the talent search, King tried to reach the president-elect to first recommend Morris Abram for solicitor general (he would end up working with Shriver and Wofford as the Peace Corps's first counsel) and to recommend his mentor Dr. Mays be appointed to the Civil Rights Commission or as ambassador to Israel. Wofford and Martin came up short on those. The Georgia senators, Richard Russell and Herman Talmadge, blocked Mays from moving forward.

At the same time, Wofford was dismayed to learn that Vandiver was being considered for secretary of the Army. When Wofford implored Kennedy not to appoint him—at least not until he integrated Georgia's schools—it turned out Vandiver had already turned down the administration.

250   *"Who's Who of Negro experts"*: Martin, interview by Grele, #3, JFKL.

250   *"There was an opportunity"*: Martin, interview by Edwin, #3, Columbia University Oral History Collection. Martin's daughters, Dr. Toni Martin and Trudy Martin Hatter, told us that the suspicion in their family was that their father was kept out of the administration because of his closeness with Detroit labor unions. Dr. Martin later requested her father's FBI file, but did not find any record of vetting that got that far. One of Martin's first projects during the Kennedy administration was pressuring Attorney General Robert Kennedy to have J. Edgar Hoover take the NAACP off the FBI's subversives list. He did so because false connections to communism caused Black apointees and nominees vetting and security clearance problems.

250   *a generation of Black presidential appointees*: Eisenhower made more notable appointments than previous presidents had managed, such as Jewel Rogers as Assistant U.S. Attorney, J. Ernest Wilkins as assistant secretary of labor, and Roberta Church to a policy-making role in the same agency. See Gellman, *The President and the Apprentice*, 137. But Martin's ambitions and success were on a scale more impressive than in the earlier Eisenhower years. The Kennedys had a long way to go; important administration appointments went almost exclusively to those Kennedy was at ease with: white men, mostly in their thirties and forties—smart without being dull; witty instead of self-righteous. There were Black men who served on White House staff during the Kennedy administration in fairly uninfluential positions, such as Andrew Hatcher as a

Salinger press aide and the CRS's Frank Reeves briefly, before being forced out over a personal tax issue.

250 *"some black sitting in the White House"*: Draft, Speech File, LMP.

250 *"Louis and I continued"*: Wofford, "Remembering Shriver on JFK's Inauguration Day." Though not part of their official duties, multiple times a week Wofford and Martin convened in Shriver's Mayflower hotel room to help shape what would become the Peace Corps. The *Chicago Daily Defender* wrote that Martin, Shriver, and Wofford's vision "will be reassuring in Africa and in underdeveloped countries where the Peace Corps will meet its real tests" (Robert G. Spivack, "Watch on the Potomac," *Chicago Daily Defender*, March 29, 1961). Robert Troutman, the Kennedys' Atlanta contact who tried to derail involvement in the King case, stopped in to see Shriver and, after admitting things worked out unexpectedly well, added, "But I hope all you bomb-throwers will now be corralled in one place, like the Peace Corps, so all your energies can be directed overseas instead of toward Georgia." Wofford, *Of Kennedys and Kings*, 99.

251 *"His career would have been bright"*: Booker, "Richard Nixon Tells."

251 *"be in it but not of it"*: Morrow, *Forty Years a Guinea Pig*, 6.

251 *"a certain nuisance value"*: Ibid., 7.

252 *"As I turned to go inside"*: Nixon, *Memoirs of Richard Nixon*, 227–28.

252 *The Georgia Court of Appeals*: "King's Sentence Ruled in Error," *ADW*, March 8, 1961.

252 *Daddy King was out there*: "Adults Join Youth on Picket Lines," *AI*, Dec. 15, 1961.

252 *"with dignity and without incident"*: Burns, "Integration of Atlanta Public Schools."

252 *Days later, Black customers*: Clemmons, *Rich's*, 130–31.

253 *"Today, a Negro stands no chance"*: A. S. "Doc" Young, "The Big Beat: Final Election Comments," *Los Angeles Sentinel*, Nov. 17, 1960.

253 *"There's no question"*: Sabato, *Kennedy Half-Century*, 395.

EPILOGUE: THE DUNGEON SHOOK

256 *"not surprise, but shock"*: King, *My Life with Martin Luther King Jr.*, 293.

256 *"Well, I tell you, it's pretty bad"*: King, *My Life, My Love, My Legacy*, 161.

256 *"I always thought I would go"*: Ibid., 163.

256 *When the news reached him*: Lonnie King, interview.

257 *"Wyatt Tee will be handling"*: Ibid. As the sit-in campaign wound down, Lonnie believed his leadership team had forged the best agreement they could to integrate downtown businesses; the catch was that city leaders felt it should be implemented only after vital school desegregation in the fall. The student activist feared the reaction this compromise he helped forge might receive. At a final mass meeting on March 10, 1961, Daddy King tried to sell the student community on the new compromise terms, but the crowd grew so unruly that even his preacher's voice could not be heard. Worse, King senior lost his temper, bellowing toward the students' disrespect, "I've been working for civil rights for over thirty years." From the upper balcony, a woman shouted out, "That's what's wrong." Lonnie thought he saw Daddy King's heart breaking, and he quickly went out of the room to call Dr. King, pleading, "We need you to come over here to calm this crowd down." One more time, King did what Lonnie asked. Lonnie remembers the way King entered the angry meeting, personally shaken that his father, after all he had done for them, should be exposed to this fury. Lonnie describes what King did: "This man took the crowd up the hill and back to the valley . . . with tears in his eyes." Lonnie watched with amazement at how King eased people's frustration, until they could finally accept a painful path to progress.

Recovering from having had acid thrown in his face while picketing, Lonnie felt so exhausted from his efforts that he, as well as Herschelle Sullivan, tried to resign. In an acrimonious session, students refused to let them, but feeling burned out from all he had risked, Lonnie left Atlanta a few months later for a new start at Howard Law School.

258   *Harris Wofford, by then president of SUNY*: Wofford, *Of Kennedys and Kings*, 201.

258   *"I felt that he was a friend"*: Stein and Plimpton, *American Journey*, 257.

258   *"I still had the feeling"*: Coretta King, interview by Jean Stein, *American Journey* interview transcript, Jean Stein Personal Papers, JFKL.

259   *"My family has experience"*: Burns, *Burial for a King*, 39.

259   *"I don't really see anything"*: Stein and Plimpton, *American Journey*, 257.

259   *"Although they were political figures"*: Schlesinger, *Robert Kennedy and His Times*, 876.

259   *"You will never know the meaning"*: Carson, *Autobiography of Martin Luther King Jr.*, 184.

260   *Kennedy's death being the first*: Martin memoir draft, Speeches and Writings File, LMP. As he records in his unpublished autobiographical papers, when Martin heard the news Kennedy had been shot, he was at a work lunch. He immediately took off running down K Street to the DNC offices. After an aimless hour there, he decided to go to the White House, not knowing what else to do. There he encountered Shriver, who was already working on funeral arrangements, having been selected by the family to head up this unimaginably difficult task. Even in his shock, Shriver was relieved to see an old trusted partner like Martin arrive; Martin remembered fondly how then Shriver referenced the "magic" Martin helped create in the old CRS days. Over the next four days, emotionally wrought, they worked together under incredible pressure.

They heard the sound of Marine One landing on the South Lawn, bringing President Johnson to the White House, his new home. As he always did, Shriver gathered ideas from everyone, arranging everything for the arrival of the president's casket at the East Room. Working deep into the night, Martin finally saw the headlights of the motorcade approaching the North Lawn. Soldiers carried the flag-covered bier, with Jackie and Bobby led by Shriver, to where the casket would rest in the center of the darkened East Room. Martin looked on as Jackie lit the candles, still in her bloodstained pink suit, and at last he then wept. He went home for four hours of sleep, then returned to assist the family however he could.

The third member of the CRS team almost made it back to America to be with them. When Wofford was awakened in Addis Ababa, Ethiopia, with the sickening news that the president was dead, he rushed to turn on his shortwave radio. Hearing that the emperor Haile Selassie would be flying to the funeral, he rushed to the airport to talk himself onto the plane, but it was taking off just as Wofford arrived.

On the day of the burial, Martin marched in the funeral procession, walking alongside other Kennedy friends and staffers down Connecticut Avenue toward St. Matthew's in cold sunlight. Reaching the Arlington National Cemetery burial site, dark leaves strewn everywhere, he noticed Nixon standing in the back of the throng. Martin thought that Kennedy's rival seemed younger than he had imagined, and wondered what Nixon must be pondering, watching his opponent honored among the nation's fallen.

260   *his daughter Anita's wedding*: Poinsett, *Walking with Presidents*, 165.

261   *"it's not credible"*: Dwight Chapin, interview by Timothy Naftali, April 2, 2007, Richard Nixon Oral History Project, RNL.

261   *"a prisoner of the moment"*: Perlstein, *Nixonland*, 263.

261   *"The danger of the Republican Party"*: Rampersad, *Jackie Robinson*, 384.

261   *Goldwater supporters in Georgia*: Farrington, *Black Republicans and the Transformation of the GOP*, 131.

261   *to attend would be "grandstanding"*: Safire, *Before the Fall*, 59–60; Safire, "View from the Grandstand."

262   *"This can never be talked about"*: Chapin, interview by Naftali, April 2, 2007.

262   *"Dwight, how's our trip to Atlanta"*: This and the exchange that follows also come from ibid. Nixon barked at Chapin what was supposed to have been deduced: "The whole purpose in our doing it was so that we would do it privately, we were not taking advantage of it, and we would not have to go to the funeral."

263 *"Many have said you helped"*: WSB-TV newsfilm clip of an interview with Dr. Martin Luther King Jr., Nov. 22, 1963, UGA Libraries, Digital Library of Georgia. King said, "I was very upset and couldn't adjust to it, and could hardly believe it in the very beginning." He was asked what it was like to live under the threat of his own assassination: "This is where I have decided to stand, and I believe firmly that this cause is right. And that someone must have the courage and the fortitude to stand up for it, even if it means suffering or even if it means death." This was his reality. If he had to die for this movement, it would be worth it, "to free the soul of our nation and free our children from a permanent spiritual death."

264 *memorial march in Memphis*: Wofford, *Of Kennedys and Kings*, 203.

264 *put King's interests above his brother's*: In Bobby's oral history interview, when asked why Wofford was not named to the post, Bobby was cutting to the extreme: "Harris Wofford was very emotionally involved in all these matters and was rather in some areas a slight madman." Bobby amplified this in his oral history, saying, "And the person who was logical for the position was Harris Wofford, who wanted the position, and who Sargent Shriver and everybody who was associated with our fight on civil rights wanted for that job." A tape of Bobby's caustic assessment is featured in the documentary on Wofford's life titled, after this quotation, *Slightly Mad*.

Bobby justified choosing the white corporate lawyer Burke Marshall over Wofford (a man Wofford magnanimously suggested) by saying, "I didn't want to have someone in the Civil Rights Division who was dealing not from fact but was dealing from emotion and who wasn't going to give what was in the best interest of President Kennedy . . . I wanted advice and ideas from somebody who had the same interests and motivation that I did." Under further prompting, Bobby added, in reference to Wofford's work founding the Peace Corps with Shriver, that Wofford was "a fine fellow. And he did a terrific job . . . I just don't think that he would have been fitted for the position."

Just to make sure his instinct was correct, Bobby had Byron White, the new deputy attorney general, have a drink with Wofford. White asked, "What did you think of Bob Kennedy's call to the judge in the Martin Luther King case?" Wofford, perhaps thinking he should appear tough-minded, offered, "I thought it was unprofessional, but not enough to disbar him, but it was pretty bad." White said, "Well, you'll be pleased to know that I'm the one who recommended to Bob that he call the judge." (Wofford, interview by Hackman, #3, JFKL.) As a cautious Kennedy adviser, White was making a quite unlikely claim, about a call that was only later seen as a wise move. Hearing this dubious claim, Wofford realized another avenue into power was likely closed to him. Sorensen would be one of the few Kennedy staffers to ever admit being against Kennedy calling Coretta, something he later confessed had been a personal oversight. Sorensen remembered a staff debate over whether the call should be made, which was more likely some discussion of whether the call should have been made (*Counselor*, 271). Others, like O'Donnell and Richard Goodwin, would in later years remember themselves as having been open to, or even encouraging, the call.

265 *he asked the president to let him*: Wofford to President Kennedy, Jan. 23 and March 7, 1962, Papers of John F. Kennedy, Presidential Papers, President's Office Files, JFKL. In bidding farewell to Wofford, the president said, "It will take some more time, but I want you to know that we are going to do all these things" (Wofford, *Of Kennedys and Kings*, 125). The habitually ironic Kennedy sounded uncharacteristically earnest: "You will see, with time, I'm going to do them all." He was right that Wofford's list would eventually be realized, but time was not what he had. It was the last time they would ever speak.

265 *It was on Ethiopian radio*: Wofford, *Of Kennedys and Kings*, 171.

265 *"They say that his call"*: Ibid., 11.

266 *"I let Nixon in"*: Lonnie King, interview. Daddy King's autobiography lists a number of famous people at his son's funeral, but interestingly omits Nixon's name. King Sr., *Daddy King*, 173.

267 *Atlanta in 1964 on political business*: Martin flew down to Atlanta in 1964 to ensure the minister's cooperation nixing a fraudulent RNC leaflet telling Black voters that they should write in

King for president. Martin sat across from King in his humble Sunset Avenue home, impressed by how the leader made you feel you were important by how he listened. On that visit, Martin was in Atlanta only three hours, with King happy to denounce any claim he was in any way a candidate, so Martin set up a King press conference and heard it on the radio in his taxi back to the airport.

267 *"an apostle of love"*: Remarks by Louis Martin, Deputy Chairman, Democratic National Committee. Speech at the Colorado State Young Democrats Convention, Denver, April 27, 1968, LMP.

267 *"turning point in King's life"*: Martin memoir draft, LMP.

267 *"Our time seems to be"*: Speech at the Colorado State Young Democrats Convention, Denver, April 27, 1968, LMP.

268 *"How had it all come to this?"*: Wofford, *Of Kennedys and Kings*, 203.

268 *"Are you going to march"*: Thomas, *Being Nixon*, 158.

269 *"For Martin King marching was"*: Wofford, *Of Kennedys and Kings*, 201.

269 *"Can I get a ride?"*: Chapin, interview by Naftali, RNL. It was surreal for the cabdriver that the presidential candidate Richard Nixon and Wilt Chamberlain were packing into his car.

270 *"Could you put things aside"*: Wofford, interview.

270 a *"monkey wrench" into the talks*: Farrell, *Richard Nixon*, 638.

270 *"lay off pro-Negro crap"*: Ibid., 332.

271 *"Nixon always couched his views"*: Kotlowski, *Nixon's Civil Rights*, 268.

271 *"The GOP didn't give a damn"*: Farrington, *Black Republicans and the Transformation of the GOP*, 181.

271 *"The Richard Nixon I met"*: Robinson, *I Never Had It Made*, 135.

272 *"The best political writing"*: Woodward and Bernstein, *Final Days*, 450. Whether Nixon actually meant to order a specific Watergate break-in remains a disputed point, but the president's obsession over O'Brien, and his rants that encouraged the establishing of a political operation that undertook a range of crimes, are certain.

272 *Wofford said that Shriver*: Wofford, interview.

272 *"I have to do this"*: Garrow, *Bearing the Cross*, 500.

272 *"It ends with me getting killed"*: Ibid., 469.

273 *"The details and symbols of your life"*: James Baldwin, "My Dungeon Shook" (1962), in *Collected Essays*, 294–95.

273 *"jail cells are not dungeons"*: Carson, *Autobiography of Martin Luther King Jr.*, 307.

273 *"He shared very little"*: Young, interview by the authors.

273 *"paralyzing fear of being alone"*: Young, *Easy Burden*, 175.

274 *"an old Christian idea"*: Ibid.

274 *"was going to be one challenge"*: Young, interview by the authors.

274 *"was crucial to his decision"*: Ibid.

275 *"a good case can be made"*: Stossel, "Good Works of Sargent Shriver."

275 *"We need dramatic action"*: "Kennedy White House" document, June 16, 1963, LMP.

275 *"If one of my daughters"*: Martin, interview by Grele, #3, JFKL.

275 *Martin never asked for any credit*: Dr. Toni Martin, interview.

276 *Vernon Jordan and Andrew Young advised him*: Jordan, interview; Young, interview.

276 *"a pinch hitter"*: "'Godfather of Black Politics' Returns to Capital," *Chicago Sun Times*, Oct. 29, 1978, clipping in LMP.

276 *"godfather of many of the specific"*: Shriver to Martin, April 17, 1990, LMP.

276 *DNC's Lawrence O'Brien Achievement Award*: *New York Voice Harlem USA*, Oct. 8–14, 1992, clipping in LMP.

277 *"Kennedy would never have telephoned"*: Shriver remarks at Martin funeral, provided by Trudy Martin Hatter to the authors. Lady Bird Johnson attended Martin's D.C. service and former president Jimmy Carter called Gertrude Martin.

277 *"the unsung, unheralded, and to some, unknown"*: Vernon Jordan remarks at Louis Martin's fu-
     neral, provided by Jordan to the authors.
277 *"imagination and guts"*: Louis Martin, "New Senator, a Friend of King," *Chicago Defender*, May
     18, 1991.
278 *"Is this the Lonnie King"*: Lonnie King, interview.
278 *In 2017, Lonnie and Charles Black*: Jeremy Redmon, "Georgia Activists, Immigrants Without
     Legal Status Find Common Cause," *AJC*, March 29, 2016.
279 *"That's my last hurrah"*: Lonnie King, interview.
279 *"Well done, brave warrior"*: Lonnie King, obituary, www.legacy.com/obituaries/name/lonnie
     -king-obituary?pid=191739403&page=3.
279 *writing a* New York Times *op-ed*: Harris Wofford, "Finding Love Again, This Time with a
     Man," *NYT*, April 24, 2016.
280 *"It wasn't just a job"*: Poinsett, *Walking with Presidents*, 11.

SELECTED BIBLIOGRAPHY

BOOKS

Abernathy, Ralph David. *And the Walls Came Tumbling Down: An Autobiography*. New York: Harper & Row, 1989.

Abram, Morris B. *The Day Is Short: An Autobiography*. New York: Harcourt Brace Jovanovich, 1982.

Aitken, Jonathan. *Nixon: A Life*. Washington, D.C.: Regnery History, 1993.

Allen, Ivan, Jr. *Mayor: Notes on the Sixties*. With Paul Hemphill. New York: Simon & Schuster, 1971.

Ambrose, Stephen E. *Nixon: The Education of a Politician, 1913–1962*. New York: Simon & Schuster, 1987.

Baldwin, James. *Collected Essays*. Edited by Toni Morrison. New York: Library of America, 1998.

Bass, Jack. *Taming the Storm: The Life and Times of Judge Frank M. Johnson Jr. and the South's Fight over Civil Rights*. New York: Doubleday, 1993.

Bass, S. Jonathan. *Blessed Are the Peacemakers: Martin Luther King Jr., Eight White Religious Leaders, and the "Letter from Birmingham Jail."* Baton Rouge: Louisiana State University Press, 2001.

Belafonte, Harry. *My Song: A Memoir*. With Michael Shnayerson. New York: Alfred A. Knopf, 2011.

Bishop, Jim. *The Days of Martin Luther King Jr.* New York: G. P. Putnam's Sons, 1971.

Black, Conrad. *Richard M. Nixon: A Life in Full*. New York: PublicAffairs, 2007.

Booker, Simeon. *Shocking the Conscience: A Reporter's Account of the Civil Rights Movement*. With Carol McCabe Booker. Jackson: University Press of Mississippi, 2013.

Branch, Taylor. *At Canaan's Edge: America in the King Years, 1965–68*. New York: Simon & Schuster, 2006.

———. *Parting the Waters: America in the King Years, 1954–63*. New York: Simon & Schuster, 1988.

———. *Pillar of Fire: America in the King Years, 1963–65*. New York: Simon & Schuster, 1998.

Brauer, Carl M. *John F. Kennedy and the Second Reconstruction*. New York: Columbia University Press, 1977.

Brown-Nagin, Tomiko. *Courage to Dissent: Atlanta and the Long History of the Civil Rights Movement*. New York: Oxford University Press, 2011.

Bryant, Nick. *The Bystander: John F. Kennedy and the Struggle for Black Equality*. New York: Basic Books, 2006.

Burns, Rebecca. *Burial for a King: Martin Luther King Jr.'s Funeral and the Week That Transformed Atlanta and Rocked the Nation*. New York: Scribner, 2011.

Burns, Stewart. *To the Mountaintop: Martin Luther King Jr.'s Mission to Save America*. San Francisco: HarperOne, 2003.

Carson, Clayborne, ed. *The Autobiography of Martin Luther King Jr.* New York: Warner Books, 1998.

———. *The Eyes on the Prize: Civil Rights Reader: Documents, Speeches, and Firsthand Accounts from the Black Freedom Struggle, 1954–1990*. New York: Viking, 1991.

Carson, Clayborne, Tenisha Armstrong, Susan Carson, Adrienne Clay, and Kieran Taylor, eds. *The Papers of Martin Luther King Jr. Vol. 5, Threshold of a New Decade, January 1959–December 1960*. Berkeley: University of California Press, 2005.

Carson, Clayborne, Stewart Burns, Susan Carson, Dana Powell, and Peter Holloran, eds. *The Papers of Martin Luther King, Jr. Vol. 3, Birth of a New Age, December 1955–December 1956*. Berkeley: University of California Press, 1997.

Carson, Clayborne, Susan Carson, Adrienne Clay, Virginia Shadron, and Kieran Taylor, eds. *The Papers of Martin Luther King Jr. Vol. 4, Symbol of the Movement, January 1957–December 1958*. Berkeley: University of California Press, 2000.

Carson, Clayborne, Ralph E. Luker, Peter Holloran, and Penny A. Russell, eds. *The Papers of Martin Luther King Jr. Vol. 7, To Save the Soul of America, January 1961–August 1962*. Oakland: University of California Press, 1992.

Clemmons, Jeff. *Rich's: A Southern Institution*. Charleston, S.C.: History Press, 2012.

Cohen, Andrew. *Two Days in June: John F. Kennedy and the 48 Hours That Made History*. Toronto: McClelland & Stewart, 2014.

Dallek, Robert. *Camelot's Court: Inside the Kennedy White House*. New York: HarperCollins, 2013.

———. *An Unfinished Life: John F. Kennedy, 1917–1963*. New York: Oxford University Press, 2003.

Daniels, Maurice Charles. *Saving the Soul of Georgia: Donald L. Hollowell and the Struggle for Civil Rights*. Athens: University of Georgia Press, 2013.

Donaldson, Gary A. *The First Modern Campaign: Kennedy, Nixon, and the Election of 1960*. Lanham, Md.: Rowman & Littlefield, 2007.

Dyson, Michael Eric. *I May Not Get There with You: The True Martin Luther King Jr.* New York: Simon & Schuster, 2000.

Edelman, Marian Wright. *Lanterns: A Memoir of Mentors*. Boston: Beacon Press, 1999.

Fairclough, Adam. *Martin Luther King Jr.* Athens: University of Georgia Press, 1995.

———. *To Redeem the Soul of America: The Southern Christian Leadership Conference and Martin Luther King Jr.* Athens: University of Georgia Press, 1987.

Farrell, John A. *Richard Nixon: The Life*. New York: Doubleday, 2017.

Farrington, Joshua. *Black Republicans and the Transformation of the GOP*. Philadelphia: University of Pennsylvania Press, 2016.

Flanigan, William H., Nancy H. Zingale, Elizabeth A. Theiss-Morse, and Michael W. Wagner. *Political Behavior of the American Electorate*. 13th ed. Los Angeles: Sage/CQ Press, 2015.

Fleming, Cynthia. *Soon We Will Not Cry: The Liberation of Ruby Doris Smith Robinson*. Lanham, Md.: Rowman & Littlefield, 1998.

Frady, Marshall. *Martin Luther King Jr.: A Life*. New York: Viking, 2002.

Frank, Jeffrey. *Ike and Dick: Portrait of a Strange Political Marriage*. New York: Simon & Schuster, 2013.

Galbraith, John Kenneth. *Ambassador's Journal: A Personal Account of the Kennedy Years*. Boston: Houghton Mifflin, 1969.

Gallup, George H. *The Gallup Poll: Public Opinion, 1935–1971*. New York: Random House, 1972.

Garrow, David. *Atlanta, Georgia, 1960–1961: Sit-Ins and Student Activism*. Brooklyn: Carlson, 1989.

———. *Bearing the Cross: Martin Luther King Jr. and the Southern Christian Leadership Conference*. New York: William Morrow, 1986.

Gellman, Irwin F. *The President and the Apprentice: Eisenhower and Nixon, 1952–1961*. New Haven, Conn.: Yale University Press, 2015.

Gladney, Margaret Rose, ed. *How Am I to Be Heard? Letters of Lillian Smith*. Chapel Hill: University of North Carolina Press, 1993.

Gladney, Margaret Rose, and Lisa Hodgens, eds. *A Lillian Smith Reader*. Athens: University of Georgia Press, 2016.

Goodwin, Richard. *Remembering America: A Voice from the Sixties*. Boston: Little, Brown, 1988.

Gould, Lewis, ed. *Documentary History of the John F. Kennedy Presidency*. Vol. 14. Bethesda: LexisNexis, 2006.

Guthman, Edwin O., and Jeffrey Shulman, eds. *Robert Kennedy in His Own Words: The Unpublished Recollections of the Kennedy Years*. New York: Bantam Books, 1988.

Hansen, Drew. *The Dream: Martin Luther King Jr. and the Speech That Inspired a Nation*. New York: HarperCollins, 2003.

Haygood, Wil. *King of the Cats: The Life and Times of Adam Clayton Powell Jr.* New York: Amistad, 1993.

Henderson, Harold Paulk. *Ernest Vandiver: Governor of Georgia*. Athens: University of Georgia Press, 2000.

Hollowell, Louise, and Martin C. Lehfeldt. *A Sacred Call: A Tribute to Donald L. Hollowell—Civil Rights Champion*. Winter Park, Fla.: Four-G, 1997.

Hunter-Gault, Charlayne. *To the Mountaintop: My Journey Through the Civil Rights Movement*. New York: Roaring Brook Press, 2012.

Jordan, Vernon. *Vernon Can Read: A Memoir*. With Annette Gordon-Reed. New York: Basic Books, 2003.

Kallina, Edmund F., Jr. *Kennedy v. Nixon: The Presidential Election of 1960*. Gainesville: University Press of Florida, 2010.

Kamin, Ben. *Dangerous Friendship: Stanley Levison, Martin Luther King Jr., and the Kennedy Brothers*. East Lansing: Michigan State University Press, 2004.

King, Coretta Scott. *My Life, My Love, My Legacy*. As told to the Rev. Dr. Barbara Reynolds. New York: Henry Holt, 2017.

———. *My Life with Martin Luther King Jr.* New York: Henry Holt, 1969.

King, Martin Luther, Sr. *Daddy King: An Autobiography*. Boston: Beacon Press, 1980.

Klein, Herbert G. *Making It Perfectly Clear*. New York: Doubleday, 1980.

Kotlowski, Dean J. *Nixon's Civil Rights: Politics, Principle, and Policy*. Cambridge, Mass.: Harvard University Press, 2001.

Kotz, Nick. *Judgment Days: Lyndon Baines Johnson, Martin Luther King Jr., and the Laws That Changed America*. Boston: Houghton Mifflin, 2005.

Lefever, Harry G. *Undaunted by the Fight: Spelman College and the Civil Rights Movement, 1957–1967*. Macon, Ga.: Mercer University Press, 2005.

Lemann, Nicholas. *The Promised Land: The Great Black Migration and How It Changed America*. New York: Vintage, 1992.

Levingston, Steven. *Kennedy and King: The President, the Pastor, and the Battle over Civil Rights*. New York: Hachette Books, 2017.

Lewis, Anthony, and the *New York Times*. *Portrait of a Decade: The Second American Revolution*. New York: Random House, 1964.

Lewis, David Levering. *King: A Biography*. 1970. Reprint, Urbana: University of Illinois Press, 1978.

Lewis, John. *Walking with the Wind: A Memoir of the Movement*. With Michael D'Orso. New York: Simon & Schuster, 1998.

Liston, Robert. *Sargent Shriver: A Candid Portrait*. New York: Farrar, Straus, 1964.

Long, Michael G., ed. *First Class Citizenship: The Civil Rights Letters of Jackie Robinson*. New York: Times Books, 2007.

Loveland, Anne C. *Lillian Smith: A Southerner Confronting the South*. Baton Rouge: Louisiana State University Press, 1986.

Martin, Harold H. *William Berry Hartsfield: Mayor of Atlanta*. Athens: University of Georgia Press, 1978.

Matthews, Chris. *Jack Kennedy: Elusive Hero*. New York: Simon & Schuster, 2011.

———. *Kennedy & Nixon: The Rivalry That Shaped Postwar America*. New York: Simon & Schuster, 1997.

McAdam, Doug. *Political Process and the Development of Black Insurgency, 1930–1970*. 2nd ed. Chicago: University of Chicago Press, 1999.

McGuire, Danielle. *At the Dark End of the Street: Black Women, Rape, and Resistance*. New York: Alfred A. Knopf, 2010.

Michaeli, Ethan. *"The Defender": How the Legendary Black Newspaper Changed America: From the Age of the Pullman Porters to the Age of Obama*. New York: Houghton Mifflin Harcourt, 2016.

Michener, James. *Report of the County Chairman*. New York: Random House, 1961.

Morrow, E. Frederic. *Black Man in the White House: A Diary of the Eisenhower Years by the Administrative Officer for Special Projects, the White House, 1955–1961*. New York: Coward-McCann, 1963.

———. *Forty Years a Guinea Pig*. New York: Pilgrim Press, 1980.

Neary, John. *Julian Bond: Black Rebel*. New York: William Morrow, 1971.

Newman, Richard. *Go Down, Moses: A Celebration of the African-American Spiritual*. New York: Roundtable Press, 1998.

Newton, Michael. *Unsolved Civil Rights Murder Cases, 1934–1970*. Jefferson, N.C.: McFarland, 2016.

Nichols, David A. *A Matter of Justice: Eisenhower and the Beginning of the Civil Rights Revolution*. New York: Simon & Schuster, 2007.

Niven, David. *The Politics of Injustice: The Kennedys, the Freedom Rides, and the Electoral Consequences of a Moral Compromise*. Knoxville: University of Tennessee Press, 2003.

Nixon, Richard. *The Memoirs of Richard Nixon*. New York: Grosset & Dunlap, 1978.

———. *Six Crises*. 1962. Reprint, New York: Touchstone, 1990.

Oates, Stephen. *Let the Trumpet Sound: A Life of Martin Luther King Jr.* New York: Harper & Row, 1982.

O'Brien, Michael. *John F. Kennedy: A Biography*. New York: Thomas Dunne Books, 2005.

O'Donnell, Helen. *The Irish Brotherhood: John F. Kennedy, His Inner Circle, and the Improbable Rise to the Presidency*. With Kenneth O'Donnell. Berkeley, Calif.: Counterpoint, 2015.

O'Donnell, Kenneth P., and David F. Powers. *"Johnny, We Hardly Knew Ye": Memories of John Fitzgerald Kennedy*. With Joe McCarthy. 1970. Reprint, Boston: Little, Brown, 1972.

Oliphant, Thomas, and Curtis Wilkie. *The Road to Camelot: Inside JFK's Five-Year Campaign*. New York: Simon & Schuster, 2017.

O'Reilly, Kenneth. *Nixon's Piano: Presidents and Racial Politics from Washington to Clinton*. New York: Free Press, 1995.

Perlstein, Rick. *Nixonland: The Rise of a President and the Fracturing of America*. New York: Scribner, 2008.

Pietrusza, David. *1960: LBJ vs. JFK vs. Nixon: The Epic Campaign That Forged Three Presidencies*. New York: Union Square Press, 2008.

Poinsett, Alex. *Walking with Presidents: Louis Martin and the Rise of Black Political Power*. Lanham, Md.: Rowman & Littlefield, 1997.

Pomerantz, Gary M. *Where Peachtree Meets Sweet Auburn: The Saga of Two Families and the Making of Atlanta*. New York: Scribner, 1996.

Raines, Howell. *My Soul Is Rested: Movement Days in the Deep South Remembered*. 1977. Reprint, New York: Penguin Books, 1983.

Rampersad, Arnold. *Jackie Robinson: A Biography*. New York: Ballantine Books, 1997.

Raymond, Emilie. *Stars for Freedom: Hollywood, Black Celebrities, and the Civil Rights Movement*. Seattle: University of Washington Press, 2015.

Rieder, Jonathan. *Gospel of Freedom: Martin Luther King Jr.'s Letter from Birmingham Jail and the Struggle That Changed a Nation*. New York: Bloomsbury, 2013.

———. *The Word of the Lord Is Upon Me: The Righteous Performance of Martin Luther King Jr.* Cambridge, Mass.: Belknap Press of Harvard University Press, 2008.

Rigueur, Leah Wright. *The Loneliness of the Black Republican: Pragmatic Politics and the Pursuit of Power*. Princeton, N.J.: Princeton University Press, 2014.

Risen, Clay. *A Nation on Fire: America in the Wake of the King Assassination*. Hoboken, N.J.: John Wiley & Sons, 2009.

Robinson, Jackie. *I Never Had It Made: An Autobiography of Jackie Robinson*. As told to Alfred Duckett. 1972. Reprint, Hopewell, N.J.: Ecco Press, 1995.

Rorabaugh, W. J. *The Real Making of the President: Kennedy, Nixon, and the 1960 Election*. Lawrence: University Press of Kansas, 2009.

Sabato, Larry J. *The Kennedy Half-Century: The Presidency, Assassination, and Lasting Legacy*. New York: Bloomsbury, 2013.

Safire, William. *Before the Fall: An Inside View of the Pre-Watergate White House*. New York: Ballantine Books, 1977.

Salinger, Pierre. *With Kennedy*. Garden City, N.Y.: Doubleday, 1966.

Sandler, Martin, ed. *The Letters of John F. Kennedy*. New York: Bloomsbury, 2013.

Schlesinger, Arthur M., Jr. *Robert Kennedy and His Times*. 1978. Reprint, New York: First Mariner Books, 2002.

———. *A Thousand Days: John F. Kennedy in the White House*. 1965. Reprint, New York: Fawcett Premier, 1992.

Shriver, Mark. *A Good Man: Rediscovering My Father, Sargent Shriver*. New York: Henry Holt, 2012.

Smith, Judith E. *Becoming Belafonte: Black Artist, Public Radical*. Austin: University of Texas Press, 2014.

Sorensen, Ted. *Counselor: A Life at the Edge of History*. New York: Hyperion, 2008.

———. *Kennedy*. New York: Harper & Row, 1965.

Stein, Jean, and George Plimpton, eds. *American Journey: The Times of Robert Kennedy*. New York: Harcourt Brace Jovanovich, 1970.

Stern, Mark. *Calculating Visions: Kennedy, Johnson, and Civil Rights*. New Brunswick, N.J.: Rutgers University Press, 1992.

Stossel, Scott. *Sarge: The Life and Times of Sargent Shriver*. New York: Other Press, 2004.

Strober, Gerald S., and Deborah H. Strober. *"Let Us Begin Anew": An Oral History of the Kennedy Presidency*. New York: HarperCollins, 1993.

Sullivan, Patricia, ed. *Freedom Writer: Virginia Foster Durr, Letters from the Civil Rights Years*. Athens: University of Georgia Press, 2006.

Thomas, Evan. *Being Nixon: A Man Divided*. New York: Random House, 2015.

———. *Robert Kennedy: His Life*. New York: Simon & Schuster, 2000.

Thomas, G. Scott. *A New World to Be Won: John Kennedy, Richard Nixon, and the Tumultuous Year of 1960*. Santa Barbara, Calif.: Praeger, 2011.

Thompson, Kenneth W., ed. *The Kennedy Presidency: Seventeen Intimate Perspectives of John F. Kennedy*. Lanham, Md.: University Press of America, 1985.

Thurber, Timothy N. *Republicans and Race: The GOP's Frayed Relationship with African Americans, 1945–1974*. Lawrence: University Press of Kansas, 2013.

Tuck, Stephen G. N. *Beyond Atlanta: The Struggle for Racial Equality in Georgia, 1940–1980*. Athens: University of Georgia Press, 2001.

Tushnet, Mark, ed. *Thurgood Marshall: His Speeches, Writings, Arguments, Opinions, and Reminiscences*. Chicago: Lawrence Hill Books, 2001.

U.S. Senate. *The Speeches, Remarks, Press Conferences, and Statements of Senator John F. Kennedy, Presidential Campaign of 1960, August 1 Through November 7, 1960*. Washington, D.C.: U.S. Government Printing Office, 1961.

Watters, Pat. *Down to Now: Reflections on the Southern Civil Rights Movement*. New York: Pantheon Books, 1971.

White, Theodore H. *The Making of the President, 1960*. New York: Athenaeum, 1961.

Wicker, Tom. *One of Us: Richard Nixon and the American Dream*. New York: Random House, 1991.

Widmer, Ted, ed. *Listening In: The Secret White House Recordings of John F. Kennedy*. New York: Grand Central Press, 2012.

Williams, Juan. *Thurgood Marshall, American Revolutionary*. New York: Times Books, 1998.

Wofford, Harris. *Of Kennedys and Kings*. 1980. Reprint, Pittsburgh: University of Pittsburgh Press, 1992.

Woodward, Bob, and Carl Bernstein. *The Final Days*. New York: Simon & Schuster, 1976.

Young, Andrew. *An Easy Burden: The Civil Rights Movement and the Transformation of America*. New York: HarperCollins, 1996.

Zinn, Howard. *The Southern Mystique*. New York: Alfred A. Knopf, 1964.

ARTICLES

Alexander, Blayne. "New Footage: Julian Bond's Final Atlanta Interview." *USA Today*, Aug. 17, 2015. www.usatoday.com/story/news/local/2015/08/17/julian-bond-interview/31853041/.

Burns, Rebecca. "The Integration of Atlanta Public Schools." *Atlanta Magazine*, Aug. 1, 2011. www.atlantamagazine.com/civilrights/the-integration-of-atlanta-public-schools/.

Grier, Peter. "Martin Luther King Jr. and John F. Kennedy: Civil Rights' Wary Allies." *Christian Science Monitor*, Jan. 20, 2014. www.csmonitor.com/USA/Politics/DC-Decoder/2014/0120/Martin-Luther-King-Jr.-and-John-F.-Kennedy-civil-rights-wary-allies.

Jones, Joyce. "The Activist Gene." *Clark Atlanta University Magazine*, Fall 2014. issuu.com/clarkatlantauniversity/docs/cau_14_fall_oct20.

Kuhn, Clifford M. "'There's a Footnote to History!' Memory and the History of Martin Luther King's October 1960 Arrest and Its Aftermath." *Journal of American History* 84, no. 2 (Sept. 1997): 583–95.

Lebovich, William. "Pelli's Renewed Investment Building." *ArchitectureWeek*, Feb. 6, 2002. www.architectureweek.com/2002/0206/design_1-1.html.

Looney, Ginny. "Segregation Order at Reidsville Prison." *Southern Changes: The Journal of the Southern Regional Council* 1, no. 7 (1979): 19–21.

Roosevelt, Eleanor. "My Day, Nov. 14, 1960." The Eleanor Roosevelt Papers Digital Edition (2017), www2.gwu.edu/~erpapers/myday/displaydoc.cfm?_y=1960&_f=md004876.

Scammon, Richard M. "How the Negroes Voted." *New Republic*, Nov. 21, 1960.

Stossel, Scott. "The Good Works of Sargent Shriver." *Atlantic*, Jan. 18, 2011. www.theatlantic.com/politics/archive/2011/01/the-good-works-of-sargent-shriver/69677.

Tatum, Gloria. "Atlanta Student Movement Historical Trail to Be Unveiled with Interactive Markers." *Atlanta Progressive News*, Oct. 31, 2014. atlantaprogressivenews.com/2014/10/31/atlanta-student-movement-historical-trail-to-be-unveiled-with-interactive-markers/.

Weaver, Amy. "Auburn University Student Recalls Being One of MLK Jr.'s Foot Soldiers." *Opelika-Auburn News*, Feb. 18, 2008. www.oanow.com/news/auburn-university-student-recalls-being-one-of-mlk-jr-s/article_e020c376-f900-5559-ab77-aa6a2ba1226f.html.

Williamson, Heidi. "Julian Bond: A Final Interview." *Newsweek*, Aug. 17, 2015. www.newsweek.com/julian-bond-final-interview-363577.

Wofford, Harris. "Remembering Shriver on JFK's Inauguration Day." cnn.com, Jan. 21, 2011. www.cnn.com/2011/OPINION/01/20/wofford.shriver.speech/index.html.

Zengerle, Jason. "The Man Who Was Everywhere." *New Republic*, Nov. 20, 2014. newrepublic.com/article/120160/harris-wofford-20th-centurys-most-serendipitous-man.

INTERVIEWS

Black, Charles, by the authors, May 18, 2017.

Goodwin, Richard, by the authors, Jan. 23, 2017.

Jordan, Vernon, by the authors, June 23, 2017.

King, Lonnie, by the authors, 2017–2018.
Martin, Toni, by the authors, May 16, 2017.
Moss, Otis, by the authors, May 27, 2017.
Orbert, Blondean, by Jeff Clemmons, shared with the authors.
Person, Charles, by the authors, May 12, 2017.
Rich, Sally, by the authors, June 28, 2017.
Seigenthaler, John, by Larry Tye, Aug. 30, 2011, shared with the authors.
Wofford, Harris, by the authors, 2016–2017.
Wofford, Harris, by Taylor Branch, interview notes, Wofford Folder 957 in the Taylor Branch Papers #5047, Southern Historical Collection, Wilson Library, University of North Carolina at Chapel Hill.
Young, Andrew, by the authors, Aug. 29, 2017.

NEWSPAPERS AND PERIODICALS

Atlanta Constitution
Atlanta Daily World
Atlanta Inquirer
Atlanta Journal
The Atlanta Journal-Constitution
Baltimore Afro-American
Baltimore Sun
Boston Globe
Chicago Daily Defender
Chicago Daily Tribune
Chicago Defender
Chicago Sun Times
Christian Science Monitor
The Cincinnati Enquirer
Cleveland Call and Post
Daily News (New York)
DeKalb New Era
Ebony
Fort Worth Star-Telegram
Jet
Kansas City Times
The Knoxville News-Sentinel
Los Angeles Sentinel
Lubbock Avalanche-Journal
Negro Digest
New York Amsterdam News
New York Herald Tribune
New York Times
New York Voice Harlem USA
The Philadelphia Daily News
The Philadelphia Inquirer
Philadelphia Tribune
Pittsburgh Courier
Republican and Herald (Pottsville, Pennsylvania)
Rome News-Tribune
St. Louis Globe-Democrat
Suffolk County News

Tri-State Defender (Memphis)
Washington Post
Women's Wear Daily
The York Dispatch

ORAL HISTORIES

Bond, Julian. "Discusses History of the Student Nonviolent Coordinating Committee," Feb. 2, 2010, University of Virginia School of Law. www.youtube.com/watch?v=UtVPgK_5UmU.

———. Interview by Bob Short, Feb. 27, 2012, Georgia Politics Oral History Collection, Russell Library, University of Georgia.

Booker, Simeon. Interview by John Stewart, April 24, 1967, JFKL Oral History Program.

Calhoun, John. Interview by John Britton, May 23, 1968, Ralph Bunch Oral History Collection, Howard University.

Challenor, Herschelle. Interview by Jeanne Law Bohannon, Aug. 25, 2017, Atlanta Student Movement Project, Kennesaw State University.

———. Interview by Vicki Crawford, June 14, 2017, King Collection. www.youtube.com/watch?v=qdFEA2ftqRI.

Chapin, Dwight. Interview by Timothy Naftali, April 2, 2007, Richard Nixon Oral History Project, Richard Nixon Presidential Library.

Curry, Constance. "Circle of Trust," unpublished memoir chapter, provided to the authors.

Davis, June Wilson. Interview by Jeanne Law Bohannon, May 19, 2017, Atlanta Student Movement, Kennesaw State University. Stories from the Trenches: Women on the Move(ments), 1940s–2018. 2018 Women's History Month Finale Panel, March 28, 2018, Atlanta Student Movement, Kennesaw State University.

Fort, Vincent Dean. "The Atlanta Sit-In Movement, 1960–1961: An Oral Study" (1980). ETD Collection for AUC Robert W. Woodruff Library. Paper 2433.

Hartsfield, William B. Interview by Charles T. Morrissey, Jan. 6, 1966, JFKL Oral History Program.

Hesburgh, Theodore M. Interview by Joseph E. O'Connor, March 27, 1966, JFKL Oral History Program.

Hoytt, Marilyn Pryce. Interview by Jeanne Law Bohannon, July 13, 2018, Atlanta Student Movement Project, Kennesaw State University. soar.kennesaw.edu/handle/11360/2384.

Iles-Foster, Gwendolyn. Interview by Junior and Senior Everest High School students, D. C. Everest Oral History Project, 2012. www.crmvet.org/nars/fosterg.htm.

King, Lonnie. Interview by Jeanne Law Bohannon, July 19, 2017, Atlanta Student Movement Project, Kennesaw State University.

———. Interview by Ashley Burke, Georgia State University.

———. Interview by Emilye Crosby, May 29, 2013, U.S. Civil Rights History Project, Library of Congress. www.loc.gov/item/afc2010039_crhp0090/.

———. Interview by Bob Short, Sept. 28, 2009, Reflections on Georgia Politics Oral History Collection, ROGP 086, Richard B. Russell Library for Political Research and Studies, University of Georgia Libraries, Athens.

———. Interview by Voices Across the Color Line Oral History Project, Atlanta History Center.

———. King Collection Oral History, Morehouse College. www.youtube.com/watch?v=ZCIjGroKWzI.

———. "On Student Movements and the Civil Rights Movement," Feb. 18, 2012, University of Georgia Social Work. www.youtube.com/watch?v=RfYVXgJAiow.

King, Martin Luther, Jr. Interview by Berl I. Bernhard, March 9, 1964, JFKL Oral History Program.

Lawson, Belford V. Interview by Ronald J. Grele, Jan. 11, 1966, JFKL Oral History Program.

Lawson, Marjorie McKenzie. Interview by Ronald J. Grele, Oct. 25, 1965, JFKL Oral History Program.

————. Interview by Ronald J. Grele, #2, JFKL Oral History Program.

Martin, Louis. Interview by Ed Edwin, #3, May 2, 1985, Columbia University Oral History Collection, JFKL Oral History Program.

————. Interview by Ed Edwin, #10, Sept. 18, 1986, Columbia University Oral History Collection.

————. Interview by Ronald Grele, #1, March 14, 1966, JFKL Oral History Program.

————. Interview by Ronald Grele, #2, April 7, 1966, JFKL Oral History Program.

————. Interview by Ronald Grele, #3, May 11, 1966, JFKL Oral History Program.

————. Interview by David G. McComb, #1, May 14, 1969, LBJ Library Oral Histories, LBJ Presidential Library.

————. Interview by Anthony K. Shriver, JFKL Oral History Program.

————. Interview by Robert Wright, March 25, 1970, Civil Rights Documentation Project, Bunch Collection, Howard University.

McGill, Ralph E. Interview by Charles T. Morrissey, Jan. 6, 1966, JFKL Oral History Program.

Mitchell, Clarence M. Interview by John Stewart, Feb. 9 and 23, 1967, JFKL Oral History Program.

Morrow, E. Frederic. Interview by Ed Erwin, April 15, 1968, Columbia Center for Oral History Archives, Rare Book and Manuscript Library, Columbia University.

Morton, Thruston B. Interview by Stephen Hess, Aug. 4, 1964, JFKL Oral History Program.

Moss, Otis. Atlanta Student Movement, City of Atlanta. vimeo.com/110629334.

————. Interview by Jeanne Law Bohannon, Aug. 25, 2017, Atlanta Student Movement Project, Kennesaw State University.

Reeves, Frank. Interview by John F. Stewart, March 29, 1967, JFKL Oral History Program.

Rogers, William P. Interview by John T. Mason Jr., June 28, 1968, Eisenhower Administration Project, Butler Library Oral History Collection, Columbia University.

Seigenthaler, John. Interview by William A. Geoghegan, #1, July 22, 1964, JFKL Oral History Program.

————. Interview by Ronald J. Grele, #2, Feb. 21, 1966, JFKL Oral History Program.

Shriver, Sargent, Louis Martin, Harris Wofford, Franklin Williams, Sam Proctor, and Parren Mitchell. Interview by Anthony K. Shriver, *Kennedy's Call to King: Six Perspectives*, fall 1988, Independent Study, Georgetown University, JFKL Oral History Program.

Tubby, Roger W. Interview by Joseph E. O'Connor, Jan. 16, 1967, JFKL Oral History Program.

Vandiver, Ernest. Interview by Clifford Kuhn, Jan. 25, 1994, P1994–02, Series A. Georgia Governors, Georgia Government Documentation Project, Special Collections and Archives, Georgia State University Library (GSU), Atlanta.

————. Interview by Charles Pyle, March 20 and July 28, 1986, Georgia Government Documentation Project, Special Collections and Archives, GSU, Atlanta.

————. Interview by John F. Stewart, May 22, 1967, JFKL Oral History Program.

Wilkins, Roy. Interview by Berl Bernhard, Aug. 13, 1964, JFKL Oral History Program.

Williams, Franklin. Interview by Anthony K. Shriver, fall 1988, JFKL Oral History Program.

Wofford, Harris. Interview by Berl Bernhard, #1, Nov. 29, 1965, JFKL Oral History Program.

————. Interview by Blackside Inc., Oct. 31, 1985, for "Eyes on the Prize: America's Civil Rights Years (1954–1965)," Washington University Libraries, Film and Media Archive, Henry Hampton Collection.

————. Interview by Larry Hackman, #2, May 22, 1968, JFKL Oral History Program.

————. Interview by Larry Hackman, #3, Feb. 3, 1969, JFKL Oral History Program.

————. Interview by Carol Quirke, Dec. 19, 2011, SUNY Old Westbury Oral History. www.oldwestburyoralhistory.org/wp-content/uploads/2013/03/wofford-h-transcript.pdf.

————. Interview by Voices of the Civil Rights Movement, "Participating with Dr. King," Dec. 4, 2015. voicesofthecivilrightsmovement.com/Video-Collection/2015/12/04/participating-with-dr-king.

Women of the Atlanta Student Movement, 2017 Women's History Month Finale Panel, March 31, 2017, Kennesaw State University. soar.kennesaw.edu/bitstream/handle/11360/2407/WHM2017-transcription.pdf.

MANUSCRIPT COLLECTIONS

Taylor Branch Papers, Southern Historical Collection, Wilson Library, University of North Carolina at Chapel Hill.
Donald Hollowell Papers, Auburn Avenue Research Library on African American Culture and History, Atlanta-Fulton Public Library System.
John F. Kennedy Presidential Library.
Louis Martin Papers, Library of Congress.
E. Frederic Morrow Papers, Amistad Research Center, Tulane University.
E. Frederic Morrow Papers, Vivian G. Harsh Research Collection, Chicago Public Library.
NAACP Papers, Manuscript Division, Library of Congress.
Richard Nixon Presidential Library.

TV AND FILM

American Idealist: The Story of Sargent Shriver, PBS, 2008. Documentary.
Harris Wofford: Slightly Mad. Dir. Jacob Finkel. Corporation for Civic Documentaries, 2017. Documentary.
King. History Channel, 2008. Documentary.
WSB-TV (Atlanta television station) newsfilm clip of an interview with Dr. Martin Luther King Jr. following the assassination of President John F. Kennedy in Atlanta, Nov. 22, 1963, WSB-TV newsfilm collection, reel 1116, 22:35/30:13, Walter J. Brown Media Archives and Peabody Awards Collection, University of Georgia Libraries, Athens, as presented in the Digital Library of Georgia.
WSB-TV newsfilm clip of Dr. Martin Luther King Jr. leaving the Georgia State Prison in the company of Donald Hollowell, Ralph D. Abernathy, and Wyatt T. Walker, Reidsville, Georgia, Oct. 27, 1960, WSB-TV newsfilm collection, reel 0767, 28:41/29:40, Walter J. Brown Media Archives and Peabody Awards Collection, University of Georgia Libraries, Athens, as presented in the Digital Library of Georgia.
WSB-TV newsfilm clip of Dr. Martin Luther King Jr. speaking about the civil rights movement after being arrested during a sit-in at Rich's department store, Atlanta, Oct. 19, 1960, WSB-TV newsfilm collection, reel 0826, 50:16/51:19, Walter J. Brown Media Archives and Peabody Awards Collection, University of Georgia Libraries, Athens, as presented in the Digital Library of Georgia.
WSB-TV newsfilm clip of Mayor William B. Hartsfield speaking to reporters about recent civil rights demonstrations and the arrest of Dr. Martin Luther King Jr. in Atlanta, Oct. 24, 1960, WSB-TV newsfilm collection, reel 0962, 45:39/53:08, Walter J. Brown Media Archives and Peabody Awards Collection, University of Georgia Libraries, Athens, as presented in the Digital Library of Georgia.

DISSERTATIONS AND THESES

Curry, Kristina. "The Rhetoric of Louis E. Martin, 'Godfather of Black Politics.'" PhD diss., Georgia State University, 2013.
Griffin, Willie James. "Courier of Crisis, Messenger of Hope: Trezzvant W. Anderson and the Black Freedom Struggle for Economic Justice." PhD diss., University of North Carolina at Chapel Hill, 2016.
Sullivan, Matthew E. "A Symbol of Virtue or a Strategy for Votes? John F. Kennedy's Telephone Call to Coretta King and Its Social and Political Consequences." Master's thesis, Brandeis University, 2013.

ACKNOWLEDGMENTS

We saw the story of these nine days of crisis, of possibility, as one that needed to be told, a story we Americans need to remember: that decency and a moral compass actually can make a difference in our national life. There is real human cost in this story; three of our protagonists would, in the end, be killed. Yet we embarked on this book believing these nine days provide a profound reminder that friendship, sacrifice, and moral courage are essential elements of our heritage.

We feel lucky to have had the opportunity to tell the largely forgotten saga of the CRS team and of the Atlanta circle around MLK before the years of his blinding fame. We have sought to tell it truthfully, as it deserves.

We are grateful to Louis Martin's daughters for their generosity of time and invaluable help in this project. Dr. Toni Martin and Trudy Martin Hatter shared moving memories of their father. We are particularly grateful for Mrs. Hatter's sending us a program from her father's funeral, where Shriver's and Wofford's names appear as a last notation of a consequential bond. Mrs. Hatter also had the crucial idea of helping us get in touch with a legendary figure who revered her father, Vernon Jordan. Once Jordan heard the name Louis Martin, he was eager to talk about his political mentor, as well as his legal mentor: Donald Hollowell. Jordan conveyed the underappreciated greatness of both men, even finding his eulogy from Martin's funeral, which he movingly read in his office as if he were delivering the eulogy again.

We thank Ambassador Andrew Young for taking the time to give us perceptive recollections of King, and Patra Marsden for arranging our meeting.

Ambassador Young was one of the few people with whom King reflected about the ride to Reidsville, so his testimony was a key authentication of our telling of it. He affirmed our sense of how transformative this experience was for King, reinforcing our belief that his facing down death during these days showed King his path forward.

For interviews and other crucial help, we thank Jack Bass, Timuel Black, Jeanne Law Bohannon of the Atlanta Student Movement Project at Kennesaw State University, Charles Calloway, Dr. Clayborne Carson of the indispensable King Papers at Stanford University, Andrew Cohen, Georgia Secretary of the Senate David A. Cook, Adam Conner, Joshua Farrington, Richard and Doris Kearns Goodwin, Peter Hanig, Vicki Heyman, Chris Kennedy, Kerry Kennedy, Raja Krishnamoorthi, Rabbi Robert Marx, Walter Massey, Mike Naple, Steven Puzzo, Sally Rich and Julia Shivers, Mark Shriver, Christian Washington, and Jim Whitters.

The author of *Rich's: A Southern Institution*, Jeff Clemmons, was always available to answer questions about the fabled department store and Atlanta in 1960, and provided us with his interview of Blondean Orbert before her passing, for which we are grateful.

Larry Tye, author of *Bobby Kennedy: The Making of a Liberal Icon*, was generous to provide us with the interview he did with John Seigenthaler shortly before the death of Bobby's 1960 assistant.

The civil rights movement participant Constance Curry was present at the Rich's arrest. It was so kind of her to share with us, before her passing, what she drafted about that day for her memoirs.

Thank you to the outstanding, helpful staff of the Amistad Research Center at Tulane University, Atlanta University Library, Auburn Avenue Research Library, Chicago Public Library, Georgia State Library, Library of Congress, John F. Kennedy Presidential Library (Maryrose Grossman and James Hill), Nixon Library (Meghan Lee-Parker), the King Center, and the Moorland-Spingarn Research Center at Howard University (Meaghan Alston). In this, our third book together, we are aware that nothing good happens without librarians.

Thank you to our readers for their wise feedback: Emma Cronin, Lindsay Holst, Callie Siskel, and Jamia Wilson.

Our agents Katherine Flynn and Ike Williams were immediately supportive of the notion of *Nine Days*, and Katherine's intrepid efforts to make this book a reality are deeply appreciated. Without her intelligent focus, the proposal would never have gone beyond mere hope and into the hands of a remarkable editor. We are beyond grateful to Colin Dickerman, an editor of keen eye and generous spirit, who took us and our manuscript along on his own professional journey—a ride that we will be forever grateful for. The book at every stage was greatly improved by his team at Farrar, Straus and Giroux, in the daily care and scrutiny of Dominique Lear and Ian Van Wye. We particularly appreciate Ian stewarding the book through its last stages and Alex Star's support.

There are two people without whom this book would not be possible: Lonnie King and Harris Wofford. Though they both died before this book was published, we feel blessed to have shared hours of conversation with these two. Spending time with both was a joy. They taught us a simple but bold lesson: it is possible to change history, but you must be brave enough to put your life and reputation on the line, heedless of fame.

We treasure our afternoons with Lonnie King in his Atlanta home as he, with smiling gusto, shared memories of activist days, along with ruminations on America, past and present. Lonnie would dial up Atlanta Student Movement compatriots and enthusiastically ask that they talk with us. It was like watching him organize in 1960 as he searched for telephone numbers of those whom he thought we needed to interview. We are grateful to Charles Black, the Reverend Otis Moss, and Charles Person for their insightful memories, which we felt fortunate to record. We thank Theresa Ann Walker, who made an effort beyond that which we could ask for, to try to arrange for us to talk to her husband, the Reverend Wyatt Tee Walker, in his last days. We were lucky in so many ways, but we regret just missing the chance to interview the towering figures of Walker and Julian Bond.

And to the one whose help and openness gave impetus to this project: Harris Wofford. Harris came into our lives because our friend and neighbor Dr. Carl Marci thought we would enjoy meeting his longtime mentor, given our interest in civil rights. Carl was right, and his introduction gave us not only entrée to many long and searching sessions with Harris but access to a man who taught us a great deal about the human heart. There is a reason people have loved (and sometimes been perplexed by) this gentleman, the central link between Martin Luther King and John F. Kennedy. The earnest humility of Harris's kindness was so striking that one sometimes forgot how crucial he was to the American history of the past seventy years. His gentle directness and humor, his truly generous spirit, snuck up on you, until you remembered that you were sitting with a former senator, a renowned lawyer and writer, and one of the most important voices for national health care and citizen volunteerism in America.

Jacob Finkel, director of the documentary that we highly recommend watching about Harris's life, *Slightly Mad*, and Harris's loving partner, Matthew Charlton, were always helpful in scheduling time for us to sit with Harris. Jacob also assisted us in finding amazing images of Wofford and Shriver during their Peace Corps years. Harris enjoyed telling stories and could keep us laughing but was dutiful in answering the detailed questions we had. Eventually, we reached a point in our interviews where we would ask something so specific that he could not recall it; then he told us in a proud tone that we now knew more about these days that he lived through than he did. He loved hearing all we were learning from Louis Martin's notes from an unpublished memoir in his Library of Congress papers, and we came to see his friends Sarge and Louis as he fondly still did.

We asked Wofford if he felt lucky to have worked with King, JFK, and Bobby—or somehow cursed, having befriended figures slain each in turn. He considered, looking out over Rock Creek Park, winding for miles from his living room vista. In his earnest way, he answered by gesturing. "Well, I'm looking at these red leaves in the wind outside the window, and that's where I walk, to the river down there, most mornings, when I can. So I feel very lucky." He could walk each day, remembering; they were not so spared.

Harris told us once about how he would take the towpath along the Potomac River to a spot on the Georgetown waterfront facing the Kennedy Center. He would stop to contemplate what appeared to be three striking, lovely trees, which were actually one, sharing a twisting root system. Wofford would ponder this tree, where students, professionals, and families strolled and children played in a fountain nearby. Once a boy came to him, curious as to what he was looking at. Wofford said to the child, "These are the trinity trees."

Pointing to each one, Wofford added, "Faith, Hope, and Charity." When Wofford was arrested outside the 1968 Democratic National Convention in Chicago, a reporter asked him to explain why he was going to jail in three words. He replied, "Bob Kennedy, John Kennedy, and Martin Luther King."

The boy walked back toward his father, leaving Wofford bemused that he, a man with a limited instinct for religion compared with King, or, for that matter, Shriver and Martin, had summoned such a spiritual allusion. He overheard the child speak with great seriousness, "Daddy, I saw the trinity tree."

With infinite gratitude, we acknowledge the unwavering support of our family that made this book possible: Anna, Elizabeth, and Liz Kendrick; Elana, Haley, Marc, Maureen, and Kori Schulman. Their belief in us got us through, and their own dedication to the sustaining idea that politics can actually lift us up, make our society more just and forgiving, inspired us at every point.

TOP: Lonnie King at home in Atlanta in 2017
(photograph by Paul Kendrick)

BOTTOM: Harris Wofford at home in Washington, D.C.,
in 2017 (photograph by Kelly Jo Smart)

INDEX

Abernathy, Ralph, 36, 69, 71, 90, 186, 187, 196, 197, 200, 203, 213, 218, 256, 266, 269

Abram, Morris, 100–104, 106, 107, 109–11, 113, 133, 162, 163, 169, 173, 184, 217, 298n, 317n; Wofford and, 100–101, 103, 107–108, 185, 296n

ACLU, 159

Adams, Sherman, 124, 126

AFL-CIO, 192

Allen, Ivan, Jr., 256

American Jewish Congress, 192

American Legion, 15

AmeriCorps, 277

Anderson, Trezzvant, 93–94

Angola (Louisiana State Penitentiary), 141

anti-Semitism, 101, 102, 313–14n

AP (Associated Press), 84, 201

"Appeal for Human Rights, An," 78–79

Ashmore, Ann, 77–78

Atlanta, Ga., 13, 15, 24, 36, 42–43, 72, 100, 102, 121, 161, 223, 246, 288n; King's return to, 33–35, 47; Nixon's

appearance in, 27–28; Republicans in, 35; voters in, 229, 234, 296n, 313n

Atlanta Constitution, The, 53, 78, 84–85, 92, 116, 159, 161, 187, 191–92, 211, 222–23, 235, 311n

Atlanta Daily World, 41, 48–49, 78, 83, 229

Atlanta Inquirer, The, 83, 85, 234, 247

Atlanta Journal, The, 53, 55, 78, 84–85, 92, 116, 159, 204, 234, 248

Atlanta Journal-Constitution, The, 114–15

Atlanta Life Insurance Company, 140

Atlanta Prison Farm, 76, 77, 110

Atlanta Student Movement, 82

Atlanta University, 4, 40, 41, 51–52, 78–79, 90, 140, 257

Baker, Ella, 59

Baldwin, James, 159; "My Dungeon Shook," 272–73, 280

Balkcom, R. P., 153, 160, 183, 191, 199

Barnett, Claude, 297n

Barry, Marion, 42

Bass, Jack, 307n

Bassett, Jim, 312*n*
Belafonte, Harry, 14, 32, 90, 147–48, 192, 217–18, 266
Bell, Griffin, 113–14, 146, 178, 192, 311*n*
Bevel, James, 42
Big Rock Jail at Fulton Tower, 66–67, 77, 82
Biko, Steve, 274
Birmingham campaign, 259–60, 275
Black, Charles, 257, 265, 278
Black Man in the White House (Morrow), 251
Black media and journalists, 17, 20, 21, 86, 125–26, 174, 176–77, 209–11, 220, 299*n*
Black Republicans and the Transformation of the GOP (Farrington), 242
Blackshear, Otis, 56, 294*n*
Black soldiers, 61
Black voters, 10, 35, 223, 243, 284*n*, 296*n*, 313*n*, 315*n*, 320*n*; Blue Bomb pamphlets and, 210–13, 218–21, 224–25, 244; Democratic Party and, 12, 124, 220, 222, 234–35, 242, 243, 313*n*; Eisenhower and, 12, 25, 105; election turnout of, 243; in Georgia, 234–35; JFK's campaign and, 10, 11–12, 14, 16–19, 22–23, 27, 85, 100, 104, 114, 174–76, 189, 198, 209–14, 218–20, 233–35, 237–45, 263, 313*n*, 315*n*, 316*n*; Nixon's campaign and, 12, 25, 26, 28–30, 38, 175–76, 85, 114, 127, 128, 175–76, 194, 195, 209–10, 217–19, 221–22, 234, 237–38, 242, 243, 251, 297*n*, 313*n*, 315*n*; Republican Party and, 25, 35, 36, 87, 105, 123, 126, 127, 175, 195, 219–22, 234–35, 239–40, 242
Blair, Ed, 197, 200
Blue Bomb pamphlets, 210–13, 218–21, 224–25, 242, 244, 272
Bond, Julian, 62, 78, 82–83, 92, 279, 293*n*; Hollowell and, 62, 83; Lonnie King and, 82
Bondurant, Joan, 81

Booker, Simeon, 86, 177, 194–95, 221–22
Bowles, Chester, 150, 162, 163, 192
Brando, Marlon, 230, 266
Brazier, James, 151–52
Brinkley, David, 199
Broome, C. J., 92
Brown, Benjamin, 55
Brown v. Board of Education, 42, 71, 101, 105, 125, 154, 221, 252
buffalo soldiers, 61

Calhoun, John, 36, 91, 104–106, 128, 175, 195, 235, 246, 261; Hartsfield and, 104–105
Califano, Joseph, 260
Carter, Jimmy, 113–14, 276
Case of Martin Luther King, The (Blue Bomb pamphlets), 210–13, 218–21, 224–25, 242, 244, 272
Castro, Fidel, 109
Cavanaugh, John, 99
Celler, Emanuel, 192
Chamberlain, Wilt, 266, 268, 269
Chapin, Dwight, 262, 319*n*
Charlton, Matthew, 279
Chicago, Ill., 167, 225, 227, 231, 233, 244, 272, 313*n*, 315*n*
Chicago Daily Tribune, 90
Chicago Defender, The, 17, 21, 93, 225, 277, 313*n*
China, 23
Christian Science Monitor, The, 192
Church, Roberta, 317*n*
Civil Rights Act of 1957, 29, 86, 126
Civil Rights Act of 1964, 235
Civil Rights Commission, 13, 98–100, 317*n*
civil rights movement, 4, 8, 10, 20, 31, 34, 54, 82, 154, 226, 278, 292*n*, 318*n*; Birmingham campaign, 259–60, 275; Democratic Party and, 150, 156, 226; Eisenhower and, 125, 126, 147, 161, 195, 239; Freedom Rides, 8; jail and, 32, 41, 43; JFK's campaign and, 3–4,

9, 10, 13–15, 20, 23–24, 26, 36–39, 42, 85, 86, 114, 147, 156–57, 176, 177, 222; JFK's presidency and, 241, 244, 252, 260, 263–65, 275; King's Birmingham jail letter and, 260; March on Washington, 29, 267, 272; Montgomery bus boycott, 14, 31–32, 34, 41, 78, 81, 82, 118, 119, 142; National Conference on Constitutional Rights, 37–39, 45, 210, 213–15; Nixon's 1960 campaign and, 3–4, 11–12, 23–26, 29–30, 38, 42, 85–87, 95, 114, 128, 157; Nixon's true feelings about, 270–71; Selma to Montgomery march, 265; SNCC and, 42–43; "We Shall Overcome" in, 52, 60, 204, 205; women's centrality to, 78–79, 292n; women's suffering of sexual violence during, 77; see also segregation and integration; sit-ins

Civil Rights Section (CRS), 11–13, 16–20, 26, 37, 98, 115, 128, 129, 147, 149, 162, 163, 174, 178, 180, 198–99, 202, 209, 214, 220, 225, 234, 241–46, 285n, 296n, 317n, 319n; Blue Bomb pamphlets of, 210–13, 218–21, 224–25, 242, 244, 272; conservative elements and, 37; Dawson in, 18; King's imprisonment and, 70; Nixon telegram proposal and, 70; Reeves-Lawson rivalry in, 68–69; see also Martin, Louis E.; Shriver, Sargent; Wofford, Harris

Clark, Kenneth, 221
Clayton, Charles, 119, 138, 139
Clayton, Xernona, 259
Clement, Rufus, 78, 102
Committee on Appeal for Human Rights, 78, 81
Congressional Record, 79
Congress of Racial Equality, 161
Connor, Bull, 259
Conquest of Violence (Bondurant), 81
Corporation for National and Community Service, 277
Craig, Calvin, 59

Cross, Lonnie, 287n
CRS, see Civil Rights Section
Crusade for Citizenship, 34
Cuba, 95, 109
Curry, Constance "Connie," 58–59

Daley, Richard, 167, 227, 233
Dawson, William, 18
Decatur, Ga., 131–32
DeKalb County, Ga., 6, 132, 162, 204; King released from, 197; King's court hearings in, 130, 131–41, 161; King's sentence appealed in, 183–84, 196, 216, 252; King's sentencing in, 141–44, 146–48, 161, 183; King's traffic citation in, 6, 47, 48, 74, 115, 116, 118–20, 121–23, 130, 137–41, 155, 161, 171, 172, 179, 181, 184–85, 200, 202, 292n, 298n, 300n; Republicans in, 235; white voters in, 235
DeKalb County Jail, 6–7, 120, 130
Democratic National Committee (DNC), 17, 250, 271, 276
Democratic National Convention, 14, 16, 155
Democratic Party, Democrats, 12, 27, 28, 38, 105, 113–14, 124, 146, 177–79, 181, 226, 233, 239; Black voters and, 12, 124, 220, 222, 234–35, 242, 243, 313n; civil rights and, 150, 156, 226; King's imprisonment and, 156–57; segregationist, 12, 15, 35, 105; southern, 12, 35, 92, 105, 127, 148, 271
Depression, Great, 147
desegregation, see segregation and integration
DeWolf, L. Harold, 226
Dexter Avenue Baptist Church, 31
Dobbs, John Wesley, 91, 132, 140
Dorsey, Thomas, 313n
Douglass, Frederick, 271, 276
DREAM Act, 278
Du Bois, W. E. B., 273
Duke University, 87

Ebenezer Baptist Church, 4, 33, 48,
  63, 115, 205–206, 218, 257, 278,
  279; King's "Eight Days Behind Bars"
  sermon at, 225–26; King's funeral at,
  257, 264–69
Ebony, 87, 238
Edelman, Marian Wright, 41, 262–63
Edelman, Peter, 262
Ehrlichman, John, 271
Eisenhower, Dwight D., 28, 235, 239,
  317*n*; Black voters and, 12, 25, 105;
  civil rights and, 125, 126, 147, 161,
  195, 239; JFK and, 219; King's
  imprisonment and, 144, 145, 192,
  194–95; Morrow and, 24, 124–27, 176,
  250–51, 276; Nixon and, 85–87, 215;
  Nixon's campaign and, 215, 219
Eisenhower, Mamie, 215
Evers, Medgar, 218

Farrell, John, 270
Farrington, Joshua, 242
Farris, Christine King, 103, 131, 142
Farris, Isaac, 131
Fauntroy, Walter, 262
FBI, 317*n*
Finch, Robert, 127, 128, 193–94, 232,
  237, 238, 299*n*
First Amendment, 137
Flanigan, Peter, 175
Forty Years a Guinea Pig (Morrow), 251
Fourteenth Amendment, 137
Frank, Leo, 101
Franklin, Aretha, 266
Freedom Crusade Committee, 213
Freedom Rides, 8
Fulton County, Ga.: Big Rock Jail at
  Fulton Tower, 66–67, 77, 82; Fulton
  County Jail, 3–6, 66–74, 76–85,
  90–95, 110, 120, 121–22, 292*n*; voters
  in, 229, 235

Galbraith, John Kenneth, 248–49
Gallup, 227

Gandhi, Mahatma, 14, 32, 34, 64, 81,
  98, 119, 165, 222, 223, 300*n*
Georgia, 6, 10, 35, 92, 113, 161, 176, 178,
  229, 232, 278–79; Atlanta, *see* Atlanta,
  Ga.; Black voters in, 234–35; criminal
  justice system in, 6, 8; Decatur, 131–32;
  DeKalb County, *see* DeKalb County,
  Ga.; Fulton County, *see* Fulton County,
  Ga.; State Prison in Reidsville, *see*
  Reidsville, Georgia State Prison in
Georgia Council on Human Relations, 66
Georgia State Board of Corrections, 152
Ghana, 28–29
Goldwater, Barry, 239, 261
Goodwin, Richard, 249, 317*n*, 320*n*
Gordy, Barry, 266
Granger, Lester, 126, 222
Graves, John Temple, II, 28
Gray, James, 311*n*
Gray, William, 213

Haldeman, H. R., 270, 312*n*
Harris, Louis, 243
Hartsfield, William, 3–6, 59, 72,
  74, 90–91, 106–107, 113, 234;
  Calhoun and, 104–105; desegregation
  negotiations of, 4, 6, 91–92, 102,
  106, 110, 116, 121–22, 137, 252,
  300*n*; King's imprisonment and, 3–4,
  100–104, 106–11, 116, 121–23, 127,
  133, 160–61, 163, 191, 246, 296*n*,
  297*n*; King Sr. and, 102–103
Harvey's Restaurant, 148–49
Hatcher, Andrew, 317*n*
health care, 277
Hermann, A. B., 299*n*
Herter, Christian, 90
Hesburgh, Ted, 99
Heston, Charlton, 266
Hill, Jesse, 4
Hoffa, Jimmy, 180
Hollings, Fritz, 107
Hollowell, Donald, 7, 9, 54, 56, 58, 134,
  247, 252; Bond and, 62, 83; Brazier
  and, 151; Johnson and, 160; King

and students represented by, 62–65,
67, 76, 81–82, 117; in King's court
hearings, 132–43, 169–72; and King's
imprisonment at Reidsville, 159–60;
King's release and, 196, 197, 199, 200,
203, 205; King's traffic citation and,
116, 121; Mitchell called by, 184; Nash
and, 61–62; in World War II, 61
Hollowell, Louise, 63
Holmes, Hamilton, 76
Holt Street Baptist Church, 31–32
Hoover, J. Edgar, 317n
Hopkins, Gerard Manley, 149
Hotel Theresa, 38
Howard University, 20–21, 45, 277,
285n; JFK's appearance at, 22–23, 37
Hoytt, Marilyn Pryce, 279
Humphrey, Hubert, 270, 274
Hunter, Charlayne, 76

India, 98
India Afire (Wofford and Wofford), 98
integration, *see* segregation and
integration

Jackson, Jesse, 256
Jackson, J. H., 90
Jackson, Mahalia, 192, 266
Javits, Jacob, 79
Jefferson Memorial, 280
Jenkins, Herbert, 40, 133, 256
Jet, 25–26, 86, 177, 221–22,
310n
Jewish Labor Committee, 161
Jews, 101, 102, 313–14n
Jim Crow, 12, 21, 57, 205; *see also*
segregation and integration
Johnson, Ernest, 140
Johnson, Lyndon B., 17, 36, 37, 156,
166–67, 176, 219–20, 231, 270, 319n;
and Civil Rights Act of 1964, 235;
King's assassination and, 260; Martin
and, 250; Shriver in administration of,
266–67, 274; War on Poverty, 274

Johnson, Nathaniel, 160
Joint Center for Political and Economic
Studies, 276
Jones, Clarence, 217
Jones, Raymond "Silver Fox," 220, 226,
230
Jordan, Vernon, 63, 104, 132, 160, 276,
277
Justice Department, U.S., 144, 192, 264,
275

Kansas City Times, The, 84
Kelley, John, 113
Kennedy, Caroline, 214
Kennedy, Ethel, 248, 263, 264, 268
Kennedy, Jacqueline, 22, 167, 169, 229,
319n
Kennedy, John F., 231, 248, 255;
assassination of, 260, 263, 319n; back
surgery of, 94; Catholicism of, 28, 165,
173, 206, 214–15, 233, 243, 278; civil
rights and presidency of, 241, 244,
252, 260, 263–65, 275; Coretta King
called by, 149–50, 162–63, 168–70,
172–74, 177–78, 187, 191, 205–206,
209, 211, 212, 214–15, 217–20, 239,
241–46, 259, 261–63, 265, 277, 304n,
306n, 313n, 316n, 320n; Eisenhower
and, 219; elected president, 232–35,
242, 244, 253; funeral for, 319n;
illnesses of, 167; inauguration of, 252;
Irish heritage of, 15, 147; King on,
216; King's Birmingham campaign
and, 259, 260; King's meetings with,
14–15; March on Washington and,
267; Nixon's relationship with, 44–45,
94–95; presidency of, 10, 17, 238, 241,
244, 249, 252, 253, 259, 260, 263–65,
274, 275, 317n; racism as viewed by,
147; RFK's character contrasted with,
202–203; *The Strategy of Peace*, 99;
Vandiver called by, 155–56, 169–70,
174, 185, 246, 272, 298n, 305n;
Wofford's meeting of, 98–99; in World
War II, 167

Kennedy, John F., presidential campaign
of, 3–4, 8–10, 23, 27, 37–39, 49, 85,
94–95, 109, 164, 166–67, 209–15,
223–24, 226–27, 271; Black voters
and, 10, 11–12, 14, 16–19, 22–23,
27, 85, 100, 104, 114, 174–76, 189,
198, 209–14, 218–20, 233–35,
237–45, 263, 313*n*, 315*n*, 316*n*; Blue
Bomb pamphlets in, 210–13, 218–21,
224–25, 242, 244, 272; and Bowles's
call to Coretta King, 162, 163; civil
rights and, 3–4, 9, 10, 13–15, 20,
23–24, 26, 36–39, 42, 85, 86, 114,
147, 156–57, 176, 177, 222; debates
with Nixon, 23–24, 74, 94, 95, 219,
234; Election Day, 229–33; hectic
schedule in, 166; Howard University
appearance, 22–23, 37; JFK's call
to Coretta King, 149–50, 162–63,
168–70, 172–74, 177–78, 187, 191,
205–206, 209, 211, 212, 214–15,
217–20, 239, 241–46, 259, 261–63,
265, 277, 304*n*, 306*n*, 313*n*, 316*n*,
320*n*; JFK's final televised statement
in, 226–27; King and, 13–16, 44–45,
69, 98; King's father and, 36; King's
imprisonment and, 49, 68–72, 92, 101,
103–4, 106–109, 113–15, 122–23,
127–30, 145–50, 155–58, 162–63,
168–70, 172–74, 177–81, 184–87,
191–92, 197–203, 205–206, 209–23,
237–50, 272, 288*n*, 296*n*, 313*n*, 316*n*;
King's lack of endorsement for, 217–18;
National Conference on Constitutional
Rights and, 37–39, 45, 210, 213–15;
Nixon telegram proposal and, 70;
Robinson and, 14, 26–27; Troutman
and, 106–107; Wofford recruited for,
99–100; *see also* Civil Rights Section
Kennedy, Joseph, Jr., 107
Kennedy, Joseph, Sr., 99, 233, 248,
313–14*n*; Shriver and, 164
Kennedy, Robert F., 8, 11–13, 44, 45,
68, 107, 155–56, 165, 167, 170, 174,
177–80, 184–86, 216, 218, 229–34,
245, 247–49, 253, 255, 258, 259,

267, 269–70, 296*n*, 317*n*, 320*n*;
assassination of, 267; Blue Bomb
pamphlets and, 211, 212; Coretta King
visited by, 263; JFK's assassination and,
319*n*; and JFK's call to Coretta King,
163, 306*n*; JFK's character contrasted
with, 202–203; King's assassination
and, 258–59; at King's funeral, 268;
King's traffic citation sentence and,
179, 184–85, 202; Martin and, 17–19,
178–80, 182, 185, 210, 211, 275,
285*n*, 307*n*; Mitchell called by, 181,
182, 185–87, 189–90, 193, 197–99,
201–203, 209, 213, 222–23, 234, 237,
239, 242, 245, 246, 248–49, 307*n*,
308–309*n*, 311*n*, 320*n*; presidential
campaign of, 259, 264, 270; Rachel
Robinson and, 195; on racial inequality,
15; Stewart and, 186, 189, 193, 307*n*;
Vandiver and, 182; Wofford and, 45,
182, 185, 210, 211, 264, 269–70
Kennedy, Rose, 165
Kennedy, Ted, 197, 199
Kennedy Library, 247
Kenya, 116
Khrushchev, Nikita, 161, 180
Killers of the Dream (Smith), 118
King, A. D., 7, 36, 65, 75–76, 81, 131,
158, 171, 196–98, 203, 293*n*
King, Alberta Williams, 115
King, Alice, 170–71
King, Bernice, 259
King, Christine, 103, 131, 142
King, Coretta Scott, 4, 7, 32, 33, 72, 81,
117–18, 265; Blue Bomb pamphlets
and, 212, 213; Bowles's call to, 162,
163; early life of, 117; JFK's call to,
149–50, 162–63, 168–70, 172–74,
177–78, 187, 191, 205–206, 209,
211, 212, 214–15, 217–20, 239,
241–46, 259, 261–63, 265, 277, 304*n*,
306*n*, 313*n*, 316*n*, 320*n*; Martin's
assassination and, 255–58, 261;
Martin's court hearing and, 131; and
Martin's imprisonment in Birmingham
jail, 259; and Martin's imprisonment

following Rich's sit-in arrest, 3–5, 68, 71, 84, 117, 153, 158, 162–63, 182–83; Martin's letter to, 182–83; Martin's marriage to, 117; Martin's release and, 203–4; Martin's sentencing and, 142–44, 147–48; Nixon's visit to, 261–62; and release of Rich's sit-in protestors, 3, 117; RFK's visit to, 263

King, Lonnie, 78, 80, 81, 94, 95, 104, 120, 154, 187, 253, 257, 278–79, 287n, 292n, 293n, 295n, 298n, 318n; Bond and, 82; death of, 279; early life of, 80; imprisonment of, 74, 76, 83–84, 92; Jordan and, 63; and King's assassination and funeral, 256–57, 265–66; King's release and, 205, 207; in Navy, 80; off-duty police incident and, 170–71; post office job of, 51, 128–29; in Rich's sit-in, 4–7, 39–42, 46–48, 51–53, 56–59, 62, 65–67, 94, 128, 279, 289n

King, Martin Luther, III ("Marty"), 4, 68, 117–18, 183, 203–4, 277

King, Martin Luther, Jr., 4, 31–36, 39–44, 255, 272–73, 313n; arrest and incarceration in Montgomery, 79–80; assassination of, 255–61; Atlanta return of, 33–35, 47; Birmingham campaign of, 259–60, 275; in Birmingham jail, 259–60; and Civil Rights Act of 1964, 235; Coretta's marriage to, 117; funerals for, 257, 261–69, 319n; grandmother of, 81; humility and guilt of, 81; "I Have a Dream" speech of, 273; Jackson and, 90; on jail, 84, 259–60, 273, 293n; on JFK, 216; JFK's campaign and, 13–16, 44–45, 69, 98; JFK's meetings with, 14–15; leadership, fame, and prestige of, 32–33, 223, 292n; Lee as body man for, 54, 293n; in Montgomery bus boycott, 14, 31–32, 34, 41, 81, 118, 119, 142; name change of, 31; on Nixon, 30; Nixon's campaign and, 35–36; Nixon's relationship with, 9, 13, 28–30, 35, 126, 175, 217, 238, 261; Nobel

Peace Prize awarded to, 267; political neutrality of, 13, 36, 44, 45, 71, 192, 204, 217–18; radio interview of, 222; in Rich's sit-in, 4, 39–40, 42–49, 52–53, 56–60, 73, 94, 134–37, 206–207, 289n, 295n; as SCLC head, 33, 34, 41; sit-in movement and, 40–41; SNCC and, 43; stabbing attack on, 30; *Stride Toward Freedom*, 14, 30; tax indictment of, 47, 48, 119; voting problem of, 218; wiretapping of, 245; Wofford's relationship with, 14, 71–72, 98, 100

King, Martin Luther, Jr., imprisonment of: arrest, 4, 6, 8, 58–60, 68, 69, 90, 102, 115, 116, 119, 271, 272, 279, 294n; bail refusal and, 4, 10, 64, 114; bond payment and, 196, 197; *The Case of Martin Luther King* (Blue Bomb pamphlets), 210–13, 218–21, 224–25, 242, 244, 272; Coretta and, 3–5, 68, 71, 84, 117, 153, 158, 162–63, 182–83; court hearings and, 130, 131–41, 161, 170–72; in DeKalb County Jail, 6–7, 120, 130; and dropping of charges, 110–11, 122, 130, 133; Eisenhower and, 144, 145, 192, 194–95; in Fulton County Jail, 3–6, 67–74, 77, 79–85, 90–94, 110, 120, 121–22, 292n; Hartsfield and, 3–4, 100–104, 106–11, 116, 121–23, 127, 133, 160–61, 163, 191, 246, 296n, 297n; homecoming from, 197, 201, 205–206, 226; JFK's call to Coretta on, 149–50, 162–63, 168–70, 172–74, 177–78, 187, 191, 205–206, 209, 211, 212, 214–15, 217–20, 239, 241–46, 259, 261–63, 265, 277, 304n, 306n, 313n, 316n, 320n; JFK's call to Vandiver on, 155–56, 169–70, 174, 185, 246, 272, 298n, 305n; JFK's campaign and, 49, 68–72, 92, 101, 103–4, 106–9, 113–15, 122–23, 127–30, 145–50, 155–58, 162–63, 168–70, 172–74, 177–81, 184–87, 191–92, 197–203, 205–206, 209–23, 237–50, 272, 288n, 296n, 313n, 316n;

King, Martin Luther, Jr., (*cont.*)
  King's fasting during, 73; King's letter
  to Coretta during, 182–83; King's
  sermon on, 225–26; King's television
  interview during, 73; King's written
  statements during, 64, 79, 85; "leave
  the premises" trespassing charge in,
  63–64, 85, 110, 114, 135–37, 294*n*;
  media condemnation of, 192; Mitchell's
  decision reversal and, 184, 185, 193,
  196–97, 216; Nixon's campaign and,
  49, 85–87, 92, 104–106, 127–30,
  144–46, 175–77, 179, 186, 192–95,
  197, 201, 210–13, 215, 17, 218,
  221, 238–39, 245, 248, 261, 287*n*;
  288*n*; plot against King's life in, 158;
  prisoners' notes to King in, 190; Reeves
  and, 69–71; in Reidsville, 6, 8, 9,
  144, 151–53, 155–62, 167, 171, 179,
  182–87, 190–91, 206, 222, 259, 267,
  273–74, 287*n*; release from prison,
  196–201, 203–7, 210, 246–48, 281,
  305*n*; and release of fellow protestors,
  3–7; RFK's call to Mitchell on, 181,
  182, 185–87, 189–90, 193, 197–99,
  201–203, 209, 213, 222–23, 234, 237,
  239, 242, 245, 246, 248–49, 307*n*,
  308–309*n*, 311*n*, 320*n*; sentencing
  in, 141–44, 146–48, 161; in solitary
  confinement, 153, 191; telegrams sent
  to JFK and Nixon about, 49, 92; traffic
  citation and, 6, 47, 48, 74, 115, 116,
  118–20, 121–23, 130, 137–41, 155,
  161, 171, 172, 179, 181, 184–85,
  200, 202, 292*n*, 298*n*, 300*n*; traffic
  sentence appealed, 183–84, 196, 216,
  252; Vandiver and, 115, 122, 123, 146,
  155–58, 160, 169–70, 174, 181–82,
  185, 192, 246–49, 272, 298*n*, 305*n*;
  visits during, 84; Wofford and, 68–70,
  72, 97–98, 100–101
King, Martin Luther, Sr. ("Daddy King"),
  4, 28, 31, 33–36, 42, 75, 91, 115–16,
  183, 216, 217, 246, 252, 267, 318*n*;
  Blue Bomb pamphlets and, 212, 213;
  Coretta and, 117; early life of, 115;
  Hartsfield and, 102–103; and JFK's
  call to Coretta, 173, 205–206, 214–15;
  and JFK's Catholicism, 173, 206,
  214–15; Martin's assassination and,
  256; Martin's court hearings and, 131,
  169; Martin's imprisonment and, 7, 8,
  115, 120; Martin's imprisonment at
  Reidsville and, 158–59, 162, 186–87;
  Martin's sentencing and, 142–43;
  Martin's traffic citation and, 119; name
  change of, 31; Nixon's visit to, 262;
  Rich's sit-in and, 43–44, 46–49
King, Yolanda "Yoki," 68, 117–18, 183,
  203–204, 256
Klein, Herb, 176, 177, 186, 297*n*
Kuhn, Clifford, 287*n*
Ku Klux Klan (KKK), 6, 55, 59, 74, 75,
  87, 89, 97, 101–102, 111, 131, 132,
  154, 252, 313*n*

labor camps, *see* prison farms and labor
  camps
labor unions, 220, 317*n*
Lawson, Belford, 68
Lawson, James, 43, 64
Lawson, Marjorie, 16, 68–69, 212, 241;
  Reeves' rivalry with, 68–69
Lee, Bernard, 54, 80; as King's body man,
  54, 293*n*
Lee, George W., 128
Levison, Stanley, 81, 217
Lewis, Anthony, 173–74, 191, 244
Lewis, John, 42, 43, 95, 264, 265, 277,
  295*n*
Life, 223
Lincoln, Abraham, 12, 35, 271, 276
Little, R. E., 56, 58, 60, 76, 136
Little Rock, Ark., 126, 144
Lodge, Henry Cabot, 26, 36; pledge on
  Black cabinet member made by, 38, 39,
  194, 216, 239, 271
Long, Carolyn, 7, 53
Los Angeles Sentinel, 86, 240–41, 253
Louisiana State Penitentiary (Angola), 141
lynchings, 72, 101, 115, 211

Mackay, James, 181
Making of the President, 1960, The (White), 244, 284*n*
March on Washington, 29, 267, 272
Marshall, Burke, 320*n*
Marshall, Thurgood, 71, 77, 116–17, 134, 205, 260
Martin, F. M., 140–41
Martin, Gertrude, 21, 275, 276
Martin, Louis E., 9–10, 16–23, 26, 37, 44, 68–69, 70, 97, 98, 149, 195, 209, 226, 227, 230–32, 238, 241, 242, 244–46, 249, 253, 255, 265, 267–68, 270, 272, 275–77, 279, 280, 284*n*, 304*n*, 310*n*, 313*n*, 317*n*, 318*n*; Black elected officials mentored by, 249–50, 276, 317*n*; Black voter outreach by, 10, 16–17, 22–23, 174–76, 198, 209–13, 240, 243, 299*n*, 320*n*; Blue Bomb pamphlets and, 210–13, 218–21, 224, 225; Carter and, 276; Conference on Constitutional Rights and, 213; Dawson and, 18; death of, 277; FDR and, 210; JFK's assassination and, 260, 319*n*; and JFK's call to Coretta King, 149–50, 163, 177, 277; Johnson and, 250; King's assassination and, 260–61; at King's funeral, 266; King's imprisonment and, 68, 70, 127–30, 145, 148, 174, 189; on King's Reidsville experience, 267; King's sentencing and, 145, 148; and Lodge's pledge of Black cabinet member, 38–39; Nixon telegram proposal of, 70; racism confronted by, 211; RFK and, 17–19, 178–80, 182, 185, 210, 211, 275, 285*n*, 307*n*; and RFK's call to Mitchell, 182, 198–99, 201, 203, 307*n*, 309*n*; Shriver and, 16–17, 22; at University of Michigan, 21; Wofford and, 17, 19–22, 285*n*; *see also* Civil Rights Section
Martin, Toni, 231
Martin Luther King Day, 277, 280
Martin Luther King Jr. Memorial, 279–80

Mays, Benjamin, 102, 110, 132, 140, 171, 257, 317*n*
Meany, George, 192
McCarthy, Eugene, 270
McDonald, Dora, 218, 256
McGill, Ralph, 222–23
McGovern, George, 274
media, 209; Black, 17, 20, 21, 86, 125–26, 174, 176–77, 209–11, 220, 299*n*; King's imprisonment condemned in, 192
Metropolitan AME Church, 26, 27
Miami, Fla., 15–16, 44–46
Michigan Chronicle, 21
Ministers' Alliance, 94
Mitchell, Clarence, 176
Mitchell, John, 261
Mitchell, Oscar, 47, 74, 115, 116, 119, 120, 123, 130, 157, 162, 174, 181–82, 192, 223, 234, 249; decision reversal and release of King by, 184, 185, 193, 196–97, 216; Hollowell's call to, 184; in King's hearings, 132–44, 170–72, 196; RFK's call to, 181, 182, 185–87, 189–90, 193, 197–99, 201–203, 209, 213, 222–23, 234, 237, 239, 242, 245, 246, 248–49, 307*n*, 308–309*n*, 311*n*, 320*n*; Stewart and, 181–82, 272
Montgomery bus boycott, 14, 31–32, 34, 41, 78, 81, 82, 118, 119, 142
Moore, Howard, 205
Morehouse College, 4, 41, 51, 66, 82, 92, 110, 115, 132, 140, 142, 257, 268, 269
Morrow, Catherine, 25
Morrow, E. Frederic, 24–26, 123–28, 219, 222, 240, 250–51, 261, 299*n*, 305*n*; *Black Man in the White House*, 251; Eisenhower and, 24, 124–27, 176, 250–51, 276; Finch and, 127; *Forty Years a Guinea Pig*, 251; King and, 28–29; Nixon and, 25, 251; Nixon's presidential campaign and, 24–26, 123, 127, 175–76, 251; Robinson and, 125; White House staff appointment of, 124
Moss, Otis, Jr., 49, 81, 92–93, 106, 131, 206

Mount Moriah Baptist Church, 85
Mount Zion Second Baptist Church,
   186–87
Mussolini, Benito, 98
"My Dungeon Shook" (Baldwin),
   272–73, 280

NAACP, 36, 37, 54, 62, 71, 77, 82, 84,
   85, 87, 90–91, 104, 116–17, 128, 132,
   176, 192, 218, 293*n*, 317*n*; King's
   sentencing and, 142–44
Nash, Diane, 42
Nash, Willie, 61–62
Nation, The, 79
National Conference on Constitutional
   Rights, 37–39, 45, 210, 213–15
National Guard, 87, 262
National Newspaper Publishers
   Association, 125–26
National Urban League, 37, 63, 222, 266
Neely, Frank, 55–56
New Deal, 12, 35, 105, 123, 235
New Republic, 244
New York Amsterdam News, 174, 183,
   219, 220, 222
New York, N.Y., 85, 219, 223–24,
   315*n*; Harlem, 38, 39, 176, 194, 220;
   National Conference on Constitutional
   Rights in, 37–39, 45, 210, 213–15
New York Post, 180, 240
New York Times, The, 34, 39, 79, 84, 114,
   131, 173, 180, 191–92, 211, 226, 233,
   243–44, 279
Nigeria, 161, 216
1984 (Orwell), 143
Niven, David, 243
Nix, Robert, 215
Nixon, Pat, 232
Nixon, Richard, 86–87, 231, 251–52,
   255, 305*n*, 313*n*; civil rights movement
   as viewed by, 270–71; Coretta King
   visited by, 261–62; early life of, 86;
   Eisenhower and, 85–87, 215; Finch
   and, 127; at JFK's funeral, 319*n*, 319*n*;
   JFK's relationship with, 44–45, 94–95;

JFK's surgery and, 94; King on, 30;
   King's funeral and, 261–62, 266, 268,
   269; King's relationship with, 9, 13,
   28–30, 35, 126, 175, 217, 238, 261;
   Martin's telegram proposal and, 70;
   Mexico trip of, 230, 231; Morrow and,
   25, 251; 1968 presidential campaign
   of, 270–71, 275; 1972 presidential
   campaign of, 271, 274; presidency of,
   271; segregation condemned by, 86,
   87; *Six Crises*, 194; southern strategy of,
   271; Watergate and, 271–72
Nixon, Richard, 1960 presidential
   campaign of, 3–4, 11–13, 23, 27, 37,
   44–45, 48–49, 94–95, 105, 109, 113,
   166, 167, 175, 179, 180, 223, 224,
   226–27, 237–41, 271, 313*n*; Atlanta
   appearance, 27–28; Black journalists
   and, 176–77; Black voters and, 12,
   25, 26, 28–30, 38, 175–76, 85, 114,
   127, 128, 175–76, 194, 195, 209–10,
   217–19, 221–22, 234, 237–38, 242,
   243, 251, 297*n*, 313*n*, 315*n*; civil rights
   and, 3–4, 11–12, 23–26, 29–30, 38,
   42, 85–87, 95, 114, 128, 157; debates
   with JFK, 23–24, 74, 94, 95, 219, 234;
   Eisenhower and, 215, 219; Election
   Day, 229–33; Finch and, 127, 128;
   Harlem and, 38, 39, 176, 194; Howard
   University forum and, 22, 45, 286*n*;
   King and, 35–36; King's father and, 36;
   King's imprisonment and, 49, 85–87,
   92, 104–106, 127–30, 144–46, 175–77,
   179, 186, 192–95, 197, 201, 210–13,
   215, 217, 218, 221, 238–39, 245, 248,
   261, 287*n*, 288*n*; and Lodge's pledge
   of Black cabinet member, 38–39, 194,
   216, 239, 271; Morrow and, 24–26,
   123, 127, 175–76, 251; Nixon's closing
   appeal in, 226; Quinn Chapel invitation
   and, 312*n*; Republican National
   Committee and, 105; Robinson and,
   26, 27, 176, 179, 193–95, 221, 222,
   240–41, 261, 271
Nixon Library, 194
Northwestern University, 132

Obama, Barack, 253, 272, 277–78
O'Brien, Lawrence, 178, 271
O'Donnell, Ken, 109, 167–68, 170, 202, 304*n*, 320*n*
Orbert, Agnes "Blondean," 56–57, 59, 67
Orwell, George, 143

Parchman Farm, 141
Parks, Rosa, 31, 40–41, 77
Paschal's Restaurant, 3–5, 117
Patterson, John, 154
Peace Corps, 250, 265, 274, 317*n*, 318*n*, 320*n*
Person, Charles, 67
Pittsburgh Courier, The, 93, 223
Politics of Injustice, The (Niven), 243
Poor People's Campaign, 263
Pope, Roslyn, 78
Powell, Adam Clayton, 20, 38, 90
presidential election of 1960, 3–5, 8–10, 23, 95, 229–35, 237, 271, 315*n*; as close contest, 3, 219, 226, 232, 242, 243; Election Day, 229–33; Electoral College count in, 232, 243; JFK's victory in, 232–35, 242, 244, 253; King's neutrality on, 13, 36, 44, 45, 71, 192, 204, 217–18; polling on, 227, 242–43; voter turnout for, 23, 229, 243; *see also* Kennedy, John F., presidential campaign of; Nixon, Richard, 1960 presidential campaign of
presidential election of 1968, 270–71, 275
presidential election of 1972, 271, 274
presidential election of 1976, 274–75
prison farms and labor camps, 119–20, 141, 158; Atlanta Prison Farm, 76, 77, 110; King sentenced to, 141–44, 146–48, 183
Proctor, Sam, 242
Pryce, Marilyn, 56–57, 59–60, 67

Ramsay, Richard, 65–66
Randolph, A. Philip, 126, 223
Reeves, Frank, 16, 68, 69, 71, 285*n*,

318*n*; King's imprisonment and, 69–71, 129–30; Lawson's rivalry with, 68–69
Reidsville, Georgia State Prison in, 158–60, 162; guards at, 158, 159, 190–91; King at, 6, 8, 9, 144, 151–53, 155–62, 167, 171, 179, 182–87, 190–91, 206, 222, 259, 267, 273–74, 287*n*; King's release from, 196–201, 203–207, 210, 246–48, 281; plot against King's life in, 158; prisoners' notes to King in, 190
Republican National Committee (RNC), 104, 105, 123, 175, 299*n*, 320*n*
Republican Party, Republicans, 12, 13, 35–38, 87, 92, 105, 123–28, 144, 177, 186, 220, 239, 261, 271, 299*n*, 300*n*, 315*n*; in Atlanta, 35; Blacks and, 25, 35, 36, 87, 105, 123, 126, 127, 175, 195, 219–22, 234–35, 239–40, 242; in DeKalb County, 235; South and, 27–28, 271
Rich, Dick, 6, 40, 57, 91, 110–11, 113, 119; charges against King dropped by, 122, 130, 133
Rich's department store, 39–40, 57, 101, 287*n*; Crystal Bridge, 52; Magnolia Room, 40, 55–58, 60, 66, 119, 134–36, 252–53, 279; Sam Nunn Federal Center at site of, 279
Rich's department store sit-in, 4, 37, 51–74, 89, 206–207, 252–53, 289*n*; arrests of protestors, 3, 4, 56, 58, 60, 66, 67, 75, 90, 294*n*; imprisonment of protestors, 4–5, 60–61, 64, 66–68, 72–74, 76–83, 90–95, 110; King in, 4, 39–40, 42–49, 52–53, 56–60, 73, 94, 134–37, 206–207, 289*n*, 295*n*; King's arrest in, 4, 6, 8, 58–60, 68, 69, 90, 102, 115, 116, 119, 271, 272, 279, 294*n*; King's court hearing and, 134–36; King's imprisonment following, *see* King, Martin Luther, Jr., imprisonment of; "leave the premises" trespassing charges in, 63–64, 76, 85, 110, 114, 135–37, 294*n*; Lonnie King in, 4–7, 39–42, 46–48, 51–53, 56–59, 62, 65–67, 94,

Rich's department store sit-in, (*cont.*)
128, 279, 289*n*; planning of, 39–40,
42–49, 52; release of protestors, 3–7,
110, 117, 294*n*
Rickey, Branch, 195
Robeson, Paul, 117
Robinson, Jackie, 14, 26–27, 114, 125,
126, 176, 177, 179, 193–95, 221–22,
237, 240–41, 261, 266, 271
Robinson, Rachel, 194, 195
Rockefeller, Nelson, 114
Rogers, Jewel, 317*n*
Rogers, William, 144–46, 161, 194
Roosevelt, Eleanor, 37–38, 90, 160, 241
Roosevelt, Franklin Delano, 17, 251–52,
284*n*; Martin and, 210; New Deal of,
12, 35, 105, 123, 235
Rush Church, 54
Russell, Bob, 156, 157, 247
Russell, Richard, 156, 317*n*
Ruwe, Nick, 262

Safire, William, 193, 194, 237, 261
Salinger, Pierre, 109, 167–68, 170
Sam Nunn Federal Center, 279
Saturday Review, 119
Schlesinger, Arthur M., 203, 230,
284*n*
Schley, Bobby, 56
segregation and integration, 62, 85, 86,
90, 206, 222, 252; *Brown v. Board of
Education*, 42, 71, 101, 105, 125, 154,
221, 252; Democrats and, 12, 15, 35,
105; Hartsfield's negotiations on, 4, 6,
91–92, 102, 106, 110, 116, 121–22,
127, 252, 300*n*; JFK's administration
and, 241; Jim Crow, 12, 21, 57, 205;
in Little Rock, 126, 144; of lunch
counters, 4, 6, 40, 41, 54, 50, 83,
89, 91, 93; Nixon on, 86, 87; Nixon
telegram proposal and, 70; States'
Rights Council of Georgia and, 157;
Vandiver and, 154, 156; in workplace
break rooms, 129; *see also* civil rights
movement; sit-ins

Seigenthaler, John, 19, 177–78, 184–86,
298–99, 201–203, 296*n*, 306*n*, 308*n*,
309*n*, 317*n*
Selassie, Haile, 319*n*
Selma to Montgomery march, 265
Semple, Cecil, 58, 136
Sengstacke, John, 21
Shriver, Eunice Kennedy, 164, 229,
267, 27
Shriver, Maria, 225
Shriver, Robert, 225, 277
Shriver, Sargent, 8–10, 11, 16, 19, 20,
44, 68, 69, 97, 108, 128, 145, 148–49,
163–66, 175, 185, 244–46, 249–50,
255, 272, 274–77, 280, 299*n*, 304*n*,
313*n*, 318*n*, 320*n*; Blue Bomb pamphlets
and, 211–13, 218–19, 224–25; Catholic
faith of, 149, 164–65; Conference on
Constitutional Rights and, 213; JFK's
assassination and, 260, 319*n*; and JFK's
call to Coretta King, 162–63, 168–70,
172–74, 177, 178, 246, 304*n*, 306*n*; in
Johnson administration, 266–67, 274;
Joseph Kennedy Sr. and, 164; at King's
funeral, 266; Martin and, 16–17, 22;
Peace Corps and, 250, 265, 274, 317*n*,
318*n*, 320*n*; presidential campaign of,
274–75; RFK's assassination and, 267;
Special Olympics and, 275; Wofford and,
165; in World War II, 164; *see also* Civil
Rights Section
Siegel, Jacob, 161
sit-ins, 23, 40–41, 52, 54–55, 60–62, 70,
74, 78, 82, 89–92, 95, 116, 246, 252,
278, 293*n*, 318*n*; Atlanta newspapers
on, 84–85; Hartsfield's negotiations
on, 4, 6, 91–92, 102, 106, 110, 116, 121–22,
127, 252, 300*n*; Nixon on, 226; at
post office break room, 129; at Rich's
department store, *see* Rich's department
store sit-in; at Terminal Station
restaurant, 75, 76; trespassing law and,
63–64, 76, 85; voter registration, 34
Six Crises (Nixon), 194
Smith, Jack, 130, 133–38, 140, 141,
171–72, 196

Smith, Lillian, 118–19; King's driving of, 47, 118

Sorensen, Ted, 99, 168, 284n, 320n

South, 12, 15, 18, 23, 44, 107, 114, 124, 176, 217, 218, 222, 226, 232, 234, 239, 240, 311n; Democrats in, 12, 35, 92, 105, 127, 148, 271; Nixon's strategy for, 271; political realignment in, 235; Republicans and, 27–28, 271

Southern California–Nevada Council of Churches, 238

Southern Christian Leadership Conference (SCLC), 33, 34, 41, 47, 69, 70, 85, 90, 143, 198, 216, 247, 259, 262

Southern Regional Council, 159, 205

Soviet Union, 23, 161

Special Olympics, 275

Spelman College, 40, 41, 46, 56, 57, 78, 256, 263

States' Rights Council of Georgia, 157

Stevenson, Adlai, 150, 162, 315n

Stewart, George, 157–58, 172, 174, 180–84, 247, 248; Mitchell and, 181–82, 272; RFK and, 186, 189, 193, 307n

Stossel, Scott, 275

Strange Fruit (Smith), 118

Strategy of Peace, The (Kennedy), 99

Stride Toward Freedom (King), 14, 30

Student Nonviolent Coordinating Committee (SNCC), 42–43, 59, 65, 84, 90, 288n

Sullivan, Herschelle, 46, 53, 77, 83, 92, 289n, 295n, 318n

Supreme Court, 32; *Brown v. Board of Education*, 42, 71, 101, 105, 125, 154, 221, 252

Talmadge, Herman, 317n

Taylor, Gardner, 213

Temple University, 215

Tenth Cavalry, 61

Terminal Station restaurant, 75, 76

Till, Emmett, 82–83, 125, 151

Time, 82

Thoreau, Henry David, 81

Thurman, Howard, 273

Thurmond, Strom, 270–71

Today, 216

Trevor Arnett Library, 51

Troutman, Bobby, 106–107, 109, 113, 318n; Wofford and, 114

Truman, Harry, 210–11

Tubby, Roger, 198–99, 201

Tuck, Bennett, 57–58, 134–36

unions, 220, 317n

United Nations, 161

United Press International, 64

University of Georgia, 76, 132, 252

University of Michigan, 21

U.S. Commission on Civil Rights, 13, 98–100

Vandiver, Betty, 155, 156

Vandiver, Ernest, 35, 42, 87, 153–58, 245, 287n, 307n, 317n; JFK's call to, 155–56, 169–70, 174, 185, 246, 272, 298n, 305n; King's imprisonment and, 115, 122, 123, 146, 155–58, 160, 169–70, 174, 181–82, 185, 192, 246–49, 272, 298n, 305n; RFK and, 182; Stewart and, 157–58

Vietnam War, 270

Viva Zapata, 230–31

voting rights and registration, 34, 86, 242, 296n

Wagner, Robert F., Jr., 90

Walden, A. T., 183

Walker, Wyatt Tee, 47, 70–71, 90, 132, 143, 161, 171, 172, 183, 197, 200, 203, 247, 257

Wallace, George, 154

Walsh, Lawrence, 144–45, 301n

Ward, Horace, 121, 132

Wardlaw, John, 237

Washington, Val, 105, 175
Washington Post, The, 192
Watergate, 271–72
Watters, Pat, 204–205
Webb, James, 60, 61, 63–66, 76, 110
"We Shall Overcome," 52, 60, 204, 205
Wheat Street Baptist Church, 116
White, Byron, 320*n*
White, Theodore, 244, 248, 284*n*
Whittier College, 87
Wilkins, J. Ernest, 317*n*
Wilkins, Roy, 84, 91, 126, 132, 143, 223
Williams, Franklin, 221, 242
Williams, Samuel W., 142
Wilson, Norma June, 77
Wilson, Woodrow, 233
Wittenstein, Charles, 183–84
Wofford, Clare, 72, 98, 100, 265, 279
Wofford, Daniel, 97, 214
Wofford, Harris, 8–10, 11–16, 19–21, 37, 44–46, 97–100, 106–109, 115, 118, 149, 180, 210, 217, 226, 227, 230, 233–34, 244–47, 249–50, 255, 264–65, 268, 269, 272, 276, 278–80, 284*n*, 295*n*, 299*n*, 316*n*, 317*n*, 320*n*; Abram and, 100–101, 103, 107–108, 185, 296*n*; and appeal of King's sentence, 183–84; Blue Bomb pamphlets and, 211, 212, 218–19, 221, 224; Conference on Constitutional Rights and, 213–15; Dawson and, 18; death of, 280; Gandhi admired by, 14, 34, 64, 81, 98, 165, 223; health care and, 277; JFK's assassination and, 319*n*; and JFK's call to Coretta King, 149–50, 162–63, 172–74,

177, 304*n*; JFK's meeting of, 98–99; JFK's meetings with King arranged by, 14–15; King's assassination and, 258; at King's funeral, 266–67; King's imprisonment and, 68–70, 72, 97–98, 100–101, 127–30, 144–50, 162–63, 173–74; King's relationship with, 14, 71–72, 98, 100; King's sentencing and, 144–50; and Lodge's pledge of Black cabinet member, 38–39; Martin and, 17, 19–22, 285*n*; Obama and, 277–78; Peace Corps and, 265, 317*n*, 318*n*, 320*n*; recruited for JFK's campaign, 99–100; remarriage of, 279; RFK and, 45, 182, 185, 210, 211, 264, 269–70; and RFK's call to Mitchell, 182, 202, 203, 308*n*, 309*n*; Senate campaign of, 277; Shriver and, 165; Troutman and, 114; *Viva Zapata* watched by, 230–31; *see also* Civil Rights Section
Wofford, Susanne, 97, 264, 268
Wonder, Stevie, 266
work camps, *see* prison farms and labor camps
World War II, 93, 98, 107, 133, 276; black soldiers in, 61; Hollowell in, 61; JFK in, 167; Shriver in, 164
Wright, Jeremiah, 278

Young, Andrew, 134, 242, 256, 273–74, 276
Young, A. S. "Doc," 253
Young, Whitney, 266

Zinn, Howard, 40, 78

A NOTE ABOUT THE AUTHORS

Stephen Kendrick and Paul Kendrick are the coauthors of *Douglass and Lincoln: How a Revolutionary Black Leader and a Reluctant Liberator Struggled to End Slavery and Save the Union*, named one of *Kirkus Reviews'* best books of 2008, and *Sarah's Long Walk: The Free Blacks of Boston and How Their Struggle for Equality Changed America*, designated one of the best nonfiction books of 2005 by *The Christian Science Monitor*. Their work has appeared in publications that include *The New York Times*, *The Washington Post*, *The Boston Globe*, *USA Today*, and *American Heritage*.